JOURNAL FOR THE STUDY OF THE NEW TESTAMENT SUPPLEMENT SERIES
187

Sheffield Academic Press

Prodigality, Liberality and Meanness in the Parable of the Prodigal Son

A Greco-Roman Perspective on Luke 15.11-32

David A. Holgate

Journal for the Study of the New Testament
Supplement Series 187

BT
378
.P8
H64
1999

To Patricia, Sarah and Elinor

Copyright © 1999 Sheffield Academic Press

Published by
Sheffield Academic Press Ltd
Mansion House
19 Kingfield Road
Sheffield S11 9AS
England

Typeset by Sheffield Academic Press
and
Printed on acid-free paper in Great Britain
by Bookcraft Ltd
Midsomer Norton, Bath

British Library Cataloguing in Publication Data

A catalogue record for this book is available
from the British Library

ISBN 1-84127-025-3

CONTENTS

Abbreviations   9
Preface   13

Part I
THE PARABLE

Chapter 1
PRIOR GRECO-ROMAN PERSPECTIVES ON LUKE 15.11-32:
AN OVERVIEW   16
   1. Introduction   16
   2. The Origins and Antecedents of Greco-Roman Perspectives   18
   3. Prior Readings of Luke 15.11-32 from a Greco-Roman
      Perspective   26
   4. From Parallel Plots to Related Patterns of Moral Thought   31

Chapter 2
THE COMPOSITION AND MESSAGE OF LUKE 15.11-32   39
   1. The Text of Luke 15.11-32   41
   2. Major Divisions   44
   3. Colon Divisions   46
   4. Analysis of the Composition of Luke 15.11-32   50
   5. Results   65

Chapter 3
CO-TEXTS: LUKE 15.11-32 AND THE OTHER L PARABLES   69
   1. Luke's Teaching on Possessions and Luke 15.11-32   69
   2. A Wider Co-Text for Luke 15.11-32: The L Parables 73
   3. Results of Adopting the L Parables as the Co-Text 87

Part II
THE TOPOS

Chapter 4
THE TOPOS 'ON COVETOUSNESS' IN MORAL PHILOSOPHY	90
  1. Topoi: Definitions and Uses	92
  2. The Topos On Covetousness	99
  3. Moral-Philosophical Texts Reflecting the
     Influence of the Topos On Covetousness	101
  4. Characteristic Features of the Topos On Covetousness	128

Part III
THE PARABLE AND THE TOPOS

Chapter 5
THE PRODIGAL YOUNGER SON	132
  1. The Rejection of the Ideal of Common Ownership	133
  2. Gathering and Scattering	139
  3. Prodigal Living	142
  4. Famine, Hunger and Want	148
  5. Desire and Degradation	153
  6. Moral Death and Ruin	158

Chapter 6
THE LIBERAL FATHER	168
  1. The Ideal of Liberality	168
  2. Indicators of the Father's Liberality	169
  3. Liberality Shown by Example and Word	174

Chapter 7
THE YOUNGER SON LEARNS LIBERALITY	192
  1. Desperation	192
  2. Turning and Returning	198
  3. Acknowledgment of Culpability and Confession	206
  4. Moral Choice	211
  5. Restoration	214
  6. Harmony	218
  7. Good Health	221

Chapter 8
THE MEAN ELDER SON   227
  1. The Meanness of the Elder Son   228
  2. Philosophical Views of Meanness   230
  3. The Consequences of Meanness   236

Chapter 9
CONCLUSION   247
  1. Similarities and Differences between the Parable
      and the Topos   247
  2. Luke's Philosophical Affiliation   249
  3. Gains from Recognizing the Relationship between the
      Parable and the Topos   250
  4. Further Research   251

Bibliography   253
Index of References   278
Index of Authors   296

The abbreviations given in the Instructions for Contributors to the *Journal of Biblical Literature*, as published in its *Membership Directory and Handbook* for 1990, have been followed. For classical citations those given in the *TDNT*, I, pp. xvi-xxxix, have been used. Abbreviations not found there have been taken from N.G.L. Hammond and H.H. Scullard (eds.), *The Oxford Classical Dictionary* (2nd edn; Oxford: Clarendon Press, 1970), pp. ix-xxii[1] and H.G. Liddell and R. Scott, *A Greek-English Lexicon*, 9th edn. by H.S. Jones, with *A Supplement*, edn. E.A. Barber (Oxford: Clarendon Press, 1968), pp. xvi-xxxviii, in that order. In addition to these, the following abbreviations have been used:

AB	Anchor Bible
AJP	*American Journal of Philology*
AJT	*American Journal of Theology*
AnBib	Analecta biblica
ANRW	Hildegard Temporini and Wolfgang Haase (eds.), *Aufstieg und Niedergang der römischen Welt: Geschichte und Kultur Roms im Spiegel der neueren Forschung* (Berlin: W. de Gruyter, 1972–)
APAT	*American Philological Association—Transactions*
ATLA	American Theological Library Association
ASNU	Acta seminarii neotestamentici upsaliensis
BAGD	Walter Bauer, William F. Arndt, F. William Gingrich and Frederick W. Danker, *A Greek–English Lexicon of the New Testament and Other Early Christian Literature* (Chicago: University of Chicago Press, 2nd edn, 1958)
BDF	Friedrich Blass, A. Debrunner and Robert W. Funk, *A Greek Grammar of the New Testament and Other Early Christian Literature* (Cambridge: Cambridge University Press, 1961)
BETL	Bibliotheca ephemeridum theologicarum lovaniensium
Bib	*Biblica*

---

1. Equivalent abbreviations used by S. Hornblower and A. Spawforth (eds.), *The Oxford Classical Dictionary* (Oxford and New York: Oxford University Press, 3rd edn, 1996), xxix-liv, are given in brackets.

BJRL	*Bulletin of the John Rylands University Library of Manchester*
BNTC	Black's New Testament Commentaries
BT	*The Bible Translator*
BTB	*Biblical Theology Bulletin*
BULICS	*Bulletin of the University of London Institute of Classical Studies*
CBQ	*Catholic Biblical Quarterly*
CBQMS	*Catholic Biblical Quarterly*, Monograph Series
CGTC	Cambridge Greek Testament Commentary
CJ	*The Classical Journal*
CQ	*The Classical Quarterly*
CP	*Classical Philology*
CSCP	*Cornell Studies in Classical Philology*
CWCurTM	*Currents in Theology and Mission*
EBib	Etudes bibliques
EvQ	*Evangelical Quarterly*
ExpTim	*Expository Times*
FRLANT	Forschungen zur Religion und Literatur des Alten und Neuen Testaments
GR	*Greece and Rome*
HeyJ	*Heythrop Journal*
HSCP	Harvard Studies in Classical Philology
HNT	Handbuch zum Neuen Testament
HR	*History of Religions*
HTS	Hervormde Teologiese Studies
ICC	International Critical Commentary
Int	*Interpretation*
IPQ	*International Philosophical Quarterly*
ITL	*International Theological Library*
JAC	*Jahrbuch für Antike und Christentum*
JBL	*Journal of Biblical Literature*
JEH	*Journal of Ecclesiastical History*
JHS	*Journal of Hellenic Studies*
JSNT	*Journal for the Study of the New Testament*
JSNTSup	*Journal for the Study of the New Testament*, Supplement Series
JSOT	*Journal for the Study of the Old Testament*
JSOTSup	*Journal for the Study of the Old Testament*, Supplement Series
JTS	*Journal of Theological Studies*
KEK	Kritisch-Exegetischer Kommentar über das Neue Testament
LCL	Loeb Classical Library
LNSM	J.P. Louw, et al., eds., *Greek-English Lexicon of the New Testament Based on Semantic Domains*
LSJ	H.G. Liddell, Robert Scott and H. Stuart Jones, *Greek-English Lexicon* (Oxford: Clarendon Press, 9th edn, 1968)
MH	*Museum Helveticum*
MM	J.H. Moulton and G. Milligan, *The Vocabulary of the Greek Testament* (Grand Rapids: Eerdmans, 1982)

NA26	Nestle-Aland, *Novum Testamentum graece*. 26th edn.
NAK	*Nederlandsch Archief voor Kerkgeschiedenis*
NCB	New Century Bible
Neot	*Neotestamentica*
NIDNTT	Colin Brown (ed.), *The New International Dictionary of New Testament Theology* (3 vols.; Exeter: Paternoster Press, 1975)
NIGTC	The New International Greek Testament Commentary
NovT	*Novum Testamentum*
NovTSup	*Novum Testamentum*, Supplements
NTS	*New Testament Studies*
NTT	*Nederlands Theologisch Tijdschrift*
OBO	Orbis biblicus et orientalis
OBT	Overtures to Biblical Theology
OCD	*Oxford Classical Dictionary*
OTP	James Charlesworth (ed.), *Old Testament Pseudepigrapha*
PA	*Philosophia Antiqua*
RAC	*Reallexikon für Antike und Christentum*
RB	*Revue biblique*
RhM	*Rheinisches Museum für Philologie*
RP	Religions Perspectives
RSR	*Recherches de science religieuse*
RVV	Religionsgeschichtliche Versuche und Vorarbeiten
SAJP	*South African Journal of Philosophy*
SBLMS	SBL Monograph Series
SBLDS	SBL Dissertation Series
SBLSBS	SBL Sources for Biblical Study
SBLSCS	SBL Septuagint and Cognate Studies
SBLSP	SBL Seminar Papers
SBLTT	SBL Texts and Translations
SEÅ	*Svensk exegetisk årsbok*
SP	*Studia Patristica*
SCHNT	Studia ad corpus hellenisticum Novi Testamenti
SJT	*Scottish Journal of Theology*
SNTSMS	Society for New Testament Studies Monograph Series
ST	*Studia theologica*
SUNT	Studien zur Umwelt des Neuen Testaments
SVF	*Stoicorum veterum fragmenta*
SVTP	Studia in Veteris Testamenti pseudepigrapha
TAPA	*Transactions of the American Philological Association*
TD	*Theology Digest*
TDNT	Gerhard Kittel and Gerhard Friedrich (eds.), *Theological Dictionary of the New Testament* (trans. Geoffrey W. Bromiley; 10 vols.; Grand Rapids: Eerdmans, 1964–)
THKNT	Theologischer Handkommentar zum Neuen Testament
TNT	Texte zum Neuen Testament
TSFBul	*TSF Bulletin*
TU	Texte und Untersuchungen
TZ	*Theologische Zeitschrift*

WUNT	Wissenschaftliche Untersuchungen zum Neuen Testament
YCS	*Yale Classical Studies*
ZNW	*Zeitschrift für die neutestamentliche Wissenschaft*
ZTK	*Zeitschrift für Theologie und Kirche*

PREFACE

This monograph is a lightly revised version of my doctoral dissertation, completed in Grahamstown, South Africa, in early 1993. Commentary on the New Testament as Hellenistic literature has continued in the intervening period of course but, apart from a few references to some recent publications, I have not attempted to interact with it here. The moral-philosophical dimension of Lk. 15.11-32 remains an overlooked area of Lukan study.

In the course of writing the dissertation I experienced the generosity of many people and institutions. The warden of St Paul's College, Canon Chich Hewitt, enabled me to be in Grahamstown during the time of my research and writing by giving me part-time employment on his staff. His successor, the rector of the College of the Transfiguration, Canon Luke Lungile Pato, graciously allowed that arrangement to continue for part of 1993, to enable me to complete my writing without disruption. I received financial assistance from the Theological Teachers' Training Fund of the Church of the Province of Southern Africa, Reginald Dryden Scholarships from the Faculty of Divinity of Rhodes University, Grahamstown, and a doctoral bursary from the South African Centre for Science Development. I am glad to acknowledge the assistance of the latter towards this research, and to make clear that the opinions expressed and conclusions arrived at here are my own, and are not necessarily to be attributed to the Centre for Science Development.

Generosity takes many forms. My supervisor, Professor P.G.R. de Villiers, was consistently encouraging and helpful during the years that he guided my graduate research. I benefited from the insights of a number of visiting scholars, especially Professor A.J. Malherbe, Professor J.H. Petzer and Dr J. Thom. My debt to each of them is evident in the following pages. Other staff members of Rhodes University were also generous with their time and assistance. Mr J. Jackson and Mr M. Vermaak gave me guidance and advice in the areas of classics and philosophy respectively, and the inter-library Loans staff of Rhodes

University Library enabled me to have prompt access to many publications not available in Grahamstown.

As this study shows, friendship and family life are the contexts in which generosity is most richly given and received. Through friends and family members I was often given help to take the next step, or to sit down at my computer for another day. In addition to people already mentioned, I wish to express my thanks to the Reverend Allan Williams, Mr Ian Dore and Professor Chris de Wet, who, together with the members of their families, gave me and my family great practical help and encouragement. My parents-in-law, Johan and Cathy Besseling, also gave generous financial and moral support to us during the years I was studying.

Since this thesis was completed I have been living and working in the UK, where I have again had cause to give thanks for the generosity of many. The publication of this work was set aside for four years while I devoted myself to church leadership and clergy in-service training in a new country. I am grateful to my friends and colleagues at the Southern Theological Education and Training Scheme for encouraging me to take up this matter once again, to the editors of the JSNT Supplement Series for accepting this monograph for publication and to the Revd Tim Reader and Mr Keith Hubbard for their assistance with the proofreading.

I must acknowledge a personal debt to Lk. 15.11-32. Since first hearing it retold at a time of crisis in my adolescence, I have consistently experienced it as a parable which gives guidance and joy. I shall always be grateful to John and Heather Harrison for telling me and showing me what the story means.

Above all, I am deeply grateful to my wife, Patricia, and my daughters, Sarah and Elinor. This book is dedicated to them.

Part I

THE PARABLE

Chapter 1

PRIOR GRECO-ROMAN PERSPECTIVES ON LUKE 15.11-32:
AN OVERVIEW

1. *Introduction*

This study opens up a new perspective on Lk. 15.11-32 by relating the structure and language of the parable of the prodigal son to the Greco-Roman topos On Covetousness.[1] It argues that Luke employs this relationship with an important field of moral debate in the late first century CE as a deliberate strategy to facilitate communication with his intended readership.[2] In the central section of his Gospel (Lk. 9.51-19.27) he assembles a large number of sayings of Jesus, including a number of parables found only in this Gospel. These parables may be viewed as a collection with many formal, linguistic and thematic similarities, and many points of contact with the topos On Covetousness. One of these, the parable in Lk. 15.11-32, deals with a particular aspect of this topos: the ideal of liberality. This ideal is presented to Luke's readers by means of a story about the relationship between a compassionate and liberal man and his two covetous sons.

---

1.   A definition of the term 'topos' and a full description of the topos On Covetousness are given in Chapter 4 below.

2.   Neither the Gospel of Luke nor the Acts of the Apostles identifies its author. This study adopts the conclusions of Fitzmyer that (1) Luke the companion of Paul is the author; (2) a date of composition of c. 80–85 CE is most likely; (3) the place of composition is unknown; and (4) his intended readers are Gentile Christians. See J.A. Fitzmyer, *The Gospel According to Luke* (AB, 28, 28A; New York: Doubleday, 1983), pp. 35-62. However, this study also accepts the view of Johnson that the most helpful information about the author comes from the character of his writings. See L.T. Johnson, *The Gospel of Luke* (Sacra Pagina, 3; Collegeville, MN: Michael Glazier, 1991), p. 3.

The parable and its co-texts give many indications that Luke made use of the conventions and concerns of Greco-Roman morality to facilitate the proclamation of the Christian gospel. These will be noted in the course of this study. Hock's comment, made in connection with Lk. 16.19-31, applies just as readily to Lk. 15.11-32: 'After all the text of the parable is in Greek, and it is part of a larger two-volume work that was intended for persons whose familiarity with Greco-Roman society is not in doubt'.[3] In this respect his practice resembles that of the popular moralists, who also engaged with these conventions and concerns in their efforts to promote the moral views associated with their particular philosophical associations. In both Luke and the popular philosophers this engagement is not an uncritical echoing of popular viewpoints, but a creative interaction with them. The approach to the parable of the prodigal son taken here therefore involves comparing it with a wide range of Greco-Roman and Hellenistic Jewish moral writings which have similar moral concerns.

Implicit in this approach are the further assumptions that the author had some knowledge of Greco-Roman literature and culture, and that he was free to produce a text in which parables attributed to Jesus could be told in such a way that they would relate closely to the structure and terminology of Greco-Roman moral thought. There are a number of reasons why these assumptions are not examined in any detail here. First, they are not particularly novel. The practice of comparing the paraenesis of Paul and the speeches of Acts with forms and teachings found in Greco-Roman moral philosophy is widely accepted today.[4]

---

3.   R.F. Hock, 'Lazarus and Micyllus: Greco-Roman Backgrounds to Luke 16.19-31', *JBL* 106 (1987), 447-63 (456). Alexander argues that the literature of the Hellenistic schools, the 'middlebrow' literature of the trades and professions, provides a convincing literary context for Luke (L. Alexander, 'The Living Voice: Scepticism towards the Written Word in Early Christian and in Graeco-Roman Texts', in D.J.A. Clines, S.E. Fowl and S.E. Porter [eds.], *The Bible in Three Dimensions: Essays in Celebration of Forty Years of Biblical Studies in the University of Sheffield* [JSOTSup, 87; Sheffield: Sheffield Academic Press, 1990], pp. 221-47 [245]; and 'Luke's Preface in the Context of Greek Preface Writing', *NovT* 28 [1986], pp. 48-73 [60-69]).

4.   A seminal example of the latter is the 1939 essay by M. Dibelius, 'Paul on the Areopagus', in *idem, Studies in the Acts of the Apostles* (ed. H. Greeven; London: SCM Press, 1956), pp. 26-77. A recent study of the same speech in the

Secondly, the process of examining these assumptions would take us away from the question under discussion, into questions relating to the historical Jesus, the Hellenization of Palestine in the first century CE, the origins of Luke's sources, the content of Jesus' original teaching and the composition of his original audiences. These questions are important but lie outside the area of focus here, which is Luke's efforts to communicate his understanding of the gospel to his intended readers. Thirdly, the assumption that Luke was engaging with Greco-Roman philosophy and morality is best proved by demonstrating the relationship between the Lukan text and moral philosophical literature, both at the level of concrete details and at the level of overall perspective. This is done in Part 3.

This study shows that Luke uses the structures, themes and language of Greco-Roman morality consistently throughout Lk. 15.11-32. It further argues that these points of contact are themselves part of a well-established moral structure: the topos On Covetousness. This network of relationships between Luke and his moral milieu yields a coherent reading of the parable which: (1) addresses the long-standing exegetical question of the unity of the parable; (2) sheds new light on many of its most familiar but enigmatic motifs; (3) relates well to a major theological concern of Luke's Gospel; (4) explains how the parable might have been received by Luke's readers; and (5) suggests that Greco-Roman morality was regarded as an important point of contact between Christians and pagans in the Hellenized cities of the late first century CE.

Because this study is based on the relationship between Lk. 15.11-32 and Greco-Roman moral literature, I begin with a survey of the roots and fruits of this approach, and a critical sketch of prior studies of Lk. 15.11-32 which have been made from a Greco-Roman perspective.

2. The Origins and Antecedents of Greco-Roman Perspectives

a. From the Church Fathers to the Renaissance

The contemporary exploration of the relationship between Greco-Roman and early Christian literature finds its origins in the Renaissance, in the work of humanist scholars such as Erasmus (1466–1536)

same tradition is that of D.L. Balch, 'The Areopagus Speech: An Appeal to the Stoic Historian Posidonius against Later Stoics and the Epicureans', in D.L. Balch, E. Ferguson and W.A. Meeks (eds.), *Greeks, Romans and Christians: Essays in Honor of Abraham J. Malherbe* (Minneapolis: Fortress Press, 1990), pp. 52-79.

and Hugo Grotius (1583–1645).[5] Jaeger has pointed out that Erasmus's Christian humanism goes back to the works of the fourth-century Greek Fathers, which were brought to Italy after the fall of Constantinople in 1453.[6] The Cappadocians were noted for their rich classical education, their positive view of Greek literature and philosophy, and their use of Middle and Neo-Platonism, and Stoicism.[7] Prior to the Greek and Latin Fathers of the fourth and fifth centuries, patristic exegetes drew on Greek and Roman literature and philosophy more for apologetic purposes, seeing philosophy as a means of preparing the world for the truth of Christianity.[8] Some, like Tatian and Tertullian, were hostile to Greek philosophy, but most, including Aelius Aristides, Justin, Athenagoras and Minucius Felix, thought of philosophy as containing some truth which was perfectly revealed in the Christian gospel. However, both those who opposed Greek philosophy and those who valued it were influenced by aspects of its language and thought.

The most important representatives of the early relationship between Christianity and Greco-Roman culture are the leaders of the Alexandrian school, Clement and Origen.[9] Both interpret Lk. 15.11-32 in a Platonic way.[10] Clement, for example, interprets the best robe in v. 22 as the robe of immortality, and the shoes as imperishable and suitable for the journey to heaven.[11] Origen describes the younger son's prodigal spending as evidence that he had fled from the Law of Nature itself. His

5.   See W.C. van Unnik, 'Hugo Grotius als uitlegger van het Nieuwe Testament', *NAK* NS 25 (1932), pp. 1-48.

6.   W. Jaeger, *Early Christianity and Greek Paideia* (Cambridge, MA: Harvard University Press; London: Oxford University Press, 1962), pp. 100-101.

7.   F. Copleston, *A History of Philosophy*. I. *Greece and Rome* (London: Burns & Oates, 1966), p. 38.

8.   Nock finds in *1 Clem.* 'a foretaste of the later Clement and of the Christian humanism of the great Cappadocians' ('Christianity and Classical Culture', in Z. Stewart [ed.], *Arthur Darby Nock: Essays on Religion and the Ancient World* [Oxford: Clarendon Press, 1972], II, pp. 676-81 [680]).

9.   Jaeger, *Early Christianity*, p. 112.

10.   For the Platonist orientation of Clement and Origen see H. Chadwick, *Early Christian Thought and the Classical Tradition: Studies in Justin, Clement and Origen* (Oxford: Oxford University Press, 1966), pp. 40-41 and 71-72.

11.   Cited in I.J. du Plessis, *'n Kykie in die Hart van God* (Pretoria: N.G. Kerkboekhandel, 1990), p. 7; and W.S. Kissinger, *The Parables of Jesus: A History of Interpretation and Bibliography* (ATLA Bibliography Series, 4; Metuchen, NJ: Scarecrow Press, 1979), pp. 10-11.

hunger for the carob pods eaten by the pigs is interpreted as the longing of his rational nature to return to rationality, even if of an inferior kind. The carob pods, which are sweet and fattening, are likened to the 'persuasive words of those who love the material and corporeal, who call pleasure a good thing, having itching ears and turning to fables'.[12]

Wiles has shown that there was a large gap between theory and practice in ante-Nicene parable exegesis.[13] Their canons of interpretation have much in common with the prevailing historical approaches of the twentieth century, from Jülicher to Jeremias:[14] (1) not every detail of the parable should be interpreted; some are there only for the sake of the story; (2) established doctrine should be used to guide interpretation; (3) the historical context of the parables in the Gospels should be taken into account;[15] (4) a deeper meaning beyond the surface meaning should be sought; (5) a true understanding of the parables can only be attained with the help of Christ and the gift of the Spirit of God.

However, in practice, the following five principles were determinative: (1) allegorical interpretation was dominant, because of the example of the evangelists, the tradition of the elders,[16] the influence of gnostic interpretations, and because allegorical interpretations were felt to be more satisfying and more complete; (2) there was a tendency to generalize the significance of the parables; (3) parables tended to be grouped together and interpreted in terms of one another; (4) the point of comparison was taken to be the main item in the parable rather than

12. These examples are taken from H. Smith, *Ante-Nicene Exegesis of the Gospels* (Translations of Christian Literature, 6; London: SPCK, 1928), pp. 135-36.

13. M.F. Wiles, 'Early Exegesis of the Parables', *SJT* 11 (1958), pp. 287-301.

14. See J.C. Little, 'Parable Research in the Twentieth Century. II. The Contribution of J. Jeremias', *ExpTim* 88 (1976), pp. 40-44; and 'Parable Research in the Twentieth Century. III. Developments since J. Jeremias', *ExpTim* 88 (1976), pp. 71-75.

15. Using this principle, Tertullian (*Pud.* 8, 9) argued that the parables of Lk. 15 were concerned with Christ's acceptance of the heathen tax-collectors and sinners of Lk. 15.1, and hence could not be applied to the forgiveness of post-baptismal sin. Wiles ('Early Exegesis', p. 290 n. 3) comments, 'Yet in his pre-Montanist days he had himself used them for this very purpose (*De Poenitentia* 8).'

16. Some allegorical interpretations are assumed rather than argued, suggesting that pre-literary oral traditions are being followed. 'The fact that the interpretation of the fatted calf in the parable of the Prodigal Son as meaning Christ is given alike by Irenaeus, Tertullian and Origen suggests the possibility that that interpretation ... derives from an early oral tradition' (Wiles, 'Early Exegesis', p. 294).

the situation as a whole; (5) interpretations were aimed at meeting immediate needs or resolving current controversies.[17]

Derrett rejects the patristic allegories of Lk. 15.11-32 as arbitrary and fanciful, and advances the view that the allegorical associations found in Jewish midrash are closer to the meanings intended by Jesus.[18] However, Tissot's study of patristic allegories of Lk. 15.11-32 shows that it is inaccurate to contrast patristic allegories with those of the Jewish midrashic tradition. The former are rooted in the latter though, as patristic allegories developed, they came to reflect the theology and life of the church.[19]

Derrett's exegesis suffers from the now-outdated assumption that there is a dichotomy between 'Palestinian' and 'Hellenistic' Christianity.[20] It is also flawed by positivistic assumptions about interpretation.[21] He fails to recognize that because interpretation is an ongoing process, patristic exegetes legitimately attempted to make scripture intelligible

---

17. Wiles notes that these correspond substantially with Jeremias's view of how the church interpreted the parables prior to the writing of the Gospels (Wiles, 'Early Exegesis', pp. 299-301).

18. J.D.M. Derrett, 'The Parable of the Prodigal Son: Patristic Allegories and Jewish Midrashim', *SP* 10, pp. 219-24.

19. Y. Tissot, 'Patristic Allegories of the Lukan Parable of the Two Sons', in F. Bovon and G. Rouiller (eds.), *Exegesis: Problems of Method and Exercises in Reading* (trans. D.G. Miller; Pittsburgh: Pickwick Press, 1978), pp. 362-409 (384-85).

20. 'The problem is why the church, when it spread amongst non-Jews, dropped so much of the inbuilt learning and insinuation, and substituted for it allegories which are purely imaginary and do not, cannot, go back to Christ himself' (Derrett, 'Patristic Allegories', p. 219). For the inappropriateness of the Palestinian–Hellenistic distinction, see M. Hengel, *The 'Hellenization' of Judaea in the First Century after Christ* (London: SCM Press; Philadelphia: Trinity Press International, 1989) passim; and I.H. Marshall, 'Palestinian and Hellenistic Christianity: Some Critical Comments', *NTS* 19 (1972–73), pp. 271-87. Van Unnik observes that one of the advantages of the perspective fostered by the Corpus Hellenisticum project (see below) is that it helps 'to get rid of all sorts of schematization like "Jewish"—"Hellenistic"—"Jewish Hellenistic" as though these were watertight compartments' (W.C. van Unnik, 'Words Come to Life: The Work for the "Corpus Hellenisticum Novi Testamenti"', *NovT* 13 [1971], pp. 199-216 [215]).

21. For example, 'There is no doubt but that the elder brother represents the pious Jew and the younger represents the Jew who has fallen away from Jewish observance ... There is no ground whatsoever for supposing that the brothers *mean* anything more than that' (Derrett, 'Patristic Allegories', p. 220).

for their own contexts. At the same time, as both Wiles and Tissot note, the Fathers did not neglect established traditional interpretations.

Tissot provides a good account of the patristic exegesis of Lk. 15.11-32 which includes the work of post-Nicene exegetes.[22] He identifies four basic lines of allegorical interpretation: (1) gnosticizing interpretations, in which the older son symbolizes the angels and the younger son humanity; (2) ethical interpretations, which see the two brothers as types of the righteous and the sinner; (3) ethnic approaches, which see the two as Israel and the heathen respectively; and (4) penitential perspectives, in which the older brother represents the Christian rigorist who opposes reconciliation with his penitent brother.[23]

These approaches are distinguished for the sake of theoretical clarity. However, Tissot points out that the second, third and fourth are usually used together by exegetes who are unable to interpret the whole parable with a single approach. Either exegetes switch approaches when they come to the part dealing with the elder son, or they simply neglect this section of the parable. As there are no textual grounds for viewing vv. 25-32 as a secondary addition to the parable, this indicates the real weakness of patristic allegorical exegesis of this parable. None of the interpretive approaches is able to interpret the whole parable consistently according to a single approach.

This points to the need to read the parable in terms of a prior audience, consisting of Christian converts together with interested pagans, whose primary frame of reference is neither Jewish midrash nor the practices of the patristic church, but Greco-Roman culture.

b. *The Christian Humanists: Price and Wettstein*
Two important milestones in the tradition of reading the New Testament together with the works of Greco-Roman authors, are the collections of parallels contained in the commentary by Price in the *Critici Sacri* and the edition of the New Testament by Wettstein.

The *Critici Sacri* is a collection of commentaries by humanist scholars from the sixteenth and seventeenth centuries which was published in Utrecht and Amsterdam in 1698.[24] One of the scholars represented in

22. Tissot, 'Patristic Allegories', pp. 362-409.
23. Tissot, 'Patristic Allegories', p. 366.
24. W.C. van Unnik, 'Corpus Hellenisticum Novi Testamenti', *JBL* 83 (1964), pp. 17-33 (21).

the *Critici sacri* is John Price, who provides a valuable collection of parallels from classical literature.[25] His work provides a useful supplement
to the parallels cited by Wettstein. Jülicher comments on the value of
his collection of parallels for parable exegetes, but regrets his neglect of
the broader meaning of larger units of text.[26]

J.J. Wettstein (1693–1754) devoted a lifetime of scholarship to pro-
ducing an edition of the New Testament that provided an apparatus for
improving the Textus Receptus. This was published in Amsterdam in
1751/52.[27] To this edition he added parallels from Jewish and classical
writers which he had collected over many years. These aroused great
interest, both at the time and since. His work has now been republished
in a revised, expanded and corrected form by Georg Strecker and Udo
Schnelle.[28]

c. *The* Corpus Hellenisticum Novi Testamenti *Project*
The eighteenth and nineteenth centuries produced much new material
relating to the interpretation of the New Testament: inscriptions, papyri,
Gnostic texts such as the Corpus Hermeticum, and the rediscovery
by Western scholars of extra-canonical texts preserved by the Eastern
churches. This new material shifted the framework of interpretation of

25. J. Pricaeus, *Commentarii in Varios Novi Testamenti Libros; in quibus
Vulgatae Versionis, quamplurimis locis, prae quavis alia recentiore sermo purus
Latinusque ostenditur; Contextus Graeci litera explicatur; Ejusdem Phraseologia
cum Auctorum Ethnicorum locutionibus amoene comparatur; Multorum difficilium
locorum Expositiones novae afferuntur; Sensusque non solum ex Christianis
Ecclesiae antiquissimae Doctoribus, sed et ex Graecis Latinisque Gentium Scrip-
toribus ubique illustratur* in *Annotata ad SS. Evangelia: sive Criticorum Sacrorum*,
VI (London: Flescher, 1660).

26. A. Jülicher, *Die Gleichnisreden Jesu* (Darmstadt: Wissenschaftliche Buchgesellschaft, 1976 [1910]), p. 273.

27. The full title of this work is: H KAINH ΔIAΘHKH, *Novum Testamentum
Graecum editionis receptae cum lectionibus variantibus codicum MSS, editionum
aliarum, versionum et Patrum, nec non commentario pleniore ex scriptoribus vet-
eribus Hebraeis, Graecis, et Latinis Historiam et vim verborum illustrante opera et
studio Joannis Jacobi Wetstenii* (Amstelaedami ex officina Dommeriana, MDCCLI-
MDCCLII, 2 tomi) (Graz: Akademische Druck- und Verlagsanstalt, photomechani-
cal repr., 1962).

28. G. Strecker and U. Schnelle (eds.), *Neuer Wettstein: Texte zum Neuen
Testament aus Griechentum und Hellenismus* (2 vols.; Berlin: W. de Gruyter, 1995,
1997).

the New Testament away from the Old Testament and the classical Greek tradition.

But renewed interest in the study of Hellenism and Greco-Roman culture was again evident by the end of the nineteenth century. 'Most strikingly this renewal is precipitated in Lietzmann's *Handbuch zum NT*, in Walter Bauer's lexicographical masterpiece, and in the indispensable *Theologisches Wörterbuch* of Kittel-Friedrich'.[29] These and other works recognized again the importance of Greco-Roman literature and philosophy for interpreting the language[30] and moral teaching[31] of the New Testament.

In 1910, Georg Heinrici proposed the development of a 'new Wettstein'. He intended to draw upon the enormous amount of material not assessed by Wettstein, especially in the field of the relationship between New Testament and Greco-Roman social ethics. In view of Billerbeck's *Kommentar zum NT aus Talmud und Midrash* this was to be limited to Greek and Latin texts. Heinrici died in 1915, and the project was stalled by the major shift in theology that took place after 1920 and, later,

29. Van Unnik, 'Corpus Hellenisticum', pp. 21-22, with reference to the HNT; the BAGD; MM; A. Deissmann, *Light from the Ancient East: The New Testament Illustrated by Recently Discovered Texts of the Graeco-Roman World* (trans. L.R.M. Strachan; London: Hodder & Stoughton, 4th edn, 1927).

30. See R.C. Trench, *Notes on the Parables of our Lord* (London: Macmillan, 1870); and *idem*, *Synonyms of the New Testament* (London: Macmillan, 9th edn, 1880; Grand Rapids: Eerdmans, 1948). The latter is still a rich collection of philological material. Jülicher (*Gleichnisreden*, p. 300) was not impressed by the work of his influential predecessor on the parables. He remarks, 'Im einzelnen enthält das Werk vieles Ausgezeichnete, grammatische und antiquarische Bemerkungen, aber zu wenig scharfe Begriffsbestimmung, zu viel dogmatisierende und erbauliche Ergüsse, und keine Anwandlung von Kritik.'

31. Of the original members of the Göttingen history of religions school, J. Weiss is notable for his conviction that exegetes should have a good working knowledge of Seneca, Epictetus, Plutarch, Lucian, Musonius, Marcus Aurelius, Cicero and von Arnim's collection of Stoic fragments. Other examples of this view are history of religions studies such as those of Bonhöffer and Clemen: A. Bonhöffer, *Epiktet und das Neue Testament* (Giessen: Alfred Töpelmann, 1911; repr., Berlin: Alfred Töpelmann, 1964); and C. Clemen, *Religionsgeschichtliche Erklärung des Neuen Testaments: Die Abhängigkeit des ältesten Christentums von nichtjüdischen Religionen und philosophischen Systemen* (Giessen: Alfred Töpelmann, 1924; repr., Berlin: W. de Gruyter, 1973). While the latter works illustrate the interest in the relationship between Greco-Roman philosophers and the New Testament, they provide little of direct application to the present investigation.

another world war. One dissertation on Plutarch and the New Testament was published in 1946,[32] but the project only gained momentum after W.C. van Unnik was given custody of the Greco-Roman material in 1956.

Apart from Almqvist, the following scholars have contributed explicitly to the Corpus Hellenisticum Novi Testamenti project since the end of the Second World War: H.-D. Betz, G. Mussies, J.N. Sevenster, P.W. van der Horst, and J.S. Sibinga.[33] Many other New Testament and

32. H. Almqvist, *Plutarch und das Neue Testament: Ein Beitrag zum Corpus Hellenisticum Novi Testamenti* (ASNU, 15; Uppsala: Appelbergs boktr., 1946)

33. See particularly H.D. Betz, *Lukian von Samosata und das Neue Testament: Religionsgeschichtliche und paränetische Parallelen. Ein Beitrag zum Corpus Hellenisticum Novi Testamenti* (TU, 76; Berlin: Akademie Verlag, 1961); 'Lukian von Samosata und das Christentum', *NovT* 3 (1959), pp. 226-37; his contributions to the studies of two collections of Plutarch's writings, H.D. Betz (ed.), *Plutarch's Theological Writings and Early Christian Literature* (SCHNT, 3; Leiden: E.J. Brill, 1975); and *Plutarch's Ethical Writings and Early Christian Literature* (SCHNT, 4; Leiden: E.J. Brill, 1978) and H.D. Betz, *2 Corinthians 8 and 9: A Commentary on Two Administrative Letters of the Apostle Paul* (Hermeneia; Philadelphia: Fortress Press, 1985) and H.D. Betz, *The Sermon on the Mount: A Commentary on the Sermon on the Mount, including the Sermon on the Plain (Matthew 5:3–7:27 and Luke 6:20-49)* (Hermeneia; Minneapolis: Fortress Press, 1995). G. Mussies, *Dio Chrysostom and the New Testament* (SCHNT, 2; Leiden: E.J. Brill, 1972). J.N. Sevenster, 'Waarom spreekt Paulus nooit van vrienden en vriendschap?' *NTT* 9 (1954/55), pp. 356-63; *idem, Paul and Seneca* (NovTSup, 4; Leiden: E.J. Brill, 1961); and *idem*, 'Education or Conversion: Epictetus and the Gospels', in J.N. Sevenster (ed.), *Placita Pleiadia: Opstellen aangeboden aan G. Sevenster* (Leiden: E.J. Brill, 1966), pp. 247-62. P.W. van der Horst, 'Drohung und Mord Schnabend (Acta 9.1)', *NovT* 12 (1970), pp. 257-69; *idem*, 'Macrobius and the New Testament', *NovT* 15 (1973), pp. 220-32; *idem*, 'Musonius Rufus and the New Testament', *NovT* 16 (1974), pp. 306-15; *idem*, 'Hieracles the Stoic and the New Testament', *NovT* 17 (1975), pp. 156-60; *idem*, 'Cornutus and the New Testament', *NovT* 23 (1981), pp. 165-72; *idem*, 'Chariton and the New Testament', *NovT* 25 (1983), pp. 348-55; *idem, The Sentences of Pseudo-Phocylides* (SVTP, 4; Leiden: E.J. Brill, 1978); 'Hellenistic Parallels to the Acts of the Apostles (1.1-26)', *ZNW* 74 (1983), pp. 17-26; 'Hellenistic Parallels to the Acts of the Apostles (2.1-47)', *JSNT* 25 (1985), pp. 49-60; 'Hellenistic Parallels to Acts (Chapters 3 and 4)', *JSNT* 35 (1989), pp. 37-46 (the latter two reprinted in C.A. Evans and S.E. Porter (eds.), *New Testament Backgrounds: A Sheffield Reader* [The Biblical Seminar, 43; Sheffield: Sheffield Academic Press, 1997], pp. 207-19 and 220-29); J.S. Sibinga, 'Toorn en droefheid in Marcus 3.5: Een bijdrage aan het Corpus Hellenisticum', in

classical scholars have also made contributions to this area of study without directly associating themselves with the project.[34] However, with hindsight it is clear that the Corpus Hellenisticum Novi Testamenti Project played an important role in reaffirming the importance of Greco-Roman literature for the understanding of the New Testament, and in indicating fruitful avenues for research.[35]

3. *Prior Readings of Luke 15.11-32 from a Greco-Roman Perspective*

The immense popularity of the parable of the prodigal son has resulted in its often being used to test or illustrate new exegetical methods.[36] This practice often overlooks the fact that it is not typical of the synoptic parables, and belongs to a group of parables found only in Luke's Gospel, of which it is the longest. I examine the implications of this for its interpretation in the following two chapters.

a. *Parallel Stories from the* Controversiae *of Roman Declamation*
Given the fact that Lk. 15.11-32 is one of the most intensively re-searched parts of the New Testament, it is remarkable that it has received relatively little attention from a Greco-Roman perspective. This can be attributed to the strong apologetic commitment to its dominical origins and hence to its Palestinian milieu.[37]

I.B. Horst *et al.* (eds.), *De Geest in het geding* (Festschrift J.A. Oosterbaan; Alphen aan den Rijn: Tj. Willink, 1978), pp. 255-67.

34. The field has been well-reviewed by A.J. Malherbe in a variety of papers. The most comprehensive and recent survey is given in 'Hellenistic Moral Philosophy and the New Testament: A Retrospective Analysis', keynote SBL paper, 1990. See also 'Greco-Roman Religion and Philosophy and the New Testament', in E.J. Epp and G.W. MacRae (eds.), *The New Testament and its Modern Interpreters* (Atlanta: Scholars Press, 1989), pp. 3-26; the introduction to *Paul and the Popular Philosophers* (Minneapolis: Fortress Press, 1989), pp. 1-9; and 'Hellenistic Moralists and the New Testament', *ANRW*, II.26.1 (1992): 267-333.

35. D. Dormeyer provides an overview of the links between the New Testament and Hellenistic literature in *The New Testament among the Writings of Antiquity* (trans. R. Kossov; Biblical Seminar, 55; Sheffield: Sheffield Academic Press, 1998). Chapters 5–7 are of particular relevance to this study.

36. See, for example, the articles in F. Bovon and G. Rouiller (eds.), *Exegesis: Problems of Method and Exercises in Reading (Genesis 22 and Luke 15)* (trans. D.G. Miller; Pittsburgh: Pickwick Press, 1978) and J.D. Crossan, (ed.), *Polyvalent Narration* (Semeia; Missoula: Scholars Press, 1977).

37. The most influential twentieth-century interpreter to take this view is of

The most important recent studies from a Greco-Roman viewpoint are those of Schottroff, Berger and Rau.[38]

(i) *L. Schottroff*. Schottroff considers the parable to be a Lukan composition, because it reflects the soteriology and Christology of Luke, has the function of integrating the three parables of Luke 15, and has a wider moral framework than either the traditions of Jesus's fellowship with sinners or Paul's teaching on justification.[39] She thinks it is best understood within the context of Greco-Roman rhetoric and identifies a number of parallels of content and form between Luke's parable and the fifth declamation of Pseudo-Quintilian (*Aeger redemptus*).[40] She argues that this parallel demonstrates that the parable relates to conventions well known to Luke's readers: the paradigm of love between parents and children and the familiar rhetorical theme of *filius abdicatus*. The father's love in the parable does not represent extraordinary divine love, but normal paternal love.[41] Similarly, the objections

course Jeremias. See J. Jeremias, *The Parables of Jesus* (London: SCM Press, 3rd edn, 1972), pp. 128-32. Rau mentions the strong apologetic commitment of Jülicher and Jeremias to the incomparability of Jesus. See E. Rau, *Reden in Vollmacht: Hintergrund, Form und Anliegen der Gleichnisse Jesu* (FRLANT, 149; Göttingen: Vandenhoeck & Ruprecht, 1990), p. 218.

38. L. Schottroff, 'Das Gleichnis vom verlorenen Sohn', *ZTK* 68 (1971), pp. 27-52; K. Berger, 'Gleichnisse als Texte: Zum lukanischen Gleichnis vom "verlorenen Sohn"', in K.-H. Bender, K. Berger and M. Wandruszka (eds.), *Imago Linguae* (Festschrift F. Paepcke; Munich: Wilhelm Fink Verlag, 1977), pp. 61-74; and Rau, *Reden in Vollmacht*.

39. See Schottroff, 'Gleichnis vom verlorenen Sohn', pp. 51-52. Her other reason, that the elder brother presents a caricature of Jewish piety, is less persuasive. See J. Piper's criticisms in *'Love Your Enemies': Jesus' Love Command in the Synoptic Gospels and in the Early Christian Paraenesis. A History of the Tradition and Interpretation of its Uses* (SNTSMS, 38; Cambridge: Cambridge University Press, 1979), pp. 82-83; and Marshall's charge of 'unjustifiable allegorization' in I.H. Marshall, *The Gospel of Luke: A Commentary on the Greek Text* (NIGTC; Exeter: Paternoster Press, 1978), p. 606.

40. G. Lehnert, *Declamationes xix maiores* (Leipzig: Teubner, 1905), pp. 88-110.

41. Betz agrees with her identification of Luke's engagement with the literary topos of father and son. See H.D. Betz, '*De Fraterno Amore (Moralia* 478A-492D)', in H.D. Betz (ed.), *Plutarch's Ethical Writings and Early Christian Literature* (SCHNT, 4; Leiden: E.J. Brill, 1978), pp. 231-63 (236 n. 33).

of the elder brother to his father's actions are typical rhetorical objections to such love from the perspective of retribution.

Thus, while Schottroff discusses only one of many possible parallels between Greco-Roman literature and Lk. 15.11-32, she shows that such a comparison provides a different horizon of interpretation (*Verstehenshorizont*) which strongly challenges many cherished exegetical traditions relating to the parable.[42] In focusing almost exclusively on her claim that the parable illustrates Lukan soteriology and her conclusion that the parable is a completely Lukan composition, critics have failed to credit Schottroff with breaking significant new ground in showing how the parable might have been understood by audiences with a fundamentally Greco-Roman cultural perspective.[43] If those addressed by Luke's Gospel are rooted in Greco-Roman culture, it is beside the point for Bovon to say that, 'The themes of the return from a trip, the father who forgives and the rivalry between brothers are too much anchored in the Biblical tradition to make us venture into another tradition',[44] or for Rau to accuse her of ignoring the perspective of the hearers.[45] The point is that Hellenized readers would read the parable against other traditions, and the question is whether Luke made use of this fact in his shaping or reshaping of this parable.

(ii) *K. Berger*. Berger brings his wide knowledge of Hellenistic literature to bear on his analysis of the parable and cites a number of Greco-Roman, Hellenistic Jewish and rabbinic parallel stories. He describes the basic elements of the parable, a father with two sons, as a common rhetorical form in later Hellenism,[46] and gives three examples of paral-

---

42. Schottroff, 'Gleichnis vom verlorenen Sohn', p. 47.

43. See Marshall, *Gospel of Luke*, pp. 605-606; Fitzmyer, *Luke*, p. 1085; B.B. Scott, *Hear Then the Parable: A Commentary on the Parables of Jesus* (Minneapolis: Fortress Press, 1989), p. 105; and Rau, *Reden in Vollmacht*, p. 183.

44. F. Bovon, *Luke the Theologian: Thirty-Three Years of Research (1950–1983)* (trans. K. McKinney; Allison Park: Pickwick Publications, 1987), p. 286.

45. Rau, *Reden in Vollmacht*, p. 204.

46. He cites, among others, Pseudo-Quintilian, *Declam.* 5; Philo, *Quaest. in Gen.* 4.198 (on Gen. 27.3-4); and *Omn. Prob. Lib.* 57 ('Gleichnisse als Texte', p. 62 n. 1).

lel plots.[47] In addition to these he cites many points of contact with Hellenistic Jewish or Greco-Roman literature.[48]

Berger's study is a model of concise but acute exegetical observation,[49] with extensive interaction with the secondary literature, including the study by Schottroff. However, he interprets the parable solely in the context of Luke 15, and argues that the closest external points of contact with the parable are found in Philo. It is a call to the Lukan community to rejoice together over the conversion of new members.[50]

Thus, although he identifies parallels of content and motif with narratives in the rhetorical tradition of Hellenism, his interpretation remains dominated by traditional theological themes, particularly those of repentance and mutual acceptance. He does not make any mention of the relationship between the moral issues discussed by these parallel Greco-Roman texts and those addressed in Lk. 15.11-32.[51]

(iii) *E. Rau.* Rau's monograph on the background, form and concerns of Jesus' parables contains an extensive discussion of parallels to Lk. 15.11-32.[52] He accepts the linguistic arguments that the parable derives from pre-Lukan tradition and thinks of it as a parable of Jesus that has been reworked by Luke.

47. Pseudo-Quintilian, *Declam.* 5, *Apoc. Sedr.* 6 and Philo, *Prov.* 2.15 ('Gleichnisse als Texte', pp. 65-67). Further examples of Philo, *Virt.* 179; Teles, *Autark.* Περὶ αὐταρκείας 95-96; and two rabbinic parables are given in K. Berger and C. Colpe, *Religionsgeschichtliches Textbuch zum Neuen Testament* (TNT, 1; Göttingen: Vandenhoeck & Ruprecht, 1987), pp. 137-40. No further examples are given in M.E. Boring, K. Berger and C. Colpe, *Hellenistic Commentary to the New Testament* (Nashville: Abingdon Press, 1995), pp. 223-26.

48. See the references to *Joseph and Asenath*, Sentences of Sextus, *4 Ezra*, *Pseudo-Philo*, *Assumption of Moses* and Artemidorus, *Oneirocr.*, among others, in Berger, 'Gleichnisse als Texte', p. 64 nn. 10-14.

49. For example, the comments on narrative method and techniques in Berger, 'Gleichnisse als Texte', p. 62 n. 2.

50. Berger, 'Gleichnisse als Texte', pp. 72-74.

51. For example, his reference to Philo, *Virt.* 179, made in connection with the motif of rejoicing together, points to the topos On Friendship (see φιλτάτους καὶ συγγενεστάτους and φιλία καὶ οἰκειότης). However, Berger makes no link between the motifs of rejoicing together and friendship, though they are found together in Lk. 15.29.

52. Rau, *Reden in Vollmacht*, pp. 216-408.

However, he also recognizes the existence of many parallels to the plot of the parable in Greco-Roman and Jewish thought. Here he reveals the influence of Schottroff and Berger in finding his parallels principally in Greco-Roman declamations, Philo and rabbinic literature.[53] He attributes the links between Roman rhetoric and Lk. 15.11-32 to the influence of Hellenistic and Roman rhetoric on Palestinian Jewish parables.

While this does point to an important element in the origins of rabbinic and New Testament parable forms, it has the effect of relegating the Greco-Roman elements somewhat to the background. In the case of Lk. 15.11-32 this results in the parable being read in terms of its fictional audience of the scribes and the Pharisees. Despite his extensive examination of parallels, Rau comes to the traditional exegetical conclusion that the parable is aimed at justifying Jesus' table-fellowship with sinners, to those who objected that such behaviour was an attack on the purity law undergirding Pharisaic piety.[54]

However, as Scott has pointed out, the fictional audience and the original, historical audience need not be identical. He argues that it is essential to retain the distinctions between: (1) what happens to the elder son within Lk. 15.11-32; (2) the association of the elder son with the Pharisees in the intermediate narrative of Lk. 15 as a whole; and (3) the identification of Luke's readers, and subsequent readers, with the younger son. These literary considerations mean that the interpretive focus should be placed not on the interaction between Jesus and his hearers within Luke 15, but on Luke as 'the first available reader/ performer'.[55] Rau's focus on the relationship between Jesus and the Pharisees within Luke's narrative thus neglects the process of communication between Luke and his implied readers. The strong possibility that the Greco-Roman features of the parable were inserted by Luke with his readers in mind, makes it important for literary-historical studies such as this to take cognizance of the distinctions between extra-textual and intra-textual authors and readers.[56]

---

53. Of the 21 parallels discussed, the only exceptions to this are two papyri, a fable, a dream report and a chapter from the *Apocalypse of Sedrach*. Rau, *Reden in Vollmacht*, pp. 244-52.

54. Rau, *Reden in Vollmacht*, pp. 402-403.

55. Scott, *Hear Then the Parable*, pp. 100-105.

56. See, for example, the diagram of these relationships given in N.R. Petersen, 'The Reader in the Gospel', *Neot* 18 (1984), pp. 38-51 (39).

4. *From Parallel Plots to Related Patterns of Moral Thought*

These three studies all compare the plot of the parable with similar plots found in a variety of other genres. If we set aside the rabbinic parables, they are drawn principally from the *controversiae* of Roman declamation[57] and the paradigm of a father and two sons in Philo.[58] However, these examples do not in any way exhaust the range of possible parallels, for there are many other stories in Greco-Roman literature which contain either similar plots or similar motifs.[59]

The plot of the parable, especially the part dealing with the younger son, can be compared with the structure of heroic myths such as the *Odyssey*. It follows the universal formula for the adventure of the hero, described by Campbell as: departure, initiation and return.[60] In the parable the younger son journeys to a far country, where he is thought to be lost and 'dead' and where he suffers many hardships, before returning safely. There are also many similar motifs and descriptions that could be compared, without suggesting any direct literary dependence.[61] With

---

57. W. Schmithals (*Das Evangelium nach Lukas* [Zürcher Bibelkommentare; Zürich: Theologische Verlag, 1980], p. 165) comments that the parable appears to make use of illustrative material from Hellenistic rhetoric, but this does not affect his reading of the parable.

58. In addition to the examples given by Berger and Rau, Downing suggests that Philo, *Prov.* 2.4 and *Praem. Poen.* 116, may be compared with Lk. 15.18-20. See F.G. Downing, *Strangely Familiar: An Introductory Reader to the First Century* (Manchester: F. Gerald Downing, 1985), p. 124.

59. Given the frequency with which stories about fathers with two sons are found in Greco-Roman and Hellenistic-Jewish literature, and the slightness of the other resemblances, I do not think there is any literary relationship between the parable of the two sons in Mt. 21.28-32 and Lk. 15.11-32. *Pace* M.D. Goulder, *Luke: A New Paradigm* (JSNTSup, 20; Sheffield: JSOT Press, 1989), pp. 75, 609-14

60. There are significant correspondences of detail between aspects of the plot of the adventure of the hero and the parable. For example, 'Initiation' deals with themes such as: the Road of Trials, the Meeting with the Goddess, the Woman as Temptress, Atonement with the Father, Apotheosis and the Ultimate Boon (J. Campbell, *The Hero with a Thousand Faces* [Bollingen Series, 17; New York: Pantheon Books, 1949], pp. ix-x).

61. Compare, for example, the motifs of the loving father and the importance of the right use of inherited property. Wettstein (*Novum Testamentum Graecum*, vol. 1, p. 761) compares the father's greeting in Lk. 15.20d-e with the joyful embrace

the exception of the love theme, the plot of the parable also resembles that of the Hellenistic romances: boy-meets-girl, travel, separation, tribulations and final reunion.[62] Many of the motifs or details found in the parable can also be paralleled in the romances.[63] The resemblances of narrative technique are illustrated in Chapter 2 below.

Many of the themes of the parable can be traced in these, and other genres.[64] The Greco-Roman fable tradition is a relatively neglected field of comparison.[65] This Greco-Roman genre is particularly closely related to Luke's special parables, because it employs purely invented stories (while most other Greco-Roman genres draw on historical and/or mythological events or characters),[66] and because fables are stories with morals.[67]

---

which Penelope gives to Odysseus on being sure of his identity in Homer, *Od.* 23.207-208. There is a similar description of joyful welcomes in *Od.* 17.31-35.

62. B.P. Reardon, 'Aspects of the Greek Novel', *GR* NS 23 (1976), pp. 118-31 (121).

63. See the examples cited in R.F. Hock, 'The Greek Novel', in D.E. Aune (ed.), *Greco-Roman Literature and the New Testament: Selected Forms and Genres* (SBLSBS, 21; Atlanta: Scholars Press, 1988), pp. 127-46 (140-41).

64. Prominent among the comparable themes found in all these different genres are those of the relationship between fathers and their sons, the fathers' methods of upbringing and the resultant behavior of the sons, particularly their use of their inheritances. The typical contrast is between the right use of such resources and the twin excesses of the miser and the prodigal.

65. Compare the following examples from the *Aesopica*: the farmer and his sons (42); the farmer's sons: a lesson on the strength of unity (with the associated moral that harmony, ὁμόνοια, is a guarantee of strength) (53); the prodigal young man and the swallow (169); Plato's myth of plenty and poverty from the *Symposium* (203b-c) (466); the fable of the domestic snake has a related plot of poverty-riches-pride-repentance (573); and the fable of the covetous and the envious man, a fable from Avianus (580). The numbering is that given in B.E. Perry, *Aesopica: A Series of Texts Relating to Aesop or Ascribed to Him or Closely Connected with the Literary Tradition That Bears his Name. Collected and Critically Edited, in Part Translated from Original Languages, with a Commentary and Historical Essay.* I. *Greek and Latin Texts* (Urbana: University of Illinois Press, 1952); and B.E. Perry, *Babrius and Phaedrus* (LCL; Cambridge, MA: Harvard University Press, 1965). Also to be compared is the man with an ugly daughter and beautiful son in *Phaedr.* 3.8.

66. See J. Breech, *Jesus and Postmodernism* (Minneapolis: Fortress Press, 1989), p. 58.

67. Beavis compares a number of fables with parables of the L source, especially those that have a moral at the end, such as the rich fool (Lk. 12.15-21), the

Gnomic literature also provides examples of comparable themes. One of the earliest examples of a story about two brothers who make differing uses of their inheritances, is the contrast between Hesiod and his brother Perses found in Hesiod's *Works and Days*.[68]

Histories, satires and comedies also provide many thematic points of comparison. Hopkins notes that because relations between Roman fathers and sons were strained, stories of conflict between fathers and sons are frequent in Roman folklore and history. He gives examples, from Dionysius of Halicarnassus, Livy, Valerius Maximus and Seneca, of fathers who had their sons executed or flogged to death for disobedience, and of other fathers who acted indulgently towards sons who had plotted against their lives. He cites P. Veyne's remark that Roman men essentially belonged to two groups, the fortunate and unfortunate. 'The fortunate comprised those whose fathers had died when they were still young, leaving their sons as masters of their estates. The unfortunate were those who remained long under the thumb of their fathers'.[69] The discussion of notorious prodigals in *The Deipnosophists* of Athenaeus gives a number of examples of temperate and intemperate leaders mentioned by historians.[70] Polybius, Dio Cassius and Herodian[71] all make reference to prodigal rulers. Dionysius of Halicarnassus uses the theme of the prodigal as a metaphor for the takeover of the Hellenistic world by a debased form of rhetoric.[72]

Satires, especially those of Horace, also provide us with a number of descriptions of the relationships between prodigal sons and their fathers. These are particularly valuable for this study because they can

---

unjust steward (Lk. 16.1-9), the persistent widow (Lk. 18.1-8), and the Pharisee and the tax-collector (Lk. 18.9-14). See M.A. Beavis, 'Parable and Fable', *CBQ* 52 (1990), pp. 473-98.

68. Hesiod, *Op.* 27-41 and 286-372.

69. See K. Hopkins, 'Death in Rome', in *idem, Death and Renewal* (Sociological Studies in Roman History; Cambridge: Cambridge University Press, 1983), II, pp. 201-56 (244-45).

70. Those mentioned in Athenaeus, *Deipn.* 166d-168e are Theopompus of Chios, Duris, Demetrius of Skepsis, Hegesander of Delphi, Agatharchides of Cnidus and Poseidonius. This section of Athenaeus contains many of the indicators of the topos On Covetousness which are identified in Chapter 4 below.

71. Polybius, *Hist.* 14.12.3; 32.11.10; 39.7.7; Dio Cassius, 65.20.3; 67.6.3, 4, (cited by Foerster, 'ἄσωτος, ἀσωτία', *TDNT*, I, pp. 506-507); and Herodian, *Hist.* 2.5.1-2.

72. Dionysius of Halicarnassus, *Ancient Orators* 1.

be more closely related to the moral approaches of Stoic or Cynic philosophy.[73]

However, Greek and Roman comedies and mimes provide most points of contact both in terms of plot, theme and detail. Via describes the plot of the parable as 'a comedy in which tragedy is included and overcome'.[74] Referring to Horace's *The Art of Poetry*, ll.189-192, Sibinga compares Lk. 15.12-16 to a conventional five-act drama depicting the theme of 'rise and fall'.[75]

Athenaeus[76] refers to other plays of Middle and New Comedy which contain prodigals and misers as part of their representation of contemporary types and manners: two plays by Alexis, *The Women of Cnidus* and *Phaedrus*;[77] Axionicus's *The Etruscan*; Anaxandrides' *Tereus* and a citation from Amphis.[78] Aulus Gellius quotes eight lines from a mime by Laberius called *The Ropemaker*, in which a rich and stingy miser bewails his son's prodigality.[79] Beare mentions a lost play by Afranius, a writer of *fabulae togatae* who drew on the work of Menander and Terence, called *The Prodigal*.[80]

Many details from the comedies of Menander, Plautus and Terence can be related to the parable. Two of Terence's plays, *The Brothers* and *The Self-Tormentor*, address the issue of the correct way for a father to bring up his son and deal with the theme of the correct use of money.[81]

---

73. Horace, *Sat.* 2.3.168-86, 224-46, 253-57; *Sat.* 1.1.28-119; *Sat.* 1.2.1-24; and *Sat.* 1.4.48-54, 105-11.

74. D.O. Via, Jr, *The Parables: Their Literary and Existential Dimension* (Philadelphia: Fortress Press, 1967), pp. 104 and 165.

75. J.S. Sibinga, 'Zur Kompositionstechnik des Lukas in Lk. 15.11-32', in J.W. van Henten (ed.), *Tradition and Re-Interpretation in Jewish and Early Christian Literature* (Festschrift J.C.H. Lebram; Leiden: E.J. Brill, 1986), pp. 97-113 (108).

76. Athenaeus, *Deipn.* 4.165d-169b.

77. LSJ, s.v. ἀσωτοδιδάσκαλος, cite another play by Alexis with the title Ἀσωτοδιδάσκαλος.

78. Compare the description of prodigality as ὑγρότης in Crobylus, a New Comedy poet in LSJ, s.v. ἀσωτία.

79. Aulus Gellius, *NA* 10.17.3-4

80. W. Beare, *The Roman Stage: A Short History of Latin Drama in the Time of the Republic* (London: Methuen, 3rd edn, 1964), p. 131.

81. See Terence, *Adelph.* 500-504: wealthy people must be just. In ll. 831-34 the tendency for older people to become too concerned with money is criticized: 'Oh my dear Demea, in all other respects we get wiser as we get older: there is only this one flaw that old age brings on a man, we all think too much of money.' The point is referred to again in ll. 953-54. At the end of the play (ll. 985-95) the

The Brothers in particular, which is modelled on plays of the same name by Menander and others,[82] has much in common with the parable. It contains two generations of brothers, each generation having one who is a thoughtless and irresponsible town-dweller[83] and the other a thrifty and sober country-dweller.[84] Relationships between fathers, sons, brothers and friends constitute the core relationships.[85] The country-dwelling father has a family farm which resembles that suggested by Lk. 15.11-32 in size, with slaves and house servants as part of the household. The mother of the two sons is no longer part of the story. Money is often mentioned. In the character of the prodigal son Aeschinus, we are given a broad sketch of the behavior of a prodigal son: he gets a girl pregnant, visits prostitutes and is generally easy-going; yet he is also kind and helps his brother even when it is to his own disadvantage.

This wide range of parallels of all kinds, some of which have been noted as far back as Price and Wettstein, reveals that the important hermeneutical question is not which of these are the closest, but how to account for the relationships which exist between all of them and the contents of the parable.[86] I have not found any studies that widen the

---

importance of paternal guidance in the right use of money is affirmed. Compare Terence, *Haut.* 439-41: 'Ah, my friend, you are too impetuous both ways, by turns [in] excessive profuseness and excessive parsimony (*es nimis aut largitate nimia aut parsimonia*) ...'

82. Apart from the play by Menander, Allinson mentions six other Greek comic poets who wrote plays of the same name. 'Terence's play, although ascribed in the didascalia wholly to Menander, was indebted in part at least (see prologue) to the *Companions in Death* by Diphilus' (*Menander, the Principal Fragments* [trans. F.G. Allinson; LCL; New York: G.P. Putnam, 1921], p. 313).

83. Terence, *Adelph.* 757-62.

84. Radice says that the two forms of upbringing represent two rival Roman educational policies: the strict discipline of Cato versus the new liberal Hellenism (*Terence: The Comedies* [trans. B. Radice; Harmondsworth: Penguin Books, 1976], p. 333).

85. 'Is this to be a father or this to be a son? Had he been my brother or my friend could he have been more complaisant? Is he not a man to be loved, to be next to one's heart? It's wonderful, and so his kindness fills me with the most vehement desire not to do from want of thought anything to displease him' (Terence, *Adelph.* 707-10).

86. The importance of providing the right conceptual framework for the interpretation of parallels between Greco-Roman and Jewish literature and the Gospels is stressed by Aune. See D.E. Aune, 'The Literary Background of the Gospels', review of *Documents for the Study of the Gospels*, by David Cartlidge and David

range of comparison in this way for Lk. 15.11-32.[87] Danker's recent commentary on Luke, alone among recent commentaries, reads Luke in dialogue with Greco-Roman literature—but in an unfocused way that fails to advance the question of how parallels are to be interpreted.[88] Some steps toward this have been taken with regard to some of the other parables found only in Luke. Hock and Bauckham (Lk. 16.19-31) and Downing (Lk. 18.9-14) have shown that it is necessary to include parallels from Greco-Roman literature in the discussion and to be careful to note resemblances and differences. These studies also tend to focus upon parallel plots rather than related moral issues. Downing's study moves away from parallel narratives, but does not establish another framework for considering the parallels which he notes.[89]

The recognition that the range of parallels cited by previous researchers is too limited, leads me beyond pointing out the many other possible kinds of parallels that exist between the parable and Greco-Roman literature, to seek a comprehensive explanation for this relationship.[90] This involves a shift of perspective away from parallel stories to

Dungan, *Documents for the Study of the Gospels* (Cleveland: Collins, 1980) in *Int* 35 (1981), pp. 293-97 (295).

87. Betz ('*De Fraterno Amore*', pp. 231-63) makes many references to Lk. 15.11-32 in his study of the topos On Brotherly Love, but they are not drawn together or developed. Wolfgang Pöhlmann's *Der verlorene Sohn und das Haus: Studien zu Lukas 15.11-32 im Horizont der antiken Lehre von Haus, Erziehung und Ackerbau* (WUNT, 68; Tübingen: J.C.B. Mohr [Paul Siebeck], 1993), appeared after this study was completed.

88. See F.W. Danker, *Jesus and the New Age: A Commentary on St. Luke's Gospel* (Philadelphia: Fortress Press, rev. edn, 1988). The various possible kinds of relationship between early Christian texts and their *Umwelt* (10 types of contrast and 14 of resemblance) are distinguished in Berger and Colpe, *Religionsgeschichtliches Textbuch*, pp. 18-26. For the English translation see Boring, Berger and Colpe, *Hellenistic Commentary*, pp. 23-32.

89. See R. Hock, 'Lazarus and Micyllus', pp. 447-63; R. Bauckham, 'The Rich Man and Lazarus: The Parable and the Parallels', *NTS* 37 (1991), pp. 225-46. F.G. Downing, 'The Ambiguity of "The Pharisee and the Toll-collector" (Luke 18:9-14) in the Greco-Roman World of Late Antiquity', *CBQ* 54 (1992), pp. 80-99. While thematic relationships between the L parables are noted in Chapter 3 below, it is beyond the scope of this study to engage in an extensive critical evaluation of the Greco-Roman readings of these and other L parables.

90. Compare Malherbe's criticism of Spicq's collection of non-Christian parallels to the terminology of the Pastorals: 'Ceslaus Spicq, while citing many parallels indicating that the terminology was not unusual in antiquity, did not present a unified

questions of the underlying moral attitudes and assumptions, the place of such views within a wider moral frame of reference, and the sources of such morality.

One of the most important sources of such information is the teaching of the moral philosophers. While there are a number of accounts of philosophical conversion which provide a thematic point of comparison with the conversion of the prodigal younger son and the absence of change in his mean elder brother,[91] the relationship between the writings of the moral philosophers and Lk. 15.11-32 is much wider. In the following pages, I identify a common framework of moral teaching which is used in different ways by each of the philosophers, and also by Luke. This framework, the topos On Covetousness, explains and integrates a wide range of formal, thematic and terminological correspondences between Luke and other moral texts. Thus, via the writings of Greco-Roman moral philosophy, the question of the basis of Luke's interaction with popular morality in Lk. 15.11-32 is focused on the question: Within what moral frame of reference would questions of fathers and sons, inheritances, right training in the use of possessions, and prodigal or miserly behavior, have been addressed?[92]

In Chapter 2 I turn to the parable itself and show, by means of a close literary reading of the text, that it does emphasize the moral issue of the right use of possessions. Chapter 3 places the parable within its literary context in Luke's Gospel, and shows that it should be read not only

picture that helps in understanding the language' (A.J. Malherbe, 'Medical Imagery in the Pastoral Epistles', in *idem, Paul and the Popular Philosophers*, pp. 121-36 [122]). This is one of the reasons Tuckett is unconvinced by the parallels of vocabulary and imagery which Downing identifies between Q and the Cynic traditions. See F.G. Downing, 'Quite like Q: A Genre for "Q": The "Lives" of the Cynic Philosophers', *Bib* 69 (1988), pp. 196-225; and C.M. Tuckett, 'A Cynic Q?' *Bib* 70 (1989), pp. 349-76 (372-73).

91. Plutarch, *Mor.* 563b-f, cited in Chapters 5 and 7 below; Teles 2 (12, 94-98), discussed in Chapter 6 below; Epictetus, *Diss.* 3.1.14-15; 3.23.16, 37; 4.9.13-16, discussed in Chapter 7 below; and Dio Chrysostom, *Or.* 66.13, discussed in Chapter 8 below.

92. Chapters 4–9 make extensive reference to Greco-Roman primary sources. At times more references are given than are strictly necessary to establish the point being made. These extra references are retained in the tradition of Wettstein and the Corpus Hellenisticum Novi Testamenti Project for their intrinsic interest and possible future usefulness to other exegetes.

with the other parables of Luke 15, but with all of Luke's special parables. This also serves to confirm that there is a relationship between Lk. 15.11-32 and the topos On Covetousness. Chapter 4 looks at the nature and function of this topos in moral philosophy, and illustrates its influence upon a wide range of philosophical texts. Chapters 5 to 8 then explore Luke's creative interaction with this topos in Lk. 15.11-32, and Chapter 9 concludes with a summary and evaluation of the results of the study.

Chapter 2

THE COMPOSITION AND MESSAGE OF LUKE 15.11-32

In this chapter I turn my attention to the contents of Lk. 15.11-32. By a close examination of the text itself, I seek to answer the question: What is the parable intended to teach? Evans notes that this is not self-evident: 'Surprisingly for a story that has often been hailed as a literary masterpiece, or as containing "the gospel within the gospel", this is by no means easy to establish'.[1] This has led to a wide variety of descriptions of its message.[2] One reason why it is difficult to establish the message of the parable is that it lacks the typically Lukan summary statement, [3] but a more important cause of this difficulty is one that I have already noted: the confusion of the audience within Luke's Gospel with Luke's intended readers. The Entrevernes group distinguishes between

---

1.   C.F. Evans, *Saint Luke* (London: SCM Press; Philadelphia: Trinity Press International, 1990), p. 589.

2.   Some modern interpreters argue that it addresses the universal issues of human life. Jones says that the story 'combines into a succinct pattern such themes as Freedom and Responsibility, Estrangement, the Personalness of Life, Longing and Return, Grace, Anguish, and Reconciliation' (G.V. Jones, *The Art and Truth of the Parables: A Study in their Literary Form and Modern Interpretation* [London: SPCK, 1964], p. 174, cited by Fitzmyer, *Luke*, p. 1084). Harrison believes that the story 'makes nonsense of common considerations of fairness and justice in the management of family affairs.' He resolves this problem by saying that the parable is about the gap between everyday morality, in which prodigal sons are disciplined and faithful sons rewarded, and the extraordinary outlook of Christ, in which a wastrel child is of immense intrinsic value (B. Harrison, 'Parable and Transcendence', in M. Wadsworth [ed.], *Ways of Reading the Bible* [Brighton, UK: Harvester Press; Totowa, NJ: Barnes & Noble Books, 1981], pp. 190-212 [202-203]).

3.   See Lk. 12.21; 14.33; 15.10; 16.9; 17.10; 18.6-8; 18.14b. Schweizer argues, existentially, that the content of this parable 'cannot be captured in a summary statement' and that its truth is only evident when Jesus is 'alive in the particular situation of the listener or reader' (E. Schweizer, *The Good News According to Luke* [trans. D.E. Green; Atlanta: John Knox Press, 1984], p. 252).

the primary narrative scene, which presents the interaction of Jesus, the sinners, the scribes and the Pharisees; the secondary scene in which the characters in the parable interact with one another; and the 'intermediary story'. This intermediary story consists of the *relationship* between the characters and roles in the primary narrative and in the parable, and is variously constructed by different audiences: (1) the sinners and the religious leaders in the primary story; (2) Luke's implied readers; and (3) subsequent Christian readers.[4] Because of the wide variety of possible interests that readers might bring to the text, this study places the emphasis on Luke's implied readers. That is, it seeks to identify what Luke was trying to teach his Greco-Roman hearers.

Can this be established by a literary-critical study of the parable? Reardon illustrates how this may be done with the Hellenistic romance *Chaereas and Callirhoe*. He is able to show, by means of a study of its plot and narrative technique, that Chariton engages with the popular philosophical and theological notions of the Hellenistic world while adopting his own position on these issues.[5] I take a similar approach here. While Reardon does not make any link between Chariton's novel and Luke's Gospel, Cadbury has pointed out the value of Hellenistic romances, and *Chaereas and Callirhoe* in particular, for illustrating Luke's idiom and ideas.[6] There are, however, also correspondences at the level of narrative technique.

This literary approach is a good point of departure for this study because it roots the discussion of what Luke intended to teach his readers in the text itself. In the following chapter I move beyond the bounds of Lk. 15.11-32 to look at the parable's relationship with its immediate co-text, and examine other parts of the same work that are syntagmati-

---

4. The Entrevernes Group, *Signs and Parables: Semiotics and Gospel Texts* (trans. G. Phillips; Pittsburgh: Pickwick Press, 1978), p. 120.

5. See B.P. Reardon 'Theme, Structure and Narrative in Chariton', *YCS* 27 (1982), pp. 1-27 (7, 23-27). He describes what Chariton has to say as: 'Life can bring isolation and grief; but if Fortune is kind, they can be overcome; let us, for our comfort, suppose that Fortune is kind.'

6. 'I do not know where one can get so many illustrations of the idiom and ideas of the author of Acts in 150 pages as the love story of his near contemporary, Chariton of Aphrodisias' (H.J. Cadbury, *The Book of Acts in History* [New York: Harper & Brothers, 1955]), p. 8, cited by L.T. Johnson, *The Literary Function of Possessions in Luke–Acts* [SBLDS, 39; Missoula: Scholars Press, 1977], p. 20).

cally and paradigmatically related to it. The results of these two processes are then used as a basis for studying how Luke enables the
parable to resonate with the moral world of his intended readers.

1. *The Text of Luke 15.11-32*

Before we look at the internal structure and narrative techniques of Lk.
15.11-32, we need to establish the text. This is essential, as much of the
case argued and illustrated below is based on Luke's use of particular
terminology. Such arguments must be built upon reliable textual traditions. At the same time, the study of variant textual traditions serves as
a reminder that variant receptions of the parable are themselves reflected in the different manuscript traditions used to establish a working
text.[7] As a result of a textual analysis my working text turns out to
be that of NA[26] (unchanged in NA[27]), an eclectic text, based on the
Alexandrian tradition, with two changes.[8]

The two changes to NA[26] which are necessary for my moral study of
Lk. 15.11-32 are these:

1. In Lk. 15.16, instead of the Alexandrian χορτασθῆναι ἐκ, we read,
with the Western tradition, γεμίσαι τὴν κοιλίαν αὐτοῦ ἀπό.[9] A third
reading, a singular conflation of these two given by W, γεμίσαι τὴν
κοιλίαν καὶ χορτασθῆναι ἀπό, can be ignored.

Scholars are divided on which of the two traditions to follow. Metzger prefers χορτασθῆναι ἐκ, 'on the basis of age and diversity of text-

---

7. I wish to acknowledge the help and advice of Dr J.H. Petzer, who com-
mented very fully on an earlier paper in which I examined 40 textual variants in Lk.
15.11-32. For a full list of textual variants see *The New Testament in Greek*. III. *The
Gospel According to St Luke*. Part 2. *Chapters 13–24*, ed. American and British
Committees of the International Greek New Testament Project (Oxford: Oxford
University Press, 1987).

8. I have essentially followed the principles guiding the text-critical practice of
K. and B. Aland as outlined in their 'twelve basic rules for textual criticism' in
K. Aland and B. Aland, *The Text of the New Testament: An Introduction to the
Critical Editions and to the Theory and Practice of Modern Textual Criticism*
(trans. E.F. Rhodes; Grand Rapids: Eerdmans; Leiden: E.J. Brill, 1987), pp. 275-77.
My only reservation is that I doubt whether we can establish 'the original reading'
when reconstructing a text on the basis of third-century witnesses.

9. χορτασθῆναι ἐκ is found in: P[75]; ℵ; B; D; L; R; f[1]; f[13]; and γεμίσαι τὴν
κοιλίαν αὐτοῦ ἀπό in: A; Θ; Ψ; Old Latin; sy[s]; sy[b]; sy[p]; sy[l].

type of witnesses',[10] and he is followed by Aland in NA[26], Fitzmyer and others.[11] However, despite the solid external support for this reading, many other scholars prefer the Western reading. Marshall considers it more likely that the 'strong, almost crude' expression γεμίσαι τὴν κοιλίαν was corrected by scribes than that it was later added to the text.[12] Bovon argues, 'At verse 16 we prefer γεμίσαι τὴν κοιλίαν ('filled his belly') to χορτασθῆναι ('to be filled'), for this common expression would have shocked the copyists who, taking their cue from Luke 16.21, have substituted a more decorous word'.[13] Sibinga agrees, citing the agreement of Westcott and Hort, Jülicher, Baljon, Zahn, Jeremias and Bovon.[14]

I propose retaining the Western reading, adding the following lexical considerations to those already given by Marshall and Bovon above: (1) κοιλία is a word found in texts which interact with the topos On Covetousness.[15] (2) Luke describes the father's compassion

---

10. B.M. Metzger, *A Textual Commentary on the Greek New Testament* (London: United Bible Societies, 2nd edn, 1994), p. 139.

11. Fitzmyer, *Luke*, p. 1088. In a personal conversation, Petzer suggested to me that Western scribes or redactors might have introduced the second reading to make the implicit degradation of the son more explicit. Another example of this tendency to make the implicit more explicit in the Western tradition is the longer Western rewriting of v. 30.

12. Marshall, *Gospel of Luke*, p. 609.

13. F. Bovon, 'The Parable of the Prodigal Son (Luke 15.11-32): First Reading', in F. Bovon and G. Rouiller (eds.), *Exegesis: Problems of Method and Exercises in Reading (Genesis 22 and Luke 15)* (trans. D.G. Miller; Pittsburgh: Pickwick Press, 1978), pp. 43-73 (50).

14. Sibinga, 'Kompositionstechnik', p. 100 n. 14.

15. See, for example, Plutarch's discussion of prodigals and misers in *De Cupiditate Divitiarum* (*Mor.* 525c): 'For Demas himself played the demagogue to fill his belly (γαστέρα) and regarding Athens as not adequate for his prodigality (ἀσωτία) laid in supplies from Macedon as well. (Hence Antipater, seeing him in his old age, said that like a carcass when the butchers had finished, nothing remained but the tongue and the gut [κοιλία]).' See also Pseudo-Crates, *Ep.* 17 (66, 15-25); and, in the New Testament, Rom. 16.18; 1 Cor. 6.13; and perhaps also Mt. 15.17; Mk 7.19; Phil. 3.19. The term κοιλία is also associated with another indicator of the influence of the topos On Covetousness, the noun ἐπιθυμία. For obvious reasons, desire and the stomach are often found together. Sir. 23.5, 6 mention κοιλία and ἐπιθυμία in successive verses. In *T. Reub.* 3.3, the second of

with σπλαγχνίζομαι, a verb which Menken has shown to be central in the three places it is used in Luke's Gospel.[16] Because of the importance of σπλαγχνίζομαι in the parable, Luke may have been using κοιλία and σπλαγχνίζομαι as a stereotypical word-pair.[17] The pair would have been familiar to Greco-Roman readers[18] through the literal pairing of σπλάγχνα (nobler inward parts, eaten by sacrificers at the beginning of a feast) and κοιλία (the other inward parts) in sacrificial practice.[19] In Pseudo-Heraclitus, *Epistle* 9, the heart and the bowels are paired in this way: 'Nor does the heart (καρδία), the most sacred organ, scorn the bowels (σπλάγχνα), the most common parts of the body'.[20]

2. In Lk. 15.21, instead of the shorter reading, υἱός σου, I adopt the longer Alexandrian reading ποίησόν με ὡς ἕνα τῶν μισθίων σου.[21]

the deceitful spirits, that of insatiate desire, is located in the belly (δεύτερον πνεῦμα ἀπληστίας ἐν τῇ γαστρί). H.W. Hollander and M. de Jonge, *The Testaments of the Twelve Patriarchs: A Commentary* (SVTP, 8; Leiden: E.J. Brill, 1985), p. 95, refer to the link between desire and the belly in Philo, *Ebr.* 22; and *Spec. Leg.* 1.150.

16. M.J.J. Menken, 'The Position of Σπλαγχνίζεσθαι and Σπλάγχνα in the Gospel of Luke', *NovT* 30 (1988), pp. 107-114. He cites H. Koester, σπλάγχνον, σπλαγχνίζομαι, κτλ., *TDNT*, VII, pp. 548-59 (553), who says of Mt. 18.27 and Lk. 10.33 and 15.20, 'In drei Gleichnisse Jesu steht das Verbum an zentrale Stelle.'

17. Jeremias points out Luke's fondness for word pairs. See J. Jeremias, *Die Sprache des Lukasevangeliums: Redaktion und Tradition im Nicht-Markusstoff des dritten Evangeliums* (Göttingen: Vandenhoeck & Ruprecht, 1980), p. 252. This is an aspect of his use of parallelism for emphasis. Other pairs found in this parable are συνάγω and διασκορπίζω in v. 13a-b (also found in Lk. 11.23); νεκρός and ἀναζάω, or ζάω, in vv. 24a-b and 32b-c; ἀπόλλυμι and εὑρίσκω in vv. 24c-d and 32d; συμφωνία and χοροί in v. 25c; and εὐφραίνω and χαίρω in v. 32a. As I note in Chapter 6, Stoics think of compassion as one of the ways in which cosmic harmony is maintained.

18. Weiss warns against dismissing ancient Roman religion as an insignificant factor in the religious scene of the first century CE. H. Weiss, 'The *Pagani* among the Contemporaries of the First Christians', *JBL* 86 (1976), pp. 42-52 (50).

19. The seventh edition of LSJ describes the σπλάγχνα as the '*inward parts*, esp. the nobler pieces, the heart, lungs, liver, kidneys (*viscera thoracis*) which in sacrifices were reserved to be eaten by the sacrificers at the beginning of their feast (distinguished from the ἔντερα or κοιλία [*viscera abdominis*] as Lat. *viscera* from *intestina* by Cels., cf. Hdt. 2.40, Aesch. Ag. 1221, Arist. P.A. 3.4, 1 sq.)'. See also J.B. Lightfoot, *Saint Paul's Epistle to the Philippians* (London: Macmillan, 8th edn, 1888), p. 86.

20. Pseudo-Heraclitus, *Ep.* 9 (214, 9).

21. υἱός σου is found in: P[75]; A; L; W; Θ; Ψ; f[1]; f[13]; Majority; lat; sy[s]; sy[c]; sy[p];

The shorter reading is favoured by Metzger: 'While recognizing that several good manuscripts (ℵ, B, D, 700 al) combine to support the reading ποίησόν με ὡς ἕνα τῶν μισθίων σου, the Committee thought it more probable that the words were added (from ver 19) by punctilious scribes than omitted, either accidentally or deliberately'.[22] Similar comments are made by Greenlee, Marshall, Fitzmyer, Jeremias and Bovon.[23]

My reasons for retaining the longer reading are: (1) it is favoured on the grounds of external evidence, both in the texts that support it and in the good distribution of its support; (2) the longer reading may have been omitted through homoioteleuton;[24] (3) Luke's stylistic fondness for parallelism, which is marked in this passage, provides internal evidence for the retention of this phrase: it is not necessary to attribute it to a learned scribal correction; (4) it is important for this moral reading of the parable because it stresses that the converted younger son is now willing to take on humble and insecure employment, and it expresses his confidence in his father as a good employer. This point is discussed in Chapter 7 below.

With these two modifications to the text of NA[26], I now examine how the parable has been composed.

2. *Major Divisions*

a. *Luke 15.11-32 as One Unit*
For the purpose of my analysis of the narrative composition of the parable, I treat Lk. 15.11-32 as a single unit.[25] It consists of a single

co. ποίησόν με ὡς ἕνα τῶν μισθίων σου is added by the following witnesses: ℵ; B; D; U; X; 33; 700; 1241; *pc*; vg[mss]; sy[h].

22. Metzger, *Textual Commentary*, p. 139.

23. J.H. Greenlee, *Introduction to New Testament Textual Criticism* (Grand Rapids: Eerdmans, 1964), p. 132; Marshall, *Gospel of Luke*, p. 610; Fitzmyer, *Luke*, pp. 1089-90; Jeremias, *Parables*, p. 130; and Bovon, 'First Reading', p. 50.

24. As the omitted passage and the previous two phrases end on the word σου, a scribe's eye could easily have jumped from the second σου to the third. The fact that the omitted phrase is about the length of a line in certain manuscripts adds to the likelihood that it could have been omitted through a combination of parablepsis and homoioteleuton. The case for this omission is strengthened by the fact that v. 21 otherwise exactly repeats the confession of v. 19. I owe this observation to Professor J.H. Petzer.

25. Since Wellhausen some have held that the story of the elder brother (vv. 25-32) is an appendix which does not belong to the original story. See J. Wellhausen's

pronouncement of Jesus, from the introductory words εἶπεν δέ (11a) to the start of a new unit at Lk. 16.1 with the words Ἔλεγεν δὲ καὶ πρὸς τοὺς μαθητάς.

The most basic division is into two parts, each dealing with one of the sons. After an introductory section of vv. 11 and 12, the story of the younger son is told in vv. 13-24 and the older in vv. 25-32. Some scholars, considering the father to be a, or the, central character, propose a three-part division, with one section for each of the main characters. In this scheme, vv. 20b-24 is allocated to the father.[26] Other divisions of three, four or more major subsections have been proposed. A

Das Evangelium Lucae (Berlin: G. Reimer, 1904), pp. 81-85. Bultmann however correctly noted the importance of the second part as a contrast which highlights the message of the first. See R. Bultmann, *The History of the Synoptic Tradition* (trans. J. Marsh; Oxford: Basil Blackwell, 1972), p. 96. J.T. Sanders argued for a concentration of Lukan terms in the second part. See J.T. Sanders, 'Tradition and Redaction in Luke XV.11-32', *NTS* 15 (1968–69), pp. 433-38. This has been questioned by Schweizer, Jeremias, Carlston and O'Rourke.

Scott sums up the process of this debate about the second part thus: 'Schweizer rejects the elder brother episode, in "Zur Frage", pp. 469-71; Jeremias defends the integrity of the parable, in "Zum Gleichnis", pp. 228-31; Schweizer responds in "Antwort an Joachim Jeremias", pp. 231-33. Sanders summarizes Schweizer and Jeremias, agreeing with Schweizer, in "Tradition and Redaction", pp. 433-38; O'Rourke rejects Sanders' arguments in "Some Notes", pp. 431-33. See also my rejection of Sanders in "The Prodigal Son", pp. 186-89' (*Hear Then the Parable*, p. 104 n. 14). See also Fitzmyer, *Luke*, pp. 1084-85. The references are to E. Schweizer, 'Zur Frage der Lukasquellen, Analyse von Luk. 15, 11-32', *TZ* 4 (1948), pp. 469-71; and 'Antwort', *TZ* 5 (1949), pp. 231-33; J. Jeremias, 'Zum Gleichnis vom verlorenen Sohn, Luk. 15, 11-32', *TZ* 5 (1949), pp. 228-31; C.E. Carlston, 'Reminiscence and Redaction in Luke 15.11-32', *JBL* 94 (1975), pp. 368-90; and J.J. O'Rourke, 'Some Notes on Luke XV.11-32', *NTS* 18 (1971–72), pp. 431-33.

26. Blomberg's description is typical of many: 'verses 11-20a—the younger son's departure and return; verses 20b-24—the father's welcome; verses 25-32—the older son's reaction' (C.L. Blomberg, *Interpreting the Parables* [Downer's Grove, IL: InterVarsity Press, 1990], p. 174). Some try to combine the two by dividing the parable into two stories, but still reading it in terms of the roles and relationships of the three main characters. See, for example, du Plessis, *Kykie*, pp. 92-99 and 118-35. Grelot becomes too schematic when he claims to detect the three trials of the father, the three trials of the younger son and the three trials of the older son. See P. Grelot, 'Le père et ses deux fils: Luc, XV, 11-32: Essai d'analyse structurale', *RB* 84 (1977), pp. 321-48 (326-47).

representative selection of the range of divisions, which could be expanded with many other variations, is presented schematically by Sibinga.[27] There is no scholarly consensus on the most satisfactory subdivision of this, the most widely-studied of the New Testament parables.

b. *Four Parts*

Here, following the words which link the parable to the primary story, εἶπεν δέ, I follow a fourfold division, with the additional refinement that the story of the elder son can be divided into two parts. Verses 11b-12c should be viewed as an introduction to the parable, presenting the characters and the event that triggers the subsequent events of the parable. There are some indicators of a division within the story of the younger son, such as a change of subject at v. 17a, but other formal considerations, such as a regular pattern of sections containing a summary, a scene and a passage in direct speech, suggest that his story does not fall as easily into two parts. Thus, after the linking words in v. 11a, I divide the parable into: (1) vv. 11b-12c: introduction of characters and plot; (2) vv. 13a-20a: the younger son; (3) vv. 20b-24e: the father; (4) vv. 25a-28b and 28c-32d: the elder son.

3. *Colon Divisions*

To facilitate the discussion of the syntactic and stylistic features that reveal the composition of the parable, I divide the text into units smaller than sentences. Here it is divided into basic semantic units, termed 'cola' in South African discourse analysis. A colon is defined as an independent grammatical construction consisting of a noun phrase and a verb phrase, often with further embedded sentences. Embedded sentences are repetitions or qualifications of the nominal subject or object. Each colon or subcolon in the text below is therefore distinguished by having only one main verb, which is printed in bold.[28]

27. See Sibinga, 'Kompositionstechnik', p. 99. He objects that scholars frequently do not make clear their reasons for dividing the parable up in a particular way. However, his own divisions (vv. 11a, 11b-16c, 17a-24d, 24e-32d) arrived at on the basis of a count of syllables and verbal forms, overlook other important narrative markers of structure, particularly patterns of summary and direct speech.

28. See the definition given by G.M.M. Pelser *et al.* in the Preface to 'Discourse Analysis of Galatians', addendum to *Neot* 26.2 (1992). The principles of South

In the analysis below, the cola and subcola are identified by verse number and letter. The start of each new colon is marked by a blank line, and subcola within each verse are lettered.[29] By this means, it is evident that single verses often contain more than one colon (as in vv. 11a, 11b, 12a-b, 12c and so on), while sometimes, particularly in passages of direct or indirect speech, a single colon extends over a number of verses (as in vv. 17a-19b).

v. 11a   **Εἶπεν δέ·**

Part 1   ....

v. 11b   ἄνθρωπός τις **εἶχεν** δύο υἱούς.

v. 12a   καὶ **εἶπεν** ὁ νεώτερος αὐτῶν τῷ πατρί·

v. 12b   πάτερ, **δός** μοι τὸ ἐπιβάλλον μέρος τῆς οὐσίας.

v. 12c   ὁ δὲ **διεῖλεν** αὐτοῖς τὸν βίον.

Part 2   ....

v. 13a   καὶ μετ᾽ οὐ πολλὰς ἡμέρας συναγαγὼν πάντα ὁ νεώτερος υἱὸς **ἀπεδήμησεν** εἰς χώραν μακρὰν

African discourse analysis are set out and illustrated in J.P. Louw, *Semantics of New Testament Greek* (Philadelphia: Fortress Press, 1983). See also J. Botha, *Semeion: Inleiding tot die Interpretasie van die Griekse Nuwe Testament* (Potchefstroom: Dept. Sentrale Publikasie, PU vir CHO, 1989).

29. This is a departure from the conventions of colon numbering in South African discourse analysis, where the cola are usually numbered, with subcola being numbered alphabetically according to their subcomponents on the same level, or with additional numbers to reflect the levels of embeddedness of their constituent parts. This system is explained in the Preface to the 'Discourse Analysis of Galatians' cited above. The system adopted here is intended to combine the benefits of distinguishing smaller units of the text with the need to retain traditional verse numbering for ease of reference. Such a compromise is possible because this chapter is not a formal discourse analysis. Conversely, it needs to be stressed that division into cola and subcola is done for convenience of reference. It is not meant to imply that discourse analysis is more scientific than other forms of composition analysis, such as that adopted by H.D. Betz in 'Cosmogeny and Ethics in the Sermon on the Mount', in *Essays on the Sermon on the Mount* (trans. L.L. Welborn; Philadelphia: Fortress Press, 1985), pp. 89-123 (98-103); and J.C. Thom, 'The Golden Verses of Pythagoras: Its Literary Composition and Religio-Historical Significance' (PhD dissertation, University of Chicago, 1990, pp. 60-67).

v. 13b   καὶ ἐκεῖ **διεσκόρπισεν** τὴν οὐσίαν αὐτοῦ ζῶν ἀσώτως.

v. 14a   δαπανήσαντος δὲ αὐτοῦ πάντα **ἐγένετο** λιμὸς ἰσχυρὰ κατὰ τὴν χώραν ἐκείνην,

v. 14b   καὶ αὐτὸς **ἤρξατο** ὑστερεῖσθαι.

v. 15a   καὶ πορευθεὶς **ἐκολλήθη** ἑνὶ τῶν πολιτῶν τῆς χώρας ἐκείνης,

v. 15b   καὶ **ἔπεμψεν** αὐτὸν εἰς τοὺς ἀγροὺς αὐτοῦ βόσκειν χοίρους,

v. 16a   καὶ **ἐπεθύμει** γεμίσαι τὴν κοιλίαν αὐτοῦ ἀπὸ τῶν κερατίων

v. 16b   ὧν **ἤσθιον** οἱ χοῖροι,

v. 16c   καὶ οὐδεὶς **ἐδίδου** αὐτῷ.

v. 17a   εἰς ἑαυτὸν δὲ ἐλθὼν **ἔφη**·
v. 17b   πόσοι μίσθιοι τοῦ πατρός μου **περισσεύονται** ἄρτων,
v. 17c   ἐγὼ δὲ λιμῷ ὧδε **ἀπόλλυμαι**.
v. 18a   ἀναστὰς **πορεύσομαι** πρὸς τὸν πατέρα μου
v. 18b   καὶ **ἐρῶ** αὐτῷ·
v. 18c   πάτερ, **ἥμαρτον** εἰς τὸν οὐρανὸν καὶ ἐνώπιόν σου,
v. 19a   οὐκέτι **εἰμὶ** ἄξιος κληθῆναι υἱός σου·
v. 19b   **ποίησόν** με ὡς ἕνα τῶν μισθίων σου.

v. 20a   καὶ ἀναστὰς **ἦλθεν** πρὸς τὸν πατέρα ἑαυτοῦ.

Part 3   ....

v. 20b   Ἔτι δὲ αὐτοῦ μακρὰν ἀπέχοντος **εἶδεν** αὐτὸν ὁ πατὴρ αὐτοῦ
v. 20c   καὶ **ἐσπλαγχνίσθη**
v. 20d   καὶ δραμὼν **ἐπέπεσεν** ἐπὶ τὸν τράχηλον αὐτοῦ
v. 20e   καὶ **κατεφίλησεν** αὐτόν.

v. 21a   **εἶπεν** δὲ ὁ υἱὸς αὐτῷ·
v. 21b   πάτερ, **ἥμαρτον** εἰς τὸν οὐρανὸν καὶ ἐνώπιόν σου,
v. 21c   οὐκέτι **εἰμὶ** ἄξιος κληθῆναι υἱός σου.
v. 21d   **ποίησόν** με ὡς ἕνα τῶν μισθίων σου.

v. 22a   **εἶπεν** δὲ ὁ πατὴρ πρὸς τοὺς δούλους αὐτοῦ·
v. 22b   ταχὺ **ἐξενέγκατε** στολὴν τὴν πρώτην

v. 22c   καὶ **ἐνδύσατε** αὐτόν,
v. 22d   καὶ **δότε** δακτύλιον εἰς τὴν χεῖρα αὐτοῦ καὶ ὑποδήματα εἰς τοὺς πόδας,

v. 23a   καὶ **φέρετε** τὸν μόσχον τὸν σιτευτόν,
v. 23b   **θύσατε,**
v. 23c   καὶ φαγόντες **εὐφρανθῶμεν,**
v. 24a   ὅτι οὗτος ὁ υἱός μου νεκρὸς **ἦν**
v. 24b   καὶ **ἀνέζησεν,**
v. 24c   **ἦν** ἀπολωλὼς
v. 24d   καὶ **εὑρέθη.**

v. 24e   καὶ **ἤρξαντο** εὐφραίνεσθαι.

Part 4   ....

v. 25a   **᾽Ην** δὲ ὁ υἱὸς αὐτοῦ ὁ πρεσβύτερος ἐν ἀγρῷ·

v. 25b   καὶ ὡς ἐρχόμενος **ἤγγισεν** τῇ οἰκίᾳ,

v. 25c   **ἤκουσεν** συμφωνίας καὶ χορῶν,

v. 26a   καὶ προσκαλεσάμενος ἕνα τῶν παίδων **ἐπυνθάνετο**
v. 26b   τί ἂν **εἴη** ταῦτα.

v. 27a   ὁ δὲ **εἶπεν** αὐτῷ
v. 27b   ὅτι ὁ ἀδελφός σου **ἥκει,**
v. 27c   καὶ **ἔθυσεν** ὁ πατήρ σου τὸν μόσχον τὸν σιτευτόν,
v. 27d   ὅτι ὑγιαίνοντα αὐτὸν **ἀπέλαβεν.**

v. 28a   **ὠργίσθη** δὲ

v. 28b   καὶ οὐκ **ἤθελεν** εἰσελθεῖν,

....

v. 28c   ὁ δὲ πατὴρ αὐτοῦ ἐξελθὼν **παρεκάλει** αὐτόν.

v. 29a   ὁ δὲ ἀποκριθεὶς **εἶπεν** τῷ πατρὶ αὐτοῦ·
v. 29b   **ἰδοὺ**
v. 29c   τοσαῦτα ἔτη **δουλεύω** σοι
v. 29d   καὶ οὐδέποτε ἐντολήν σου **παρῆλθον,**
v. 29e   καὶ ἐμοὶ οὐδέποτε **ἔδωκας** ἔριφον
v. 29f   ἵνα μετὰ τῶν φίλων μου **εὐφρανθῶ**·
v. 30a   ὅτε δὲ ὁ υἱός σου οὗτος ὁ καταφαγών σου τὸν βίον μετὰ πορνῶν **ἦλθεν,**

v. 30b   ἔθυσας αὐτῷ τὸν σιτευτὸν μόσχον.

v. 31a   ὁ δὲ εἶπεν αὐτῷ·
v. 31b   τέκνον, σὺ πάντοτε μετ' ἐμοῦ εἶ,
v. 31c   καὶ πάντα τὰ ἐμὰ σά ἐστιν·
v. 32a   εὐφρανθῆναι δὲ καὶ χαρῆναι ἔδει,
v. 32b   ὅτι ὁ ἀδελφός σου οὗτος νεκρὸς ἦν
v. 32c   καὶ ἔζησεν,
v. 32d   καὶ ἀπολωλὼς καὶ εὑρέθη.

4. Analysis of the Composition of Luke 15.11-32

I now turn to a closer analysis of the composition of the text, looking first at syntactical matters, and then at narrative considerations. By this means I explain the divisions stated above and provisionally identify the message of the parable. The syntactic and stylistic arrangement of the text has the effect of emphasizing certain parts of the text, thus indicating what the parable is intended to teach.

a. *Syntax*
The most important way in which the constitutive elements of the parable are combined is by means of paratactic and hypotactic constructions.

(i) *Parataxis*. Simple parataxis is evident in the frequent use of the particles καί and δέ. καί occurs 35 times and δέ 16 times.

This frequency of usage limits the usefulness of either of these particles as markers of structure. However, they do have a mimetic and narrative function. Luke's more frequent use of simple parataxis here than in Acts is often taken as evidence that he used a source written in Semitic Greek. Yet, as BDF and Turner make clear, paratactic sentence structure is typical of plain and unsophisticated language in all periods, and is found in the earliest Greek prose. Thus, the fact that it resembles Semitic style does not require us to assume Luke's dependence upon a Semitic source. He may well have been imitating Semitic Greek or simple speech in secular Greek.[30] In addition, it has a narrative function.

---

30. See BDF, p. 239. Turner, p. 58, comments that 'in secular Greek simple speech favors καί' (N. Turner, 'The Style of Luke–Acts', in *A Grammar of New Testament Greek*. IV. *Style* [Edinburgh: T. & T. Clark, 1976]). Black says that

Scott notes that sections with paratactic constructions take the reader/ hearer through the narrative at great speed. This is particularly true of vv. 12a-24e.[31]

Because of the frequency with which καί and δέ are used, it is possible to view their absence from a colon as a significant change indicating emphasis, once we have eliminated those instances where the absence of these particles is obviously due to other reasons.[32] This leads to the observation that the particles are absent at the start of sections of direct or indirect speech: vv. 12b, 17b, 18c, 19a, 19b, 21b, 21c, 21d, 22b, 29b, 29c and 31b. Verse 26b, in which indirect speech is reported, also belongs to this category. The other instances are at v. 18a (the son's decision to return to his father) and v. 25c (the elder son hears music and dancing). The absence of particles here lends emphasis to these statements, in the former, emphasizing that the decision to return involves a break with what has gone before, and in the latter, serving to highlight a reference to the important Greco-Roman ideal of concord.

(ii) *Hypotaxis.* A more useful syntactic structural marker is the recurrent pattern in which subordinate participial clauses are each followed by one or more main verbs, usually aorists.[33] This is one of the most striking examples of the careful composition of the parable.[34] Scott uses this

temporal and consecutive uses of καί also reflect Greek usage. See M. Black, *An Aramaic Approach to the Gospels and Acts* (Oxford: Clarendon Press, 3rd edn, 1967), pp. 66-67. Evans (*Luke*, p. 40) lists the markers of Semitic idiom in Greek as 'parataxis of sentences, the verb at the beginning of the sentence, the redundant pronoun, pleonasm such as "answered and said", prepositions such as "in the face of"'. He illustrates Luke's ability to imitate Semitic idiom by referring to Acts 5.12-16 which resembles Mk 6.56 linguistically.

31. Scott, *Hear Then the Parable*, p. 106.

32. The following are excluded for other reasons. Verse 11b introduces the parable. In v. 16b, ὧν introduces a relative clause. In v. 23b, the absence of the particle emphasizes the imperative. Other conjunctions are used in vv. 27b and 27d (ὅτι) and 29f (ἵνα). In v. 30b, the colon follows the temporal particle ὅτε.

33. Black (*Aramaic Approach*, p. 63) notes that 'the subordinating aorist participle occurs no less that 11 times in 21 verses'.

34. Scott, *Hear Then the Parable*, p. 272 n. 21, cites the opinion of Thompson that the use of participles and main verbs to organize sentence structure is more characteristic of written than oral composition (W. Thompson, *Matthew's Advice to a Divided Community: Mt 17, 22-18, 35* [AnBib, 44; Rome: Biblical Institute Press, 1970], p. 221). Black (*Aramaic Approach*, p. 69) says that such constructions are acceptable idiomatic Greek.

feature alone to sketch the surface structure of the parable,[35] showing that the following sections belong together:

v. 13a-b:	συναγαγὼν... ἀπεδήμησεν... διεσκόρπισεν
v. 14a-b:	δαπανήσαντος... ἐγένετο... ἤρξατο
vv. 15a-16c:	πορευθεὶς ἐκολλήθη... ἔπεμψεν... ἐπεθύμει... ἐδίδου
v. 17a:	ἐλθὼν ἔφη
v. 18a-b:	ἀναστὰς πορεύσομαι... ἐρῶ
v. 20a:	ἀναστὰς ἦλθεν
v. 20b-c:	ἀπέχοντος... εἶδεν... ἐσπλαγχνίσθη
v. 20d-e:	δραμὼν ἐπέπεσεν... κατεφίλησεν
vv. 22b-23b:	(ταχὺ) ἐξενέγκατε... ἐνδύσατε... δότε... φέρετε... θύσατε
v. 23c:	φαγόντες εὐφρανθῶμεν[36]
v. 25b-c:	ἐρχόμενος ἤγγισεν... ἤκουσεν
v. 26a-b:	προσκαλεσάμενος... ἐπυνθάνετο... εἴη[37]

There is then a break in the pattern of parataxis and finite verbs, in order to emphasize the angry response of the elder son. The pattern is resumed when the father comes out:

v. 28c:	ἐξελθὼν παρεκάλει
v. 29a:	ἀποκριθεὶς εἶπεν

(iii) *Verbal Tenses*. The dominant verbal tense of the parable is aorist. There are 60 aorists (including infinitives), compared with 19 present tenses, 13 imperfects, 2 futures and 1 optative. While these tenses are of exegetical importance, they do not present an obvious pattern. There are two exceptions to this. In vv. 16a-c we find a string of imperfects. In the father's refrain in vv. 24a-d there is a pattern of alternating imperfects and aorists, with the imperfects referring to being dead and lost and the aorists to being alive and found. The emphasis shifts in vv. 32b-d to

acceptable idiomatic Greek.

35. Scott, *Hear Then the Parable*, pp. 106-108.

36. 'Paratactic imperatives are not uncommon in Greek when they are connected by simple καί. The more literary construction, however, puts the first verb in the participle, subordinated to the second imperative'. Black (*Aramaic Approach*, p. 65) cites Lk. 15.23, θύσατε, καὶ φαγόντες εὐφρανθῶμεν, as an example of this. However, εὐφρανθῶμεν is not an imperative, but a subjunctive used to express an injunction or wish. See C.F.D. Moule, *An Idiom Book of New Testament Greek* (Cambridge: Cambridge University Press, 1953), p. 136.

37. Here εἴη is a potential optative with the protasis omitted. See E. de W. Burton, *Syntax of the Moods and Tenses in New Testament Greek* (Edinburgh: T. & T. Clark, 3rd edn, 1898), p. 133.

Sibinga counts the occurrence of verbal forms to determine the structural composition of the parable. On the basis of a count of 24 aorist
indicative forms (excluding the εἶπεν in 11a), he finds that the four
central ones are found in v. 20b-e: εἶδεν, ἐσπλαγχνίσθη, ἐπέπεσεν,
κατεφίλησεν. On this basis he places the dramatic centre of the parable
there.[38] Menken corrects this to 23 aorist indicatives and shows that the
central one is ἐσπλαγχνίσθη.[39] As we see below, Luke places the father
at the centre of his parable, and emphasizes his exemplary liberal
behavior. Through the central placement of the aorist indicative ἐσπλαγχνίσθη, he emphasizes the father's compassionate nature. This adds a
Christian dimension to the Greco-Roman ideal of liberality.

b. *Plot*

We have already decided that the three major parts of the parable, from
v. 13 onwards, present the actions of each of the three major characters:
the younger son, the father and the elder son. Yet, strictly speaking, this
is only true of part of the sections dealing with the sons, vv. 13a-20a
and 25a-28b. In the section allocated to the father, vv. 20b-24e, he
interacts with his younger son and the wider community. The father
is also present in the first and last sections of the parable. In the first,
vv. 11b-12c, he relates to both sons, and in the last, vv. 28c-32d, he
appeals to his elder son. Thus, the actions of the father do not fit neatly
into a simple one-part-per-character description of the plot.[40]

The same criticism applies to the view that the actions of the younger
son shape the plot. This view is based on substantial evidence: the
younger son's request sets all the subsequent events in motion; his story

---

38. 'Es scheint mir nicht abwegig, hier einen oder vielleicht den Gipfel der
dramatischen Handlung zu erblicken' (Sibinga, 'Kompositionstechnik', p. 107). This
is one of a number of observations which Sibinga makes on the basis of counting
verbal forms which can be verified on other grounds.

39. Sibinga apparently counted ἤθελεν as an aorist, instead of an imperfect.
Menken, 'Σπλαγχνίζεσθαι', p. 108.

40. Antoine divides the parable into two parts, vv. 11-24 and 25-32, but sees
'the figure and attitude of the father' as affirming the unity of the two. See
G. Antoine, 'The Three Parables of Mercy. Exposition of Luke 15.11-32', in
F. Bovon and G. Rouiller (eds.), *Exegesis: Problems of Method and Exercises in
Reading (Genesis 22 and Luke 15)* (trans. by D.G. Miller; Pittsburgh: Pickwick
Press, 1978), pp. 183-96 (184).

has the formal shape of a quest myth;[41] and his story exhibits perfect closure.[42] From this perspective, the story of the elder brother is a negative mirror-image of this plot. But these arguments overlook the central role of the father. *It is the father's actions which drive the plot.* The younger son's request would have come to nothing without his father's generous willingness to accede to it. His return would have never happened without the memory of his father's fair employment practices. His homecoming is made memorable by the warmth and generosity of his father's welcome. The plot focuses on the father's generosity: his division of his property between the two sons; his giving of fine clothing and a feast to mark his younger son's return; his appeal to his elder son to remember that he has always shared everything with him.

This pattern is noted by Bovon, but he fails to recognize that it is central. His exegesis, vivid and insightful as it is, remains dominated by an understanding of the plot which relates primarily to the younger son. He describes the three main axes of the plot as the intersecting themes of the heroic journey, the loss and recovery of goods and the fault that is pardoned. In summing up the plot of the parable as: 'a viable equilibrium, which is followed by a pernicious disequilibrium and then a joyous recovery of stability', he only describes the plot as it relates to the younger son, and quite overlooks the function of the elder son's anger and the father's appeal in the plot as a whole.[43]

Thus, although there are three stories being told, the stories of the two sons are woven together as part of the father's story. In this way, the plot gives greatest emphasis to *his* actions and values.

41. R.C. Tannehill, *The Narrative Unity of Luke–Acts: A Literary Interpretation*. I. *The Gospel According to Luke* (Philadelphia: Fortress Press, 1986), pp. 111-12.

42. 'From the standpoint of plot The Prodigal Son has a rounded and complete beginning, middle and end without the elder brother episode' (Via, *Parables*, p. 167).

43. The same is true of his argument that there is a structural correspondence between the parable of the prodigal son and the Emmaus story in Lk. 24 (F. Bovon, 'The Parable of the Prodigal Son [Luke 15.11-32]: Second Reading', in F. Bovon and G. Rouiller (eds.), *Exegesis: Problems of Method and Exercises in Reading (Genesis 22 and Luke 15)* [trans. D.G. Miller; Pittsburgh: Pickwick Press, 1978], pp. 441-66 [454-56]).

c. *Characterization*

Luke's characterization also draws attention to the father. Studies of the comic characters of Menander and Terence have shown that certain characters are individualized by acting counter to their conventional typology.[44] Luke uses this technique to differentiate the character of the father from that of his two sons. Both sons act according to type, behaving as a prodigal and a miser in ways which would have been familiar to Luke's readers.[45] The father, however, acts quite differently from the way fathers with covetous sons were conventionally portrayed, as the examples given in Chapter 1 indicate.[46] His liberality is all the more striking for being unexpected. The atypicality of his behavior also means that his character carries most of what Reardon terms the 'emotional action'.[47]

Despite a fondness for stereotyping his characters,[48] Luke does not 'label' them explicitly. Even the younger son is not called a prodigal directly: prodigality is an epithet of his way of life in the far country. As elsewhere in his Gospel, Luke leaves his readers to infer the moral condition of his characters.[49]

The secondary characters in the story also belong to two opposing groups. The various members of the household represent aspects of the father's liberality: the good wages of the hired servants (μίσθιοι) inspire the impoverished son to join them; the slaves (δοῦλοι) are the

44. See W.G. Arnott, 'Time, Plot and Character in Menander', in F. Cairns (ed.), *Papers of the Liverpool Latin Seminar: Second Volume 1979* (ARCA Classical and Medieval Texts, Papers and Monographs, 3; Liverpool: Francis Cairns, 1979), pp. 343-60 (353-54).

45. As I note below, even the attribution of prodigality to the younger son and meanness to the elder son is conventional.

46. It is this mixture of conventional and unconventional behavior which reveals that the parable ought to be read as fiction. This mixture also confounds those who seek to interpret all the characters allegorically, or identify a particular Jewish legal situation underlying the narrative.

47. Of *Chaereas and Callirhoe*, Reardon says that it does not only consist of events. 'The other pole of the story is emotion' ('Theme', p. 10).

48. Johnson emphasizes this characteristic of the Lukan style. See L.T. Johnson, 'On Finding the Lukan Community: A Cautious Cautionary Essay', P. Achtemeier (ed.), *Society for Biblical Literature Seminar Papers 1979* (Atlanta, GA: Scholars Press, 1979), pp. 87-100 (93). He illustrates this from Lk. 15.1–16.31 (*Literary Function*, pp. 109-10).

49. J.D. Kingsbury, Conflict *in Luke: Jesus, Authorities, Disciples* (Minneapolis: Fortress Press, 1991), p. 16.

agents of the father's welcome; and the young servant (παῖς) explains the father's generous welcome to the elder son. The other group consists of impersonal or anonymous actants:[50] the famine, which intervenes from outside as 'a cosmic agent'; the foreign employer, who is the other agent of the younger son's degradation;[51] and the 'no one' (οὐδείς), mentioned in v.16c. They are all found in the foreign country, and are images of illiberality.

I have already mentioned the importance of direct speech in the parable. In a further device, also used by Menander, Luke makes the early words of each of the sons reveal their central weakness.[52] The younger son says, 'Father, give me...' (v. 12b) and the elder, 'Lo, these many years I have served you... yet you never gave me ...' (v. 29b-e).

Because the bulk of this study is devoted to the exploration of the moral behavior of the three central characters, no description of the characterization of each of them is necessary here. In Chapters 5–8 I discuss fully how Luke relates their behavior to themes belonging to the topos On Covetousness.

d. *Narrative Devices*

Apart from orientating the action around the central characters, Luke also uses a number of narrative techniques to give order and emphasis to his plot and to highlight specific themes.

(i) *Summaries, Scenes and Close-Ups*. The most prominent narrative technique used by Luke in the parable is that of alternating summary (reporting) with description (representation).[53] He sketches parts of the

---

50. In structuralism and semiotics, actants are the basic logical categories of a story which generate the narrative. They occur in opposing pairs and represent the basic functions (such as Subject–Object, Giver–Receiver, Helper–Opponent) fulfilled by the characters. See F. Deist, *A Concise Dictionary of Theological Terms* (Pretoria: J.L. van Schaik, 1984), s.v. 'Actants'. Within a narrative, actants may change from being Sender to Subject, Opponent or whatever, depending on which main character is in the forefront. Scott's structuralist reading of the parable demonstrates this. See B.B. Scott, 'The Prodigal Son: A Structuralist Interpretation', *Semeia* 9 (1977), pp. 45-73; and the summary in du Plessis, *Kykie*, pp. 86-90.

51. Entrevernes, *Signs and Parables*, pp. 148-55.

52. Arnott ('Time, Plot and Character in Menander', p. 360 n. 44) cites the example of the way the greed of Smikrines in *Aspis* is revealed by his comments in ll. 82-86, before he is described as avaricious in ll. 114-89.

53. This Hellenistic narrative technique is identified by Hägg in his study of the

story in barest outline and fills other parts with life and detail.[54] By means of summaries he moves his readers quickly to the important scenes.[55] Within them, he zooms into close-up by means of direct speech.[56] The effect of this device is to focus the attention of his readers on particular events within the parable:

v. 11b	summary
v. 12a-b	scene with direct speech
v. 12c	transitional summary
v. 13a-b	summary
vv. 14a-16c	scene
vv. 17a-19b	scene with direct speech
v. 20a	transitional summary
v. 20b-e	scene
vv. 21a-24d	scene with direct speech
v. 24e	transitional summary
v. 25a	summary
v. 25b-c	scene

novel *Chaereas and Callirhoe*: 'Characteristically, it proceeds by means, first, of rapid narrative summarizing a sequence of events; then, by degrees, the tempo slows; and finally a "scene" materializes, displaying the actions, thoughts, utterances of an important character at an important juncture of events ... Then the story proceeds—perhaps the subject is changed—and the process is repeated' (Reardon, 'Theme', p. 11, summarizing the 'Syncrisis' on 'Tempo and Phases of Narrative' in T. Hägg, *Narrative Technique in Ancient Greek Romances* [Göteborg: Paul Astrom, 1971]).

54. The same is true of the Parable of the Good Samaritan. Noorda shows that this narrative technique is found in Acts 4.32–5.16. See S.J. Noorda, 'Scene and Summary: A Proposal for Reading Acts 4, 32–5, 16', in J. Kremer (ed.), *Les actes des apôtres: Traditions, rédaction, théologie* (BETL, 48; Leuven: Leuven University Press, 1979), pp. 475-83. Johnson (*Luke*, p. 13) identifies summaries and speeches as two of Luke's most important narrative devices.

55. These scenes are given further emphasis by being vividly described, a literary device termed διατύπωσις, by Longinus. See Longinus, *Subl.* 20.1.

56. Goulder notes Luke's liking for 'prolonged exchanges and conversations'. He comments that in Lk. 15.11-32 there are exchanges between the father and each of the sons, and the elder son and a servant, and that all three members of the family make short speeches. He observes further on that Luke generally repeats the moral of his story in the direct speech of his characters. This is correct, though by referring only to the repeated confession of the younger son and the refrain of the father, he overlooks the complaint of the elder brother in vv. 29b-30b (Goulder, *Luke*, pp. 95 and 103-104).

vv. 26a-27d	scene with indirect speech[57]
v. 28a-b	transitional summary
v. 28c	summary
vv. 29a-32d	scene with direct speech
	[absence of transitional summary]

The parable begins with a unit, vv. 11a-12c, containing a summary, a scene with direct speech and a transitional summary. The ending, vv. 28c-32d, is the same, but omits the summary following the direct speech. Within the parable are three units which each develop from a summary (or scene at v. 20b) to a 'close-up' in direct speech, and are followed by a transitional summary of the action flowing from the speech. As we would expect, the bulk of the parable is made up of scenes, rather than the summaries.[58] Each of the three central units exhibits a similar pattern: (1) an outline of events as they relate to one of the central characters (omitted in vv. 20b-24e); (2) more detailed description of his actions; and (3) his inner, psychological, interpretation. In a detail of characterization, the elder son has to ask a young servant (παῖς) to interpret the prevailing events and actions, while both the younger son and the father are able to interpret these for themselves.[59]

The emphasis thus given to the passages of direct speech means that we should pay particular attention in our quest for the message or teaching of the parable. They reveal, for example, that it is not to be sought in the prodigal living of the younger son, for this is quickly disposed of in the summary in v. 13. The focus, as far as the younger son is concerned, is on his greed in v. 12a-b, the destructive consequences of that greed in v. 17a-c, and his decision to return home as a hired worker in vv. 18a-19b.

---

57. This scene also summarizes the events of vv. 20a-24e, but the summary is for the benefit of the elder son, not the readers.

58. Of a total of 402 words in our text, 335 words (83%) are devoted to scenes, with 201 of these words (50% of the total, or 60% of the scenes) in direct speech. (For the purposes of this analysis v. 26a-b is classified as part of a scene with speech, though the four words in the indirect question τί ἂν εἴη ταῦτα are not counted as words of direct speech.)

59. In Greek comedy utterances that reveal character in the form of questions have particular force. See E.G. Turner, 'The Rhetoric of Question and Answer in Menander', *Themes in Drama* 2 (1980), pp. 1-23 (5).

This technique of giving greatest emphasis to scenes in direct speech also means that the conversation between the father and the elder son in vv. 29a-32d deserves greater exegetical attention than it usually receives. It is not a mere appendix to the story, but the climax.[60] This is evident in a variety of ways: (1) it is the only actual conversation in the parable; (2) each speaker begins emphatically, the brother with ἰδού in v. 29b, and the father with σύ in v. 31b, softened somewhat by the affectionate τέκνον; (3) the father's response reverses and corrects aspects of what his son says: the elder son's repeated οὐδέποτε in v. 29d-e is answered by the father's πάντοτε in v. 31a. The son's pejorative οὗτος in ὁ υἱός σου οὗτος in v. 30a is corrected by the non-pejorative οὗτος of the father in ὁ ἀδελφός σου οὗτος in v. 32b; (4) the parallelism in the father's words in v. 31b-c is varied by the chiastic crossing of the 'you' and 'me' references:

$$\text{σύ } \underline{\text{πάντοτε}} \text{ μετ' } \underline{\text{ἐμοῦ}} \text{ εἶ,}$$
$$\text{καὶ } \underline{\text{πάντα}} \text{ τὰ } \underline{\text{ἐμὰ}} \text{ σά ἐστιν}$$

This summary of his liberality is thus emphasized stylistically; (5) finally, as I note below, both son and father echo phrases from his speech in vv. 23a-24d, including the important dead-alive, lost-found refrain.

(ii) *Parallelism.* Within the passages of direct speech, further emphasis is given to certain elements by means of parallelism.

The first lengthy passage of direct speech (after v. 12b) is the younger son's soliloquy in vv. 17b-19b. Part of this, vv. 18c-19b: πάτερ, ἥμαρτον... μισθίων σου, is exactly paralleled in v. 21b-d. Other key words and phrases from this soliloquy are also repeated: the λιμός in v. 17c echoes an earlier reference in v. 14a; the use of ἀπόλλυμι in v. 17c anticipates its use later in vv. 24c and 32d; and the use of ἀνίστημι in v. 18a is echoed in v. 20a.[61]

In the first speech of the father, in vv. 22b-24d, the double antithetical parallelism found in v. 24a-d is itself almost exactly paralleled in v. 32b-d.[62] Other phrases from this speech are echoed: μόσχον τὸν

---

60. Johnson notes this intuitively when he comments: 'What gives this story its true poignancy, however, is the final scene between the father and the elder son' (*Luke*, p. 241).

61. F.W. Danker discusses Luke's fondness for echo diction and anticipation in his *Luke* (Philadelphia: Fortress Press, 2nd edn, 1987), pp. 21-24.

62. See Jeremias, *Sprache*, pp. 251-53.

σιτευτόν in v. 23a, and θύω in v. 23b, are echoed by the servant and the elder son in vv. 27c and 30b, and the father himself repeats the verb εὐφραίνω in v. 23c and parallels it with the synonym χαίρω in v. 32a.

The pattern of these paralleled words and motifs can be represented as follows:

vv. 18c-19b:	**confession of sin, make me a servant**
v. 21b-d:	**confession of sin, make me a servant**
v. 23a-b:	*slaughter the prize calf*
v. 23c:	**rejoice**
v. 24a-d:	dead-alive, lost-found
v. 24e:	**rejoice**
v. 27c:	*slaughter the prize calf*
v. 30b:	*slaughter the prize calf*
v. 32a:	**rejoice**
v. 32b-d:	dead-alive, lost-found

These motifs are significant in being related, as we shall see in the following chapters, both to the topos On Covetousness and to the Christian dimension which Luke adds to it.

(iii) *Inclusio.* A further device that Luke uses to order and unify the parable is the inclusio. Verses 11b-12c and vv. 28c-32d each form an inclusio by beginning and ending with the father as subject. By resembling one another in this way, they also form an inclusio in the parable as a whole.

The part dealing with the elder brother also contains two inclusios. In vv. 25a-28b an inclusio is created by having the older brother as the subject of vv. 25a and 28a-b (together with the pair of imperfects, ἦν and ἤθελεν). Similarly, vv. 28c-32d form an inclusio by beginning and ending with the father. This is one of the reasons for dividing this section in two.

(iv) *Changes of Subject, Place and Time.* The narrative is also structured by changes of subject, place or time.[63]

---

63. Schnider presents some of the features discussed here in schematic form. He combines the changes of place and time into one category, 'circumstances', which obscures the way the changes of place clearly mark the strucure of this parable, while changes of time do not. See F. Schnider, *Die verlorenen Söhne: Strukturanalytische und historisch-kritische Untersuchungen zu Lk 15* (OBO, 17;

Change of Subject. The parable begins and ends with two sections, vv. 11b-12c and vv. 28c-32d, in which there is a father-son-father pattern.

In the section following the opening one (vv. 13a-20a) the subject alternates between the younger son and something else. In the far country the alternation is between the younger son and the negative subjects of the famine, the foreign employer, the pigs and 'no one'.

The section dealing with the younger son's return (vv. 20b-24e) is central. There, the subject alternates between the father and the younger son, culminating in the subject of the whole household.

In the penultimate section (25a-28b), the subject of the elder son alternates with that of his servant.

This reveals a clear set of patterns. The change of subject divides the parable into units, in which the younger and elder sons each first interact with other people and then with their father.[64] The father–son–father sections that begin and end the parable form an inclusio. The centrality of the section, in which the converted younger son is welcomed by his father and the whole household, serves to emphasize the importance of the ideal of liberality.

Change of Place. This is an important structural marker. The central place in the parable is the father's home. This is evident in the way the actions of the central characters are all described in terms of their orientation towards it. The story begins at the father's home in vv. 11b-12c, and the part dealing with the younger son begins with his departure from there in v. 13 for a foreign (μακράν) country.

The part dealing with the father begins with the father seeing his returning son from afar (μακράν). The son's arrival is described in v. 20b from the perspective of the father's home. He is welcomed outside the home in vv. 20c-24d and then fêted within (an inference from v. 28b-c) in v. 24e.

From the point of view of place, the elder son's movements are a mirror of the younger's. His part of the parable also begins with his return home from the fields in v. 25a-b, although he has never left home. On hearing of his father's compassionate and liberal welcome of

Freiburg: Universitästverlag; Göttingen: Vandenhoeck & Ruprecht, 1977), pp. 43-46.

64. (1) vv. 11b-12c father and younger son; (2) vv. 13a-20a younger son and others; (3) vv. 20b-24e father and younger son; (4) vv 25a-28b elder son and servant; (5) vv. 28c-32d father and elder son.

his younger brother, he refuses to enter the home that he shares with his
father (v. 28a-b). His father comes outside to appeal to him, but we are
not told whether he relents or remains outside (vv. 25a-32d).[65]

This centring of the action on the father's home again reveals his
importance in the story. The moral concerns of the parable reflect this
spatial orientation, with the younger son departing from his father's
moral viewpoint and later returning to it. The elder son apparently
shares his father's viewpoint, but is revealed at the end to be unwilling
or unable to adopt it.

Change of Time. The chronology of the parable is vague. Most of the
time indicators are not stated explicitly and have to be inferred from the
action of the verbs, the class or meaning of other words, and the overall
shape of the narrative.[66] While the details of the chronology remain unspecified, they do correspond to the divisions I have already established
by other means. The clearest indications of change are numbered below.

(1) The action begins at a specific but unspecified moment (εἶπεν,
aorist) when the son asks for his share of his father's living (vv. 12a-
12c).

(2) Not long after (μετ' οὐ πολλὰς ἡμέρας) the younger son has received his share he turns it into cash and departs (vv. 13a-13b).[67]

---

65. The Entrevernes Group segments the story in terms of changes of *place*
(foreign country, house, outside the house), *action* (leaving and lack, return and
attribution, refusal to enter and denunciation) and *actors* (father and two sons,
father and younger son, father and older son) (Entrevernes Group, *Signs and Parables*, p. 142).

66. Compare Reardon's comment on *Chaereas and Callirhoe*: 'Chariton offers
very little indication of the "real" chronological framework—the calendar time
taken by events. Deprived, thus, of a firm, objective "handrail" to guide us through
events, we turn the more readily to what the author wants to present as important,
namely his characters' psychological reactions as set in the emotional *sequence* of
events—this is of course an aspect of the gliding-and-close-up technique discussed
above' ('Theme', p. 20).

67. This typically Lukan phrase (see Fitzmyer, *Luke*, p. 1087; and Jeremias,
Sprache, p. 249), and the elder brother's reference to the years he has served the
father, are the only explicit references to time in the parable. For a discussion of
Lukan and Hellenistic phrases similar to usage of μετ' οὐ πολλὰς ἡμέρας, see D.L.
Mealand, ' "After not Many Days" in Acts 1.5 and its Hellenistic Context', *JSNT* 42
(1991), pp. 69-77. However, because of the word order he specifies for his searches
of the *Thesaurus Linguae Graecae* compact disk, he fails to identify the reference
in Lk. 15.13.

Luke's use of the device of litotes (understatement, especially affir-
mation by negation of the contrary) is used here to emphasize the
strength of the younger son's prodigal desires.

(3) As soon as he has spent all the money a famine arrives. λιμὸς ἰσ-
χυρά refers to a widespread lack of food over a considerable period of
time. He becomes increasingly hungry: ἐπεθύμει is a durative imperfect[68] and ἐδίδου a progressive imperfect (vv. 14a-16c).[69] After an unspecified length of time he comes to himself and decides to go home.
He recognizes that his behavior during his time away from home has
changed his status: οὐκέτι is an adverb of time (vv. 17a-20a).

(4) While he is still at a distance (ἔτι is an adverb of time) his father
runs to meet him and welcomes him home: ἀνέζησεν, like ἔζησεν at
v. 32c, is an aorist, which indicates that the younger son *began* to live
once again (vv. 20b-24d).[70] In v. 24e, the household begins to rejoice
(ἤρξαντο, aorist).

(5) The elder son approaches the home (vv. 25a-27d). When he hears
what has happened he is angry and refuses to go inside. The imperfect,
ἤθελεν, suggests an ongoing, continuous unwillingness to go in (v. 28a-
b). When the father learns of this, he comes out to appeal to him. The
elder son refers back to the whole period during which he has been at
home (vv. 28c-32d).[71]

The importance of the younger son's taking up of a life of virtue at
home is emphasized by the way most of the action takes place on the
day of his return, although the plot as a whole ranges over a considerable time.

e. *Diction*
One of the most important means of demonstrating Luke's engagement
with the topos On Covetousness is his use of words with distinctive

68. J. Reiling and J.L. Swellengrebel, *A Translator's Handbook on the Gospel
of Luke* (Leiden: E.J. Brill, 1971), p. 548.

69. 'The progressive imperfect is sometimes used of action attempted, but not
accomplished' (Burton, *Syntax*, p. 12). Other Lukan examples of this are Lk. 1.59;
Acts 7.26; 26.11.

70. Verbs that express 'a state or condition are employed in the aorist tense to
indicate the action which is the point of entrance into that state' (N. Turner, *Grammatical Insights into the New Testament* [Edinburgh: T. & T. Clark, 1965], p. 150).

71. As noted above, the phrases τοσαῦτα ἔτη and πάντοτε parallel one another.
The two occurrences of οὐδέποτε parallel the πάντοτε antithetically, and also stand
in opposition to the ὅτε δέ.

moral associations for his Greco-Roman readers. Chapters 5–8 show that much of the vocabulary found in the parable is widely used by other writers when addressing issues relating to the issue of covetousness.

Luke is often described as being fond of giving colourful details,[72] with the assumption that they are non-allegorical and essentially decorative. However, the fact that many exegetes and preachers have wished to know more,[73] suggests that Luke has been conservative in his use of details and that those which he has included are functional. We shall see that the details have been carefully chosen for their moral resonance and shared semantic domains. This ought not to surprise us. The importance of the Lukan choice of words has been known since the work of Cadbury in the 1920s.[74]

The broad semantic domain to which the parable belongs is suggested by the semantic domains to which the most frequently used words belong.[75] These are described by the LNSM lexicon as: kinship terms;[76] terms referring to possession, transfer and exchange;[77] and

72. For example, Goulder (*Luke*, p. 97) mentions 'the far country, the famine, the swine, the boy's hunger even for the pods, the father's running, the best robe, the ring, the shoes, the lack of a kid for the faithful elder brother and so on' as examples of 'non-allegorical details' which give 'colour and realism' to Luke's writing.

73. What were the terms of the property division at the start of the story? How exactly did the younger son behave in the far country before he ran out of money? How true is the elder brother's accusation that he had consorted with harlots? What was life like at home in his absence? Why did the father not go looking for his son? And so on.

74. See H.J. Cadbury, *The Style and Literary Method of Luke* (HTS, 6; Cambridge, MA: Harvard University Press, 1920; and *idem*, *The Making of Luke–Acts* (New York: MacMillan, 1927).

75. The semantic domains cited are those used in J.P. Louw *et al.* (eds.), *Greek-English Lexicon of the New Testament Based on Semantic Domains*. I. *Introduction and Domains* (New York: United Bible Societies, 1988), hereafter 'LNSM'. They have the merit of relating different words which have a similar meaning and of distinguishing variant meanings within a single word more explicitly. While these domains are not watertight, and areas of overlap are noted in the lexicon itself, they do provide a standardized point of departure.

76. *Kinship terms* (LNSM domain 10): πάτηρ (twelve times), υἱός (eight times), ἀδελφός (twice).

77. *Possess, transfer, exchange* (LNSM domain 57): δίδωμι (four times), ἐπιβάλλω, διαιρέω, συνάγω, διασκορπίζω, δαπανάω, πάντα τὰ ἐμὰ σά ἐστιν, βίος

physiological processes and states.[78] While it would be a methodological error to identify the message of the parable on such grounds alone, these results nevertheless support the idea that the teaching of the parable deals with the moral and physical well-being of family members and their use of their possessions.

However, the only conclusive way of showing that much of the language of the parable belongs to the topos On Covetousness, is to discuss a wide range of examples in detail. In Chapters 5–8 below, the following terms are shown to be related by their frequent use in texts on the topos On Covetousness: a brother, ἀδελφός; to do wrong, to sin, ἁμαρτάνω; to be lost, ἀπόλλυμι; wastefully, ἀσώτως; living, means, βίος; to feed (a herd of animals), βόσκω; a ring, δακτύλιος; to spend, squander, δαπανάω; to distribute, διαίρεω; to scatter or squander, διασκόρπιζω; to give, δίδωμι; to serve, δουλεύω; to disobey a command, ἐντολὴν παρέρχομαι; to return to oneself, εἰς ἑαυτον ἔρχεσθαι; to fall to one's share, τὸ ἐπιβάλλον; to desire, covet, ἐπιθυμέω; to rejoice, make merry, εὐφραίνω; famine, hunger, λιμός; a hired servant, μίσθιος; dead, νεκρός; to be angry, ὀργίζομαι; substance, property, οὐσία; to be or have in abundance, περισσεύω; a prostitute, πορνή; to feel compassion or pity, σπλαγχνίζομαι; a robe, στολή; music, symphony, συμφωνία; to gather together, συνάγω; a child, τέκνον; to be healthy, ὑγιαίνω; a sandal, ὑποδήμα; to be in want, ὑστερέω; a friend, φίλος; a pig, χοίρος; a dance, χορός; to live, be alive, ζάω; and to regain life, ἀναζαω.[79] Many of these are everyday words, but they have specific, often metaphorical, meanings when used in texts interacting with the topos On Covetousness.

5. *Results*

a. *The Composition of the Parable*
I now summarize my findings. The most important indicators of the compositional structure are: hypotaxis; summary, scene and close-up; changes of subject and place; and the rhetorical devices of parallelism

(twice), οὐσία (twice), ὑστερέω, ἀπόλλυμι (thrice), περισσεύω, μίσθιος (thrice), δοῦλος and κατεσθίω.

78. *Physiological processes and states* (LNSM domain 23): λιμός (twice), κοιλία, ὑγιαίνω, νεκρός, ἀνέζησεν/ἔζησεν, ζῶν ἀσώτως, βόσκω, ἀπόλλυμι and ἐσθίω.

79. This list excludes phrases which are significant but which cannot be short-

and inclusio. Of secondary importance are: syntactic constructions; the tenses of verbs; and changes of time. If we weigh these considerations together, we are able to account for the divisions of the parable mentioned in section 2.2 above:

v. 11a: does not belong to the parable itself, but is part of Luke's primary narrative.

vv. 11b-12c: The parable itself begins without a particle at 11b. The three central characters of the parable are introduced, and the event which leads to all the subsequent events in the story is narrated by means of a summary, a close-up and a transitional summary. The father as the subject at the start and the end produces an inclusio.

vv. 13a-20a: There is a change of subject, place and time at v. 13a. The unit consists of a summary, scene and close-up and a transitional summary. It is further bound together by the hypotactic constructions found in vv. 13a-b, 14a-b and 15a-16c. The change of subject and time between vv. 16c and 17a is also accompanied by the use of verbs in the imperfect tense in v. 16a-c.

vv. 20b-24e: There is a change of subject, place and time at v. 20b. The unit consists of a scene, close-up and transitional summary. Patterns of hypotactic construction continue in vv. 20b-e and 22b-23c.

vv. 25a-28b: There is a change of subject, place and time at v. 25a. The unit consists of a summary, scene, close-up and transitional summary. The elder son as the subject of vv. 25a and 28a-b forms an inclusio. The pattern of hypotactic construction is still present, but not as marked (vv. 25b-c and 26a-b).

vv. 28c-32d: The subject changes at v. 28c. The unit consists of a summary and close-up. Again hypotactic constructions are found in vv. 28c and 29a, but this feature is not marked. The absence of the expected transitional summary is a formal parallel to the lack of narrative closure to the elder son's story. However, it begins and ends with the father as the subject, forming an inclusio.

---

ened to one or two characteristic words, such as σὺ πάντοτε μετ᾽ ἐμοῦ εἶ, καὶ πάντα τὰ ἐμὰ σά ἐστιν in v. 31b-c.

The use of similar structural patterns throughout the parable gives it a structural unity. The parable is further unified by the repetition, in anticipation and echo-diction, of phrases found in the passages of direct speech.

b. *What the Parable Teaches*

Through the above study of the composition of Lk. 15.11-32, we have been able to identify which sections and aspects are emphasized by Luke. If we draw a composite picture of the sections, characters and themes thus accented, we are given some idea of what the parable is intended to teach. This picture is provisional because it takes no account of the influence of the co-text upon the meaning of the parable, nor of the pre-understanding of its intended readers. These matters are dealt with in the succeeding chapters.

The most important character is the father.[80] His central structural position and individualization concentrate attention upon him, and suggest that Luke intended his behavior to be a positive example for his readers. He forms the standard by which all other behavior is to be judged. His home is the central place. His workers and servants reveal his liberality, and his sons evoke his compassion. Luke emphasizes both of these virtues, so that each qualifies the other. The subjects of his speech make this clear: his gifts, his joy at his younger son's recovery from ruin, and his concern at his elder son's criticism of the celebration to mark his brother's return.

The presentation of the sons as opposing stereotypes reveals Luke's rejection of such behavior. His rejection of prodigality is shown by his brief mention of prodigal behavior. He prefers to focus on the negative consequences of such behavior, and places greater stress on the younger son's conversion and return. This emphasis is also evident in the way most of the action in the parable is related to his return and takes place on the day of his return. Luke's rejection of meanness is seen in the way he places the father's appeal to his elder son at the climax of the parable. In this important section the narrative is slowed down by having fewer hypotactic constructions. Through the father's appeal to his elder son, Luke appeals to his readers.

---

80. This point is recognized by many exegetes. See H. Weder, *Die Gleichnisse Jesu als Metaphern* (FRLANT, 120; Göttingen: Vandenhoeck & Ruprecht, 1978), p. 259 n. 76.

The unacceptability of both prodigal and miserly behavior is seen in the direct speech of the two sons. The younger's first words are, 'Father, give me ... ' and his elder brother complains about what he has *not* been given. The younger son's admission that he has been wrong, and his request to be taken on as a hired worker, are emphasized by being repeated. In contrast, the elder son only complains.

The semantic domains of the most frequently used words add the supplementary consideration that the parable somehow relates the moral and physical well-being of family members to their use of possessions.

Thus, I conclude that the parable teaches the virtue of compassionate liberality and rejects the opposing vices of prodigality and meanness. It illustrates that liberality is a source of physical and moral health and harmony, for the individual and for the community. Through the creative use of a simple plot, conventional characters and familiar moral language, Luke appeals to his readers to behave with liberality, particularly towards their Christian brothers and sisters.

Chapter 3

CO-TEXTS: LUKE 15.11-32 AND THE OTHER L PARABLES

In the study of the construction and language of Lk. 15.11-32 in the previous chapter, we came to the conclusion that the parable teaches the virtue of compassionate liberality and rejects the opposing vices of prodigality and meanness. However, this view has not been widely held by exegetes, who have largely interpreted the parable theologically, placing the emphasis on the lost-found motif and relating the message to the intra-textual hearers mentioned in Lk. 15.11-32. These are all consequences of taking Luke 15 as the sole co-text for the parable. I argue here that when it is interpreted together with the other L parables, its moral orientation and paraenetic function become more clearly evident.

1. Luke's Teaching on Possessions and Luke 15.11-32

Most scholars fail to recognize that Lk. 15.11-32 relates directly to the Lukan theme of the right use of possessions. This is true even of studies that are specifically focused on this aspect of Luke's theology.[1]

1. Fitzmyer (*Luke*, pp. 247-51) emphasizes the Lukan theme of 'the disciple's right use of material possessions'; makes specific mention of parables such as Lk. 12.16-20; 16.1-8a; and 16.19-31; and mentions the story of the Good Samaritan as one 'which exemplifies a right use of material possessions to aid an unfortunate human being, 10.35-37', though it is told for another purpose. However, he does not make a similar claim for Lk. 15.11-32.

In an article aimed at reconstructing the rich-and-poor aspect of the Lukan *Sitz im Leben*, Karris refers to Lk. 12.13-21 and 16.1-31 in his discussion of a large collection of passages from the travel narrative. However, his analysis jumps from Lk. 14.33 to 16.1 without a mention of Lk. 15. See R.J. Karris, 'Poor and Rich: The Lukan *Sitz im Leben*', in C.H. Talbert (ed.), *Perspectives on Luke–Acts* (Danville, VA: Association of Baptist Professors of Religion, 1978), pp. 112-25.

Pilgrim lists a number of parables on the dangers of wealth and the right use of

This state of affairs arises from a circular method of describing this aspect of Luke's theology. Passages that seem to address the issue of the use of possessions specifically are identified and the teaching of these units is systemized.[2] The results are then used to identify which passages ought to be studied more closely to refine the picture. This description oversimplifies the procedure, but does illustrate the way certain passages are excluded a priori.

Certain passages that make mention of wealth or possessions are excluded on the grounds that they do not give explicit teaching on these issues, but are intended to teach something else. However, when the reasons for this 'other emphasis' are examined, they are found not to derive from the text itself. Theological presuppositions, for example, lead to a passage being classified as having a particular theological theme. This results in those elements of the text that support this classification being given undue emphasis, while other data are simply set aside.

As an example of how the exclusion process takes place, I examine the line of argument of L.T. Johnson, the scholar who comes closest to acknowledging that Lk. 15.11-32 teaches the right use of possessions.

Johnson recognizes that the parable has much to say about possessions. He observes that 'each development in the relationship between father and sons, is expressed through the imagery of possessions', citing

possessions from L: Lk. 7.10-43; 10.25-37; 12.13-21; 16.1-13, and 16.19-31; but omits Lk. 15.11-32. See W.E. Pilgrim *Good News to the Poor: Wealth and Poverty in Luke–Acts* (Minneapolis: Augsburg, 1981), pp. 109-19, 125-29, 138-39, 141-43 and 184 n.3.

Similarly, Horn's full-scale study of the theme of possessions in Luke–Acts completely overlooks Lk. 15.11-32. He thinks of it, together with the other two parables of Lk. 15, as, 'Eine einfache Umkehrung der Verlorenen zum Heil.' The only L parables studied are those in Lk. 10.30-37 and 12.16-20 and the two in ch. 16 (F.W. Horn, *Glaube und Handeln in der Theologie des Lukas* [GTA, 26; Göttingen: Vandenhoeck & Ruprecht, 2nd edn, 1986], pp. 58-87, 107-115 and 154).

Marshall's discussion of the Lukan theme of the rich and the poor makes no mention of the theme of possessions in Lk. 15.11-32, though he interprets the Pharisee in Lk. 18.10-14 in terms of Luke's reference to Pharisaic avarice in Lk. 16.14. See I.H. Marshall, *Luke: Historian and Theologian* (Exeter: Paternoster Press, 1970), p. 143.

Mealand's discussion of L material relating to possessions makes no mention of Lk. 15.11-32. D.L. Mealand, *Poverty and Expectation in the Gospels* (London: SPCK, 1980), pp. 27-33.

2.   See Johnson's discussion of this problem in *Literary Function*, pp. 127-30.

examples of this from vv. 11, 13, 14-16, 17, 22-23, and that the 'alien-
ation, conversion and return [of the younger son] are all expressed by
possessions'. He also emphasizes the importance of v.31. 'It cannot go
unnoticed how strikingly 15.31 anticipates the language and thought of
Acts 4.32ff., particularly in the note that those who are together in unity
share *all* with each other'.[3] Yet despite these observations, he denies
that the parable is aimed at teaching the right use of possessions:

> No-one would claim that the story is 'about' possessions, or that Luke
> intended to convey a particular lesson about possessions through the
> story. It is likely therefore that whatever is said about possessions in the
> story flows not from any paraenetic intent, but from the spontaneous un-
> derstanding and instinctive literary art of the author. There might have
> been any number of ways for Luke to tell this story; that he did so in the
> way he did shows something of his appreciation of the metaphorical
> strength of possessions language.[4]

His rejection of the idea that Lk. 15.11-32 has a paraenetic function
related to the use of possessions is based on two prior exegetical deci-
sions. The first is the process of classifying texts which he himself criticizes.[5] By classifying Lk. 15.11-32 as a parable that does not have the
theme of possessions as its main point of reference, he makes it virtu-
ally impossible for any conflicting exegetical data to disturb this classification. This forces him into the position in which he has to attribute
the possessions language in the parable to Luke's 'spontaneous' and
'instinctive' use of such language as a metaphor for 'human relations in
a dynamic of separation and unity'.[6] Thus, he uses the device of metaphor to say that the parable is *not* about possessions, but something
else.[7]

---

3.   Johnson, *Literary Function*, p. 161.
4.   Johnson, *Literary Function*, p. 160.
5.   Johnson (*Literary Function*, p. 128) distinguishes five different kinds of passages in Luke's Gospel dealing with possessions. Of the two that refer to stories, he
distinguishes 'stories in which possessions or the use of possessions appear to be
the point of the story (e.g. 16.1-13; 16.19-31; 19.11-27)' from 'statements or stories
which do not have as their main point of reference the use of possessions but within
which possessions play a role (e.g. 11.21-22; 15.11-32)'.
6.   Johnson, *Literary Function*, pp. 159-61.
7.   The process of evading Luke's concrete language of possessions by reinter-
preting it as metaphor is taken to extreme by J.T. Sanders. He denies Luke's special
interest in the use of money, and argues that every reference to money is actually an
illustration of something else. The parable in Lk. 7.41-43 is a defence of Jesus'

The second, related, exegetical decision is his acceptance of the traditional schema which classifies Lk. 15.11-32 as one of 'three parables of "the lost"' told by Jesus in defence of his mission to the outcasts. This classification retains its hold upon his exegesis even though he observes that the second and third parables in Luke 15 involve possessions, and that the whole unit from Lk. 15.1–16.31 is addressed to the Pharisees who are described as lovers of money, φιλάργυροι, in Lk. 16.14.[8]

Thus, the twin processes of classifying Lk. 15.11-32 as a parable which does not deal with possessions directly, and of reading it only in terms of the rest of Luke 15, have the effect of preventing other elements of the parable from being heard. Reading the parable in terms of Luke 15 alone results in the problem of focusing on Jesus' hearers in the primary story, instead of Luke's intended audience, a problem I have already discussed. The message of the parable has to be sought in terms of Luke's intended readers.[9] This point becomes clearer the more we identify the extent of Luke's influence upon its present form.

association with unrighteous people, the parables in Lk. 16.1-9 and 16.19-31 are told to show how the Pharisees cannot interpret the law rightly, and so on (J.T. Sanders, *Ethics in the New Testament: Change and Development* [London: SCM Press, 1975], pp. 36-37). Sanders takes a similar approach in 'Tradition and Redaction', *NTS* 15 (1968-1969), pp. 437-38. Unlike Johnson, he fails to see that it is hermeneutically unsatisfactory just to speak of Luke's possessions language as metaphor without seeking to understand what that language was intended to signify to his audience. If Luke's repeated association of the Pharisees with accusations of injustice and avarice were only slander, as Sanders insists, this would still tell us something important about Luke's attitude to money. Even if Luke's stories about riches and possessions were always really about something else, it would still be necessary to explain why he chose to present his teaching in that way.

8.	Johnson, *Literary Function*, pp. 109-10. He thinks of the parable in its present form as a Lukan composition. See *Literary Function*, p. 159.

9.	Verhey, the only author of a work on New Testament ethics to recognize that Lk. 15.11-32 addresses the vices of 'profligacy and stinginess', and the virtues of 'magnanimity and forgiveness', does so by thinking of the use of the parable in the early church: 'the story assumes and elicits rebukes of the younger son's profligacy and the elder son's stinginess and praise for the father's magnanimity and forgiveness. The sermonic tradition which uses the parable to reinforce those judgments and to strengthen them into dispositions surely began already in the early church.' However, he too thinks that the parable was originally told to justify Jesus' preaching of the good news to sinners and to condemn those who could not accept

2. *A Wider Co-Text for Luke 15.11-32: The L Parables*

The interpretation of Lk. 15.11-32 as the climax of the unit of three parables on the theme 'lost and found' in Luke 15 leads to the neglect of a number of significant exegetical factors relating to its co-text. These are: (1) the relationship between Lk. 15.11-32 and part of its immediate co-text, Luke 16; (2) the different sources of the first two parables in Luke 15 (the lost sheep from Q and the lost coin from L);[10] (3) the relationship between Lk. 15.11-32 and the other parables found only in Luke; and (4) the function of Lk. 15.11-32 within the major unit distinctive to Luke, the so-called Travel Narrative (Lk. 9.51–19.27).

In the remainder of this chapter I argue that the most appropriate primary co-texts with which Lk. 15.11-32 should be interpreted are the other L parables.[11] This obviously does not exclude references to other parts of Luke–Acts. Johnson rightly emphasizes that when a pericope from Luke or Acts is being studied, its function within the whole plot of Luke–Acts must be taken into account.[12] However, part of the process

---

this. This, and his retention of the conventional view that the three parables of Lk. 15 share the theme of 'joy in heaven over one sinner who repents', prevents him from exploring a moral teaching of Lk. 15.11-32 further. See A. Verhey, *The Great Reversal: Ethics and the New Testament* (Grand Rapids: Eerdmans, 1984), pp. 46, 92-97.

10. On the question of whether Lk. 15.4-6 should be considered part of Q or not, see Fitzmyer, *Luke*, pp. 1073-74.

11. Following the conventions of English-language New Testament scholarship, L refers here to material which, out of the three Synoptic Gospels, is found only in Luke's Gospel. I agree with the current scholarly consensus that it is unlikely that all the L material originally existed as a separate written document, though parts of it, such as a parable collection, may have existed as a separate collection prior to their inclusion in the Gospel. See Fitzmyer, *Luke*, pp. 82-91.

12. L.T. Johnson, 'The Lukan Kingship Parable', *NovT* 24 (1982), pp. 139-59 (141-43). Johnson ('Lukan Community', p. 93) identifies the following major literary features of Luke–Acts: (1) It is a linear story. (2) The story is carried by the main characters, who are uniformly presented by literary stereotyping. (3) Because the storyline has a consistent pattern of acceptance and rejection, the location of each pericope in this pattern should be recognized. (4) Fulfillment of prophecy is a literary mechanism; thus whole series of passages flow from and illuminate thematic (prophetic) statements within the narrative. See further Johnson, *Literary Function*, pp. 9-126.

of relating Lk. 15.11-32 to the whole of Luke–Acts involves determining which parts of that whole it interacts with most closely; in other words, what other parts of Luke–Acts are most similar in form, language and theme.

A focus upon the L parables also helps to narrow the range of the syntagmatic co-text, for, with one small exception (Lk. 7.41-42),[13] all the L parables are found between Lk. 10.30 and 18.14, that is, well within the Travel Narrative.[14] More narrowly, the focus on the L parables has the effect of ensuring that the parable in Lk. 16.1-8a is included as an important *syntagmatic* co-text.

The L parables which form the paradigmatic co-text for Lk. 15.11-32 are:

Lk. 7.41-42	The Two Debtors
Lk. 10.30-36	The Good Samaritan
Lk. 11.5-8	The Reluctant Friend at Midnight
Lk. 12.16-20	The Foolish Rich Man
Lk. 13.6-9	The Barren Fig Tree
Lk. 14.28-32	The Tower and Embassy (two parables)
Lk. 15.8-10	The Lost Coin
Lk. 16.1-8a	The Dishonest Steward
Lk. 16.19-31	The Rich Man and Lazarus
Lk. 17.7-10	The Dutiful Servant
Lk. 18.2-5	The Unrighteous Judge
Lk. 18.10-14a	The Pharisee and the Tax Collector[15]

I now turn to a more detailed consideration of the reasons for this choice, and the effect this has on our understanding of Lk. 15.11-32.

---

13. The Parable of the Two Debtors in Lk. 7.41-42 is further distinguished by being embedded within the account of the forgiveness of the sinful woman in Lk. 7.36-50.

14. It is part of a section from Lk. 9.51–18.14 known as 'the great insertion'.

15. Parrott, who uses the L parables as the co-text for his study of the Dishonest Steward, adds two additional parables to those listed below: Lk. 14.8-10, Not Seeking Honour at Table; and 14.12-14, Inviting the Poor to Table. See D.M. Parrott, 'The Dishonest Steward (Luke 16.1-8a) and Luke's Special Parable Collection', *NTS* 37 (1991), pp. 499-515 (505-506). However, with Fitzmyer (*Luke*, pp. 1044-45), I do not think that these two sayings are parables. They should be classified as a pair of 'hortatory counsels', joined together by a wisdom saying from Q (14.11), which share a common structure.

a. *The Limitations of Luke 15 as the Co-Text*
As I have already indicated, most exegetes simply use the rest of Luke 15 as a co-text for Lk. 15.11-32. Although many also note the thematic affinities between it and other L parables, these observations seldom if ever lead them to widen the range of its co-text.

Marshall's comment is typical of many scholars who regard the unity of Luke 15 as axiomatic: 'There can be no doubt that ch. 15 forms one self-contained and artistically constructed unit with a single theme... the joy which is experienced by a person who recovers what he has lost'.[16] The view is usually taken that Lk. 15.11-32 develops the theme of the first two parables, illustrating God's attitude towards the penitent in terms of human behavior.[17] Giblin varies this slightly by reading Lk. 15.11-32 in the light of Lk. 15.4-10, especially vv. 8-10. He argues that Luke has edited the two parables in Lk. 15.4-10 to produce their parallel structures and that the second parable forms a thematic inclusio for the whole chapter. This shifts the emphasis onto: 'the invitation to *share in joy* over the conversion of sinners'.[18]

The view that Lk. 15.11-32 ought to be interpreted with the parables in Lk. 15.3-11 usually carries with it the assumption that Lk. 15.1-2 provides the 'communicative setting' for all three parables. This results almost inevitably in a degree of allegorizing wherein the triad of the

---

16. Marshall, *The Gospel of Luke*, p. 597. Compare du Plessis (*Kykie*, p. 135), who says that Lk. 15.11-32 is part of a trilogy of parables that illustrate the joy of finding what was lost, a joy shared by neighbours and friends; and Schmithals (*Lukas*, p. 165) who associates the third parable both with the first two parables and with the frame of Lk. 15.1-2. L. Ramaroson ('Le coeur du troisième evangile: Lc 15', *Bib* 60 [1979], pp. 348-60 [348]) and Fitzmyer (*Luke*, p. 1071) speak of Lk. 15 as the heart of Luke's Gospel. Tannehill is content merely to observe that the three parables are united by the image of something lost: a sheep, a coin, a son. Tannehill, *Narrative Unity*, p. 106.

17. J.M. Creed, *The Gospel According to St Luke: The Greek Text with Introduction, Notes and Indices* (London: MacMillan, 1930), p. 196. Lambrecht reverses the process and argues that Luke reinterprets the first two similitudes 'by placing them in the context of his fifteenth chapter and addressing them to the same persons who heard the Parable of the Prodigal Son' (J. Lambrecht, *Once More Astonished: The Parables of Jesus* [New York: Crossroad, 1981], p. 51).

18. C.H. Giblin, 'Structural and Theological Considerations on Luke 15'. *CBQ* 24 (1962), pp. 15-31 (19, 22).

father—younger son—older son is taken to represent the triad of Jesus —disciples—Pharisees and scribes, or God—Christians—unbelievers.[19] A Bible Society publication intended to introduce newer exegetical principles upholds this traditional viewpoint:

> Moreover, there is a dyadic relationship between the three sets in the triad: Jesus speaks to his disciples who hear him gladly and who have repented. The Pharisees, on the other hand, listen to Jesus but are hostile toward what he says and are unrepentant. Furthermore, the Pharisees are hostile toward the followers of Jesus whom they regard as condemned by God since they do not practice the commandments of the law.[20]

This particular schema fails to distinguish the tax collectors and sinners from the disciples. Other allegorical schemas omit the disciples, who are not mentioned in Lk. 15.1-2, but who are mentioned in Lk. 16.1 as if they had also been listening to the preceding parables.[21] This again points to the need to widen the co-text to include Lk. 16.1-8a, 19-31.

The view that Luke 15 is a unit is based on some limited exegetical evidence. Principally, this is the lost-found motif which concludes all three parables and is emphasized in Lk. 15.24c-d and 32d. However, there are important differences between the first two parables and the third,[22] and important similarities between the third and many of the

19. This is a trend that can be observed even among scholars who are wary of allegory. For example, speaking of the parables of Lk. 15, E.P. Sanders comments: 'I do not wish to allegorize these parables, but it is hard not to see the Lost Coin and the Lost Sheep as corresponding to the tax-collectors and sinners that Jesus associated with' (E.P. Sanders, *Jesus and Judaism* [London: SCM Press, 1985], p. 179).

20. E.A. Nida *et al.*, *Style and Discourse: With Special Reference to the Text of the New Testament* (Cape Town: Bible Society, 1983), p. 143.

21. This is suggested by the καί in Lk. 16.1. Marshall (*Gospel of Luke*, p. 617) says, 'No change of scene from the previous section is implied ...' Fitzmyer (*Luke*, p. 1099) comments that because of Lk. 16.14, the Scribes and the Pharisees must be 'presupposed to be listening to all this. On the other hand what is said to them is also said to the disciples.'

22. Nida, for example, comments: 'In the first two parables, it is the property which has been lost and found, but in the third parable, the property of the younger son is lost but the son is found, while the property of the older son is not lost, but the older son is "lost"' (Nida *et al.*, *Style*, p. 143). Blomberg glosses over the differences too easily when he says, 'Despite important differences in imagery, all three parables of Lk. 15 teach about God's initiative in saving the lost, the joy of discovery of that which was lost, and the need for those who are not lost not to begrudge

other L parables. The obvious examples of this are those in Lk. 12.16-20 and 16.1-8a.

b. *Indicators of a Wider Co-Text*

In his recent commentary, Evans retains the traditional view that Luke 15 contains three parables of 'lost and found',[23] but shows that he is well aware of the unresolved exegetical problems that result from placing the emphasis on the sin, repentance and forgiveness of the younger son: (1) What is the nature of the younger son's rebellion? (2) Why is his repentance expressed in the 'curiously neutral' phrase *he came to himself*? (3) Why is his confession less evidence of repentance than 'the basis for the statement *I am no longer worthy to be called your son*, which in turn is the basis for the request to be taken back as a hired labourer'? (4) Why is there no close connection between the penitence of the son and the love of the father? (5) How can the sympathetic words of the father in Lk. 15.31 be understood to refer to the hostile, loveless and self-righteous, or to the Pharisees as they are described by Luke?[24]

While Evans notes that Lk. 15.11-32 combines the themes of repentance and wealth (the themes of the two preceding parables in Luke 15 and the two following parables in Luke 16),[25] and while he is well aware of the theme of poverty and wealth in Luke's teaching, he does not examine the theme of possessions in Lk. 15.11-32.[26] As I noted with regard to Johnson above, once again a powerful exegetical consensus is

God's concerns for those who are.' See C.L. Blomberg, 'Interpreting the Parables of Jesus: Where Are We and Where Do We Go from Here?' *CBQ* 53 (1991), pp. 50-78 (63).

23. Evans, *Luke*, p. vi.

24. Evans, *Luke*, pp. 590-92.

25. 'In 15-16 five parables are assembled (with sayings between the fourth and fifth), the first three on repentance, the fourth on wealth and the fifth on both, as rejoinders to the Pharisees (and scribes), as those who both oppose Jesus' treatment of sinners, and are lovers of money (15.2; 16.14)' (Evans, *Luke*, p. 37).

26. In the same way, Nickelsburg summarizes the teaching of Luke's Gospel on riches and the rich, yet also fails to identify Lk. 15.11-32 as teaching on the use of possessions. See G.W.E. Nickelsburg, 'Riches, the Rich and God's Judgment in 1 Enoch 92-105 and the Gospel According to Luke', *NTS* 25 (1978), pp. 322-44 (333-40).

maintained, even at the expense of other important exegetical observations.[27]

Similarly, Beck argues that Luke arranges his material thematically. He thinks that Luke 14–16 form a unit, in which Luke 16 combines the themes of 14 and 15.[28] The Pharisees symbolize the evils being attacked, evils such as 'wealth, arrogance, the interpretation of the law against the advantage of those in need, hostility to sinners, contrasted with their welcome in the kingdom of God as expressed by Jesus, and the need to hear the call to repent'.[29] As I note at the end of Chapter 4, these themes all belong to the Greco-Roman topos On Covetousness.

A number of other scholars have also drawn attention to the relationship between Lk. 15.11-32 and Luke 14 and 16. Austin proposes pairing Lk. 15.11-32 with Lk. 16.3-8 and Porter notes the correlations between 15.11-32 and 16.1-13 and 16.19-31.[30] Despite stating his support for the traditional view of the unity of Luke 15, Fitzmyer comments that Lk. 15.11-32 introduces the dominant theme of Luke 16, namely 'the proper attitude toward and use of material possessions'.[31] As we noted above, Karris recognizes that all the sections of Lk. 14.12-33 and Luke 16 are related to the Lukan theme of the rich and the poor,

27. This process can often be observed simply by comparing what commentators say in their separate introductions to Lk. 15 and 16. At the start of Lk. 15, Danker, for example says, 'Luke joins three stories linked by a common theme: rejoicing over the lost.' However, he introduces Lk. 16.1 by saying that it 'continues the theme of a proper sense of values' (*Luke*, pp. 274, 279).

28. B.E. Beck, 'Luke's Structure', in *idem, Christian Character in the Gospel of Luke* (London: Epworth Press, 1989), pp. 145-69. Compare F.W. Farrar, *The Gospel According to St Luke* (CGTC; Cambridge: Cambridge University Press, 1893), p. xliii, who places Lk. 15.11-32 within a collection of parables extending from Lk. 14.15 to Lk. 16.31.

29. Beck, 'Luke's Structure', pp. 148-49 and 155-56.

30. M.R. Austin, 'The Hypocritical Son', *EvQ* 57 (1985), pp. 307-15; S.E. Porter, 'The Parable of the Unjust Steward (Luke 16.1-13): Irony *is* the Key', in D.J.A. Clines, S.E. Fowl and S.E. Porter (eds.), *The Bible in Three Dimensions: Essays in Celebration of Forty Years of Biblical Studies in the University of Sheffield* (JSOTSup, 87; Sheffield: Sheffield Academic Press, 1990), pp. 127-153. See also C.J.A. Hickling, 'A Tract on Jesus and the Pharisees? A Conjecture on the Redaction of Luke 15 and 16', *HeyJ* 16 (1975), pp. 253-65, cited in Fitzmyer, *Luke*, p. 1072.

31. 'In a way, this new theme was foreshadowed in chap. 15 in the example given by the younger son who squandered his possessions by dissolute living' (*Luke*, p. 1095).

but he does not examine the possibility that the three parables of Luke 15 may also deal with this theme in some way.[32] Ellis also groups Lk. 15.1-32 together, but then points out the more important links which exist between Lk. 15.11-32 and Lk. 16.1-13.[33]

c. *Common Features of the L Parables*

The L parables share many common features which invite comparison with one another.

(i) *A Common Context and Hortatory Purpose.* The L parables are not scattered throughout the Gospel. With the exception of Lk. 7.41-42, all are found within Lk. 9.51–18.14, a section that is primarily a collection of the sayings of Jesus. This suggests a closer relationship with one another than has usually been recognized. Because of the failure of scholars to detect a narrative structure to the material contained in the Travel Narrative,[34] it is all the more important to compare material within it which is clearly related in terms of source and genre.[35] Farrar mentions that Lk. 9.51–19.27 is sometimes called the *Gnomology*, or 'collection of moral teaching'.[36] In addition to whatever narrative relationship the elements of this collection have with one another, they may fruitfully be regarded as a gnomological collection of the sayings of

32. Karris, 'Poor and Rich', pp. 120-23.

33. 'The story of the prodigal calls forth another parable in which a worldly-wise man makes a prudent use of money entrusted to him ... The words of exhortation appear to gather around the catchwords, "mammon" and "*adikia*"' (E.E. Ellis, *The Gospel of Luke* [NCB; Grand Rapids: Eerdmans; London: Marshall, Morgan & Scott, rev edn, 1974], p. 198).

34. For literature, see the list of studies in Johnson, *Literary Function*, p. 104 n. 3, and the bibliography in Fitzmyer, *Luke*, pp. 830-32, which contains and extends the references given by Johnson. While the study of the travel narrative by D.P. Moessner, *The Lord of the Banquet: The Literary and Theological Significance of the Lukan Travel Narrative* (Minneapolis: Fortress Press, 1989, is newer and fuller, it does not list all the major studies of the travel narrative in a single place. But see his endnotes on pp. 33-44.

35. Blomberg ('Interpreting the Parables', p. 58) notes that Luke 'seems to employ a chiastic arrangement of parables as the pegs for arranging Jesus' teachings in topical fashion'. See also C.L. Blomberg, 'Midrash, Chiasmus and the Outline of Luke's Central Section', in R.T. France and D. Wenham (eds.), *Gospel Perspectives: Studies in Midrash and Historiography* (6 vols; Sheffield: JSOT Press, 1983), III, pp. 217-61.

36. *Luke*, p. xliii. Unfortunately he gives no further details.

Jesus with a moral function.[37] Moule observes the way Lk. 12.16-20
and Lk. 16.1-8 form apt illustrations for the teaching of wealth in 1
Tim. 6.17-19 and comments that this makes them particularly suitable
for catechesis. He also notes that most of the other examples of Gospel
material that could be used to illustrate the teaching of the epistles also
derive from Luke. However, he refrains from saying that any of Luke's
illustrative material was composed with a catechetical purpose.[38]

Goulder and Verhey both detect a strong hortatory purpose in many
of the L parables. Goulder refers to Lk. 10.30-35; 11.5-8; 12.16-20;
14.28-32; 16.1-8a; 16.19-31; 17.7-10; 18.2-5 and 18.10-14, and the
three parables of Luke 15.[39] Verhey thinks of the function of Lk. 10.30-
37; 12.16-20; 14.7-11; 16.19-31 and 18.10-14 as a subtle form of exhortation aimed at influencing the ethos of the church by a reversal of conventional values and judgments.[40]

The recognition of this hortatory purpose alone has an important
influence on how Lk. 15.11-32 and the L parables are interpreted. If one
reads Lk. 15.11-32 as moral exhortation, it is quite natural for the possessions theme to move to the foreground. This does not imply that the
appeal that these parables make is only a moral one, just that Luke
understood this moral appeal to be part of the Christian teaching he was
presenting. Thus, reading Lk. 15.11-32 together with the other L parables has the effect of helping to clarify the function of all these parables.

37. Fitzmyer (*Luke*, p. 825) notes that the travel narrative consists mostly of 'a
literary compilation of sayings of Jesus (of various sorts: proverbs, parables, legal
and wisdom sayings, criticism of his opponents, eschatological utterances), pronouncement stories, and a few miracle stories'. See also A.J. Hultgren, 'Interpreting
the Gospel of Luke', *Int* 30 (1976), pp. 353-65 (360); and G. Sellin, 'Komposition,
Quellen und Funktion des Lukanischen Reiseberichtes (Lk. ix 51-xix 28)', *NovT* 20
(1978), pp. 100-135 (105).

38. C.F.D. Moule, 'The Use of Parables and Sayings as Illustrative Material in
Early Christian Catechesis', in *idem*, *Essays in New Testament Interpretation*
(Cambridge: Cambridge University Press, 1982), pp. 50-53.

39. *Luke*, pp. 101-102. There seems no reason for excluding Lk. 7.41-42 and
13.6-9 from the list as well.

40. For example, breaking down the conventional association of wealth, wisdom, security and blessing in the parable of the rich fool. See Verhey, *Great
Reversal*, p. 47.

(ii) *A Common Source.* All these parables derive from a common source: L. It is not clear whether this means that they are a collection of parables that Luke gathered from oral tradition, whether they existed as a written collection prior to being adopted and edited by him,[41] or whether Luke is substantially responsible for the composition of all or some of them.[42]

This study leaves the question of an earlier version of the parable of the prodigal son open, but stresses Luke's creative influence upon the present text of Lk. 15.11-32. Whatever the origins of each of the L parables, in their canonical form they are all found only in Luke.

(iii) *Formal Resemblances.* The L parables share a number of formal and stylistic characteristics:

Generic Resemblances. As parables, they are all secondary stories within Luke's primary narrative. Four of them, Lk. 10.30-36; 12.16-20; 16.19-31; and 18.10-14a, have been classified form-critically as *exempla*.

Narrative Resemblances. Formally, many share similar narrative characteristics: (1) preference for a detailed story;[43] (2) memorable characterization;[44] (3) characters in contrasting situations;[45] (4) contrasting

41. Parrott believes that the collection may have existed as a separate unit prior to being edited during its inclusion in the Gospel ('Dishonest Steward', p. 507).

42. One cannot make a blanket statement that covers the origin of all the L parables. A version of Lk. 12.16-20, for example, is found in *Gos. Thom.* 63, though without the Lukan addition at v. 21. On the other hand, the strong resemblances between Lk. 15.4-6 and 15.8-10 suggest that Luke composed the latter to parallel the former.

43. See Lk. 10.30-36; 15.11-32; 16.1-8a; 16.19-31; and, perhaps, 12.16-20; and 18.10-14a.

44. When Kingsbury notes that Luke's parables are marked by memorable characterization, all the examples he cites are L parables. 'Some of the most memorable figures in Luke's gospel story exist, not as characters in his story world, but as characters in Jesus' parables. Cases in point are the good Samaritan (10.30-37), the rich fool (12.16-21), the prodigal son (15.11-32), the unjust steward (16.1-9), and the poor man Lazarus (16.19-31)' (*Conflict in Luke*, p. 32). The unjust judge in Lk. 18.2-5 and the Pharisee in 18.10-14 are also memorable characters.

45. Of all the L parables, the only ones that do *not* exhibit this are Lk. 12.16-20; 13.6-9; 14.28-32; and 15.8-9.

character types;[46] (5) soliloquies;[47] and (6) direct speech or conversation.[48] The following have at least three of the above features in common: Lk. 10.30-35; 12.16-20; 15.11-32; 16.1-8a; 16.19-31; 17.7-10; 18.2-5 and 18.10-14.

Framing Elements. Three of the L parables end with questions from Jesus that bring out the moral of the story: Lk. 7.42; 10.36; and 18.7. Luke 17.7-9 consists entirely of such questions. Beavis notes that Lk. 12.20; 13.8-9; 15.31-32; 16.30; 18.4-5 all end with a comment by the central character on the action of the parable.[49] In Lk. 7.43 and 10.37 the moral of the parable is stated by the person to whom it is addressed.

Beavis's study of the relationship between Luke's parables and the Greco-Roman fable tradition draws attention to Luke's use of *promythia* and *epimythia* (morals attached to the beginning and end of his parables). Of all the synoptic parables, only four from L exhibit this feature.[50]

(iv) *A Shared Vocabulary*. The L parables also have a considerable number of words in common. I am not concerned here with a general analysis of the lexis of the L parables,[51] but the value of interpreting Lk. 15.11-32 in dialogue with them. Therefore, I simply note here that

---

46. Parrott ('Dishonest Steward', p. 510) cites as examples Lk. 7.41-42; 10.30-36; 15.11-32; 16.19-31; and 18.10-14a. Lk. 11.5-8; 13.6-9; 16.1-8a; and 18.2-5 could be added.

47. See Lk. 12.17-19; 14.28, 31 (implied); 15.17-19; 16.3; 18.4, 11.

48. See Lk. 10.35; 11.5-7; 13.7-8; 15.9; 15.12, 21, 22-24, 26-27, 28-32; 16.2, 5-7; 16.24-31; 17.7, 8, 10; 18.3.

49. Beavis, 'Parable and Fable', pp. 482-83.

50. Lk. 12.15-21; 16.1-9; 18.1-8; and 18.9-14. Beavis singles out Lk. 12.16-20 and 13.8-9 for detailed comparison with a fable. She also notes that Lk. 12.16-20 and 16.19-31 are the only parables to deal with relations between the gods and humans, another feature of some fables. See Beavis, 'Parable and Fable', pp. 481, 484-93 and 498. Other L parables she singles out for special comparison with Greco-Roman fables are Lk. 13.8-9; 15.11-32; 18.2-5; and 18.10-14.

51. For a list of the words 'characteristic of Luke' (that is, which are found at least four times in Luke, and are not found at all in Matthew or Mark, or are found in Luke at least twice as often as in Matthew and Mark together) see the list from Hawkins reproduced in Fitzmyer, *Luke*, pp. 110-11.

many of the words found in Lk. 15.11-32 are also used in the other L parables:[52]

a field, ἀγρός (Lk. 17.7); a brother, ἀδελφός (Lk. 16.28); a person, ἄνθρωπος (Lk. 10.30; 12.16; 14.30; 16.1, 19; 18.2, 4, 10, 11); to raise up, ἀνίστημι (Lk. 11.7, 8); to answer, ἀποκρίνω (Lk. 11.7; 13.8); to be lost, ἀπόλλυμι (Lk. 15.8, 9); bread, ἄρτος (Lk. 11.5);

a ring, δακτύλιος (Lk. 16.24); to spend, squander, δαπανάω (Lk. 10.35; 14.28); to scatter, squander, διασκορπίζω (Lk. 16.1); to give, δίδωμι (Lk. 10.35; 11.7, 8); a slave, δοῦλος (Lk. 17.7, 9); two, δύο (Lk. 7.41; 18.10);

to say, εἶπον (Lk. 10.29, 30, 35; 11.5, 7; 12.16, 18, 20; 13.7; 16.2, 3, 6, 7, 24, 25, 27, 30, 31; 18.4, 9); to desire, ἐπιθυμέω (Lk. 16.21); to come, go, ἔρχομαι (Lk. 10.34; 13.6; 16.28; 17.7; 18.2); to eat, ἐσθίω, φαγεῖν (Lk. 12.19; 17.8); a year, ἔτος (Lk. 12.19; 13.8); to find, εὑρίσκω (Lk. 13.6, 7; 15.8, 9); to rejoice, εὐφραίνω (Lk. 12.19; 16.19);

to will, wish, θέλω (Lk. 14.28; 18.4);

lo, see, ἰδού (Lk. 13.7); strong, mighty, ἰσχυρός (Lk. 16.3); dead, νεκρός (Lk. 16.30, 31);

a house, οἶκος (Lk. 15.8; 16.4, 27; 18.14); heaven, οὐρανός (Lk. 18.13);

to call, summon, exhort, παρακαλέω (Lk. 16.25); a father, πατήρ (Lk. 16.24, 27, 30); a citizen, πολίτης (Lk. 18.2); to go, proceed, πορεύω (Lk. 11.5; 14.31; 16.30); to call oneself, προσκαλέω (Lk. 16.5);

to feel pity, compassion, σπλαγχνίζομαι (Lk. 10.33); to gather together, συνάγω (Lk. 12.17);

quickly, ταχύ (Lk. 16.6); a child, τέκνον (Lk. 16.25); one, a certain one, τις (Lk. 7.41; 10.30; 12;16; 13.6; 16.19; 18.2); a friend, φίλος (Lk. 11.5);

to fill (with food), χορτάζω ([Lk. 16.21]); a land, country, region, χώρα (Lk. 12.16);

52. In the lists below, phrases are given as they are found in the parables, while individual words are given in their lexical form.

Of these, ἀδελφός, ἀπόλλυμι, δακτύλιος, δαπανάω, διασκορπίζω, δίδωμι, ἐπιθυμέω, εἰς ἑαυτὸν ἔρχεσθαι, εὐφραίνω, νεκρός, σπλαγχνίζομαι, συνάγω, τέκνον and φίλος are discusssed in Chapters 5–8 as indicators of the influence of the topos On Covetousness.[53]

(v) *A Common Cluster of Themes.* The L parables mentioned above also share a common cluster of themes. Parrott describes the overall theme as 'the humbling of the proud and the raising of the humble', with the subthemes of: repentance of broken relationships; relinquishing the illusion that the source of one's ultimate security and sense of personal meaning can be possessions, status, family relationships, law-following and so on; compassionate concern for one's neighbour; joy; patience with sinners and unconditional forgiveness.[54]

As we see in Chapter 4, many of these themes are characteristic of the topos On Covetousness. A superficial glance at the L parables suggests that many of them do interact with this topos in some way:

Lk. 7.41-42:	Describes forgiveness in terms of the remission of a monetary debt.
Lk. 10.30-36:	A person injured by a robbery is brought back to health through the compassion and generous giving of someone who is under no obligation to help him.[55]
Lk. 11.5-8:	A man is reluctant to share his possessions with his friend in need but is eventually persuaded to do so.
Lk. 12.16-20:	In the context of a discussion of a dispute over the division of an inheritance and a warning against covetousness, the story is told of a man who foolishly places his trust in his wealth.[56]
Lk. 13.6-9:	A story about a fruitless fig tree in a vineyard. The owner is angry at it for using resources without bearing fruit.

53. This means that the following words, which indicate the influence of the topos On Covetousness in Lk. 15.11-32, are *not* found in the other L parables: ἄξιος, ἁμαρτάνω, ἀσώτως, βίος, βόσκω, διαίρεω, δουλεύω, ἐντολή, τὸ ἐπιβάλλον, ζάω and ἀναζάω, οὐσία, λιμός, μίσθιος, ὀργίζομαι, παρέρχομαι, περισσεύομαι, πορνή, στολή, συμφωνία, ὑπόδημα, ὑγιαίνω, ὑστερέω, χοῖρος, χορός.

54. Parrott, 'Dishonest Steward', pp. 508-509.

55. Danker (*Jesus and the New Age*, p. 223) likens the Good Samaritan to the magnificent man in Aristotle, *Eth. Nic* . 4.2.5 and 4.2.8. However, as there is no indication that the Samaritan was rich or that he spent very large sums on the injured man, he is better described as liberal, following *Eth. Nic.* 4.1.

56. Danker (*Jesus and the New Age*, p. 248) describes his attitude as a form of illiberality.

Lk. 14.28-32: The cost of discipleship is illustrated in terms of economic resources (building materials or soldiers). The attached moral in v. 33 is an important supplementary indicator of the influence of the topos here.

Lk. 15.8-10: A story is told about money lost, earnestly sought, found and rejoiced over.

Lk. 15.11-32: Two brothers, one a prodigal and the other a miser, make improper use of their inherited wealth. They are guided by the words and example of their generous father.

Lk. 16.1-8a: A manager is accused of improper management and is dismissed. Before he leaves he makes friends with those who owe his master money, by reducing their debts.

Lk. 16.19-31: A rich man does not care for a poor man outside his gate. After death he is punished and the poor man is comforted.

Lk. 17.7-10: Servants are seen only in terms of their usefulness. They are characterized as useless, ἀχρεῖος.

Lk. 18.2-5: A widow, who is symbolic of people who are economically weak and need to be protected from being exploited, struggles to get justice from an unrighteous judge (ὁ κριτὴς τῆς ἀδικίας).[57]

Lk. 18.10-14a: A Pharisee congratulates himself that he is not like other people who are guilty of the vices associated with covetousness, extortioners, unjust, adulterers, or even like this tax collector, ἅρπαγες, ἄδικοι, μοιχοί, ἢ καὶ ὡς οὗτος ὁ τελώνης. He claims to be self-controlled in his eating and giving (by fasting and tithing his income). Yet he is condemned for the greater sin of self-exaltation.

A further indicator of the influence of the topos On Covetousness is the additional range of terms related to the topos found in the L parables:

Lk. 7.41-42: a debtor, χρεοφειλέτης; a money-lender, δανειστής; to owe, ὀφείλω; denarius, δηνάριον; to give back, ἀποδίδωμι; to forgive freely, χαρίζομαι;

Lk. 10.30-36: a robber, λῃστής; to strip off, ἐκδύω; his own animal, τὸ ἴδιον κτῆνος; to take care of, ἐπιμελέομαι; to give back, ἀποδίδωμι;

Lk. 11.15-18: to lend, χράω; to need, χρῄζω.

Lk. 12.16-20: rich, πλούσιος; to be fruitful, εὐφορέω; fruit, καρπός; a storehouse, ἀποθήκη; to build a house, οἰκοδομέω; all my grain and my goods, πάντα τὸν σῖτον καὶ τὰ ἀγαθά μου; to drink, πίνω; foolish, ἄφρων; to ask back, ἀπαιτέω; to store up, θησαυρίζω;

57. Compare the accusation that scribes devour the houses of widows in Lk. 20.47.

Lk. 13.6-9:   (in) his vineyard, τῷ ἀμπελῶνι αὐτοῦ; to seek, ζητέω; fruit, καρ-
                 πός; to make idle, καταργέω;

Lk. 14.28-33:   to build a house, οἰκοδομέω; to count, ψηφίζω; cost, δαπάνη; to
                 forsake, ἀποτάσσομαι; belongings, τὰ ὑπάρχοντα;

Lk. 15.8-9:   a drachma, δραχμή; carefully, ἐπιμελῶς; a neighbour, γείτων;

Lk. 16.1-8:   rich, πλούσιος; a household manager, οἰκονόμος; belongings, τὰ
                 ὑπάρχοντα; to render, ἀποδίδωμι; account, λόγος; stewardship,
                 οἰκονομία; to manage, οἰκονομέω; to beg, ἐπαιτέω; to be
                 ashamed, αἰσχύνομαι; a debtor, χρεοφειλέτης; to owe, ὀφείλω; a
                 bill, γράμμα; a household manager, οἰκονόμος; injustice, ἀδικία;

Lk. 16.19-31   rich, πλούσιος; a beggar, πτωχός; a table, τράπεζα; to receive as
                 one's due, ἀπολαμβάνω; that which is good, τὰ ἀγαθά; that which
                 is bad, τὰ κακά;

Lk. 17.7-10:   to plough, ἀροτριάω; to tend sheep, ποιμαίνω; to serve, διακ-
                 ονέω; to drink, πίνω; useless, ἀχρεῖος; to owe, ὀφείλω;

Lk. 18.2-5:   a judge, κριτής; a widow, χήρα; to grant justice, ἐκδικέω; an
                 opponent in a lawsuit, ἀντίδικος;

Lk. 18.10-14:   a tax-collector, τελώνης; rapacious, ἅρπαξ; unjust, ἄδικος; an
                 adulterer, μοιχός; to tithe, ἀποδεκατεύω; to gain, κτάομαι; a
                 sinner, ἁμαρτωλός; to justify, δικαιόω.

The listing of the words according to their occurrence in each parable here serves to show that there is more interaction with the topos in some parables (such as Lk. 12.16-20 and Lk. 16.1-8a) than others (such as Lk. 11.5-8 or 18.2-5), and that different parables deal with different themes within the topos. The relationship between a topos and a theme is dealt with in Chapter 4 below, and is illustrated in Chapters 5 to 8 with regard to Lk. 15.11-32.

3. *Results of Adopting the L Parables as the Co-Text*

The result of widening the co-text in this way is that all the language referring to possessions in the parable is permitted to be heard, and the moral function of the parable emerges more clearly.

(1) By being released from the artificial exegetical constraint of being interpreted in terms of Luke 15 alone, problems caused by this interpretive frame, such as those raised by Evans mentioned on p. 77 above, are resolved or no longer posed.[58]

___

58. Evans, *Luke*, pp. 590-92. Of the five listed there, the first four are addressed in Chapters 5–8 below, and the fifth is a problem that falls away with the change of interpretive frame.

(2) Instead of being read as a parable addressed by Jesus to his hearers, with one son being related to two groups of sinners and the other to two groups of religious leaders, it is read as one of a group of parables gathered and placed within the Travel Narrative by Luke, as part of his attempt to communicate an important implication of the Gospel to his intended readers.

(3) As part of a section of Luke's Gospel consisting largely of the sayings of Jesus, the parable is seen to have a gnomic function.

(4) Like the other L parables found in this section of Luke, it is also seen to have a hortatory purpose.

(5) When Lk. 15.11-32 is compared with the other L parables, the moral appeal of the parable comes to the fore. At the same time, it is seen to share language and themes with them which are part of the Greco-Roman moral topos On Covetousness. Thus, all the L parables are seen to contribute to the important Lukan theme of the right use of possessions.[59]

(6) It is further instructive to note the *contrasts* between the treatment of economic themes in the different L parables.[60]

---

59. Houlden sums up the importance of this theme for Luke by saying that for him 'generosity is the heart of virtue and close-fistedness and attachment to possessions are the greatest of sins'. See J.L. Houlden, *Ethics and the New Testament* (Harmondsworth: Penguin Books, 1973; repr. London: Mowbrays, 1975), p. 90.

60. Moxnes identifies a number of details that cry out to be compared with the teaching on possessions in Lk. 15.11-32. For example, his observation that the rich fool of Lk. 12.16-20 and the father in Lk. 15.11-32 are both large landowners living on and taking part in the work on their own land, reveals the great contrast in their use of their resources, and highlights the wise behavior of the father. He notes the ethical contrast between eating and making merry in Lk. 15.23, and in Lk. 12.19 and 16.19. In the latter two parables eating and making merry is criticized because it represents the way the wealth of the rich is used, 'not for the common good, but to protect their own position as a group over and against the needy people of the village'. This enables us to see the significance of the father's actions, which show him using his wealth for the benefit of the common people and including them in his celebration. There is a similar contrast between the positive significance of the best robe in Lk. 15.22 and the negative connotations of the rich man's fine clothes in Lk. 16.19. See H. Moxnes, *The Economy of the Kingdom: Social Conflict and Economic Relations in Luke's Gospel* (OBT; Philadelphia: Fortress Press, 1988), pp. 57-58, 89-90 and 92.

(7) In the long run these considerations may contribute to our under-standing of the theme and cohesion of the Travel Narrative. That issue is beyond the scope of this study. However, as I illustrate below, the unity of Lk. 15.11-32 is confirmed by allowing the language of posses-sions to be heard afresh.

Part II

THE TOPOS

Chapter 4

THE TOPOS 'ON COVETOUSNESS' IN MORAL PHILOSOPHY

The preceding literary study of Lk. 15.11-32 and its co-texts established the importance of the language of possessions for the teaching of the parable on compassionate liberality.[1] Here I seek to account for this by examining teaching on the right use of possessions found in other Greco-Roman moral texts.[2]

These texts reveal five things of importance for my enquiry: (1) the theme of the right use of possessions is an area of widespread concern; (2) these texts, which otherwise differ in terms of author, period, genre, philosophical affiliation and rhetorical purpose, refer to a core of common attitudes; (3) they make creative use of recurrent themes, motifs, terminology and illustrations; (4) Lk. 15.11-32 makes use of the same collection of recurrent material; and (5) by reading Lk. 15.11-32 in terms of the common material, we gain new insight into the composition and function of this familiar text.

The resemblances between such a wide range of texts cannot be explained on the basis of direct literary borrowing, and are the result of sharing a common moral frame of reference and a common cultural matrix. Through the historical processes shaping the growth and dissemination of Greco-Roman culture, particular social issues gained

1. Johnson's study of the literary function of possessions in Luke–Acts recognizes the importance of the language of possessions, but cannot account for the origins of this usage. He says that we can 'only surmise' about the shape of this metaphor in Luke' imagination and at its roots in his education, culture and experience (*Literary Function*, pp. 221-22).

2. While the survey below ranges from Plato in the late fourth/early third century BCE to the *Sentences of Sextus* in the second century CE, the focus is on 'the philosophical moralists of the first and second centuries of the Empire'. See A.J. Malherbe, ' "In Season and out of Season": 2 Timothy 4.2', in *idem, Paul and the Popular Philosophers* (Minneapolis: Fortress Press, 1989), pp. 137-45 (139).

special prominence. As these were widely discussed in differing contexts over a number of centuries, later discussions of the same issues made use of what had been said before. This phenomenon is characteristic of all societies that value tradition and precedent, and accounts for recurrent patterns of thought and expression, even in authors with no direct knowledge of the earlier texts.

One aspect of this shared cultural matrix that has attracted the attention of New Testament scholars in recent years is the topos: traditional treatments of moral subjects in which authors use recurrent themes, motifs, terminology and illustrations as a rhetorical frame of reference for making their own views known.

When such recurrent themes and language cluster around a particular area of moral concern, we speak of a topos on that area. A topos is not a moral theme, but a field within an overall moral framework, which includes a cluster of related themes. Topoi are neither discrete nor entirely static, but interlock and interact within one another. Similarly, themes that recur under one topos may also be found regularly in texts that interact with the framework of a different topos, or such themes may function as their own topos. This description sounds untidy, but simply acknowledges the richly varied ways in which language and thought function within any culture.

The above points can be illustrated with reference to the topos studied here: περὶ ἀδικίας καὶ φιλαργυρίας καὶ πλεονεξίας, 'on injustice and covetousness and greed'. This topos is not simply represented by texts that deal with the themes of injustice, avarice and covetousness in combination, but represents texts with a wider area of moral concern. In Lk. 15.11-32 the themes of prodigality, liberality and meanness are prominent, but many other themes, such as life and death, celebration, care of the self, good health, brotherly love and friendship, recur in texts relating to this topos. Some of these themes are topoi in their own right and have, in turn, their own special collection of interrelated themes and language. However, each topos has its own distinctive area of focus.

Topoi are of value to the New Testament exegete because they reveal the particular moral interests that were widely shared by Greco-Roman readers and writers. They thus represent the common knowledge and shared understanding that writers and readers, and speakers and hearers, took into account when they communicated with one another. Neither side would always have been conscious of this common knowledge and the conventional structures of language and thought used to express it. However, it has been established that careful writers or speakers did make conscious rhetorical use of it.[3]

In this chapter, I first review recent uses of topoi in New Testament research and provide a definition of the term for this discussion. Next, I identify and describe the contents and features of a range of texts which reflect awareness of the topos περὶ ἀδικίας καὶ φιλαργυρίας καὶ πλεονεξίας. Only Greco-Roman or Hellenistic Jewish texts that have a clearly defined philosophical character are discussed here. The chapter ends with a summary of the characteristic features of the topos, and some remarks about its use by authors of different philosophical affiliations.

1. *Topoi: Definitions and Uses*

Although the term 'topos' is now an accepted part of critical terminology, there is still sufficient variation in usage to make a working definition necessary here. In order to arrive at a fuller understanding of the term, we need to review how it has been defined and used by New Testament scholars since the mid-twentieth century.

The current debate on the form and function of the topos in New Testament begins with Bradley.[4] He thinks of it as a form used in parenesis, and defines it as 'the treatment in independent form of the topic of a proper thought or action, or of a virtue or vice, etc'.[5] The form is sometimes introduced with a title in the form περί, followed by the genitive (*de* + the ablative in Latin). Units introduced in this way are often unrelated to and easily separable from their contexts. He gives examples from authors as diverse as Isocrates, Marcus Aurelius, Paul, and those of Sirach and the Testaments of the Twelve Patriarchs.[6]

---

3. See, for example, Karris's argument that the Pastoral epistles make use of language used in the philosophical polemic against the sophists to dissociate their teaching from that of the sophists (R.J. Karris, 'The Background and Significance of the Polemic in the Pastoral Epistles', *JBL* 92 [1973], pp. 549-64 [551-56]).

4. D.G. Bradley, 'The *Topos* as a Form in the Pauline Paraenesis', *JBL* 72 (1953), pp. 238-46.

5. Bradley, 'The *Topos* as a Form', p. 240.

6. Bradley, 'The *Topos* as a Form', pp. 241-46. The phenomenon of overlapping topoi is illustrated by the way he describes *T. Jud.* 16.1-4 as a topos on the right use of wine. While the chapter clearly deals with the right and wrong use of

On the basis of these examples, he describes the form of the topos as a loose collection of self-contained teachings that are weakly, or even arbitrarily, linked to their context.[7] It consists of a collection of proverbs or other short teachings on the same topic, which are united by a common subject and a recurrent word. Topoi cover a wide variety of topics, and always give practical but general advice on matters such as the proper attitude towards friends, sex, money, wine, parents, food and so on.[8] They are used by itinerant moral teachers to compose stock answers to frequently asked questions.[9]

Modern research into topoi is distinguished from the philological and lexical studies of the nineteenth and early twentieth centuries[10] by the recognition that similar trains of thought can be discerned in Greek literature. Van Unnik has drawn attention to the existence of similar trains of thought whenever a particular term is used in Greek literature. For example, when all the occurrences of the term μία γνώμη ('one mind') (found in Rev. 17.13, 17) are read in their contexts, they are found to share the common factors of the existence of the institution of the state and an ideal situation. While verbal correspondences can be observed (for example, one of the ways to get ὁμόνοια, 'concord', is expressed by the words μία γνώμη),[11] there are also equally important correspondences in thought.[12] Van Unnik therefore speaks of phrases and thought

---

wine, the first verse contains a cluster of terms that are part of the topos On Covetousness: ἐπιθυμία, πύρωσις, ἀσωτία and αἰσχροκερδία.

7. Bradley, 'The *Topos* as a Form', p. 243.

8. Bradley, 'The *Topos* as a Form', pp. 243-44.

9. Bradley, 'The *Topos* as a Form', p. 246.

10. From Trench's *Synonyms*, to the *TDNT* and P.C. Spicq, *Notes de lexicographie néo-testamentaire* (2 vols. with supplement; OBO 22.1-3; Fribourg: Editions universitaires, 1978–82).

11. In another example, he observes that by looking at passages from between the Wisdom of Solomon and the Pseudo-Clementines, Jewish, pagan and Christian, the word ἄξιος has a complex of ideas that is found in a wide variety of circles: special revelations are only to be handed over to 'worthy' people who have passed some very long test. He notes, 'Mind you: none of these "parallel-texts" had extensive parallelism in wording; they had little more in common than the word "worthy", but they all together fit into the same pattern' (van Unnik, 'Words Come to Life', pp. 200, 213).

12. Van Unnik, 'Words Come to Life', p. 203.

forms being 'in the air', and part of the subconscious adornment of a text by a writer.[13]

Mullins adds to Bradley's definition of the form of the topos.[14] Basing his discussion on examples from the Cynic epistles, he says that a topos consists of three formal elements: 'an *injunction* urging that a certain course of behavior be followed or avoided; a *reason* for the injunction; and a *discussion* of the logical or practical consequences of the behavior'. To these may sometimes be added an example of an analogous situation,[15] and/or a refutation of the contrary way of thinking or acting. While he considers topoi to have a stereotyped form, he believes that they were used creatively to express the individual viewpoint of the speaker.[16] The conventional form simply assured 'the speaker or writer that he had given the kind of answer to the question which his audience would be most likely to accept as valid'.[17] Mullins's definition of the form has been criticized for being too constricting, and other New Testament scholars have preferred to allow for a wider range of common patterns.

Balch compares the household code found in 1 Pet. 2.13–3.7 with classical Greek discussions of the hierarchical ordering of the city and the household, discussed under the topoi On the Constitution and On Household Management.[18] Such discussions are found in Plato and Aristotle, as well as in the Middle Platonists, Peripatetics, Stoics, Epicureans, Hellenistic Jews and Neopythagoreans.[19] Here the topoi provide a common frame of reference for the authors to present their particular views and concerns.[20] Having argued that New Testament

13. W.C. van Unnik, 'First Century A.D. Literary Culture and Early Christian Literature', *NTT* 25 (1971), pp. 28-43 (37).

14. T.Y. Mullins, 'Topos as a New Testament Form', *JBL* 99 (1980), pp. 541-47.

15. Mullins, 'Topos', p. 542.

16. Mullins, 'Topos', p. 545.

17. Mullins, 'Topos', p. 547.

18. D.L. Balch, *Let Wives Be Submissive: The Domestic Code in 1 Peter* (SBLMS, 26; Chico: Scholars Press, 1981).

19. Balch, *Wives*, pp. 61-62.

20. Malherbe, 'Greco-Roman Religion', 17, cites Balch's 'Household Ethical Codes in Peripatetic, Neopythagorean and Early Christian Moralists', in P.J. Achtemeier (ed.), *Society of Biblical Literature Seminar Papers 1977* (Missoula: Scholars Press, 1977), pp. 397-404; and 'Hellenistic Moralists and the New Testament', *ANRW*, II.26.1 (1992), pp. 267-333. See also D.L. Balch, 'Household Codes', in

household codes are shaped by such topoi, Balch goes on to show that the author of 1 Peter uses these topoi as a common frame of reference for his Christian apologetic purposes.

Apart from observing that the topos On Household Management (περὶ οἰκονομίας) is nearly identical to the form-critical category found in the New Testament, Balch's work underlines an important observation made earlier by Wilhelm, that topoi are not self-contained but often closely related to one another.[21] This has important implications for this study. Although I have selected the topos On Covetousness as the one that most adequately accounts for the themes and language of Lk. 15.11-32, some of the central themes such as the ownership and use of possessions, or family relationships, are also dealt with under other topoi such as friendship, physical health, anger, brotherly love or love for children.[22] This is inevitable when relating a narrative to a topos, and makes it important to identify which topos deals most *comprehensively* with the contents of the text.

Betz makes extensive use of the idea of the topos in his commentary on Galatians and in his studies on the relationship between the ethical writings of Plutarch and early Christian literature. For example, he explains that Gal. 4.12-20 is organized around 'a string of topoi belonging to the theme of "friendship" (περὶ φιλίας)', and he relates Plutarch's treatise *De fraterno amore* to the literary topos of father and sons.[23]

D.E. Aune (ed.), *Greco-Roman Literature and the New Testament: Selected Forms and Genres* (SBLSBS, 21; Atlanta: Scholars Press, 1988), pp. 25-50; 'The Greek Political Topos περὶ νόμων and Matthew 5.17, 19 and 16.19', in D.L. Balch (ed.), *Social History of the Matthean Community: Cross-Disciplinary Approaches* (Minneapolis: Fortress Press, 1991), pp. 68-84 and 'Neopythagorean Moralists and the New Testament Household Codes', *ANRW*, II.26.1 (1992), pp. 380-411.

21. The observation that the topoi περὶ πολιτείας, περὶ οἰκονομίας and περὶ γάμου are so combined and interrelated that it is difficult to distinguish them clearly is found in F. Wilhelm, 'Die Oeconomica der Neupythagoreer Bryson, Kallikratidas, Periktione, Phintys', *RhM* 70 (1915), pp. 161-223 (163-64, 222). Balch, *Wives*, pp. 14, 19 n. 137. There are also obvious links between opposing topoi, such as the examples of envy and friendship noted by L.T. Johnson in 'James 3.13–4.10 and the *Topos* περὶ φθόνου', *NovT* 25 (1983), pp. 327-47 (336).

22. Many of the topoi discussed in books 3 and 4 of Stobaeus have some link with the parable, from περὶ ἀρετῆς to σύγκρισις ζωῆς καὶ θανάτου.

23. See H.D. Betz, *Galatians: A Commentary on Paul's Letter to the Churches in Galatia* (Hermeneia; Philadelphia: Fortress Press, 1979), pp. 220-33; and '*De Fraterno Amore*', pp. 231-63.

However, his tendency to use the term 'topos' to mean 'cliché' is less useful than using the term in the more comprehensive sense of a traditional treatment of a moral subject, in which clichés are one of the recurring elements.[24]

Following his work on possessions in Luke–Acts, Johnson has also demonstrated the usefulness of topoi for New Testament research. For example, he uses the features of the topos On Envy, περὶ φθόνου, in Plutarch's *De invidia et odio* and the *Testament of Simeon* to show that the theme of envy runs consistently through Jas 3.13–4.10.[25] This use of the 'consistent clusters and patterns' of a topos by Betz and Johnson to demonstrate the unity of 'disorderly' passages, is also of value in demonstrating the unity of the two parts of Lk. 15.11-32, as we see below.

Brunt criticizes New Testament scholars for failing to distinguish Bradley's definition of the topos from that found in classical rhetoric.[26] He argues that it is important to remember that in classical rhetoric topoi were simply 'common topics' or arguments, which could be adapted by prosecutors and defense attorneys to meet the needs of particular courtroom situations.[27] 'Although there are differences among these classical sources [that is between Aristotle, *Rhetoric to Alexander*, Cicero and *Ad Herennium*], what they have in common is that *topoi* are

24. Like Betz, the classical scholar O'Neil also uses the term 'topos' to mean a cliché. See E.N. O'Neil, '*De Cupiditate Divitiarum (Moralia 523C-528B)*', in H.D. Betz (ed.), *Plutarch's Ethical Writings and Early Christian Literature* (SCHNT, 4; Leiden: E.J. Brill, 1978), pp. 289-362 (298 n. 42). This judgment must be revised in the light of Betz's fuller use of topoi in his monumental study of the Sermon on the Mount. See, for example, his discussion of Mt. 6.25-34 in relation to the topos On Anxiety in Betz, *The Sermon on the Mount*, pp. 459-86.

25. Johnson, 'James 3.13–4.10', pp. 346-47.

26. J.C. Brunt, 'More on the *Topos* as a New Testament Form', *JBL* 104 (1985), pp. 495-500.

27. Brunt, 'More on the *Topos*', pp. 496-98. Pogoloff says that Aristotle developed the idea of topics to enable rhetoricians to reason from the generally accepted opinions of the community. The rhetorician would appeal to a topic felt by the audience to be relevant to the case, and then form these into enthumemes, which reasoned loosely from the topics 'by assuming rather than stating any premises which would sound self-evident'. This ensured that the speaker and listeners shared the same world-view. See S.M. Pogoloff, 'Isocrates and Contemporary Hermeneutics', in D.F. Watson (ed.), *Persuasive Artistry: Studies in New Testament Rhetoric in Honor of George A. Kennedy* (JSNTSup, 50; Sheffield: JSOT Press, 1991), pp. 338-62 (352-55).

stereotyped arguments that are applied to specific cases'.[28] He does not deny the existence of the common forms which Bradley and others call *topoi*, but only calls attention to this confusion of terminology, particularly since modern texts on classical rhetoric use the term in the older sense.[29] While it is helpful to be aware of the more restricted area of usage of the term in classical rhetoric, Brunt's definition of this usage—that topoi are 'stereotyped arguments that are applied to specific cases'—relates well to the observations of other scholars.

Most New Testament scholars using topoi do not take definitions based on classical rhetoric as their point of departure, but work inductively, first reading the texts and then seeking to account for observed relationships between them.[30] There is widespread consensus that, when Greco-Roman, Hellenistic Jewish and early Christian texts discuss similar moral issues, they have much in common. These common features are found at various levels: subject matter, language, patterns of thought, formal features of the text and so on. There is also consensus that these

28. Brunt, 'More on the *Topos*', pp. 498.

29. He cites Wuellner as an example of a scholar who uses the term in Bradley's sense, but also refers to ancient and modern sources that discuss the term as Aristotle and Cicero do. See W. Wuellner, 'Paul's Rhetoric of Argumentation in Romans: An Alternative to the Donfried–Karris Debate over Romans', *CBQ* 38 (1976), pp. 330-51 (348). Both definitions are given in the *OCD*, 3rd edn, s.v. 'topos'.

30. New Testament scholars also study the contents of particular topoi via the Greek anthology tradition. The most widely used representative of this tradition is the *Anthology* of Stobaeus. The best critical text available is that edited by C. Wachsmuth (vols. 1-2) and O. Hense (vols. 3-5), *Ioannis Stobaeus Anthologium* (Berlin: Weidmann, repr., 1958). For a brief introduction to the use of Stobaeus for information about topoi see V.L. Wimbush, 'Stobaeus: Anthology (Excerpts)', in *Ascetic Behavior in Greco-Roman Antiquity* (Minneapolis: Augsburg–Fortress, 1990), pp. 169-74. Balch, *Wives*, p. 30 n. 34 refers to a list of topoi in A. Oltramare *Les origines de la diatribe romaine* (Lausanne: Librarie Payot, 1926), pp. 301-306. Topoi are also identified and studied via the titles of essays, orations and diatribes. Mitchell discusses the very common title formula περὶ δέ, in M.M. Mitchell, 'Concerning περὶ δέ, in 1 Corinthians', *NovT* 31 (1989), pp. 229-56. Baasland traces the origin of this formula to disputations between pupils and teachers in philosophical schools from Aristotle to Philo of Alexandria and Epictetus. E. Baasland, 'Die περί-Formel und die Argumentation(ssituation) des Paulus', *ST* 42 (1988), pp. 67-87 (75, 83-84).

features provide a common frame of reference which writers or speakers use when they seek to persuade their readers or hearers.[31] Thus, different definitions of the term 'topos' are not to be attributed to incorrect observations by scholars, but to different interpretations of the same data by scholars with different interests and emphases.

The definition of a topos used in this study is based on the functional one offered by Malherbe. With an eye on Hierocles' epitome of Stoic ethics, he defines topoi as:

> traditional, fairly systematic treatments of moral subjects which make use of common clichés, maxims, short definitions, and so forth, without thereby sacrificing an individual viewpoint. Thus a Stoic and an Epicurean could use much the same traditional material in discussing friendship, but the Stoic would be careful to disavow the utilitarianism he perceived in the Epicurean view of virtue.[32]

A topos then, is a broad moral subject. It can be seen in the material (such as themes, motifs, language and illustrative material) which is common to particular texts in this area, and which is used to aid the communication process between author and reader/hearer. As part of this communication process, some aspects of this common material are preserved unchanged, while others are significantly modified.

While topoi have usually been identified and studied in New Testament genres that are more closely related to those found in moral philosophy, such as epitomes, diatribes or epistles, this study demonstrates that the common features that point to the influence of a particular topos on a text can also be identified in other genres that offer moral exhortation, such as the Lukan parables. This has important implications for Gospel study. Individual parables that have been fragmented by source, form and redaction criticism may be seen to be integrated wholes, and clusters of Gospel material that have long been regarded as jumbled or unrelated, may also be seen to be an expression of a single topos. As I noted in Chapter 3, the whole Lukan Travel Narrative may be arranged on gnomic rather than narrative principles.

The use of topoi in particular texts always involves the creative use of recurrent themes, motifs and terminology. These are usually explored

---

31. Through protrepsis, parenesis or diatribe. See A.J. Malherbe (ed. and trans.), *Moral Exhortation: A Greco-Roman Sourcebook* (Library of Early Christianity, 4; Philadelphia: Westminster Press, 1986), pp. 121-34.

32. Malherbe, *Moral Exhortation*, p. 144. See also, A.J. Malherbe, 'The Christianization of a *Topos* (Luke 12:13-34)', *NovT* 38 (1996), pp. 123-35 (124).

via a range of recurrent literary devices, such as the identification of a virtue as the mean of two opposing vices, or the use of character studies and conventional examples to illustrate virtues and vices. Recognizing the stereotypical aspect of the topos form is valuable to scholars because it helps to identify the conventional features of a treatment of a moral subject. The creative adaptations to these stereotypical elements in particular texts reveal the philosophical orientation and special concerns of particular authors. This is of particular value for studying the way topoi are reworked by Christian authors.

2. The Topos On Covetousness

Stobaeus gives us evidence of the existence of a separate topos On Covetousness. He entitles it On Injustice and Covetousness and Greed, περὶ ἀδικίας καὶ φιλαργυρίας καὶ πλεονεξίας.[33] This title has the value of showing that the topos covers a broad moral area characterized by the interrelationship of the vices of covetousness (πλεονεξία), avarice (φιλαργυρία) and injustice or unfairness (ἀδικία).[34] Stobaeus considers it to be the opposite of the area covered by the topos On Justice, περὶ δικαιοσύνης.[35] Following the practice already established in earlier chapters, the topos περὶ ἀδικίας καὶ φιλαργυρίας καὶ πλεονεξίας is referred to as the topos On Covetousness, but the fuller understanding of its range is assumed throughout.

In this section, I illustrate the influence of the topos on a selection of Greco-Roman and Hellenistic Jewish texts with explicit philosophical affiliations. They are discussed chronologically and grouped according to affiliation: Plato, Aristotle and the Peripatetics, Cynics (distinguishing between mild and austere forms of Cynicism where possible), Middle and Roman Stoicism, Eclecticism, Neopythagoreanism and Middle

---

33. Stobaeus 3.10.1-77 = 3.408-429. Following the practice of Balch and Malherbe, I cite references to Stobaeus by book, chapter and excerpt number, and then the volume, pages and lines (when required) in Wachsmuth–Hense.

34. Its relevance to the other L parables may be seen from the importance of the words πλεονεξία and φιλαργυρία in the frames of the parables of the rich fool (Lk. 12.15), the dishonest steward and the rich man and Lazarus (Lk. 16.14).

35. In the list of original chapter titles supplied by Photius, found in Stobaeus 1.3-10, the titles for vol. 3 are mostly grouped in pairs of opposites, starting with περὶ ἀρετῆς and περὶ κακίας.

Platonism. The aim is to provide specific examples of the topos, illustrating their use of recurrent themes and language, while making a variety of points in accordance with the different aims of each text and the
philosophical orientation of the author.

Here, I limit myself to overtly philosophical examples, in order to
make clear that the patterns identified here are part of the common
resources of moral philosophy. However, to show that the actual range
of influence of the topos is much wider, Chapters 5–8 also refer to the
influence of the topos on other Hellenistic Jewish and early Christian
texts as well. The wider influence of the topos on texts belonging to
other Greco-Roman genres may be inferred from the examples cited in
section 3 of Chapter 1 above.

It is a fundamental assumption of this study that there are other Hellenistic Jewish and early Christian texts that also reflect the influence of
the topos, without being attached explicitly to a particular philosophical
grouping.[36] But it is central to the purpose of this study to show the
influence of the topos on the parable in Lk. 15.11-32, and thus to contribute to the process of exploring the philosophical orientation of
Luke–Acts.

Introductory questions are not discussed here beyond giving the date
and philosophical affiliation of each of the texts mentioned. The views
of the authors of the list of abbreviations in volume 1 of the *TDNT*,
compared with entries in the *OCD*, have been taken as a point of departure. In each case, these have been checked with other reference
works.[37] Where necessary, I have given reasons why it is likely that a
particular text or author was known to educated Greco-Roman readers
in the late first century CE. The chapter ends with a summary of the
characteristic features of the topos.

---

36. A few, such as Hebrews, do have a recognized philosophical orientation.
For the view that Hebrews may be classified as a Middle Platonist text, see J.W.
Thompson, *The Beginning of Christian Philosophy: The Epistle to the Hebrews*
(CBQMS, 13; Washington, DC: Catholic Biblical Association, 1982).

37. For Greco-Roman authors, I have consulted the new edition of the *OCD*
together with M8
alherbe's *Moral Exhortation*, pp. 17-21, and E. Ferguson, *Backgrounds of Early
Christianity* (Grand Rapids: Eerdmans, 1987), pp. 254-314, and for the Old
Testament Pseudepigrapha, the two volumes of Charlesworth's *OTP*. The
information given in these texts has been supplemented by information from the
introductions to the editions of individual texts cited individually below.

3. *Moral-Philosophical Texts Reflecting the Influence of the Topos On Covetousness*

a. *Plato*

Plato (429–347 BCE) is not the earliest Greek author to reflect the influence of the topos On Covetousness,[38] but his influence upon subsequent philosophy makes his works an appropriate point of departure for this study.[39] Stobaeus cites a number of short examples of the presence of this topos, containing characteristic themes and terms such as injustice (ἀδικία), money-making (χρηματίζεσθαι), desire (ἐπιθυμία), poverty, substance (οὐσία), greed (ἀπληστία), avaricious (φιλάργυρος) and uncivilized (ἀνελεύθερος).[40]

---

38. See, for example, the comparison between a stingy and a spendthrift way of life in *Theognis*, 903-30.

39. 'The first century BC saw a revival in the study of Plato and Aristotle, who returned to a position of prominence they have not lost since' (Ferguson, *Backgrounds*, 308). 'In regard to ethics or moral theory, Plato's views most likely provided 'une préfiguration de l'éthique stoicienne' and it is in this realm of thought that Plato's influence on Epictetus is found' (J.P. Hershbell, 'The Stoicism of Epictetus: Twentieth Century Perspectives', *ANRW*, II.2.36.3 (1989), pp. 2148-63 (2156).

40. Stobaeus, *Anth.* (All Wachsmuth–Hense.)

3.10.27 = 3.414, 7 (*Crit.* 49b): We ought never to requite wrong with wrong.

3.10.59 = 3.423, 3 (source not given): Do not seek to increase your share of the property, but to reduce your desire.

3.10.67 = 3.425, 9 (*Leg.* 736e): Poverty consists, not in decreasing one's substance, but in increasing one's greed.

3.10.71 = 3.426, 19 (*Resp.* 361a): For the height of injustice is to seem just without being so.

3.10.72 = 3.427, 2 (*Resp.* 347b): Don't you know that to be covetous of honour and covetous of money is said to be, and is, beyond reproach?

3.10.73 = 3.427, 5 (*Resp.* 350d); But when we did reach our conclusion that justice is virtue and wisdom and injustice vice and ignorance, 'Good', said I, 'let this be taken as established.

3.10.74 = 3.427, 9 (lacuna).

3.10.75 = 4.427, 11 (*Leg.* 941b): Theft of property is uncivilized (ἀνελεύθερος), open robbery is shameless.

3.10.76 = 3.427, 14 (*Leg.* 941c). If anyone steals any piece of public property, he shall receive the same punishment, be it great or small.

Apart from the preceding short extracts, the influence of the topos can also be seen in larger sections of Plato's writings. An example of this is his description of four defective types of society (timarchy,[41] oligarchy, democracy and tyranny), together with the typical character which represents each, in books 8 and 9 of the *Republic*.[42]

While aristocracy is typified by the truly good and just person, the other types of society are represented by unjust people. Their distinctive vices are all expressions of covetousness. In the timarchic state, wealth is loved secretly. This is represented by the individual who disdains wealth in his youth, but grows to love it more as he gets older, 'because of his participation in the covetous nature'. The oligarchic state openly prizes wealth and places the wealthy in positions of control. This system is symbolized by the young man who has seen his father ruined through the responsibilities of office. The son has to work hard to earn his own wealth, and so comes to value supremely the principles of appetite and avarice.[43] The democratic state values the indiscriminate indulgence of pleasures and desires. This is represented by the behavior of a prodigal.[44] The tyrannical state arises out of a conflict between the rich on the one hand, and the drones (who covet their wealth) and their bribed followers on the other. When a tyrant seizes power the conflict is resolved. The tyrant is represented by an individual with ever growing desires which have to be satisfied.

This brief outline indicates that the topos On Covetousness is found in discussions of social order as early as Plato. Plato illustrates particular vices found within this topos, such as the love of honour, wealth, licence and unchecked desire, by means of individual character studies. Two of his types, the older man who loves wealth secretly and the young man who indulges his desires without restraint, are found in Lk. 15.11-32.

---

41. Plato refers here to a constitution based on the love of honour (*Resp.* 545b) such as the Spartan or Cretan constitutions (see *Resp.* 544c). Shorey points out that in Aristotle, *Eth. Nic.* 1160a33-34, the term refers to the rule of those who possess a property qualification. See Plato, *The Republic* (trans. P. Shorey; LCL; Cambridge, MA: Harvard University Press, 1935), II, p. 243.

42. Plato, *Resp.* 543a-576b.

43. Plato, *Resp.* 553a-d.

44. The vice of prodigality is specifically treated in Plato, *Resp.* 559d-562a. See the discussion of prodigality in Chapter 5 below. Compare Aristotle's illustration of the oligarchic state by the relation between brothers and the democratic state by a household without a master. Aristotle, *Eth. Nic.* 8.10.6.

b. *Peripatetics*

(i) *Aristotle (384–322 BCE).* Aristotle's example of the topos On Covetousness is important for three reasons. First, peripatetic topoi dealing with various aspects of economics have been shown to have been an important influence on New Testament household codes.[45] Second, his method of defining moral terms via his doctrine of the mean is followed by many subsequent Greco-Roman moralists, even those who do not adopt liberality as their preferred virtue.[46] His view, expressed in the *Nicomachean Ethics* 4.1, that liberality is the appropriate attitude to wealth is, however, widely accepted.[47] Third, his definition of the virtue of liberality as the mean between the vices of prodigality and meanness gives us a map showing the relative position of these three moral conditions. His definition, illustration and evaluation of the key terms of ἀσωτία, ἀνελευθερία and ἐλευθεριότης illuminate the basic moral configuration underlying the parable of the prodigal son.

Aristotle defines liberality (ἐλευθεριότης) as the mean of prodigality (ἀσωτία) and meanness (ἀνελευθερία).[48] The liberal person is the one who makes best use of possessions. He or she gives to the right people, the right amounts, and at the right time. This giving is done with pleasure, or at least without pain. Such a person also takes the right amounts from the right sources. It is not easy for the liberal person to become rich, as he or she does not value money highly.

He rejects the view that prodigality is a combination of many vices, and argues that it is the one particular vice of wasting one's substance (τὸ φθείρειν τὴν οὐσίαν).[49] The prodigal gives away too much and uses up his or her resources excessively, to the point of self-ruin. He or she also takes recklessly and gives wrongly. This excess is not incurable and can return to the mean.

---

45. The studies of D. Lührmann, K. Thraede and D. Balch have been most influential in establishing this consensus. See Balch, 'Household Codes', pp. 25-36.

46. Long argues that Aristotle should be seen as an important influence upon Stoic ethics (A.A. Long, 'Aristotle's Legacy to Stoic Ethics', *BULICS* 15 [1968], pp. 72-85).

47. Aristotle, *Eth. Nic.* 4.1.1-2; also *Eth. Eud.* 1221^{a}15.

48. Other texts of importance are Aristotle, *Eth. Nic.* 2.7.4; 3.12.9; 4.2.1-22; and *Pol.* 1.3.18-19; 2.4.1; 2.6.19; 2.2.6.

49. Aristotle's view of prodigality is discussed in more detail in Chapter 5 below.

The true opposite of liberality is meanness (ἀνελευθερία), which consists of giving too little and taking too much. There are two basic forms of this. Some mean people fall short in giving, but do not covet or take the goods of others. The elder son in the parable is an example of this type. Others take as much as they can, from whatever source. Both types of meanness show the sordid love of gain (αἰσχροκέρδεια).

(ii) *Theophrastus (371–287 BCE)*. Aristotle's treatment of the deficiency of meanness is further illustrated in the *Characters* of Theophrastus (c. 370–285). Character 22 illustrates ἀνελευθερία (parsimony or illiberality),[50] while two other characters illustrate the related vices of μικρολογία (penuriousness) and αἰσχροκέρδεια (meanness, or sordid love of gain).[51] These examples show that there is a long tradition of illustrating the virtues and vices associated with the use of possessions by means of character studies.[52] From the perspective of this tradition, Lk. 15.11-32 consists of three interrelated character studies presented in the form of a single narrative.

c. *Pseudo-Anacharsis (300–250 BCE)*
An early Cynic expression of the topos is found in the ninth *Epistle* of Pseudo-Anacharsis.[53] It purports to be addressed to Croesus, and discusses the consequences of failing to recognize the principle of mutual

---

50. Theophrastus, *Char.* 22.1: 'Parsimony (ἀνελευθερία) is the neglect of honour when it comes to expense.' The illustration found in 22.4 is almost an exact opposite of the father's generous celebration of his son's return in Lk. 15. 23a-24d: 'At his daughter's wedding he will put away all the meat of the sacrificial victim except the priest's portion, and covenant with the serving-men he hires for the feast that they shall eat at home.'

51. Theophrastus, *Char.* 10 and 30.

52. Thompson points out that Plato's types in the *Republic*, the typical characters of New Comedy, Aristotle's types in the *Nicomachean Ethics*, and Theophrastus's *Characters* are all expressions of type psychology. Of Aristotle he says, 'The man who collected 158 constitutions for his *Politics* must have collected many descriptions of human types for his *Ethics*' (*The Ethics of Aristotle* [trans. J.A.K. Thompson; Harmondsworth: Penguin Books, 1955], p. 24).

53. Pseudo-Anacharsis, *Ep.* 9 (46, 13–22; 46, 26–49, 17; 49, 18–27; 48, 28–50, 11.). Extracts from these and other Cynic epistles are cited by page and line number from A.J. Malherbe (ed.), *The Cynic Epistles: A Study Edition* (trans. A.M. McGuire *et al.*; SBLSBS, 12; Missoula: Scholars Press, 1977).

participation (κοινωνία). I summarize the argument briefly, and identify themes, key words and illustrations used to show the Cynic appropriation of the topos.

The Greek poets made the error of distributing the universe among the different gods, only leaving the earth as the common possession of all (κοινὴν ἅπασιν, 46, 2-8)

This human failure to realize the principle of common (κοινός) possession led men to assign certain parts of the earth to the gods. In return the gods gave to humanity the gifts of strife, the desire for pleasure and meanness of spirit (δῶρα πρέποντα ἀντεδωρήσαντο ἔριν καὶ ἡδονὴν καὶ μικροψυχίαν). Combinations of these led to all other evils. Despite hard work, people experienced only 'short-lived luxuriousness' (ὀλιγόβιον... τρυφήν) and behaved like foolish children in their search for the treasures of the earth (46, 9-26).

The epistle then addresses Croesus and argues that the pursuit of gold and pleasure does not bring wisdom. Instead of health, 'foreign foods' of this kind bring with them diseases (νοσήματα). The way to regain the health of the soul is by the renunciation of pleasure. The alternative to this is ruin and slavery (46, 26–48, 17).

At this point, the writer illustrates his argument with a story (ἱστορία): a Syrian merchant ship ran aground on a reef and was abandoned. When some robbers with an empty ship found it, they transferred the cargo to their ship. The empty ship floated away, while the robber ship sank with the weight of foreign goods (48, 18-27). This tale is immediately followed by a moral (48, 28).

These dangers, caused by possessions, are all avoided by the Scythians, described by Anacharsis as all possessing the whole earth (γῆν ἔχομεν πᾶσαν πάντες). This is the manner of life which Anacharsis advises all tyrants to adopt if they wish to avoid ruin (48, 28-50, 11).

The preceding summary shows that the epistle deals with the ideal of the common ownership of possessions, an important theme of the topos. It contrasts the benefits enjoyed by those who follow this ideal with the evils that come upon those who do not. The use of health as a metaphor for moral well-being, which is characteristic of the topos, is prominent. The danger of covetousness is illustrated by means of a tale about foolish robbers, which has a similar hortatory function to that of the L parables.

d. *Mild Cynics*[54]

(i) *Teles (fl. c. 235 BCE)*.[55] Of the pastiches of older Cynic writings put together for his students by Teles, 4A, *A Comparison of Poverty and Wealth* is a good example of his interaction with the topos.[56]

The first characteristic feature of the topos found in this fragment is the negative evaluation of money. Its theme is: the acquisition of money does not free people from scarcity and want. Teles presents two reasons for this. Those who have great wealth either do not use it, and hence do not ever satisfy their wants, or they have insatiable desires that leave them always wanting more.

The second identifying feature is the key term of illiberality (ἀνελ-ευθερία), which recurs throughout the first half of the text, sometimes together with synonyms, such as 'meanness' (ῥυπαρία) and 'insatia-bility' (ἀπληστία), or with related mental states, such as 'despondency' (δυσελπιστία). Similarly, there are a number of references to the verb 'desire' (ἐπιθυμέω), and the word-pair 'scarcity and want' (ἔνδεια καὶ σπάνις).

The third feature is the technique of contrasting moral conditions. The Cynic philosopher is described as the only one able to change a person from being 'insatiable and extravagant to being liberal and unpreten-tious' (ἐξ ἀπλήστων καὶ πολυτελῶν ἐλευθερίους καὶ ἀφελεῖς). This

54. In addition to the three examples given here, another example of a mild Cynic treatment of the topos is found in Lucian's description of Demonax in *Demon.* 3-10. Lucian shows his approval of this mild Cynic, who prefers phi-losophy to the status of civic rank and property. He leads a life of good-natured moral health; he is self-sufficient; he does not draw attention to himself; he forgives wrongdoers without anger and only avoids the morally incurable. Wanting nothing for himself, he consoles and helps others, valuing friendship as the greatest human blessing. These virtues resemble those of the father in Lk. 15.11-32.

55. The text and translation used are taken from E.N. O'Neil, *Teles (the Cynic Teacher)* (SBLTT Graeco-Roman Religion Series, 3; Missoula: Scholars Press, 1977). References are to the line numbers in O'Neil. As with the citations of Plato above, the presence of extracts of Teles in Stobaeus allows us to assume that these fragments of Teles were known in the first century CE. O'Neil thinks it likely that the portions in Stobaeus are 'extracts from extracts' and that 'more than one other intervening compression occurred between Teles and Theodorus and between Theodorus and Stobaeus' (*Teles*, p. xvii).

56. See Stobaeus, *Anth.* 4.33.31 = 5.808.12 (Hense). The influence of the topos is also evident in 2 On Self-Sufficiency (περὶ αὐταρκείας) and 4b (untitled).

is illustrated with the example of the change that Crates was able to bring about in the life of Metrocles.

The fragment *On Self-Sufficiency* is notable for also containing a story of Xenophon (*Symposium* 4.35) in which two brothers who have divided an equal sum are described, the one being in utter distress and the other quite content (τὴν ἴσην οὐσίαν διελομένων τὸν μὲν ἐν τῇ πάσῃ ἀπορίᾳ, τὸν δὲ ἐν εὐκολίᾳ).[57]

(ii) *Dio Chrysostom (c. 40/50–after 110 CE)*. The seventeenth *Oration* of Dio Chrysostom, a mild Cynic, consists of a discussion of covetousness. Engagement with the topos is evident in its title (περὶ πλεονεξίας) and in Dio's repeated use of the term πλεονεξία.

The discourse deals with the negative consequences of covetousness. (1) Covetousness is neither expedient nor honourable (οὔτε συμφέρον οὔτε καλόν), but the greatest evil; (2) actions motivated by greed not only affect the individual who takes them but also the wider community to which he or she belongs; (3) greed destroys prosperity, property and ultimately, life; (4) covetousness can only be cured by adopting the principles of equality, right proportion and sufficiency. These negative consequences and their remedy are all exemplified in Lk. 15.11-32.

Dio's extensive use of ancient and more recent illustrations (παραδείγματα) taken from both poetry and prose (17.15) again shows the importance of illustrations in the topos. Here we find a fragment from Menander, an extract from Euripides' *Phoenician Women*, ll. 531-540, a reference to Hesiod, the story of Helen of Troy, Xerxes' designs upon Greece, Polycrates' quest for money from the mainland,[58] the Spartan request of the oracle for Arcadia, the Athenians' request for Sicily and a story about Croesus.

He also uses other types of illustrations that are quite similar to synoptic parables, which often begin καθάπερ or ὥσπερ, such as a foolish man going on a journey of two or three days who takes provisions for a year, or a man who has invited 10 or 15 guests to a banquet, but who prepares food for 500 or a 1000. Greed is also illustrated as a ship that is so heavily overloaded that it sinks. The ideals of due measure and harmony are illustrated by the harmony of all the organs of the body.

---

57. Teles, περὶ αὐταρκείας, 95-96. Also cited by Berger and Colpe, *Religionsgeschichtliches Textbuch*, pp. 137-38.
58. Herodotus, *Hist*. 3.120-25.

Apart from the central term of πλεονεξία, the most common other terms characteristic of the topos found here are: harmony (ἁρμονία); destroy/die (ἀπόλλυμι); equal (ἴσος); sickness (νόσος); insatiable desire (ἀπληστία) and desire (ἐπιθυμία).

(iii) *Pseudo-Socratic Epistles (c. 200 CE)*. The epistles pseudonymously attributed to Socrates' disciples provide further examples of the use of the topos in the writings of mild Cynics. Here I take *Epistle* 8 as an example of the teaching of this school on the right attitude to money.

Pseudo-Antisthenes contrasts the conventional view, that benefits come through having money and powerful friends, with the philosophic ideal of self-sufficiency. He questions the legitimacy of accepting money from tyrants and says that money is not necessary. Similarly, he warns Aristippus that true friendship cannot be obtained from the uneducated masses nor from tyrants. Moreover, by living with a tyrant, Aristippus lays himself open to the accusation that he values pleasure (ἡδονή).

He is advised to leave Anticyra to escape the dangers of his present circumstances, which are described in terms of the metaphor of madness (ἐλλέβορος; μανία). His departure will enable him to exchange his present state of 'sickness and folly' (νόσου τε καὶ ἀφροσύνης) for one of 'health and wisdom' (ὑγίεια τε καὶ φρόνησις).

In this epistle, therefore, the influence of the topos is seen in the negative treatment of the themes of money, false ideas of friendship and pleasure, and the positive advocacy of the ideals of self-sufficiency and true friendship. The contrast is illustrated by the metaphors of madness and wisdom, and sickness and health. In addition, the dangers of living in luxury in a foreign land are contrasted with the benefits of following the ideal of self-sufficiency at home.

e. *Austere Cynics*

(i) *Pseudo-Crates (first to second centuries CE)*. Nearly all of the austere Cynic letters attributed to Crates address the issue of possessions from the perspective of the simple lifestyle.[59] The troubles of the rich are contrasted with the blessings of the temperate, and the Cynic ideal of self-sufficiency is advocated.

---

59. The pseudonymous attribution is inappropriate, as Crates himself was a mild Cynic.

Epistles 10, 15 and 22 all contain examples of terminology that are characteristic of the topos. These are usually defined by means of contrast.

In *Epistle* 10 (62, 8-11) Pseudo-Crates speaks of those who have 'temperate souls, healthy bodies and sufficient possessions' as being thrice happy. Here the virtues of self-control (ἐγκράτεια), health (ὑγίεια) and sufficiency (αὐτάρκεια) are advocated. *Epistle* 15 says that the worst of evils (τὰ τέλη τῶν κακῶν), injustice and self-indulgence (ἀδικία καὶ ἀκρασία), are caused by pleasures (ἡδονή). These ought to be shunned, in favor of the best of goods (τὰ τέλη τῶν ἀγαθῶν), self-control and perseverance (ἐγκράτεια καὶ καρτερία), which are the result of toils (πόνοι). In the discussion of Cynic begging in *Epistle* 22 those who act prudently (σωφρόνως) are contrasted with those who act wastefully (ἀσώτως). The latter are described as squandering their money recklessly (δαπανώντως). Here profligacy (ἀσωτία) is regarded as the opposite of prudence (σωφροσύνη).

(ii) *Pseudo-Socrates.* The sixth *Epistle* of Pseudo-Socrates (first Century CE or earlier) employs the topos in an apology for the Cynic attitude to money (περὶ τοῦ χρηματισμοῦ) and poverty.

The epistle answers two queries relating to themes found in the topos: (1) Why has Socrates chosen to embrace poverty instead of pursuing wealth? (2) Why does he even refuse gifts or bequests of money from friends?

Socrates explains that his attitude to money is one expression of his commitment to a life of moderation and wisdom, which is also seen in the way he does not eat rich food, wear fine clothes or seek public fame. If there is any question about whether this is the way to happiness, he cites the example of God. If wealth were necessary for happiness, God would have chosen wealth!

He answers a further question about whether the ascetic life makes adequate provision for one's children, by again saying that because gold and silver are not good things, to leave money to one's children is to provide for their folly. The only way children can avoid hunger is by becoming good. He does not deny that parents should provide for their children until adulthood, only the idea that parents should be expected to provide for their children after their own death by means of bequests. He gives an example of a man who is angry with his lazy sons for thinking that his wealth will allow them to continue in their idleness after his death. This laziness is described as a life more inactive than the dead. The father's angry remonstration is blunt, but Socrates says that he is using his 'paternal prerogative together with civic freedom of speech'.

Socrates goes on to argue that it is better for his sons to inherit his friends than his money. In the course of this argument he discusses the nature of true friendship. By gaining friends through his life of philosophy, he is able to leave his children friends who will care for them after his death. A true friend is better than gold because he meets the material and spiritual needs of his friends. This is the answer to the second question asked at the beginning: he will not accept money from friends, because friendship is the only appropriate payment for the life of philosophy.

Thus, this text deals with the theme of the life of poverty, using motifs that are characteristic of texts on covetousness: simple living and the avoidance of fine food and clothing; God as the supreme example of the happiness of those who desire nothing; the view that money is not a good; the contrast between the poor who eventually come to their senses and the corrupted affluent who do not; the link between true living and goodness; a father's appeal to his sons; and the importance of true friendship, which is described as being far more important than money.

The significant terms used are: money (χρηματισμός), poor (πένης) and wealth (πλοῦτος); a gift (δωρεά); gain (πορισμός); forbidden pleasures (αἱ ἀπόρρητοι ἡδοναί), also the sorcery of pleasures (γοητείας ἡδονῶν); children and parents; wisdom; friends and friendship (φίλοι; φιλία).

Significant for my comparison of the topos with Lk. 15.11-32 is the way this text presents the correct attitude to possessions in terms of the happiness of the individual, his sons and his friends.

f. *Middle Stoicism*
(i) *Sirach (translated into Greek c. 132 BCE).*[60] There are many places in Sirach that reveal the author's interaction with the topos On Covetousness. I consider two examples here.[61]

---

60. Text: A. Rahlfs (ed.), *Septuaginta: Id est Vetus Testamentum graece iuxta LXX interpretes* (2 vols.; Stuttgart: Württemburgische Bibelanstalt, 5th edn, 1952). The translation of this and other texts from the Apocrypha is taken from the RSV.
61. Other examples are Sir. 3.5-7; 4.1-4; 5.1-2; 8.2; 10.8; [10.9]; 10.22; 10.30-

The first, 11.10-14, 17-28 contains the following cluster of themes, many of which are relevant to Lk. 15.11-32: an appeal of father to son; the uncertain relationship between hard work and prosperity or want; the Lord as the giver of good and bad things, including life and death, poverty and wealth; the blessing of the godly by God; the uncertainty of life and prosperity; the view that a man's character is evident in his children.

Much of the language in this extract, which discusses the theme of gaining or losing possessions, echoes the possession-language of the L parables: child (τέκνον); work and toil (κοπίαω καὶ πονέω); want (ὑστερέω); abound in poverty (πτωχεία περισσεύω); life and death (ζωή καὶ θάνατος); poverty and wealth (πτωχεία καὶ πλοῦτος); allotted reward (ἡ μερὶς τοῦ μισθοῦ); find rest (εὑρίσκω ἀνάπαυσιν); eat (ἐσθίω) one's goods; the sinner (ὁ ἁμαρτωλός); labor (πόνος); enough (αὐτάρκης); reward (ἀποδίδωμι); luxury (τρυφή).

There are three similar statements of the wrong attitude towards possessions. All of these are in soliloquy, a device also characteristic of the L parables: 'I have found rest and now I shall enjoy my goods'; 'What do I need, and what prosperity could be mine in the future?' and 'I have enough, and what calamity could happen to me in the future?' (Sir. 11.19, 23-24).[62]

In the second example, Sir. 14.3-16, mean persons are criticized for failing to spend some of their possessions upon themselves. This meanness to oneself, which corresponds with the Peripatetic category of giving too little, is considered to be the most profound kind of meanness and self-envy. People are advised to treat themselves well during their lifetimes and to give generously to other people, for there is no luxury in Hades.

This passage also deals with the theme of inheritances. It criticizes the division of inheritances by lot, that is with little consideration for the just disposal of resources, and contains the stock observation that those who inherit money often spend it on luxuries.

31; 13.3; 13.19; 13.24; 18.20; 18.25; 18.30–19.1; 22.23; 23.4-6; 25.2; 27.1; 28.10; 29.10-11; 29.21-23; 30.15-16; 31.5-6; 31.8; 33.19-21; 37.29; 40.12-13; 40.25-26; 40.28; 41.1-2; 41.14; 44.6, 7; 51.25, 28.

62. These phrases, and the following motif of the unknown day of one's death, all correspond closely with Lk. 12.17-20.

Again we find language characteristic of the topos: mean (μικρο-λογός); wealth (πλοῦτος); money (χρήματα); gather (συνάγω); live in luxury (τρυφάω); to take pleasure (εὐφραίνω); retribution (ἀντά-πόδομα); greedy (πλεονέκτης); injustice (ἀδικία); bread (ἄρτος); one-self (αὐτός); child (τέκνον); worthy (ἀξίος); death (θάνατος); friend (φίλος); give (δίδωμι) and take (λαμβάνω); deprive (ἀφυστερέω); share of desired good (μερὶς ἐπιθυμίας ἀγαθῆς); labor (πόνος); division by lot (εἰς διαίρεσιν κλήρου).

One of the striking themes of this extract is the way the use of pos-sessions is related to a person's relationship with him- or herself. Mean people have a faulty attitude to themselves. In Lk. 15.11-32, the younger son's return to a right relationship with himself is contrasted with the mean elder son's self-deprivation.

The ideal attitude to possessions in Sirach is that of sufficiency and contentment.[63] Wealth is not something to be desired, pursued, or trust-ed in (as a form of self-sufficiency), and 'insatiable desire' is thought of as the root cause of meanness and prodigality. However, Sirach does not condemn wealth entirely. Both poverty and wealth are gifts from the Lord. Those who possess wealth should use their wealth while they live. They should not be misers, but should give to the poor and hungry, and also spend money on themselves.

(ii) *The Testaments of the Twelve Patriarchs (c. second century BCE).*[64]
In its extant form, the *Testaments of the Twelve Patriarchs* is a Chris-tian text with a Jewish foundation. It is a major witness either to Jewish parenesis just prior to Christianity, or to the profoundly determinative impact of Jewish ethics upon 'Christian' parenesis in the second cen-tury CE.[65] Its use of Middle Stoic ethics has also been recognized.[66]

---

63. Hengel points out that Ben Sira reflects wisdom literature's traditional high estimate of wisdom, together with polemic against unscrupulous speculators and the hectic hunt for riches (M. Hengel, *Property and Riches in the Early Church* [trans. J. Bowden; London: SCM, 1974], pp. 16-17).

64. Text: M. de Jonge *et al.* (eds.), *The Testaments of the Twelve Patriarchs: A Critical Edition of the Greek Text* (Leiden: E.J. Brill, 1978). The translation of this and other pseudepigraphal texts is from J.H. Charlesworth (ed.), *The Old Testament Pseudepigrapha* (2 vols; London: Darton, Longman & Todd, 1983, 1985).

65. J.H. Charlesworth, 'Reflections on the SNTS Pseudepigrapha Seminar at Duke on the Testaments of the Twelve Patriarchs', *NTS* 23 (1977), pp. 296-70 (304).

66. For example, in the use of terms such as σύνεσις, σωφροσύνη and ἁπλότης.

Each of the different Testaments focuses on a different vice or virtue.[67]

The title of the *Testament of Judah*, περὶ ἀνδρείας καὶ φιλαργυρίας καὶ πορνείας (on bravery and love of money and sexual immorality), identifies the presence of three separate topoi in this testament. They are not entirely separate, however. While ch. 1–9 relate to the topos περὶ ἀνδρείας, there is a closer relationship between the latter two topoi in ch. 10–26. The relationship between the vices of φιλαργυρία and πορνεία is clearly evident in *T. Jud.* 16.1; 17.1-3; 18.1-4a; 19.1-3:[68]

First, *T. Jud.* 16.1 attributes the vices of ἐπιθυμία, πύρωσις, ἀσωτία and αἰσχροκερδία to the abuse of wine, though they are also characteristic of the topos On Covetousness. Second, in *T. Jud.* 17.1 and 18.2 the love of money and sexual promiscuity are linked together. Both of these vices are seen to have personal and social consequences: in *T. Jud.* 17, when Judah is led astray by Bathshua, his whole tribe is doomed to wickedness, and in *T. Jud.* 18, the vices lead to moral and spiritual blindness, arrogance and merciless social relationships. Third, *T. Jud.* 19 reveals φιλαργυρία is shown to be the more serious of the two vices, because it leads to idolatry, loss of sanity (εἰς ἔκστασιν ἐμπεσεῖν) and loss of children. The cure for φιλαργυρία is seen to be Judah's own repentance (μετάνοια) and humility (ταπείνωσις), the prayers of Jacob, and the compassionate mercy of God.

The relative importance of the vices of φιλαργυρία and πορνεία is illustrated by the way they are linked and contrasted. The vice of πορνεία is shifted to the background and φιλαργυρία is viewed more gravely. This has implications for the exegesis of the elder son's accusation in Lk. 15.30a.

See H.C. Kee, 'The Ethical Dimensions of the Testaments of the XII as a Clue to Provenance', *NTS* 24 (1978), pp. 259-70 (263-64).

67. *T. Reub.*: περὶ ἐννοιων; *T. Sim.*: περὶ φθόνου; *T. Levi*: περὶ ἱερωσύνης καὶ ὑπερηφανίας; *T. Jud.*: περὶ ἀνδρείας καὶ φιλαργυρίας καὶ πορνείας; *T. Iss.*: περὶ ἁπλότητος; *T. Zeb.*: περὶ εὐσπλαγχνίας καὶ ἔλεους; *T. Dan*: περὶ θυμοῦ καὶ ψεύδους; *T. Naph.*: περὶ φυσικῆς ἀγαθότητος; *T. Gad*: περὶ μίσους; *T. Ash.*: περὶ δύο πρόσωπων κακίας καὶ ἀρετῆς; *T. Jos.*: περὶ σωφροσύνης; *T. Ben.*: περὶ διάνοιας καρδίας.

68. Other references: *T. Reub.* 3.2, 6; *T. Lev.* 14, 6; 17.2, 8-11; *T. Jud.* 21.7-8; *T. Iss.* 4.2-3, 5; *T. Dan* 5.7; *T. Naph.* 3.1; *T. Gad* 2.3-5; 5.1; 5.3; 7.1, 3-4, 6; *T. Ash.* 5.1; *T. Ben.* 5.1; 6.1-3; 10.3-4; 11.1-2.

g. *Roman Stoicism*

(i) *Seneca (c. 4 BCE–65 CE)*. As examples of Seneca's Stoic treatment of the topos On Covetousness, we look at two of his *Epistles to Lucilius*, 17 and 115,[69] both of which are exhortations to adopt the philosophical life.

In *Epistle* 17, Seneca deals with the most common reasons why people delay taking up the Stoic way of life: the fear of poverty and the resultant decision to wait until one has accumulated enough to live on. He reverses the popular view of poverty and riches, saying that poverty is a good, but riches are (often) an obstacle to wisdom.

He contrasts the gains of wealth and the philosophical life. Because philosophy brings wisdom and freedom, it is insane to make it a lower priority than the accumulation of wealth.

Seneca advocates the ideal of sufficiency, sometimes using aphorisms such as: 'living simply is voluntary poverty', or 'in every age, what is enough remains the same'; or a quotation from Epicurus: 'The acquisition of riches has been for many men, not an end, but a change of troubles'.

Again we note the prominent use of good health and sanity as metaphors for the moral life: the philosophical life is a life of sanity; those who reject this way have diseased minds.

The engagement with the topos On Covetousness is still more explicit in *Epistle* 115. There he begins by contrasting true virtue with the apparent glory of high position and power. He blames the distortion of true values on money: people and things are not valued for who or what they are in themselves, but for their monetary worth. Parents and society in turn are culpable for giving children this false perception. This argument is supported by examples from the poets.

He points to the negative consequences of greed. Far from bringing benefits, Seneca argues that it brings severe penalties: 'What tears and toils does money wring from us! Greed is wretched in that which it craves and wretched in that which it wins'. Furthermore, because greed is never satisfied, no one is ever contented with prosperity. In contrast, philosophy brings the only sure happiness: the 'absence of regret for your own conduct', together with freedom from desire and fear.[70]

---

69. See also Seneca, *Epp.* 14.18; 16; 18.13; 22.12.
70. Seneca, *Ep.* 115.16, 18.

(ii) *Persius (34–62 CE)*. The satires of Persius also provide a number of examples of the Stoic interaction with the topos.[71] *Satire* 6, in the form of an epistle to the lyric poet Caesius Bassus, deals with the theme of the right attitude to wealth. Persius's own view is summed up in the statement: 'Enjoy what you have'. He rejects the opposing excesses of the stingy person and the prodigal. These options are illustrated by the different actions of twins, one of whom is miserly in his use of salt and pepper, while the other devours a huge inheritance (ll. 18-22).

From line 27 onwards, he introduces the motif of the expectations of friends and heirs. Persius asserts that it is right to use one's property to help a destitute friend, and rejects the hypothetical complaints of his heirs. It is absurd that he should be prevented from the legitimate use of his possessions, to enable his heir to waste his wealth on fine food and sexual adventures with patrician women. Here Persius shows that heirs were conventional examples of prodigal or miserly behavior.

The satire as a whole shows that Stoics endorse the Peripatetic ideal of liberality in the use of possessions.

(iii) *4 Maccabees (first century CE)*.[72] *4 Maccabees* is a good example of Stoicism in a Hellenistic Jewish text. It consists of a discussion of whether reason has supreme control over the passions. Two passages where the influence of the topos can be seen are: *4 Macc.* 1.13-27 and 2.1-9.

In *4 Macc.* 1.13-27 the author first defines reason as the mind's deliberate choice of a life of wisdom—wisdom being seen as deriving from the Law. Here the ideal of the philosophical life is expressed in Jewish terms. Wisdom controls the passions of pleasure or pain. Part of pleasure is 'the malicious moral temper (ἡ κακοήθης διάθεσις)' which expresses itself in vices of the soul such as: pretentiousness, avarice, seeking the limelight, contentiousness and backbiting (ἀλαζονεία, καὶ

---

71. See Persius, *Sat.* 3.63-72; and *Sat.* 5.104-88. In *Sat.* 5.132-60 and 161-74 should be noted. The former section describes the competing claims of *avaritia* and luxury, and the latter presents the opening scene of Menander's *Eunuch* in which a young prodigal struggles with his decision to change.

72. *4 Macc.* is variously dated from the time of Caligula to CE 100 or 117/118. See H.-J. Klauck, 'Brotherly Love in Plutarch and in 4 Maccabees', in D.L. Balch, E. Ferguson and W.A. Meeks (eds.), *Greeks, Romans and Christians: Essays in Honor of Abraham J. Malherbe* (Minneapolis: Fortress Press, 1990), pp. 144-56 (155).

φιλαργυρία, καὶ φιλοδοξία, καὶ φιλονεικία, ἀπιστία, καὶ βασκανία), and those of the body, such as various forms of gluttony (παντοφαγία, καὶ λαιμαργία, καὶ μονοφαγία).[73] Using the metaphor of a royal retinue, the author associates the vice of avarice with a cluster of related vices, all of which are negative consequences of the passion of pleasure.

4 Maccabees 2.1-9 illustrates the way the rational faculty is able to control the passions of sensuality (ἡδυπαθεία) and every other desire (πᾶσα ἐπιθυμία) by means of the Law. As examples of the change that comes when someone acts according to the Law under the power of reason, the author points to the formerly avaricious man (φιλάργυρός) who lends to the needy without interest and who cancels what is owed to him after seven years, and to the formerly niggardly man (φειδωλός) who no longer gleans his own crops. Again we observe the Stoic endorsement of the Peripatetic ideal of liberality and the distinction of different forms of meanness.

(iv) *Musonius Rufus (c. 30–101/2 CE)*.[74] The discourses of Musonius Rufus all show the influence of the topos On Covetousness, usually in the context of warnings against the dangers of wealth and extravagance and his appeals for simple living.[75] To illustrate the pervasiveness of this topos in Musonius, I here consider its function within *Fragment 17*, which discusses the best preparation for old age.[76]

Musonius bases his argument on the Stoic doctrine that people ought to live according to nature (κατὰ φύσιν), and not for pleasure. For human beings, this means living a life of virtue, in imitation of God. By means of the classic virtues of prudence, justice, courage and temperance, people are able to avoid being dominated by pleasure (ἡδονή) and

---

73. *4 Macc.* 1.21, 25-27, 30.

74. The text and translation used is that of C.E. Lutz, 'Musonius Rufus: "The Roman Socrates"', *YCS* 10 (1947), pp. 3-147. Citations are given by fragment number, then page and line number of this edition.

75. An illustration of this which is relevant to this study is found in *Frag.* 1 (34, 7-33), which compares the responses of two youths to philosophical training. One has been raised in luxury and the other in a Spartan manner. The former finds it hard to accept philosophical teaching, while the latter accepts it easily.

76. Other places where the influence of the topos is evident are *Frag.* 1 (34, 14-16; 34, 31-33); *Frag.* 3 (40, 17-20; 40, 28); *Frag.* 4 (48, 9); *Frag.* 6 (52, 15-18; 56, 8-11); *Frag.* 8 (62, 13-20); *Frag.* 14 (92, 17-25); *Frag.* 15 (98, 17-22, 27-100, 16); *Frag.* 17 (108, 11-18; 110, 16-27); *Frag.* 18b. (118, 32-34); *Frag.* 19. (122, 12-32); *Frag.* 20 (126, 4-8; 11-31); *Frag.* 34; *Frag.* 50.

greed (πλεονεξία), and are enabled to be superior to desire (ἐπιθυμία), envy (φθόνος) and jealousy (ζηλοτυπία).

The man who has been trained to live according to nature from his youth (ἔτι νέος ὢν παιδείας ὀρθῆς ἐπιμέλειαν πεποιημένος) is well-prepared to deal with the deprivations of old age, such as the loss of the pleasures of youth, his weakness of body and neglect by relatives and friends.

The fragment ends with a warning which is frequent in texts on this topos: wealth is not the greatest consolation of old age. He contrasts the only commodities that wealth can buy: the sensual pleasures of food, drink and sex, with the true needs of the elderly: cheerfulness of spirit (εὐθυμία) and freedom from sorrow (ἀλυπία).

(v) *Pseudo-Phocylides (between 200 BCE and 200 CE)*. There are two passages in *Pseudo-Phocylides* that relate particularly closely to the topos On Covetousness: ll. 42-47, on the love of money and its consequences, and ll. 59-69, on moderation in all things.[77]

In the first extract, avarice is attacked by a description of its negative consequences. After citing a variation of the common aphorism on the love of money (φιλοχρημοσύνη) and all evil (here it is 'the mother of all evil'), money is described using various metaphors. It is a lure (δόλος), the source of evil, the destroyer of life (βιοφθόρος), and a calamity (πῆμα). The destructive effects of avarice are seen in the way it causes war and violence and in the way it brings enmity between children and parents and between relatives.

The second extract, ll. 59-69, reveals the importance of the ideal of the mean. Moderation is advocated in the areas of the emotions (πάθη), luxury (τρυφή), wealth (πλοῦτος), and various types of anger (θυμός, ὀργή, μῆνις), as well as in eating, drinking and speech. All excess is bad, even excess of the good (ἀγαθόν πλεονάζον), leading to things like immoderate desires, insolence, madness, shame and folly.

77. *Sib. Or.* 2.55-149 contains an interpolation from *Ps.-Phoc.* 5-79, which includes the two sections discussed here (*Sib. Or.* 2.109-18; and 2.131-34). It is probable that the verses were inserted by a Christian, but the motive for the interpolation is not known. The fact of this insertion does, however, indicate that such material was read and valued by Christians before 150 CE. See J.J. Collins, 'Sibylline Oracles', in *OTP*, I, p. 332.

As other passages in *Pseudo-Phocylides* indicate, this text does not present a blanket condemnation of possessions.[78] The emphasis is not on the evils of possessing wealth, but its abuse. The ideal of the right use of wealth involves: honest acquisition, and generosity to oneself and those in need.

(vi) *Epictetus (55–165 CE)*. As with his teacher, Musonius Rufus, we do not possess any discourse from Epictetus devoted to the themes of covetousness or avarice. However, he makes reference to the right attitude to money, wealth, poverty, possessions and property in almost every discourse. All his teaching on property and possessions is governed by the basic Stoic doctrine that possessions are not under our control.[79]

To see how the topos functions throughout his work, I look at a *Dissertation* dealing with the fear of want.[80] Epictetus supports his argument that want (ἀπορία) is not to be feared with an illustration. 'What runaway slave ever died of hunger (λιμῷ ἀπέθανεν)?' He follows this questionable point with the irrefutable statement that death is inevitable anyway (3.26.3). He illustrates the absurdity of fearing death with a contrast: at death a beggar dies hungry and a ruler dies 'bursting with indigestion and drunkenness': this is the only difference between them (3.26.5).

Epictetus counters the objection that people fear the shame of want with another Stoic principle: want is one of the things that lies outside our control. It is therefore not shameful. At this point he employs another distinctive motif from the topos, that of inheritance. An heir has no control over whether his parents are poor, or leave their wealth to someone else (3.26.8). He argues that his hearers should rather be anxious about matters relating to their weak moral purpose: their cowardice (δειλία), ignoble character (ἀγέννεια), admiration of the rich (θαυμασμὸς τῶν πλουσίων), ineffectual desire (ἀτελὴς ὄρεξις) and aversion which 'fails of its mark' (3.26.14).

---

78. See *Ps.-Phoc.* 5-6; 27-28; 36-37; 53-54; 109-10; 199. J.J. Lewis notes the parallels between *Pseudo-Phocylides* and the table talk section of the *Epistle of Aristeas* in 'The Table Talk Section in the *Letter of Aristeas*', NTS 13 (1966–67), pp. 53-56.

79. For a discussion of the importance of *prohairesis*, the ability of human beings to make choices, see Hershbell, 'The Stoicism of Epictetus', pp. 2159-60.

80. Epictetus, *Diss.* 3.26. Other discourses that could also be examined in this way are Epictetus, *Diss.* 2.16; 2.17; 2.19; 3.7; 3.24; 4.1; 4.4; 4.6; 4.7.

He attacks his hearers for claiming to fear want, when they are actually simply fearing the loss of luxury (3.26.21-22). By fearing want they really fear good health, for what they call 'a life of want' is the life followed by slaves, and workmen—and philosophers (3.26.23). He deepens his criticism of their fear by saying good workmen are always able to find employment. He implies that their fear of want questions their value to society (3.26.25-26). This motif of the value of manual labor is also a marker of the topos.

His final argument is that God does not usually neglect his servants (3.26.28-29). However, he does not provide abundance and luxury (οὐ παρέχει μοι πολλά, οὐκ ἄφθονα, τρυφᾶν με οὐ θέλει): even Heracles, his own son, suffered labors and discipline (ἐπόνει καὶ ἐγυμνάζετο). In so doing, he removed injustice and lawlessness (ἀδικία καὶ ἀνομία) and introduced justice and righteousness (δικαιοσύνη καὶ ἰσότης) (3.26.30-32). Odysseus likewise showed the value of trusting not in reputation, money or office (οὐ δόξῃ οὐδὲ χρήμασιν οὐδ' ἀρχαῖς), but in his own might (ἀλκῇ τῇ ἑαυτοῦ) (3.26.34). These two figures are examples of the way the topos encourages the use of stock illustrations of ideals, here that of self-sufficiency.

h. *Epicurus (341–270 BCE)*

Because of the dangers of unchecked desire, treatments of the nature and function of true pleasure are important elements of the topos. In his *Letter to Menoeceus*[81] Epicurus defines the various kinds of desires (ἐπιθυμίαι). The Epicurean is only to follow those desires that lead to the attainment of the ideals of bodily health and mental tranquility. This means that pleasure (ἡδονή) is defined negatively as the absence of pain in the body and of trouble in the soul.

Because Epicureans are frequently attacked by those who misunderstand their doctrine of pleasure, it is important to note that Epicurus explicitly contrasts it with the pleasures of the prodigal or the pleasures of sensuality (οὐ τὰς τῶν ἀσώτων ἡδονὰς καὶ τὰς ἐν ἀπολαύσει κειμένας).[82] He refutes malicious popular distortions[83] of the Epicurean

81. Diogenes Laertius, 10.127-32. See also his Principal Doctrines, nos. 5, 10, 15-21 and 26-40, in Diogenes Laertius, 10.140-54.

82. In the tenth Principal Doctrine Epicurus criticizes prodigals on the grounds that their lifestyle does not free them from mental fears, nor enable them to limit their desires.

83. Epictetus (*Diss.* 3.7.20) characterizes the Epicurean δόγματα as 'bad, sub-

view of pleasure which say that they advocate drinking bouts (πότοι), revelry (κῶμοι), enjoyment of boys and women (ἀπολαύω παίδων καὶ γυναικῶν) and a luxurious table (πολυτελὴς τράπεζα).[84] For Epicurus, true pleasure only comes through living prudently (φρονίμως), honourably (καλῶς) and justly (δικαίως).[85] Here he commends virtues with are ethical commonplaces in the topos.

i. *Eclecticism*

(i) *Cicero (106–43 BCE)*. Cicero's philosophy is based on that of the Academy and the Stoics, but he treats Peripatetics as part of this combination and admires the Aristotelian doctrine of the mean: 'In summary of his eclectic approach it has been said that his intellect was with the Academy, his conscience with the Stoa and his information with the Peripatetics'.[86] Cicero addresses the theme of liberality in *On Duties* 2.52-71 when he discusses generosity to individuals, using material derived from the Middle Stoic writings of Panaetius of Rhodes (c. 185–110 BCE). This passage is significant because his discussion shows that in dealing with the theme of liberality, he draws on other motifs that are part of the topos.

He deals with acts of generosity under two main headings, gifts of money and personal service, the latter being more noble for the giver and more beneficial to the recipient. His comments on gifts of money

---

versive of the State, destructive to the family, [and] not even fit for women'. Plutarch accuses Epicureans of living like animals. See A.J. Malherbe, 'The Beasts at Ephesus', in *idem, Paul and the Popular Philosophers* (Minneapolis: Fortress Press, 1989), pp. 79-89 (84). For other critical Stoic responses to the growth of Epicureanism in Italy, see H. Jones, *The Epicurean Tradition* (London: Routledge, 1992), pp. 76-93.

84. The frugal eating habits of the Epicureans are described in Diogenes Laertius, 10.11. See A.H. Armstrong, *An Introduction to Ancient Philosophy* (University Paperbacks Series; London: Methuen, 3rd edn, 1965), p. 137.

85. The just man enjoys the greatest peace of mind. Therefore wise people do not act unjustly towards themselves or others. See J.M. Rist, 'Epicurus on Friendship', *CP* 75 (1980), pp. 121-29 (128-29).

86. Ferguson, *Backgrounds*, p. 303. See also M. Grant, *Cicero: On the Good Life* (Harmondsworth: Penguin Books, 1971), p. 24; and J. Glucker, 'Cicero's Philosophical Affiliations', in J.M. Dillon and A.A. Long (eds.), *The Question of 'Eclecticism': Studies in Later Greek Philosophy* (Hellenistic Culture and Society, 3; Berkeley: University of California Press, 1988), pp. 34-69.

show his endorsement of the ideal of moderation. Because all givers have limited resources, money should be given with discretion and moderation (diligenter atque moderate): 'For many have squandered their patrimony by indiscriminate giving' (2.54).

Of types of generous giving, he distinguishes lavish spending on public games, which he condemns, from generous giving to ransom captives, or to assist friends in various ways. He agrees with Aristotle's criticism of the lavish spending which is aimed only at winning public approval. Like Aristotle, he warns against meanness (avaritia) and advocates the golden mean (mediocritas) (2.58, 59).

Cicero advises moderation in giving even when the giver is motivated by generosity rather than necessity or expediency. The aim should be to benefit as many people as possible and to evoke true gratitude (63).[87] He sums up the ideal of liberality by saying that we should be liberal in giving and fair in business, managing our personal property well. The ideal of a liberal reputation is contrasted with the warning to avoid being thought mean or avaricious.

His discussion of the second category of generosity, namely personal service, is obviously not as closely related to this topos, though it does contain a memorable aphorism by Themistocles ('I prefer a man without money, to money without a man') and a reference to the problem of wealth in Cicero's day: '...the moral sense of today is demoralized and depraved by our worship of money' (71).

The remainder of book 2 (2.72-89) deals with service to the state through personal service to individuals. Cicero warns very strongly against avaricious behavior by those in public office and stresses the importance of justice. The influence of the standard range of themes of the topos is evident right to the end of this book, where the themes of health and sensual pleasure are introduced, apparently arbitrarily, into a comparison of expediencies.

(ii) *Horace (65–8 BCE)*. Satire 2.3 is the longest and best-constructed of Horace's satires and reflects both Stoic and Cynic influences. It is a dialogue based on the Stoic tenet: all people, except the wise, are mad.

---

87. Reciprocity is at the heart of Greco-Roman ideas of benevolence. See S.C. Mott, 'The Power of Giving and Receiving: Reciprocity in Hellenistic Benevolence', in Gerald F. Hawthorne (ed.), *Current Issues in Biblical and Patristic Interpretation* (Festschrift Merril C. Tenney; Grand Rapids: Eerdmans, 1975), pp. 60-72.

The influence of the topos is especially evident in the themes and illustrations found in ll. 77-257.[88] After identifying the most prominent forms of madness in his society—ambition, avarice, extravagance and superstition—Horace says that the covetous are the maddest of all (ll. 77-83). As an example of this he mentions Staberius who, because he considered poverty to be the greatest evil, had the full amount of his estate engraved on his tombstone. To consider wealth to be the greatest value is as foolish as throwing it away, as did Aristippus (ll. 84-102).

His most important theme is that wealth is to be used rightly, not hoarded or squandered. He first attacks the foolish consequences of meanness: misers live needlessly in want, only so that their son or freedman can 'swallow up' their inheritance. In accordance with the conventions of the topos, a number of the examples given show the miser to be hungry or in poor health (for example, ll. 111, 114, 124-126 and 142-157).

However, he adds that those who are ambitious and headstrong are just as mad. This point is illustrated by the story of a rich father with two sons, one a spendthrift and the other a miser. On his deathbed he expresses his concern at how they will manage the two farms he has left them, because he believes them each to be plagued by madness. He therefore makes a similar appeal to each of them:

> 'I therefore adjure you both, by our household gods, the one not to reduce, the other not to increase, what your father thinks is enough, and what nature sets as a limit. Further, that ambition may not tickle your fancy, I shall bind you both by an oath: whichever of you becomes aedile or praetor, let him be outlawed and accursed. Would you waste your wealth on vetches, beans and lupines, that you may play the swell and strut in the Circus, or be set up in bronze, though stripped, madman, of the money your father left: to the end, oh yes, that *you* may win the applause which Agrippa wins—a cunning fox mimicking a noble lion?' (176-186)

---

88. Other examples of his interaction with the topos can be found in Horace, *Sat.* 1.1.28-119; *Sat.* 1.2.1-24; *Sat.* 1.4.48-53, 103-11; *Sat.* 1.6.65-71. Of the philosophical content of Horace's satires, Mendell says, 'Simplicity of life is emphasised, avarice and ambition, self-indulgence, superstition, and ostentation, the life without the ideal of *virtus*, are severly arraigned' (C.W. Mendell, 'Satire as Popular Philosophy', *CP* 15 [1920], pp. 138-57 [149]). West describes Roman satire as 'an area of literature where stock material from Hellenistic popular philosophy often finds a home' (M.L. West, 'Near Eastern Material in Hellenistic and Roman Literature', *HSCP* 73 [1969], pp. 113-34).

This illustration of the twin dangers of prodigality and meanness by means of an inheritance story shares the same elements as the parable in Lk. 15.11-32, though the behavior of the father is different.

Horace then illustrates the madness of spendthrifts with examples of how sons (in one example a pair of brothers) give away or squander vast amounts of the wealth they inherit (224-246). Finally, it is worth noting his mention of the stock example of the converted prodigal Polemo in line 253-257.[89]

(iii) *Juvenal (fl. c. 100 CE)*. Juvenal's fourteenth satire begins by saying that children learn vices by example: 'There are many things of ill-repute ... which parents themselves point out and hand on to their sons' (ll. 1-3).[90] In saying this he echoes the repeated motif in the topos that avarice is a vice which is not natural but learnt.

The major part of Juvenal's fourteenth satire (lines 107-331) tackles the theme of avarice. It is the only vice that young people do not practise of their own free will, but have to learn by example.

He points out the negative consequences of avarice for individuals and society. In each case, the principle is related to the theme of parental instruction. Juvenal attacks the folly of fathers who teach their sons to worship wealth and to think that no poor person has ever been happy. Yet misers are mad fools because: (1) they live in want in order to be wealthy when they die; (2) they risk loss of all and ruin just to have more than they need; (3) the more wealth they have, the more they want.

Avarice removes all respect for laws and sense of shame and thus leads directly to acts of crime and injustice. Fathers who teach their sons to love money in practice encourage them to neglect their obligations to friends, kinsmen and society. The logical outcome of such parental teaching is that the son prays for his father's death, so that he can receive his inheritance.

Juvenal concludes by endorsing the principles of moderation and sufficiency, citing Epicurus and Socrates in support: 'Never does Nature say one thing and wisdom another' (l. 321).

89. Compare Epictetus, *Diss.* 3.1.14-15; 4.11.30; Diogenes Laertius, 4.16.
90. See also Juvenal, *Sat.* 14.31-33: 'So Nature ordains; no evil example corrupts us so soon and so rapidly as one that has been set at home, since it comes into the mind on high authority.'

j. *Neopythagoreanism*

(i) *Pseudo-Pythagoras (300–250 BCE).*[91] There are two sections in the *Golden Verses* that reflect an awareness of this topos: vv. 9-20 and vv. 32-38. The first is related to it in a more general way as a summary of the four cardinal virtues which make up σωφροσύνη: ἐγκράτεια, αἰδώς, δικαιοσύνη and φρόνησις. The wise are to be self-controlled with regard to the pleasures and passions of food, sleep, sex and anger. They are to avoid shameful acts through self-awareness. They are to practice justice. And they are not to forget the universality of death and the instability of property. The motifs of pleasures and passions, self-awareness, justice, and awareness of the instability of property all belong to the topos On Covetousness.

The second section, vv. 32-38, is part of a unit dealing with deliberation and reflection (vv. 27-44). At the centre of this unit is a set of three precepts, concerning physical health (vv. 32-34), a simple lifestyle (vv. 35-36) and spending money (vv. 37-38). The verses that refer to life style in general (vv. 35-36), are enclosed by verses dealing with the external goods of health (vv. 32-34) and money (vv. 37-38).[92] This ring structure links the motifs of health (ὑγιεία) and money, and advises moderation in both eating and spending. Pseudo-Pythagoras defines and advocates the mean by rejecting the opposing extremes of ill-timed extravagance and stinginess: 'Do not spend money at the wrong time like someone ignorant of good manners,/ nor be tight-fisted (μὴ δαπανᾶν παρὰ καιρὸν ὁποῖα καλῶν ἀδαήμων/μηδ' ἀνελεύθερος ἴσθι)' (vv. 37-38a).[93]

(ii) *The Sentences of Sextus (c. second century CE).*[94] Another example of the Neopythagorean interaction with the topos is found in the *Sen-*

---

91. Text and translation: Thom, 'Golden Verses', pp. 69-79.

92. Thom, 'Golden Verses', p. 141.

93. Thom ('Golden Verses', p. 144) comments that 'Pythagoreans were well-known for their liberal and magnanimous spending when the occasion demanded, usually in aid of Pythagoreans in need. According to Pythagoras it was possible to ensure 'liberal expenditures' (τὰ ἐλευθέρια δαπανήματα) if one practised economy'.

94. The text and translation used is that of Edwards and Wild: R.A. Edwards and R.A. Wild (eds.), *The Sentences of Sextus* (SBLTTS, 22; Chico: Scholars Press, 1981).

tences of Sextus. Because this is a loose collection of gnomic sayings, it would be artificial to identify a particular section that interacts with the topos.

Overall, the *Sentences* treat the familiar themes of the topos as follows: the love of money (φιλοχρηματία) is condemned because it reveals a love for the body and a misplaced trust. It is also a problem because avarice is an insatiable desire. Luxurious living is inhumane and contrary to the purpose of life, and it leads to ruin. The true wealth of the philosopher is self-control. The traditional virtues of temperance, freedom and self-sufficiency are advocated. Food and drink are specifically mentioned as an area in which moderation should be practised. The *Sentences* advocate the ideal of detachment from possessions (pace Edwards and Wild).[95] This is expressed in injunctions to possess only necessities, or nothing, and to give to all in need. R.L. Wilken has pointed out that all these are related to the ideal of being like God.[96]

Sometimes sentences containing themes that are characteristic of the topos are found in close proximity to one another.[97] For example, sentences 137-140 mention avarice (πλεονεξία), the longing for possessions (ὄρεξις κτήσεως), injustice (ἀδικία), self-love (φιλαυτία), love of pleasure (φιληδονία) and excess (τὸ πλέον).

k. *Middle Platonism*

(i) *Plutarch (c. 50–120 CE)*. While Plutarch makes frequent references to the use of money and wealth in the *Lives* and the *Moralia*, his principal treatment of this topos is *On the Love of Wealth*.[98] In this discourse

---

95. Edwards and Wild, *Sentences*, p. 1.

96. R.L. Wilken, 'Wisdom and Philosophy in Early Christianity', in *idem* (ed.), *Aspects of Wisdom in Judaism and Early Christianity* (University of Notre Dame Center for the Study of Judaism and Christianity in Antiquity, 1; Notre Dame: University of Notre Dame Press, 1975), pp. 143-68 (151-52).

97. This can be seen from this list: *Sent. Sextus* 13, 15, 17, 18, 19, 50, 52, 73, 76, 81, 82b, 88, 91b, 98, 116, 117, 127, 128, 137, 138, 139b, 140, 146, 192, 193, 210a, 227, 228, 260, 263, 264a, 264b, 266, 267, 268, 269, 274b, 294, 295, 300, 310, 312, 329, 330, 334, 345, 365, 371, 377, 378, 379, 382, 392, 412.

98. Plutarch, *Mor.* 523c-528b. See also the fragments ΠΕΡΙ (or ΚΑΤΑ) ΠΛΟΥΤΟΥ in Stobaeus, *Anth.* 4.31.85 (5, 765, Hense), 4.31.86 (5, 765, Hense); 4.32.16 (5, 784, Hense); and 4.32.17 (5, 784, Hense); and Plutarch, *Frag.*, pp. 276-78.

he writes in the tradition of the Cynic-Stoic diatribe.[99] O'Neil observes that greed is the central theme, and, of the associated vices of miserliness, prodigality, extravagance, ostentation and ambition, prodigality receives most attention.[100]

The influence of the topos On Covetousness is seen in the title, the themes and the language used. There are many correspondences with the ideas and terminology of Aristotle's treatment of liberality in the *Nicomachean Ethics*.

Money cannot be the greatest blessing because it cannot buy the philosophic virtues of peace of mind, greatness of spirit, serenity, confidence, and self-sufficiency. Wealth only increases the desire (ἐπιθυμία) for money, the craving for money (φιλαργυρία) and the greed for gain (πλεονεξία).

He advocates the ideal of liberality by the rejection of opposing excesses. Avaricious people either spend all they get, or spend nothing. Whether they are prodigal or miserly, they are without the necessities of life. Meanness and illiberality (μικρολογία καὶ ἀνελευθερία) are more disgusting than prodigality (ἀσωτία) because misers do not make use of what they take from others. They claim to be storing up wealth for their children to inherit, but instead they ruin them by infecting them with their own avarice. Those who use money excessively are not much better.

His endorsement of moderation is evident in his rejection of great wealth as foolish superfluity. In the use of what suffices (τῶν ἀρκούντων) the rich are no better off than those of modest means. At the end of the essay, Plutarch returns to the true source of happiness: the philosophic virtues, summed up by the ideal of σωφροσύνη.

---

99. O'Neil notes that this is demonstrable in the style, language, themes and specific points of contact with other writings in this tradition E.N. O'Neil, '*De Cupiditate Divitiarum (Moralia 523C-528B)*', in H.D. Betz (ed.), *Plutarch's Ethical Writings and Early Christian Literature* [SCHNT, 4; Leiden: E.J. Brill, 1978], pp. 289-362 [292-98]).

100. Prodigality 'receives more attention and consumes more space than any other item in the canon, and it is the subject which opens and concludes the treatise. In fact, it occurs in every chapter except 5–6, but the chief passages are ch. 1 (523d-e); ch. 2 (523f-524a); ch. 3 (524b, d); ch. 4 (524d-e); ch. 7 (526e); the whole of chs. 8-10 (527a-528d)' (O'Neil, '*De Cupiditate*', p. 300).

Much of the vocabulary of the essay is typical of texts using the topos On Covetousness. Apart from terms directly related to wealth, such as χρήματα, φιλοπλουτία, ἐπιθυμία, φιλαργυρία, ἀργύριον καὶ χρύσιον, πλοῦτος, πενία, φιλοχρηματία, οὐσία, μικρολογία and βαλλάντιον, there are many other equally significant words and phrases. Chief among these are those relating to common motifs or metaphors: sickness and health (such as προσεξεμέω in 524a and θεραπεύω, ἐκβολή, καθαρμός, ἰατρός, πυρέσσω and νόσος in 524c, d), trade (such as χρεωφειλέτης, συμβόλαιος, τόκος, ὑποθήκη in 524a), household management (such as οἰκέτης, γεωργός, χρεώστης in 525a) and inheritances (such as the many references in 526a-527a) and all the trappings of feasts, festivals and banquets (as in 527b-528b).

(ii) *Philo of Alexandria (30 BCE–50 CE)*. Philo frequently interacts with the topos On Covetousness, most often in the course of his ethical allegorization of Scripture.[101] As a non-allegorical example of his employment of the topos, I examine his description of the common life of the Essenes in *Every Good Man is Free* 76-86.

These few paragraphs contain many of the themes and much of the distinctive terminology of the topos. Cities are known for their lawlessness (ἀνομία) and their capacity to cause moral disease (νόσος), while villages are morally sound. Those who labor on farms (γεωπονέω) or who practice useful crafts benefit the community, not those who hoard (θησαυροφυλακέω) money or let out land for revenue. Instead of money and land, the conventional symbols of wealth, Philo describes the ideals of frugality and contentment (ὀλιγόδεια καὶ εὐκολία) as the greatest wealth.

The technique of contrasting vices with virtues is also employed in his account of their activities: (1) The rural community rejects all trade (ἐμπορία) as a temptation to covetousness (πλεονεξία), and all slavery as a violation of the law of human equality (ἰσότης); (2) they believe that people are brothers by nature, and that it is covetousness which has replaced affinity with estrangement and friendship with enmity (ἀντ᾽ οἰκειότητος ἀλλοτριότητα καὶ ἀντὶ φιλίας ἔχθραν ἐργασαμένη);

101. See also: *Sacr.* 32; *Det. Pot. Ins.* 32, 34; *Poster. C.* 34, 116; *Gig.* 35, 37; *Agr.* 83; *Conf. Ling.* 47-49, 166; *Mut. Nom.* 103; *Abr.* 26, 133-134; *Jos.* 216; *Vit. Mos.* 1.56, 1.324, 2.186; *Dec.* 142-53, 155; *Spec. Leg.* 1.21-27 (esp. 23-24), 1.278, 2.43, 2.52, 4.5, 4.54, 4.65, 4.129-31; *Praem. Poen.* 15, 121; *Omn. Prob. Lib.* 8, 65-67; *Vit. Cont.* 2, 70; and *Flacc.* 91.

(3) they take the ethical side of philosophy seriously, emphasizing the love of God, love of virtue and love of humanity (φιλόθεος καὶ φιλάρετος καὶ φιλανθρώπος).

He extols the merits of their lifestyle by listing a whole cluster of positive virtues. Negatively, they are free from the love of money, reputation and pleasure (ἀφιλοχρήματος, ἀφιλόδοξος καὶ ἀφιλήδονος). Positively, they exemplify such ideals as self-mastery, endurance, frugality, simple living, contentment, humility, respect for the law and steadiness. Their ideals of benevolence, equality and fellowship (κοινωνία) are given concrete expression in their sharing of their homes, money, food and meals.

4. *Characteristic Features of the Topos On Covetousness*

Before proceeding to examine the influence of the topos περὶ ἀδικίας καὶ φιλαργυρίας καὶ πλεονεξίας on Lk. 15.11-32, it is important to attempt to consolidate the observations on the texts and extracts discussed above.

Thematically, all the texts deal with the right use of possessions, but views on the correct expression of that ideal vary according to philosophical orientation. While all the texts reject covetousness, Plato emphasizes the ideal of justice and Aristotle upholds the ideal of liberality. Mild Cynics think only in terms of freedom from want, while austere Cynics positively embrace poverty. Stoics do not condemn honestly-acquired wealth, but emphasize the correct attitude to wealth and its wise use. They speak of sufficiency, contentment and moderation. The ideal of having sufficient wealth and using it liberally and wisely is also upheld by the Eclectics, Neopythagoreans and the Middle Platonists.

Aristotle's ideal of liberality is widely endorsed: wealth is neither to be hoarded nor squandered, but rightly used. Although Epicureans, with their central goal of true pleasure, appear not to fit into this overall picture, they too uphold the ideals of prudence, honour and justice.

The rejection of injustice, covetousness and avarice is a recurrent motif. There is a hierarchical relationship between these three terms: injustice is the broadest, covetousness is an expression of injustice and avarice is the surest indicator of covetousness. All are rejected because of their damaging consequences for the individual and the community. Representatives of all the philosophical affiliations also reject many associated vices: love of honour; unchecked and insatiable desire; passions; meanness and prodigality; luxury, extravagance and pleasure; self-indulgence; sexual immorality; ambition; superstition; physical and moral disease; and excesses of all kinds, particularly eating and drinking. One of the most common metaphors for covetousness is that of sickness and disease.

There is also extensive agreement on the corresponding virtues that are admired and endorsed: self-sufficiency (αὐτάρκεια); true friendship; moral and physical health; temperance, moderation (σωφροσύνη) and simple living; wisdom, reason and prudence; work; equality; and harmony. They are understood generally enough to be used to support the differing emphases of the various philosophical schools.

The vices and virtues listed above are part of a wider range of terms that are characteristic of the topos. These have been noted in the course of the discussion and do not need to be listed here. The same is true of the many terms referring to money and possessions. There are many terms describing quantity of possessions, attachment to or detachment from possessions, and the consequences of such attachment or detachment. Prominent amongst these are ἐλευθεριότης, ἀνελευθερία, ἀσωτία, ἀπόλλυμι, ἐπιθυμέω and ἐπιθυμία.

While all writers advocate the ideal of sufficiency in some form or other, there are differences of opinion on how much is sufficient. All are agreed that poverty is not an evil, but only the austere Cynics actively embrace it. At the other end of the spectrum, representatives of the Middle and Roman Stoa include generosity to oneself as part of the right use of possessions. These and other schools point out that prosperity can never be regarded as permanent but remains uncertain.

There are also differences of opinion on the best form of property ownership. Some, like the Cynics, uphold the ideal of shared ownership, while others, like Aristotle, the Roman Stoics and the Eclectics, are careful to respect private property.

Formally, ideals are advocated using similar techniques. Most often the ideal is illustrated by means of opposites or contrasts. Opposing extremes are rejected in favor of a mean which is endorsed. The negative consequences of vices are contrasted with the positive benefits of the central virtue.

The point is often supported by means of illustrations. These frequently take the form of character studies, such as the Peripatetic treatments of particular character traits, or reference to well-known examples from history and literature. The positive example of the labors and hardships of Heracles is sometimes mentioned.

A favourite subject of illustrations is the wrong use of possessions, either through extravagant excess and waste, or through miserly hoarding. Sometimes these extremes are depicted as the actions of brothers or twins. They are also frequently thought of as typical of the behavior of those who inherit money. This theme is often illustrated in some detail, exploring different aspects of inheritances, from the viewpoint both of those bequeathing the wealth and those inheriting it. Associated with these are discussions of how to train young men to have the right attitude to possessions. Examples are given of those who began with the wrong attitude to possessions, but who changed as a result of philosophical instruction or example.

Part III

THE PARABLE AND THE TOPOS

Chapter 5

THE PRODIGAL YOUNGER SON

I now begin my moral reading of Lk. 15.11-32. In Chapter 4 I outlined the shape of the topos περὶ ἀδικίας καὶ φιλαργυρίας καὶ πλεονεξίας in Greco-Roman moral philosophy, noting the cluster of related issues that are usually found in texts dealing with the topos. These I summarized as right and wrong expressions of receiving, giving and possessing.

I turn now to the Parable of the Prodigal Son to examine how language and themes found in texts dealing with the topos On Covetousness are used here by Luke. I will show that the parable illustrates three of the most frequently treated themes: the vices of prodigality and meanness, and the virtue of liberality. In Greco-Roman discussions of these moral values, certain words and themes recur. For example, texts dealing with prodigality frequently refer to waste, desire, want and ruin. Such words and themes are identified in Lk. 15.11-32, and their meaning and function within the parable, and within other moral texts and statements that are expressions of the same topos, are compared. That is, other expressions of the topos are used as paradigmatic co-texts for the parable of the prodigal son, along with the other L parables.

The benefits of this moral reading will become evident as we proceed. We will be able to see that all the constituent components of the parable, sections as well as individual words and phrases, contribute to the unified moral thrust of the parable. We know the kind of ingredients that are usually found in texts dealing with the topos On Covetousness. When these elements are found distributed throughout Lk. 15.11-32, it is possible to show that the parable was composed as a unified whole.

As well as the question of unity, we are able to identify what is conventional and what is peculiar to Luke, by comparing his treatment of the topos with those of other authors. This gives us insights into his method of communicating his Christian perspective. Many points of contact with the views and approaches of the moral philosophers show his apologetic sensitivity to his cultural milieu, and his desire to show that Christians share many of the same moral ideals and concerns as their pagan contemporaries. The similarities also enable the differences to stand out more clearly.

Thus, I am able to demonstrate the unity of the parable using a moral framework that would have been familiar to Luke's intended readers. I am also able to show that Luke was a skillful apologist and teacher, and that he used the conventions of the topos On Covetousness to facilitate communication with his intended readers and to show the relationship between Greco-Roman conceptions of the virtue of liberality and his Christian message.

1. *The Rejection of the Ideal of Common Ownership*

The parable begins, like many good stories, with the disruption of a stable, even idyllic, state of affairs. A father and his two sons live together on the family farm. Although the farm is owned by the father, the parable makes it clear that he views and treats it as a common resource, to be used for the benefit of all who live and work on it. He regards his sons as having a full share in it (vv. 31b-c), and even the humblest hired workers are generously paid (v. 17b).

This situation of common ownership and shared benefits only becomes clear as the parable unfolds, for the plot begins with an event that changes the status quo. The younger son asks his father to give him his share (μέρος) of the property.[1] Exegetes usually assume that the son was entitled to make this request, and attempt to relate it to Old Testament law, or Jewish customs prevailing in Palestine in the time of Jesus.[2] However, when the parable is read with other examples of the topos On Covetousness in mind, the first words of the younger son, 'Father, give me' (πάτερ, δός μοι), v. 12, suggest that the son might be

1. J. Schneider, 'μέρος', *TDNT*, IV, pp. 594-98 (595), defines the word here to mean the share of the proceeds of a sale.
2. See, for example, Marshall, *Gospel of Luke*, p. 607; and Fitzmyer, *Luke*, p. 1087. Compare, however, Moxnes (*Economy*, p. 61) who notes the similarity between the situation in which Luke records the parable of the rich fool (Lk. 12.13) and the situation described at the start of Lk. 15.11-32. He comments, 'For a son to claim his share of the inheritance while his father was still alive is a challenge to his father's authority, as well as an upset of the family economy. After the death of the father, of course, a division of the inheritance would be the normal procedure, but one that frequently caused conflicts between brothers (12.13).'

motivated by avarice. This impression is confirmed by the picture that
the parable subsequently paints of the generosity of the father and the
prodigality of the younger son. From this perspective, questions about
what Palestinian legal situation might underlie the plot move to the
background. It becomes evident that Luke is telling a story about a matter of considerable importance in Greco-Roman culture, namely the
destructive effects of avarice upon family life.[3] He is showing that
Christians too are concerned about it and are aware of the importance of
the virtue of liberality both for the individual and the community.

a. *Concern about Covetousness in Society*
Greco-Roman philosophers, moralists and satirists frequently expressed
concern at the immorality of the young. This is evident in their discussions on the correct way to bring up young men and women,[4] and in
their attempts to identify why the young are particularly susceptible to
the vices of prodigality and sexual immorality.[5]

3.   A.J. Malherbe, 'Exhortation in 1 Thessalonians', in *idem*, *Paul and the Popular Philosophers* (Minneapolis: Fortress Press, 1989), pp. 49-66 (53), notes that
this problem was widely discussed by ancient moralists: 'They thought that covetousness caused children to be hostile to their fathers to the point that they betrayed
(*prodidontai*) them, and that parents in turn became more demanding (*baryteroi*) of
their children.' He refers to Stobaeus, *Anth.* 4.31.84 (5.764, 2-5 and 765, 12; Wachsmuth–Hense), and the comment on the failure to respect the claims of family and
friends (οὔτε συγγενὴς οὔτε ξεῖνος) in the pursuit of wealth in G.A. Gerhard,
Phoinix von Kolophon: Texte und Untersuchungen (Leipzig: B.G. Teubner, 1909),
pp. 14-18. This motif is one of the indicators of the topos On Covetousness. Other
example are *Ps.-Phoc.* 44-47 and *Sib. Or.* 2.115-18.
4.   Musonius Rufus argues that children should be brought up austerely, and
not in luxurious circumstances. He compares two boys, one reared in luxury and the
other in a Spartan manner. The latter is more easily able to heed the philosopher's
argument that 'death, toil, poverty, and the like are not evils, or again that life,
pleasure, wealth and the like are not goods' (Musonius, *Frag.* 1 [34, 14-16, 31-33]).
As I noted in Chapter 1, this theme is also found in the plays of Terence.
5.   H.W. Hollander, 'The Ethical Character of the Patriarch Joseph: A Study in
the Ethics of *The Testaments of the XII Patriarchs*', in G.W.E. Nickelsburg, Jr
(ed.), *Studies on the Testament of Joseph* (SBLSCS, 5; Missoula: Scholars Press,
1975), pp. 47-104 (95 n. 207 and 97 n. 247) gives the following examples: *T. Reub.*
1.6; 2.9; *T. Jud.* 11.1; Prov. 7.10 LXX; 22.15; Plutarch, *Mor.* 450f; 496f-497a; Philo,
Spec. Leg. 3.51; *Virt.* 39-40.

They generally attribute prodigality to the passions of youth,[6] but the underlying vices which cause it, avarice and covetousness, are regarded as vices that are learnt from bad examples set by parents or society as a whole.[7]

Thus, they give two mutually exclusive explanations for the origins of the vice of covetousness: (1) the natural human susceptibility to the vices of intemperance and pleasure, which lead on to the more serious vices of injustice and greed;[8] and (2) the view that avarice is such an unattractive vice that it could only be learnt by outward example.[9]

In this parable, Luke does not investigate the origins of the covetousness of the two sons, nor make it clear which moral explanation he would favor. Despite being brought up by a liberal father,[10] the sons are both covetous, the younger being prodigal and the older, mean. This accords well with the view that people are naturally covetous. Yet the

6.   Prodigality is regularly viewed as a vice of the young. Plato thinks that it is the responsibility of rulers to prohibit prodigal youth from spending and wasting their substance (*Resp.* 555c [cf. 559d-561b]). This is why Aristotle says prodigals sometimes change simply by growing up, (*Eth. Nic.* 4.1.31). See too *T. Jud.* 11.1; Philo, *Somn.* 2.148: τὸν μειρακιώδη τῶν ἀσώτων; Epictetus, *Diss.* 3.1.13, 14; Pseudo-Heraclitus, *Ep.* 7 (202, 15): μειράκια τῆς οὐσίας ἐκβεβρωμένα; and the reference to νεωτερικὰς ἐπιθυμίας in 2 Tim. 2.22. Compare Demea's words to his prodigal son Aeschines in Terence, *Adelph.* 986-95. Horace (*Sat.* 2.3.238) gives this convention an ironic twist when he describes a young man who gave away his huge inheritance of one thousand talents, saying he was lazy and unworthy to possess so much.

7.   Aristotle (*Pol.* 7.15.7) says that even young children can be tainted with illiberality (ἀνελευθερία) by what they see and hear. The Stoic Seneca (*Ep.* 115.11) blames the example both parents and society set children. Eclectic moralists such as Cicero and Juvenal speak of the corruption and degradation caused by the worship of wealth. Cicero (*Off.* 2.20.[71]) says, 'But the moral sense of today is demoralized and depraved by our worship of wealth', and Juvenal (*Sat.* 14. 226-28; 250-51) blames wealth-loving fathers for their sons' depravity and premature desire for their inheritances. He recommends that parents should teach their sons to give aid to friends or relatives instead.

8.   *Ep. Arist.* 277, 278.

9.   Juvenal, *Sat.* 14.107-108 comments that avarice is the only vice which the young do not practice of their own free will, but which is urged on them against their natural inclinations.

10.   He divides his living (v. 12c); his workers have more than enough (v. 17b); he is generous in his celebration (vv. 22b-24e and 32a). See the following chapter for the discussion of these and other indicators.

parable also expresses a positive view of the self as a place where moral reflection and transformation take place (v. 17a), and Luke shows his awareness of the widespread problem of covetousness in the descriptions of the mean and unjust citizens of the foreign country (vv. 15b-16c). These factors endorse the view that covetousness is taught and sustained by wrong social attitudes.

Thus, while Luke's moral position can often be related to that of specific philosophical affiliations, particularly those of the mild Cynics and Roman Stoics, he cannot be absolutely identified with any of them. He is not a moral philosopher, but a Christian apologist and teacher who makes skillful use of prevailing moral viewpoints.[11] In telling a story about a young man who asks for, and then wastes, his inheritance, he was telling a story of current moral interest to his readers.

b. *The Ideal of Shared Possessions*
When the parable is read as a whole, it also becomes evident that the younger son's request introduces the issue of private ownership into a situation of shared ownership. The moral issues within Luke's story are seen more sharply when the parable is seen as an illustration of the way the ideal of shared possessions is destroyed by the vice of covetousness.

The utopian ideal of community of goods has a long history in Greek literature.[12] Later writers attribute it to Pythagoras[13] and the Spartans, but it is first given impetus by Plato,[14] who regards community of goods as part of his ideal society.[15] Mealand points out that this ideal was a constant theme of philosophers, poets, historians and romance-writers from the fifth century onwards,[16] as shown by the widespread

11. Compare the similar comments on Paul's relationship with moral philosophy in A.J. Malherbe, *Paul and the Thessalonians: The Philosophic Tradition of Pastoral Care* (Philadelphia: Fortress Press, 1987), pp. 108-109.

12. See van der Horst, 'Hellenistic Parallels to Acts 2.1-47', pp. 217-18.

13. Diogenes Laertius, 8.10.

14. This is pointed out by D.L. Mealand, 'Community of Goods and Utopian Allusions in Acts II–IV', *JTS* NS 28 (1977), pp. 96-97 (97), with reference to Plato, *Crit.* 110d; *Resp.* 5.464d; 8.543b.

15. It is not clear whether Plato saw communal ownership as limited to the governing class, as in *Reps.* 3.416c-17b, or as applicable to all, as in *Leg.* 5.739c. See A. Erskine, *The Hellenistic Stoa: Political Thought and Action* (Ithaca, NY: Cornell University Press, 1990), p. 104 n. 1.

16. Mealand, 'Community of Goods', p. 98 nn. 1-3, refers amongst others to

occurrence of the catch phrases: '(consider) nothing one's own (οὐδὲν, or μηδὲν, ἴδιον) and everything common' (πάντα, or ἄπαντα, κοινά):

> In ever varied form Greek and Roman writers maintained that in some long vanished golden age, or in distant climes, or in some ideal future state people had shared, or did share, or would share, everything in common.[17]

It also has a firm place in Jewish tradition, with these views and phrases being found in Philo and Josephus.[18]

Even writers who support the private ownership of property argue that possessions should be used for the common good. Aristotle teaches that possessions should be privately owned, but used as common property.[19] His arguments for private ownership are based on pleasure: private ownership gives pleasure as a legitimate form of self-love and is necessary for experiencing the pleasure of giving favors to others.[20] He

Aristophanes, *Eccl.* 590ff., 610ff. 670ff.; Euripides, *Andr.* 376-77; Aristotle, *Pol.* 2.1-2 (1261-63); Diogenes Laertius, 6.72; 7.33; 8.23; Diodorus Siculus, 5.45; Cicero, *Off.* 1.16.51; Strabo, 7.3.9; Porphyry, *V.P.* 20; Seneca, *Ep.* 90; Virgil, *Georg.* 1.125-26; Tibullus, 1.3.43-44; Ovid, *Met.* 1.89-90; Iamblichus, *V.P.* 30.167-68. See also the Cynic Pseudo-Anacharsis, *Ep.* 9. (46, 12-14); the Neopythagorean *Carm. Aur.* 38a; and *Sent. Sextus* 228.

17. Mealand, 'Community of Goods', p. 98. See also the discussion of natural law and utopia in antiquity, with examples from Aristophanes, Ovid, Virgil, Strabo and Seneca in Hengel, *Property*, pp. 3-8.

18. Mealand, 'Community of Goods', p. 98 n. 4-7, refers to Philo, *Hypoth.* 11.4; *Omn. Prob. Lib.* 85-86; and Josephus, *Ant.* 15.104 (371); 18.1.5 (20); *War* 2.8.3 (122).

19. Aristotle, *Pol.* 7.10.6.

20. 'And moreover to feel that a thing is one's private property makes an inexpressibly great difference in one's pleasure; for the universal feeling of love for oneself is surely not purposeless, but a natural instinct (μὴ γὰρ οὐ μάτην τὴν πρὸς αὐτὸν ἔχει φιλίαν ἕκαστος ἀλλ᾽ ἔστι τοῦτο φυσικόν). Selfishness (φίλαυτον), on the other hand is justly blamed; but this is not to love oneself (φιλεῖν ἑαυτὸν) but to love oneself more than one ought (ἀλλὰ τὸ μᾶλλον ἢ δεῖ φιλεῖν), just as covetousness (φιλοχρήματον) means loving money to excess—since some love of self, money and so on is practically universal (ἐπεὶ φιλοῦσί γε πάντες ὡς εἰπεῖν ἕκαστον τῶν τοιούτων). Moreover, to bestow favors and assistance (χαρίσασθαι καὶ βοηθῆσαι) on friends or visitors or comrades (φίλοις ἢ ξένοις ἢ ἑταίροις) is a great pleasure, and a condition of this is the private ownership of property (*Pol.* 2.2.6.).

Irwin is critical of Aristotle's argument that private property is a necessary condition for private generosity, and argues that it is possible to think of other systems

is more realistic about human nature, recognizing the problem of covetousness, the need for accountability and responsibility in the use of resources, and the fact that societies are not uniform in composition.[21] The eclectic Cicero wholeheartedly accepts private property.[22] However, he endorses the ideal of common ownership of all that is not legally assigned to someone for private ownership.[23] He also insists that the private accumulation of property should not hurt other people.[24]

Stoics, such as Musonius and Epictetus, stress that possessions should not be spent on luxuries, but should be used to meet the needs of relatives, friends, fellow-citizens and the gods.[25] Those who do otherwise act unjustly, and neglect their duties.[26]

> Tell me, then, is it fitting for each man to act for himself alone or to act in the interest of his neighbour also, not only that there may be homes in the city but also that the city may not be deserted and that the common good may best be served? If you say that each one should look out for his own interests alone [τὸ αὑτοῦ σκεπτέον μόνον], you represent man as no different from a wolf or any other of the wildest beasts which are born to live by violence and plunder [βίας καὶ πλεονεξίας], sparing nothing from which they may gain some advantage, having no part in a

of distribution and ownership which would also allow generosity. He notes that one such system is envisaged in the parable of the talents (Mt. 25.14-30) and the parable of the pounds (Lk. 19.12-27). See T.H. Irwin, 'Aristotle's Defense of Private Property', in D. Keyt and F.D. Miller, Jr (eds.), *A Companion to Aristotle's Politics* (Oxford: Basil Blackwell, 1991), pp. 200-225 (222-24).

21. See L.T. Johnson, *Sharing Possessions: Mandate and Symbol of Faith* (OBT; Philadelphia: Fortress Press, 1981), pp. 124-25.

22. It is the basis of his comments on generosity in Cicero, *Off.* 2.

23. Cicero, *Off.* 1.51: 'All things which nature has produced for the common use of men should be kept as common, with the proviso that those things which are assigned by statutes and civil law should be held as laid down by those laws, while everything else should be considered as in the Greek proverb, everything is common among friends' (cited and trans. by Erskine, *Hellenistic Stoa*, pp. 109-10. Erskine refers also to *Off.* 1.51; 3.53. Seneca, *Ben.* 7.4-12, also reconciles the ideals of common ownership and private property.

24. Cicero, *Off.* 1.25: 'I do not find fault with the accumulation of property if it hurts no one, but damage to others is always to be avoided.'

25. In Musonius, *Frag.* 19, 'On clothing and shelter', Musonius argues that money spent on luxurious buildings could better be spent on public and private charity (122, 12-32). Compare Musonius, *Frag.* 20 (126, 4-8).

26. Musonius, *Frag.* 20 (126, 11-31).

life in common with others, no part in cooperation with others, no share of common justice.[27]

Such criticisms of individual self-interest in the use of possessions reveal the injustice of the younger son's request.[28]

The above examples show that this parable relates closely to the conviction of many Greco-Roman moralists that the vice of covetousness is antithetical to the long-cherished ideals of shared ownership and common use of possessions. It is an issue which Luke addresses elsewhere in his Gospel (Lk. 12.15 and 16.14 and adjacent parables), and to which he returns in Acts 2 and 4.

Seen from this perspective, the younger son's request at the start of the parable and the elder son's complaint at the end are both departures from an ideal represented by their father.

The vitality of the ideal is seen in the way the father and his household do not suffer any apparent hardship, even after the younger son leaves with his share of the capital. Only the two sons suffer want, the younger through prodigal waste of his resources, and the elder because of a miserly unwillingness to use the resources which he shares with his father (v. 31b-c). They illustrate the truth of Plato's maxim that 'Poverty is a matter of increased greed and not decreased substance [πενίαν ἡγητέον εἶναι μὴ τὸ τὴν οὐσίαν ἐλάττω ποιεῖν, ἀλλὰ τὸ τὴν ἀπληστίαν πλείω]'.[29] Thus, at a moral level, the parable is a creative apology for the virtue of liberality and its ideal social expression of shared possessions.

2. Gathering and Scattering

The younger son's immediate action on receiving his share of his father's capital begins the process of confirming that his request is moti-

27. Musonius, *Frag.* 14 (92, 17-25).

28. A common definition of ἀδικία in Greek ethics is an unjust desire for more than one's fair share. Thom refers to the popular definition of δικαιοσύνη as 'to render to each his due' found in Plato, *Resp.* 331e; and Aristotle, *Rhet.* 1366b. By this definition, injustice is defined as wanting more than one's due, that is as πλεονεξία. See further, Thom, 'Golden Verses', pp. 113-14, and nn. 165-67.

29. Plato, *Leg.* 5.736e. Compare Plutarch's comment on those who spend their living on superfluous luxuries and then find themselves in want: 'For his ailment is not poverty, but insatiability and avarice (πενία γὰρ οὐκ ἔστιν ἀλλ᾽ ἀπληστία τὸ πάθος αὐτοῦ καὶ φιλοπλουτία), arising from the presence in him of a false and unreflecting judgement (διὰ κρίσιν φαύλην καὶ ἀλόγιστον ἐνοῦσαν)' (*Mor.* 524d).

vated by avarice. Without delay, he gathers up what he has been given and scatters it. The two verbs that Luke uses to describe these actions, συνάγω ('to gather everything together') and διασκορπίζω ('to scatter or squander'), are a pair that have connotations of injustice, covetousness and avarice, both in Luke's other L parables and beyond.

The first verb, συνάγω (v. 13a) is used in Lk. 12.17 and 18, where it refers to the rich fool's gathering and storing of his crops.[30] In Lk. 15.13 it is usually understood to mean 'to turn into cash'. Wettstein's reference to Plutarch, *Cato Minor* 6.7 (772c) 'κληρονομίαν ... εἰς ἀργύριον συναγαγών', has been followed by many others,[31] supported with evidence from the papyri.[32] A Latin inscription by Domitian from 82 CE reflects a similar usage in Latin.[33]

This is an attractive interpretation, and may well help explain what he did with his share of the land.[34] But it overlooks the regular moral connotations of the word, for the gathering (συνάγω) of riches such as gold and silver is frequently described in Jewish wisdom literature as an

---

30. LNSM (domain 85.48) explains συνάγω in Lk. 15.13 as 'to collect and put in a safe place'.

31. For example, BAGD, s.v. συνάγω; J.M. Creed, *The Gospel According to St. Luke: The Greek Text with Introduction, Notes and Indices* (London: MacMillan, 1930), p. 199; Jeremias, *Parables*, p. 129; Marshall, *Gospel of Luke*, p. 607; and Fitzmyer, *Luke*, p. 1087.

32. 'The verb is frequently used of the total amount, the full sum, received by sale or by purchase... It would seem, therefore, that by συναγαγὼν πάντα in Lk. 15.13 we must understand with Field (*Notes*, p. 68) that the prodigal converted his goods into money, sold all off and realized their full value, rather than that he "gathered all together" to take with him' (MM, p. 600).

33. 'And I am moved also by the letter of the deified Augustus, a most diligent and gracious Leader towards his Fourth Legionaries, in which he advises them to assemble all their unsurveyed parcels of land and sell them (*ut omnia subsiciva sua colligerent et venderent*)' (ll. 22-26) (Text: M. McCrum and A.G. Woodhead [eds.], *Select Documents of the Principates of the Flavian Emperors: Including the Year of Revolution, AD 68–96* [Cambridge: Cambridge University Press, 1961]), p. 137. Translation: R.K. Sherk [trans. and ed.], *The Roman Empire: Augustus to Hadrian* [Translated Documents of Greece and Rome, 6; Cambridge: Cambridge University Press, 1988], p. 137).

34. Exegetes tend to overlook that this interpretation of συνάγω is offered tentatively by BAGD ('perhaps') and MM ('it would seem'), and not at all by LSJ. This use of the verb does not occur in the LXX, nor have I been able to locate any examples of it in other Hellenistic Jewish texts.

activity associated with wickedness.[35] In the LXX, the word is most frequently used of gathering people together for various purposes. But when it refers to the gathering of things, these are most often spoils, riches or money. Sirach provides a good illustration of this usage.[36] Thus, συνάγω is associated with the excessive gathering of wealth, the temptation to do so unjustly, and other vices associated with avarice.[37] This association is given a humorous twist in Plutarch's *The Divine Vengeance*, when he describes a money-loving prodigal as not gathering much wealth, but a huge reputation for wickedness.[38]

The same is true of the son's next action, expressed by the natural opposite of συνάγω, διασκορπίζω.[39] Having converted his share of his father's capital[40] into cash, he wastes it.[41] Luke's moral use of διασκορπίζω is seen in the parable which immediately follows the parable of the prodigal son, the parable of the unjust steward, which we have seen

35. E.g. *T. Ben.* 6.1-3. Hollander and de Jonge, *Commentary*, p. 427 refer to Job 20.15; 27.16; Prov. 28.8; Sir. 31.3, adding references to Gen. 47.14; 2 Chron. 24.5, 11; Zech. 9.3 LXX; 1 Bar. 1.6; 1 Macc. 3.31; 2 Esd. 8.14 as examples of συνάγειν being mentioned in conjunction with things like gold and silver. To these could be added Prov. 11.24; 13.11; Eccl. 2.8; Zech. 9.3; and 1 Esd. 4.18-19. Mic. 1.7 and Ezek. 16.31 refer to wages 'gathered' from prostitution.

36. Money can and should be gathered by people during their youth (Sir. 25.3), though it should be honestly acquired (Sir. 21.8) and freely used, for wealth is of no use to the μικρολόγος (Sir. 14.3, 4). The gathering of gold and silver is associated with being led astray by women (Sir. 47.18, 19). Sir. 31.3 observes that though rich and poor both work hard, they are not equally successful in gathering wealth.

37. Such as φιληδονία, a vice not mentioned in the LXX, though see 2 Tim. 3.4. Hollander and de Jonge, *Commentary*, p. 427, refer to *T. Reub.* 2.8; 3.6; *T. Iss.* 2.3; Plutarch, *Mor.* 139b; 140f; Philo, *Omn. Prob. Lib.* 21; *Spec. Leg.* 1.281; *Abr.* 24; *Op. Mund.* 158; and Clement of Alexandria, *Paed* . 3.7 (37, 2).

38. Plutarch, *Mor.* 563c: οὐσίαν μὲν οὐ πολλήν, δόξαν δὲ πονηρίας ἐν ὀλίγῳ πλείστην συνήγαγειν.

39. See Mt. 25.24, 26; Jn 11.52; and συνάγω—σκορπίζω in Lk. 11.23.

40. For examples of οὐσία with the meaning of land, property, estate, see MM, p. 467.

41. The loss of inherited land is severely criticized in a fragment from Menander, *Nauk.*, recorded in Athenaeus, *Deipn.* 4.166b-c: 'O dearest mother earth, how very reverend a possession, and beyond price, art thou in the eyes of sensible men! For it were only right, of course, that anyone who had inherited an ancestral estate and then devoured it (πατρῴαν παραλαβὼν γῆν καταφάγοι) should from that time on for ever sail the seas, and never so much as set foot on land, that he might thus come to see how good a thing he had inherited but failed to save.'

to be closely related to it. In Lk. 16.1 the accusation brought against the steward is that he has been squandering his possessions (διασκορπίζων τὰ ὑπάρχοντα) of his master. This mismanagement of the funds is sufficient to cause his dismissal and, with his subsequent actions, is spoken of as ἀδικία in Lk. 16.8.[42]

Thus, by using a pair of verbs often associated with the abuse of wealth, Luke introduces a note of moral criticism of the younger son's actions.

3. *Prodigal Living*

As the narrative unfolds, it becomes clear that the younger son's covetousness is motivated by a particular form of that vice, prodigality. Luke makes this explicit in his description of the son's behavior as 'prodigal living' (ζῶν ἀσώτως). The importance of this phrase has long been recognized in the traditional English title of the parable. However, it has not been widely understood to be a marker of the topos On Covetousness: one of the pointers to the moral problem that the parable explores. Here I examine how Luke's reference in v. 13b to the ζῶν ἀσώτως of the younger son helps to place the parable within the topos On Covetousness, and how this in turn guides our understanding of the phrase. One of the most important points made clear by this is that prodigality belongs to a 'family' of related vices and virtues. This identification of a cluster of related vices allows us to widen our understanding of prodigality by including texts that do not use the terms ἀσωτία or ἄσωτος, but a number of other related terms.[43]

In Plato's *Republic* prodigality is mentioned as the representative vice of the democratic character.[44] A young man who has been brought up in a narrow, 'economical' way, falls in with a crowd of wild revellers who falsely praise the vices of insolence, licence, prodigality and shamelessness:

42. The link between injustice and acts of lawlessness, dishonesty and bribery often found in the topos On Covetousness is not found in Lk. 15.11-32, but is present in other L parables: Lk. 16.1-8a and 18.10-14. Luke also describes Judas as buying a field for his ἀδικία in Acts 1.18 and Peter's charge of ἀδικία when Simon the magician tries to buy God's power with money.

43. This enables the inclusion of the stories of prodigal conversions given by Plutarch in *De Sera Numinis Vindicta* (*Mor.* 563b-f); and Epictetus, *Diss.* 3.1.12-15.

44. Plato, *Resp.* 559d-562a.

...they proceed to lead home from exile insolence and anarchy and prodigality and shamelessness, resplendent in a great attendant choir [χορός] and crowned with garlands, and in celebration of their praises they euphemistically denominate insolence 'good breeding', licence 'liberty', prodigality 'magnificence', and shamelessness 'manly spirit'.[45]

Here Plato associates ἀσωτία with the vices of insolence (ὕβρις), anarchy (ἀναρχία) and shamelessness (ἀναίδεια). For him, the opposing virtue is that of magnificence (μεγαλοπρέπεια), and this he links with the virtues of good breeding (εὐπαιδευσία), liberty (ἐλευθερία) and a manly spirit (ἀνδρεία). Plato's mention of prodigality here illustrates two features often found in other discussions of prodigality: other associated vices are mentioned and these are explained with reference to corresponding virtues, sometimes with a swipe at those who would catachrestically misapply both the virtues and the vices. Plato's text is an early example of the way the topos encourages us to ask: If the younger son is an example of prodigality, what do the other characters represent? The configuration of vices and virtues in this example suggests that the father is an example of the virtue of magnificence (μεγαλοπρέπεια), and the elder brother of the vices of 'want of manhood' (ἀνανδρία), 'rusticity' (ἀγροικία) and 'illiberality' (ἀνελευθερία).[46]

Aristotle's more explicit classification in the *Nicomachean Ethics* provides a basic framework for understanding prodigality as an excess of the virtue of liberality, with meanness as the corresponding deficiency. He first explains that prodigality is the vice of wasting one's *private* means and is therefore a form of self-ruin. He also distinguishes it from the popular idea of it as an expression of general lack of restraint and debauchery.[47]

He defines it as the excess of the virtue of liberality, expressed either through excessive giving or inadequate getting. These two forms are seldom found together, for it is hard to give to all without adequate receipts of money. On the rare occasions when this does happen the prodigal is easily cured when he grows older and poorer. Luke's prodigal is an example of this process: he takes only from his father, spends excessively in the foreign country, fails to earn money there, and is driven to the point of change by his poverty.

45. Plato, *Resp.* 560e-561a.
46. Plato, *Resp.* 560d.
47. Aristotle, *Eth. Nic.* 4.1.1-36; 4.1.5, 23, 30; 4.1.4.

Aristotle notes that such a person has none of the attributes of meanness but does possess the essentials of liberality: to give, and to refrain from taking. Such a prodigal is foolish, rather than evil, and simply needs to learn to give to the right people and to refrain from taking from the wrong ones. Again this describes the behavior of Luke's prodigal. However, Aristotle says that most prodigals are characterized by ignoble forms of receiving and spending: they take from anywhere, give to the unworthy and spend on debauchery (ἀκολασία) and pleasure (ἡδονή).[48]

This distinction between different forms of prodigality helps to explain why the elder brother accuses his younger sibling of wasting his money on prostitutes, although there is no other mention of this in the parable. He is simply repeating the commonly held view that all prodigals are sexually immoral.[49] This is of course also a harsher view of prodigality than that of Aristotle, because Jewish[50] and Greco-Roman[51]

---

48. Aristotle, *Eth. Nic.* 4.1.31, 33-35.

49. Aspects of the vices of covetousness and sexual immorality are frequently found together in lists of vices; (1) Examples in Greco-Roman literature include Dio Chrysostom, *Or.* 1.14. Plutarch parallels μοιχεία and ἀσωτία in a fragment *Against Wealth* (Stobaeus, *Anth.* 4.32.16 = 5.784, 9-11): 'Hunger never begot adultery, nor lack of money riotous living.' Amid a lengthy description of the different ways people delight in wrongdoing, Pseudo-Heraclitus refers to 'youths who have devoured their substance (μειράκια τῆς οὐσίας ἐκβεβρωμένα)', various forms of sexual abuses (including a mention of a licentious young man who is the lover of an entire city), gluttony and injustices (Pseudo-Heraclitus, *Ep.* 7. [202, 15-24]).

(2) Examples in Hellenistic Jewish literature: *Ps.-Phoc.* 3-6; *T. Jud.* 18.1-4a; *T. Lev.* 17.8-11.

(3) Examples in early Christian literature: Rom. 1.29-31; 1 Cor. 5.10-11; 6.9-10; Eph. 5.3-4; Col. 3.5, 8; 1 Thess. 4.3-6; 2 Tim. 3.2-5 (and implicitly in 1 Tim. 3.2-7); Mk 7.21-22; Mt. 15.19; *Did.* 2.1-6; *Barn.* 18-20; Polycarp, *Phil.* 2.2; 4.3; Hermas, *Man.* 6.2; 8.3-5; *Sim.* 6.5.5; 9.15. Van der Horst, *Pseudo-Phocylides*, pp. 114-15, remarks that in Eph. 4.19; 5.3, 5 licentiousness and covetousness are the principal vices of the heathen.

50. See, for example, Hos. 1-4; Isa. 1.21; 23.15-18; 57.1-6; Jer. 3.3; 5.1-9; Ezek. 16.30-42; 23; Wis. 14.12-29; Philo, *Leg. All.* 3.8; *Migr. Abr.* 69; *Mut. Nom.* 205; *Sacr.* 20-21; *Ps.-Phoc.* 177. De Jonge points out that warnings against πορνεία are prominent in the *Testaments of the Twelve* (M. de Jonge, 'Rachel's Virtuous Behaviour in the *Testament of Issachar*', in D.L. Balch, E. Ferguson and W.A. Meeks [eds.], *Greeks, Romans and Christians: Essays in Honor of Abraham J. Malherbe* [Minneapolis: Fortress Press, 1990], pp. 340-52 [346]).

51. Plato advises self-control and only permitted intercourse with harlots if done

authors viewed prostitution with disapproval. (Ironically, unscrupulous misers are commonly thought of as making money out of pandering.[52]) The elder brother's use of an eating metaphor (κατεσθίω) for the waste of the property may also reflect the conventional association of excessive eating with sexual indulgence in discussions of prodigals.[53]

Cynics criticize prodigals for losing their freedom through the love of money and pleasure. Dio, a mild Cynic, associates prodigality with recklessness and intemperate spending.[54] It is typified by the excesses of a festival.[55] Instead of such excesses, they call people to learn the moderate use of wealth (an expression of liberality). Austere Cynics, represented by some of the Cynic epistles, have a greater contempt for wealth. They call for a more ascetic life and more rigorous self-control. Prodigals are thought of as imprudent spendthrifts.[56]

The *Testaments of the Twelve Patriarchs* (a Hellenistic Jewish text associated with Middle Stoicism, and later popular in early Christianity) indicates the vices associated with ἀσωτία in such milieux. In *T. Jud.*

---

in secret (Plato, *Leg.* 840a-841c.). Aristotle advocates the education of Greek women to limit prostitution (Aristotle, *Pol.* 1.13, 15; 2.9, 17). The Stoics show even greater concern for sexual morality. Epictetus rejects adultery and fornication, as part of his concern to free people from passion (Epictetus, *Diss.* 4.1.21; 4.9.12), while Musonius condemns all extramarital intercourse, *Frag.* 12 (84, 30-88, 6). The moderate Cynic Dio Chrysostom attacks brothels and brothelkeepers in *Or.* 7.133-37. For an overview, see F. Hauck and S. Schulz, 'πόρνη, κτλ', *TDNT*, VI, pp. 579-95 (583-90).

52. Aristotle says that one of the typical occupations of mean people is that of brothel keeper (πορνοβοσκός), and Dio Chrysostom likens the avaricious miser to a πορνοβοσκός. See Aristotle, *Eth. Nic.* 4.1.40; and Dio Chrysostom, *Or.* 4.96-98.

53. A speech by Aeschines which charges Timarchus with immorality, prodigality and public corruption makes a conscious play on this metaphor: Aeschines says that he devoured his patrimony (τὸ καταφαγεῖν τὴν πατρῴαν οὐσίαν). 'And not only did he eat it up, but, if one may so say, he also drank it up (καὶ οὐ μόνον κατέφαγεν, ἀλλ᾽ εἰ οἷόν τ᾽ ἐστὶν εἰπεῖν, καὶ κατέπιεν)!' (Aeschines, *Tim.* 96). See also Plutarch, *Mor.* 526b-c; and Persius, *Sat.* 6.21-22.

54. Dio Chrysostom, *Or.* 20.4 (Discourse on Retirement), Compare *Or.* 30.33-34, 43 and 33.14. The first reference is cited by G. Mussies in *Dio Chrystostom*, p. 102, where he also cites Dio Chrysostom, *Or.* 4.103-104 as relating more generally to the contents of Lk. 15.13. See also Dio Chrysostom, *Or.* 17.4, 7, for references to ἀκρασία (= ἀκράτεια) as a lesser evil than covetousness (πλεονεξία). This discourse also contains frequent references to ἀπόλλυμι.

55. Dio Chrysostom, *Or.* 33.14; 30.43.

56. Pseudo-Crates, *Ep.* 22 (72, 1-5).

16.1 temperance with wine is the preferred virtue to the vices of desire (ἐπιθυμία), heated passion (πυρῶσις), debauchery (ἀσωτία) and sordid greed (αἰσχροκερδεία). In *T. Ash.* 4.4 pleasant days spent among the convivial (ἄσωτοι) are said to disgrace the body and pollute the soul. Finally, in *T. Ben.* 5.1 the prodigal (ἄσωτος) person is grouped with the evil (πονηρός) and the greedy (πλεονέκτης), who are all contrasted with the person whose mind is set toward the good. Such goodness turns the evil person back to the good, and leads the greedy to return what they have covetously taken from the oppressed.

The Roman Stoics Musonius and Epictetus do not mention ἀσωτία, preferring to speak of the vice of ἀκολασία, together with other related vices and their contrasting virtues.[57]

Epicurus associates prodigality with sensual pleasures. His tenth principal doctrine criticizes prodigals for being unable to control or satisfy their desires, and hence unable to enjoy peace.[58]

Cicero thinks of prodigals as having very low morals. In *On the Chief Good and Evil* he apparently ignores Epicurus's own rejection of prodigality, and implies that his view of pleasure as the chief good means that he approves of prodigal behavior. He describes prodigals as immoral and utterly debauched and says that they ought to be held responsible for their behavior.[59]

Plutarch, a Middle Platonist, uses Peripatetic categories to define prodigality as an excess of the virtue of liberality.[60] Like Aristotle, he is not as hard on the excess (prodigality) as the deficiency (meanness).[61] However, he warns against flatterers who call prodigality liberality or rusticity, depending upon their purposes.[62] As I noted in Chapter 4, his discourse *On the Love of Wealth* is an important discussion of prodigals and misers.[63]

57. See Musonius, *Frag.* 3. (40, 17-20; 42, 22-29); *Frag.* 4. (44, 16-22). and *Frg.* 8; (62, 12-23). Epictetus, *Diss.* 3.1.8, 14, 33; 4.1.2, 10; and 4.9.17.

58. Diogenes Laertius, 10.131, 142.

59. Cicero, *Fin.* 2.7, 8. Cicero also uses *asotos* in *Nat. Deor.* 3.77, when he says that Aristo of Chios recognized that it was possible to leave the school of Aristippus a 'profligate (*asotos*)'.

60. Plutarch, *Mor.* 445a; and *Pelo* 3.2.

61. Plutarch, *Mor.* 525f-526a.

62. Plutarch, *Mor.* 56c; 57c, d; 60d, e; and *Galb.* 19.3.

63. Plutarch, *Mor.* 525b-e. O'Neil ('*De Cupiditate Divitiarum*', pp. 335-36) summarizes a 'series of six examples in which the emphasis alternates between prodigals and misers:

In another description of a prodigal life, Plutarch tells the story of a prodigal's conversion.[64] In this story a young man having lost his estate (τὴν οὐσίαν ἀπολέσας) through living in dissipation (ἀκολασία) becomes worse and devotes himself to avarice in earnest. However, he does eventually undergo a genuine moral conversion. He has a fall and seems dead, but on the day of his funeral he revives, and, once he returns to his senses (παρ' αὐτῷ γενόμενος), he is dramatically changed. This story is interesting for its remarkable similarities with and differences from Lk. 15.11-32,[65] but the point here is that even this extreme example of prodigality is miraculously cured.[66]

Josephus contrasts prodigal living (ἀσώτως ζῆν) with hard work and the restraint of desires.[67]

This short overview serves to show that the philosophical view of prodigality is more moderate than the popular one mentioned in Chapter

1. Stratonicus, the Athenian wit, chides the prodigal Rhodians for building as if they will live forever, and eating like there is no tomorrow.

2. Lovers of money acquire like prodigals but spend like misers.

3. Demades, the Athenian demagogue and a good example of a miser, visits the statesman Phocion, who typifies self-sufficiency.

4. An apostrophe, in good Cynic fashion, to an unnamed second person who possesses most of the evil attributes of a miser.

5. A Byzantine husband finds an adulterer with his ugly wife and exclaims, "What drives you to it? The dregs are foul!" This episode somehow introduces the main subject of the section: public figures must be prodigals to maintain their power and position.

6. A second apostrophe to the miserly second person who endures every discomfort but gets no good from it, like the bathhouse keeper's ass.'

O'Neil judges this section to be a topos on πολυτέλεια, which is possibly pre-Socratic, but found especially in the writings of the Cynics and Stoics, and, to some degree, in those of Hellenistic Judaism and Christianity.

64. Plutarch, *Mor.* 563b-e.

65. H.D. Betz, P.A. Dirkse and E.W. Smith, Jr, '*De Sera Numinis Vindicta* (*Moralia* 548A-568A)', in H.D. Betz (ed.), *Plutarch's Theological Writings and Early Christian Literature* (SCHNT, 3; Leiden: E.J. Brill, 1978), pp. 181-235 (219-21), make a number of observations on this. See the discussion of conversion in Chapter 7 below.

66. Occasionally, Plutarch uses ἀσώτως or ἄσωτος to mean 'hopeless'. For example, of illnesses, 'clever physicians know in advance from the appetites of the sick which cases are hopeless and which may recover (τοὺς ἀσώτως ἢ σωτηρίως ἔχοντας)' (*Mor.* 918d).

67. Josephus, *Ant.* 12.203. Note the cluster of πατήρ, συνάγω, οὐσία, πόνος and ἐπιθυμία within a single sentence.

1.[68] It is more carefully analytical, and more concerned with causes and cures. The form of the vice which the younger son represents—excessive spending without excessive taking from the wrong sources—is seen to be curable. As an excess of liberality, it already contains within it the ingredients of liberality. During the curative process the positive elements are retained, while the excesses are curbed. Such curbs can be external, such as discipline or hunger, or internal and rational, such as humiliation and reflection. As we shall see, the popular philosophical doctrine of the care for the self and the disciplines of withdrawal, reflection and conversion all contribute to this process. Because prodigality is seen to be a vice of the young, moral change also takes place via the normal processes of maturation. In addition, moral teachers teach that fulfillment comes not through self-indulgence, but through the control of passions, moderate living and work.[69]

The philosophers never suggest that prodigality is a virtue. Rather, they differ from popular morality in judging it to be curable, while popular usage treats it as a hopeless failing. We shall see that Luke's parable reflects the philosophical conviction that prodigality is curable, and that it reflects the curative teachings and disciplines of first-century moral philosophy, including correct attitudes to wealth, to parents and siblings, to celebrations and towards oneself.

4. *Famine, Hunger and Want*

The first curbs upon the prodigality of the younger son are external. At the same time that his money runs out (such coincidences are common in Hellenistic romances), the country he is in experiences a famine. This leads him to experience hunger and want: ἐγένετο λιμὸς ἰσχυρὰ ... ἤρξατο ὑστερεῖσθαι (vv. 14a-b).

---

68. In his discussion of the topos On Envy (φθόνος), Johnson notes, 'Typically, when ethicists are describing the nature of a particular vice or virtue, they tend to make distinctions which fall away when they are using the same categories in another context, in a less technical way.' He refers to the distinctions made by Aristotle and Plutarch between ζῆλος and φθόνος, in which ζῆλος may sometimes be seen positively, while φθόνος always remains a vice ('James 3.13-4.10', p. 335).

69. The *curability* of prodigality is an important omission from Foerster's discussion of prodigality in 'ἄσωτος', *TDNT*, I, pp. 506-507.

Luke does not attribute the arrival of the famine to the intervention of providence, at least not with the same directness found in God's confrontation of the covetous hopes of the rich fool in Lk. 12.20.[70] Nevertheless, by creating the conditions in which the younger son is able to come to a moral turning point, the famine does fulfill a positive function in this parable.

Luke's readers would have interpreted the arrival of the famine variously, depending upon their view of providence.[71] Some would be inclined to view the famine as a sign of divine judgment on the younger son's prodigality, while others would exclude any notion of divine intervention in the world. Many representatives of both these viewpoints would prefer to see it as an example of the instability of life, whether divinely ordered or not.

Plato sees the gods as having providentially ordered the world so that good actions are rewarded and bad ones are punished.[72] This view is shared by Middle and Roman Stoics. Their doctrines of determinism and universal sympathy also allow them to see a link between natural phenomena and personal behavior.[73] In Hellenistic Jewish and early Christian writings, too, famine is sometimes seen as a punishment on the rich for their avarice and social injustices.[74]

---

70. Sellew comments on the presence of divine retribution in the parables of Lk. 12.16-20; 20.9-16; and the way the characters in Lk. 15.11-32; 16.1-8a; and 18.2-5 use reason to escape punishment. He does not substantiate his view that their use of reason is 'crafty or amoral'. See P. Sellew, 'Interior Monologue as a Narrative Device', *JBL* 111 (1992), pp. 239-53 (242).

71. The Hellenistic romances suggest that the popular response might be to attribute it vaguely to τύχη. See Reardon, 'Theme', p. 22.

72. Plato, *Resp.* 10.612e-613a.

73. See Epictetus, *Frag.* 3 (LCL) 'All things obey and serve the Cosmos, both earth, and sea, and sun... The Cosmos unites us together with the universe under its governance.' See also Hierocles in Stobaeus, *Anth.* 1.3.53-54 = 1.63, 6-64, 14 who says that while pestilence, drought, rain and earthquakes are usually the result of physical causes, the gods sometimes use them to punish the masses, just as they sometimes punish an individual by loss of property.

Kleinknecht discusses the wrath of the gods in the Greek world and the *ira deum* in the Roman world in Kleinknecht *et al.*, 'ὀργή, κτλ', *TDNT*, V, pp. 389-92. A full discussion of the relationship between Roman religion, Roman Stoicism and morality from the late republic to the later empire is given in J.H.W.G. Liebeschuetz, *Continuity and Change in Roman Religion* (Oxford: Clarendon Press, 1979).

74. For example: *Sib. Or.* 3.234-5; *1 En.* 100.10-13. For the view that *1 En.* 92-105 is an 'epistle' in which the author attacks the social injustices of the rich in the

The alternate view is held by Aristotle and Epicurus, who do not consider the gods to have any effect upon ethics.[75] Cynics also reject the notion of divine interference, and teach that the will of the individual is the most important factor in the pursuit of virtue.[76] Pseudo-Heraclitus reverses the usual schema in which poverty is seen as a punishment for vice, by arguing that:

> God punishes, not by taking away wealth, but rather by giving it to the
> wicked so that, since they have the means to err, they might be con-
> victed, and by abounding in wealth, they might expose their own wicked-
> ness.[77]

Thus, from the perspective of Plato's teaching, or Stoicism, the famine would be interpreted as an act of providence (or a portent)[78] which brought the younger son to his senses and pointed him back to his homeland and father. Peripatetics, Epicureans and Cynics would prefer not to invoke providence at this point.[79]

early second century BCE, see G.W.E. Nickelsburg, *Jewish Literature between the Bible and the Mishnah: A Historical and Literary Introduction* (London: SCM Press, 1981), pp. 145-50.

75. Injustice or the delay of judgment is frequently cited by Epicureans as evidence against divine providence. See J.H. Neyrey, 'Acts 17, Epicureans and Theodicy', in D.L. Balch, E. Ferguson and W.A. Meeks (eds.), *Greeks, Romans and Christians: Essays in Honor of Abraham J. Malherbe* (Minneapolis: Fortress Press, 1990), pp. 118-34 (132 n. 44).

76. Stoic and Cynic theology is compared and contrasted in A.J. Malherbe, 'Pseudo-Heraclitus, Epistle 4: The Divinization of the Wise Man', *JAC* 21 (1978), pp. 42-64 (45-51).

77. Pseudo-Heraclitus, *Ep.* 8 (208, 5-8). The consequence of this is that to obtain wealth is to be forsaken by fortune (208, 9). Other Cynic epistles, mild and austere, make the same point. Wealth comes and goes with changes of fortune, Pseudo-Socrates, *Ep.* 1 (220, 16); 'to acquire vast sums of money through some act of fortune is not characteristic of the most noble men' (Pseudo-Aristippus, *Ep.* 29. [294, 10-13]).

78. Unusual phenomena relating to the weather, the earth or monsters were called *ostenta, portenta, monstra* or *prodigia* (Cicero *Div.* 1.93); and were considered precursors of social, political, or dynastic changes (*OCD*, s.v. 'Divinatio').

79. Balch, 'The Areopagus Speech', p. 60, cites a number of sources that reflect ancient philosophical polemic concerning providence. Cicero, *Nat. Deor.* 2.73, mentions the opposing views of Stoics and Epicureans; and Josephus, *Ant.* 10.277-79, refutes the Epicurean exclusion of providence from human life. Compare Josephus, *Apion.* 2.180. Plutarch rejects the Epicurean view of providence in *De Pyth. Or.* (*Mor.* 389b-c) and in *Suav. Viv. Ep.* (*Mor.* 1086c-1107c), and the Stoic views in

If the famine is considered from the perspective of human experience, it is seen simply as one of the many sufferings and accidents that are an inescapable part of life.[80] Philosophical and gnomic writings, even by Stoic authors, emphasize the importance of recognizing this fact and of learning to take it into account.[81]

The teaching that want can be avoided by escaping the slavery of desire, and by learning to meet only one's legitimate needs, is found in Cynic, Stoic and Christian texts dealing with the topos On Covetousness.[82] Teles gives the example of Metrocles, who, after having received the right teaching on poverty and wealth from Crates, changed from being destitute and hungry to having more than he needed.[83] His problem was diagnosed in typical Cynic fashion as that of being enslaved to insatiable desires and appetites. Once he was freed from these, he was able to escape scarcity and want (ἐνδείᾳ καὶ σπάνει) .[84] Teles thus teaches that want and scarcity are caused by wrong desires.[85] The

---

Stoic. Rep. See B. Fiore, 'Passion in Paul and Plutarch: 1 Corinthians 5-6 and the Polemic against Epicureans', in D.L. Balch, E. Ferguson and W.A. Meeks (eds.), *Greeks, Romans and Christians: Essays in Honor of Abraham J. Malherbe* (Minneapolis: Fortress Press, 1990), pp. 135-43 (141-42); and P.H. de Lacy, 'II.—Lucretius and the History of Epicureanism', *APAT* 79 (1948), pp. 12-23 (16).

80. Epictetus, *Diss.* 2.5.25. See also Plutarch, *Mor.* 5d.

81. Epictetus, *Diss.* 3.24.8-10: 'Shall we not wean ourselves at last, and call to mind ... that this universe is but a single state... and it needs must be that there is a certain periodic change and a giving place of one thing to another?' Compare *Carm. Aur.* 16: 'property is wont to be acquired now, tomorrow lost (χρήματα δ' ἄλλοτε μὲν κτᾶσθαι φιλεῖ, ἄλλοτ' ὀλέσθαι)'. See Thom, 'Golden Verses', p. 118 and nn. 194, 195. For the same view in Hellenistic Jewish texts see *Ps.-Phoc.* 27; Philo *Spec. Leg.* 1.23-24; *Ebr.* 209; *T. Ben.* 6.2; and Sir. 18.25, together with warnings against seeing wealth as a form of self-sufficiency, in Sir. 5.1-2; and 11.23-25. Van der Horst, *Pseudo-Phocylides*, p. 133, gives examples from Pindar, Euripedes, Plutarch and Pseudo-Plutarch, as well as noting τὸ τῆς τύχης ἄσατον in Josephus, *Ant.* 20.57.

82. See also Aristotle, *Eth. Eud.* 2.7, 8.

83. 'when he was studying with Theophrastus and Xenocrates, although many things were being sent to him from home, he was in constant fear of dying from hunger (μὴ τῷ λιμῷ ἀποθάνοι) and was always destitute and in want (ἀεὶ σπανίζειν καὶ ἐνδεὴς εἶναι) . But when he later changed over to Crates, he could feed even another person though nothing was sent from home' (Teles 4A [40, 103-108]).

84. Teles 4A (42, 135-44).

85. Teles 4A (36, 35-46).

ideal of self-control is seen in Pseudo-Crates' teaching that Cynic begging is to be motivated by hunger, not gluttony.[86] Moles observes that
the Cynic claim to self-sufficiency was always undermined by their
having to beg.[87]

Seneca argues (somewhat too glibly, as a rich man) that the poor find
it easy to satisfy their simple needs:

> It is easy to fill a few stomachs, when they are well-trained and crave
> nothing else but to be filled. Hunger costs but little; squeamishness costs
> much ('parvo fames constat, magno fastidium'). Poverty is content to
> meet only pressing needs.[88]

In Phil. 4.11-12, Paul explains that he is never in want because he has
learnt the secret of contentment:

> Not that I complain of want [ὑστέρησιν]; for I have learned, in whatever
> state I am, to be content [αὐτάρκης εἶναι]. I know how to be abased
> [ταπεινοῦσθαι], and I know how to abound [περισσεύειν]; in any and
> all circumstances I have learned the secret of facing plenty and hunger,
> abundance and want [χορτάζεσθαι καὶ πεινᾶν καὶ περισσεύειν καὶ
> ὑστερεῖσθαι].

This is an example of a Christian adoption of the Stoic principle
of αὐτάρκεια,[89] a virtue which is frequently placed in contrast with

---

86. 'For it is not begging that is base, but not showing oneself as worthy of what
is given (μὴ παρέχειν ἑαυτὸν ἄξιον τοῦ διδομένου). It is characteristic of
unscrupulous men to beg on account of indigestion rather than hunger (ἀπεψίαν ἢ
λιμὸν), for the former is caused by gluttony that results from wickedness (γαστρι-
μαργίαν παρὰ κακίας), but the latter by need that results from poverty (ἔνδειαν
παρ' ἀπορίας)' (Pseudo-Crates, *Ep.* 17 [66, 22-25]).

87. J. Moles, 'Cynicism in Horace *Epistles* I', in F. Cairns (eds.), *Papers of the
Liverpool Latin Seminar: Fifth Volume 1985* (Liverpool: Francis Cairns, 1986),
pp. 33-60 (44).

88. Seneca, *Ep.* 17.4. Mendell ('Satire as Popular Philosophy', p. 149) says that
Epicurus is Seneca's favourite author for quotation purposes. Seneca's own
rationale is found in *Ira* 1.6.5: 'What harm is there in using the arguments of others,
so far as they are our own?'

89. αὐτάρκεια was the favourite virtue of the Cynics and Stoics. See the references cited in the comment on 1 Tim. 6.6 in M. Dibelius, H. Conzelmann and
H. Koester (eds.), *The Pastoral Epistles: A Commentary on the Pastoral Epistles*
(trans. P. Buttolph and A. Yarbro; Hermeneia; Philadelphia: Fortress Press, 1972),
p. 84 n. 6. Lightfoot (*Philippians*, pp. 163-64) cites the additional examples of
Seneca, *Ep.* 9; and Marcus Aurelius, *Med.* 1.16. Ferguson (*Backgrounds*, p. 278)
comments that all the philosophical schools of the Hellenistic Age emphasized

φιλαργυρία in popular philosophy.[90] As in the parable under discussion (vv. 14b and 17b), Paul's statement pairs ὑστερεῖσθαι with περισ-σεύειν.[91] This pairing shows that Luke is deliberately contrasting the want that the younger son experiences as a result of his prodigal living followed by an unexpected famine, with the abundance enjoyed by even the least important members of his father's household. This familiar contrast[92] would be readily noted by readers familiar with Stoic ethics and would indicate to them that he needed to learn the virtue of αὐτάρκεια.

5. *Desire and Degradation*

The importance of the control of desire is stressed by all the philosophical schools of the Hellenistic period, particularly the Stoics. There is much debate over which desires are to be considered legitimate and which not, but there is agreement that the proper control and direction of desire is essential for the moral life.

The occurrence of ἐπιθυμέω in this parable is usually understood to refer quite simply to the younger son's need to satisfy his hunger.[93] However, the strong moral associations of the verb in popular philosophy are clearly reflected in the way the parable as a whole treats the issue of desire, by illustrating the disorders of desire in the prodigality and meanness of the two sons, and the control of desire in the father. Both sons are concerned in differing ways with getting money and

---

freedom from passion through renunciation and shared the common goal of αὐτάρκεια.

90. See Gerhard, *Phoinix*, p. 57.

91. B. Weiss, *Die Evangelien des Markus und Lukas*; Kritisch-exegetischer Kommentar über das Neuen Testament 1/2 (Göttingen: Vandenhoeck & Ruprecht, 7th edn, 1885), p. 512, comments that περισσεύω and λιμός are correlative, but it is perhaps more accurate to say that the synonymous pairs of λιμός and ὑστερ-εῖσθαι (v. 14a-b), and λιμός and ἀπόλλυμι (v. 17b-c) are correlative and are together contrasted with περισσεύω (v. 17b).

92. Compare 2 Cor. 6.9-10 and *Diogn.* 5.12-13: 'They are put to death and they gain life' (θανατοῦνται, καὶ ζωοποιοῦνται). 'They are poor and yet make many rich' (πτωχεύουσι, καὶ πλουτίζουσι); 'they lack all things and have all things in abundance' (πάντων ὑστεροῦνται, καὶ ἐν πᾶσι περισσεύουσιν).

93. F. Büchsel, 'ἐπιθυμία', *TDNT*, III, pp. 168-72 (170).

pleasure, yet they remain unsatisfied. Only the father, who is uncon-
cerned with these things, experiences true joy. Commenting on the conflicts between desire and its repression in the two sons, Bovon says:

> Schematically, we could say that with the older brother submission to the
> law surpasses desire as long as the younger brother is absent. With the
> prodigal, we witness a voluntary transgression of the law and of the
> family order in the name of desire.[94]

In the Greco-Roman moral tradition, ἐπιθυμία acquires a distinctive
sense from the time of Plato onwards. Before Plato, the word does not
have a negative connotation and refers to natural impulses, such as the
desire for food. Plato does not consider ἐπιθυμία to be bad in itself, but
says that the philosopher ought to 'stand aloof from pleasures and lusts
and griefs and fears (ἡδονῶν τε καὶ ἐπιθυμιῶν καὶ λυπῶν καὶ
φόβων)'.[95] This introduces a distinction between legitimate and illegitimate desires. In the *Gorgias*, Plato's Socrates rejects the extreme
Sophistic view expressed by Callicles, that natural good and right consist in having the strongest possible desires, and in having the courage
and intelligence fully to satisfy them, whatever they are.[96] Epicurus also
distinguishes between natural and groundless desires, and says that
even among natural desires, only those which lead to bodily health and
mental tranquillity should be preferred.[97]

Stoics go further and insist on the eradication of all desires, particularly the chief passions: pleasures, lusts, griefs and fears. There is a
close relationship between passions and possessions. Büchsel comments that passions 'arise out of a wrong attitude to possessions, with

---

94. Earlier, Bovon observes that Luke hardly tells us what the son looks for and
desires: to spend his father's goods, to live, to save himself, or what? 'In any case,
the imprecision exists, and it is heavy with meaning' ('Second Reading', pp. 445 and
449).

95. Plato, *Phaed.* 83b, cited in Büchsel, 'ἐπιθυμία', p. 168.

96. Plato, *Gorg.* 492a, c; 494c. Callicles states explicitly that luxury, excess and
licence are virtue and happiness, provided that they can get sufficient backing.
H. North, *Sophrosyne: Self-Knowledge and Self-Restraint in Greek Literature*
(CSCP, 35; Ithaca, NY: Cornell University Press, 1966), pp. 97-98, points out that a
similar argument is present in the ἀγών between the just and unjust arguments in
Aristophanes, *Nu.* 899-1104.

97. Diogenes Laertius, 10.127-28. This is in marked contrast with Plutarch's
hostile interpretation of Epicurus's views in *Mor.* 1092e-1099d.

desire and anxiety when these are present and with cupidity and fear when they are future'.[98]

The Stoic insistence on the control of all desire is based upon the observation that even legitimate desires grow into illegitimate lusts if left unchecked. Though a Middle Platonist, Plutarch reflects the influence of Stoic ethics when he argues that human desires easily move from legitimate needs to illegitimate lusts:

> Finding us in want of a loaf, a house, a modest protection from the weather, and whatever comes to hand to supplement our loaf, wealth infects us with the desire (ἐπιθυμία) for gold and silver and ivory ...[99]

Hence the Cynic definition of poverty as desiring everything (ἐπιθυμεῖν πάντων).[100] The Stoic emphasis on the dangers of ἐπιθυμία is also found in Hellenistic Judaism, such as book 2 of the *Sibylline Oracles*,[101] and Josephus,[102] and particularly in texts which exhibit Stoic influence such as Sirach[103] and Philo.[104]

The distinctive feature of desire is its insatiability. As the above quotation from Plutarch suggests, this is particularly true of the desire for money. All the philosophical movements mention this. Peripatetics, who do not stress the ethical role of ἐπιθυμία, criticize the insatiability of human craving for money.[105] Epictetus illustrates the propensity of desire to flare up more strongly each time it is satisfied, by describing the process whereby the desire for money hardens into true avarice

98. Büchsel, 'ἐπιθυμία', p. 168.

99. Plutarch, *Mor.* 523f. Compare Plato, *Phaedr.* 238a-b.

100. Pseudo-Diogenes, *Ep.* 33 (140, 28-30).

101. 'Much luxury draws toward inordinate desires' (*Sib. Or.* 2.133).

102. Josephus describes Sabinus as 'eager for gain and greedy in his desire (διὰ κέρδη καὶ πλεονεξιῶν ἐπιθυμίας)' (*Ant.* 17.253).

103. Sir. 5.1-2; 18.30-19.1; 23.4-6. Though see also Sir. 14.14-16, which advises, 'let not your share of desired good (μερὶς ἐπιθυμίας ἀγαθῆς) pass by you'.

104. Philo (*Agr.* 83) speaks of the 'virtue-hating and passion-loving mind (μισάρετος καὶ φιλοπαθὴς νοῦς), whose delight was in pleasures and cravings (ἡδοναῖς καὶ ἐπιθυμίαις), acts of injustice and rascality (ἀδικίαις τε καὶ πανουργίαις), as well as in exploits of plundering and overreaching (ἁρπαγαῖς καὶ πλεονεξίαις)'. See also Philo, *Spec. Leg.* 4.79-131 and *Dec.* 151-153.

105. 'for appetite (ἐπιθυμία) is in its nature unlimited, and the majority of mankind live for the satisfaction of appetite (ἧς πρὸς τὴν ἀναπλήρωσιν οἱ πολλοὶ ζῶσιν)' (Aristotle, *Pol.* 2.4.11). See Theophrastus, *Char.* 30.1, for a criticism of meanness as the desire for base gain (αἰσχροκέρδειά ἐστιν ἐπιθυμία κέρδους αἰσχροῦ).

(φιλαργυρία). [106] The mild Cynic Dio Chrysostom says that the great majority of people feed in their hearts a whole army of desires (οἱ γὰρ πολλοὶ βόσκουσι παρ' ἑαυτοῖς τῶν ἐπιθυμιῶν στρατόπεδον). [107] The insatiability of desire is twice mentioned in the Neopythagorean *Sentences* of Sextus. [108]

While ἐπιθυμία is not always thought of negatively in the New Testament, as Lk. 22.15 shows, the negative view predominates. This is evident in Rom. 7.7, in the omission of an object to the commandment, 'You shall not covet (οὐκ ἐπιθυμήσεις)'. Barrett comments: 'Desire means that exaltation of the *ego* which we have seen to be the essence of sin'. [109] In the Markan explanation of the parable of the sower, the thorns represent the cares (μέριμναι) of the world, the deception of riches (ἡ ἀπάτη τοῦ πλούτου), and the desire for other things (αἱ περὶ τὰ λοιπὰ ἐπιθυμίαι) (Mk 4.19). The epistle of James speaks of desire which lures and tempts people to sin, [110] the author of 1 Timothy says that the desire for wealth leads to many senseless and hurtful desires (1 Tim 6.9), and the author of Titus writes, in Tit. 3.3, of Christians having formerly been enslaved to passions and desires (δουλεύοντες

106. Epictetus, *Diss.* 2.18.8-10; 4.4.33. Compare Horace, *Sat.* 1.1.61-62, 108-112.

107. Dio Chrysostom, *Or.* 17.21.

108. For example: 'Every kind of desire is insatiable (ἀπλήστως ἐπιθυμία ἅπασα) and so remains unmanageable'; and, 'The possession of goods will not stop a longing (ἐπιθυμίαν) for possessions' (*Sent. Sextus* 146 and 274b). De Jonge ('Rachel's Virtuous Behaviour', p. 351) describes the *Sentences* as 'a document of nonsectarian Encratism'.

109. C.K. Barrett, *The Epistle to the Romans* (BNTC; London: A. & C. Black, 2nd edn, 1991), p. 132. Cranfield says that the omission of an object 'reflects the consciousness, which is evidenced in the OT and in Judaism as well as elsewhere in the NT, of the sinfulness of all inordinate desires as the expression of man's self-centredness and self-assertion over against God' (C.E.B. Cranfield, *A Critical and Exegetical Commentary on the Epistle to the Romans* (2 vols.; ICC; Edinburgh: T. & T. Clark, 1975), I, p. 349.

110. Jas 1.15-16. Dibelius and Greeven say this is not an example of the Stoic condemnation of desire in general, but of the desire to do evil. See M. Dibelius and H. Greeven, *James: A Commentary on the Epistle of James* (trans. M.A. Williams; ed. H. Koester; Hermeneia; Philadelphia: Fortress Press, 1976), p. 93. Yet the Stoic avoidance of desire is based on the view that good desires tend to grow into bad ones, and this is exactly what happens in Jas 4.2. Jas 4.1-4 illustrates the disastrous consequences of spending (δαπανᾶν) upon passions (ἡδοναί). Again the language indicates that the passage is interacting with the topos On Covetousness.

ἐπιθυμίαις καὶ ἡδοναῖς). The deceptiveness of desire is that it promises pleasure, but results in slavery.[111] This paradox is echoed in the Apostolic Fathers.[112]

From this review of the use of ἐπιθυμία in moral philosophy, it is clear that far from being a simple reference to the hunger of the younger son, it is a succinct diagnosis of his moral condition. His desires for money and pleasure have led him to the place where he is penniless and starving. Seeking pleasure, he has found grief. The distortion of perception caused by desire is vividly illustrated by the way the son now desires to eat the food of pigs, something that he never imagined when he set out from home.

The moral degradation caused by slavery to desire is seen in his occupation as a swineherd.[113] Commentators regularly comment on this as a mark of extreme moral decline for a Jew, because of postexilic purity laws.[114] However, this task would be no less humiliating for the son of a Greco-Roman landowner rich enough to employ hired workers. A number of references in the Greco-Roman moralists show that they also saw pigs as a symbol of moral degradation.[115]

---

111. This is a Stoic viewpoint, as Spicq observes: 'Les stoiciens considéraient l'esclavage des passions comme la pire des servitudes' (C. Spicq, *Saint Paul: Les épitres pastorales* (EBib; 2 vols.; Paris: J. Gabalda, 4th edn, 1969), II, p. 650.

112. Ignatius, *Rom.* 4.3: 'I am a convict ... Now I am learning in my bonds to give up all desires (μηδὲν ἐπιθυμειν).' Polycarp, *Phil.* 4.3: 'Let [the slaves] not desire to be set free at the Church's expense (ἀπὸ τοῦ κοινοῦ), that they be not found the slaves of lust (ἐπιθυμία).' Hermas, *Vis.* 1.1.8-9: Those who have evil desires in their hearts bring death and captivity upon themselves, 'especially those who obtain this world for themselves, and glory in their wealth, and do not lay hold of the good things which are to come'. Hermas, *Sim.* 9.19.3, teaches that the sin of 'the lust of gain' (ἐπιθυμίαν τοῦ λήμματος) is one that may be repented of.

113. The fact that the younger son went to work on a farm with pigs suggests that the foreign country to which he had gone was under Roman influence. Romans ate more pork than any other meat, and also farmed pigs for sacrifical and military purposes. See K.D. White, *Roman Farming* (London: Thames & Hudson, 1970), pp. 316 and 320.

114. References to χοῖρος are only found in variant readings of Lev. 11.7; Ps. 79.14; and Isa. 65.4; 66.3. Otherwise the usual term is ὗς, as in Lev 11.7. The pig is a symbol of apostasy in *4 Macc.* 5.6.

115. Cercidas (*Meliamb.* 2.14.) speaks of 'swine-befouled wealth' (συοπλουτοσύνα) to express his Cynical disapproval of rich usurers and spendthrifts whose money ought to be distributed to the poor. Horace (*Ep.* 1.2.23-24) says that if Ulysses had drunk of Circe's cups he too would have ended up living 'like a

Thus, Luke uses the moral associations of ἐπιθυμέω in v. 16a to emphasize the fact that, at this stage in the parable, the younger son illustrates the degradation experienced by those who fail to control their desires.

6. *Moral Death and Ruin*

The most prominent statement in the parable is the refrain of the father, 'this son of mine was dead and is alive again; he was lost and is found', οὗτος ὁ υἱός μου νεκρὸς ἦν καὶ ἀνέζησεν, ἦν ἀπολωλὼς καὶ εὑρέθη, found in v. 24a-d, and repeated with slight variations in v. 32b-d.[116] Apart from its stylized form, and the fact that it is repeated, Luke gives this statement prominence by placing it in direct speech, and by giving it to the most important character, the father. He forms the link between the two sons, just as the section describing his actions forms the centre of the parable. He is the moral exemplar, and his statement has the effect of unifying the parable by being the conclusion to the story of his younger son, and to the parable as a whole. Just as the younger son's repeated confession (vv. 18c-19b and 21b-21d) expresses the content of his repentance, so the father's refrain describes its significance.[117]

---

wallowing sow'. Dio Chrysostom (*Or.* 30.33) likens the dissolute and intemperate (ἀσώτους καὶ ἀκρατεῖς) to pigs in a sty (ὥσπερ ἐν συφεῷ ὗς) which show no interest in anything but food or sleep. Malherbe, 'Beasts at Ephesus', p. 84, refers to Dio Chrysostom, *Or.* 8.24-26, and comments that 'Pleasure drives the victim into a sort of sty and pens him up; henceforth the victim goes on living as a pig or wolf.' Martial (*Epigr.* 10.11) criticizes the boaster Calliodorus in a way that suggests that feeding pigs was a lowly occupation: 'You talk of nothing but Theseus and Pirithous, and think yourself, Calliodorus, the peer of Pylades. May I be hanged if you are fit to hand Pylades a chamber pot, or to feed Pirithous' swine.' Epictetus (*Diss.* 4.11.30-31) speaks of pigs, geese, worms and spiders as 'creatures furthest removed from association with human beings'.

116. The fraternal status of the younger son is emphasized in v. 32b, ζάω is used instead of ἀναζάω in v. 32c, and the imperfect ἦν is replaced with a conjunction in 32d.

117. Luke's description of the father's action of running to embrace and kiss his son when he first sees him return also resonates with the dead-alive motif. Hock comments that it corresponds exactly with the way people greet those they love but thought were long dead in Greek novels. Hock, 'The Greek Novel', p. 140 cites examples from Chariton's *Chaereas and Callirhoe* 8.6.8 ('Hermocrates leapt on board, ran to the tent, and threw his arms around his daughter. "Are you alive, my child", he cried, "or is this too an illusion?" "I am alive, Father! I am really alive

These literary markers of emphasis mean that the pairs 'dead-alive' and 'lost-found' (or, better, 'ruin-recovery') are metaphors that are central to the understanding of the parable. They are most often quite legitimately interpreted in a religious sense, as illustrations of the son's movement from spiritual death to life, thus relating the teaching of the parable to the use of death and life in some of the deutero-Pauline and Johannine writings.[118]

However, it is equally important to recognize the use of these word-pairs as metaphors for wrong/right living in Greco-Roman moral philosophy, Hellenistic Jewish writings and early Christian texts. This moral usage, often given particular expression in discussions of the wrong/right use of possessions,[119] is my focus in this section.[120]

Before looking at examples of this, we should note that, despite the frequency with which dead (νεκρός), to live (ζάω), to lose (ἀπόλλυμι) and to find (εὑρίσκω) are used individually in Luke–Acts,[121] this is the only place where Luke uses them all together. It is also the only place where he uses the pairs figuratively. Three of the four terms are found in Luke's resurrection narrative in Lk. 24.2-5 (εὑρίσκω, νεκρός, and ζάω—the words are not found in the related accounts in the other Gospels) and in Paul's Areopagus sermon in Acts 17.23-32 (εὑρίσκω, ζάω and νεκρός with ζωή in v. 24). However, in both of those accounts, the

now that I have seen you!" They all wept for joy' [trans. B.P. Reardon, *Collected Ancient Greek Novels*, p. 121]); Longus, *Daphn. Chloe* 2.30.1; 4.36.3 and 4.23.1 (to these could be added 3.7, and 4.22); and Achilles Tatius, *Leucippe and Clitophon*. 1.4.1 and 7.16.3. The motif is also vividly illustrated in the opening scene of Heliodorus's *An Ethiopian Romance* 1.2.6, where a beautiful young woman runs to embrace and kiss a young man who at first appears to be dead.

118. Eph. 2.1, 5; 5.14; Col. 2.13; Jn 5.25. See G. Braumann, 'Tot-Lebendig, Verloren-Gefunden', in W. Haubeck and M. Bachmann (eds.), *Wort in der Zeit: Neutestamentliche Studien* (Festgabe Karl Heinrich Rengstorf; Leiden: E.J. Brill, 1980), pp. 156-64 (158).

119. Cicero, for example, parallels life and death, and wealth and want (*vita mors, divitiae paupertas*) in the same sentence in *Off.* 2.10.37.

120. Gerhard (*Phoinix*, p. 62) refers to two comments by 'Socrates' in Stobaeus, *Anth.* (3.16.27, 28 = 3.488, 1-5): ' "Sokrates' illustriert den Reichtum der φιλάργυροι durch die untergegangene Sonne, die οὐδένα τῶν ζώντων εὐφραίνει, und ihr Leben durch eines Toten Mahl: πάντα γὰρ ἔχων τὸν εὐφρανθησόμενον οὐκ ἔχει.'

121. According to the *Concordance* of Moulton and Geden, the frequencies are νεκρός: Luke, 13; Acts, 17; ζάω: Luke, 9; Acts, 12; ἀναζάω is hapax legomenon in Luke–Acts; ἀπόλλυμι: Luke, 27; Acts, 2; and εὑρίσκω: Luke, 46; Acts, 34.

language is not figurative.[122] Thus, we find no clearly related usage in Luke–Acts to guide our interpretation of the combination νεκρὸς ἦν καὶ ἀνέζησεν, ἦν ἀπολωλὼς καὶ εὑρέθη found here.

Exegetes rightly point out that the parallelism between the two pairs of words means that different nuances of meaning ought not to be sought for each pair. However, each of the pairs of metaphors does contribute to the meaning of the whole statement. First, the placement of the idea of being 'first lost, then found' in parallel with that of being 'first dead, then alive' points to the need for a figurative interpretation which makes sense of *both* metaphors. Just as the second pair does not refer literally to being lost, so there is no thought of literal revivification in the first. This is one of the significant contrasts between the parable and the conversion story found in Plutarch.[123] Betz wonders whether the phrase νεκρὸς ἦν καὶ ἀνέζησεν originally belonged to a story about a journey of the soul such as this. If so, the difference in Lk. 15.24 emphasizes 'that the younger son was converted *not* by a journey to the beyond, but by remembering the goodness of his father'.[124] Second, ἀπόλλυμι-εὑρίσκω ought to be thought of in terms of ruin and recovery, rather than loss and discovery. This is suggested by the frequent idea in texts on covetousness that moral death leads to ruin, as we shall see below.

Although there are no parallels to the father's whole refrain in Luke–Acts, Luke does use ζάω, ζωή and νεκρός in other L parables which relate moral behavior to the ideas of life and death. In Lk. 10.28, Jesus promises life (τοῦτο ποίει καὶ ζήσῃ) to those who obey the law, illustrating this with the story of the compassionate Samaritan. Life is thereby given a moral meaning, and is linked with obedience to the law, as in Hellenistic Jewish literature. Bultmann cites examples of this from the *Letter of Aristeas*, Josephus, Wisdom and *4 Maccabees*.[125] The

---

122. Similarly, once we have excluded chance collocations such as Acts 26.5-8 (ζάω and νεκρός); Lk. 6.7-9; 11.51-54; Acts 5.37-39; 27.28-34 (ἀπόλλυμι and εὑρίσκω), there are few significant examples of the combination of ζάω and νεκρός (Lk. 20.35-38; 24.5; and Acts 10.42; 20.9-12, the resuscitation of Eutychus; 28.4-6, Paul's miraculous preservation from death), and ἀπόλλυμι and εὑρίσκω (Lk. 13.3-7, repent or perish; bear fruit or be cut down).

123. *De Sera Numinis Vindicta* (*Mor.* 563c-e).

124. Betz *et al.*, '*De Sera Numinis Vindicta*', p. 221.

125. R. Bultmann, 'ζάω, ζωή, κτλ', *TDNT*, II, pp. 832-75 (858). In addition he observes that Josephus, *War* 7.341-88, contains late Stoic ideas about life and

warning in Lk. 12.15, that a person's life does not consist in the abundance of possessions (οὐκ ἐν τῷ περισσεύειν τινὶ ἡ ζωὴ αὐτοῦ ἐστιν ἐκ τῶν ὑπαρχόντων αὐτῷ), explicitly links the meaning of living with the right use of possessions. This statement is particularly significant for this study, as it is made in the context of a real situation very similar to the fictional one in our parable: conflict between brothers arising out of the division of inherited wealth (Lk. 12.13). Correspondingly, this parable in Lk. 16.19-31 warns that affluence can harden people against being compassionate to the poor, and challenges the popular view that wealth is good (v. 25). The moral and spiritual danger which the rich are in is shown by the way the parable concludes, saying that those who do not obey the law will not even respond to a messenger from the dead.

These three examples show that Luke associates the idea of true life with the compassionate and unselfish use of wealth. Indeed, life and death are not simply metaphors for right and wrong living: the actual receipt of eternal life is directly related to the right use of possessions. David Seeley has recently claimed that in a sense Luke argues for 'salvation by generosity'.[126]

a. *Death and Life*
The fact that both βίος and ζάω are used in the parable, in Lk. 15.12, 13, 24, 30 and 32, indicates that of the two pairs, the dominant pair is the first: dead-alive.

A moralizing interpretation of life and death is found in Plato's *Apology*. He argues that instead of thinking of life as a good and death as an evil, we ought to think in terms of right and wrong.[127] In the *Phaedo* Plato teaches that the truly philosophical attitude to life treats it as a preparation for death.[128] A similar view is found in a late Cynic epistle by Pseudo-Diogenes:

---

death, which can be traced back to Posidonius (the choice facing the ἀνὴρ ἀγαθός is ζῆν καλῶς ἢ τεθνάναι).

126. D. Seeley, *Deconstructing the New Testament* (Leiden: E.J. Brill, 1994), p. 97.

127. Plato, *Apol.* 28b, 29a-e, 39a. Most of the references to Plato in this note and the next are taken from R. Bultmann, 'θάνατος, κτλ', *TDNT*, II, pp. 4-25 (10).

128. Plato, *Phaed.* 64a, 67e, 80e.

It is wise not to be like those who indulge their bodies [φιλοσώματοι], but to be men who are moderate [μέτριοι]. Those who want to possess more, to eat, drink and indulge their lusts [πλείονα ἔχειν καὶ ἐσθίειν καὶ πίνειν καὶ ἀφροδισιάζειν οἱ πάντες φαῦλοί εἰσί], are worthless and no different from the animals.[129]

Thus, Plato and his followers view life as a struggle against lusts and pleasures in the service of virtue or wisdom.[130]

This motif of struggle is adopted by Cynics and Stoics.[131] They are not concerned about physical death, which they view as a natural phenomenon, but they warn against the danger of moral death.[132] Life lived κατὰ φύσιν is, or ought to be, moral. Bultmann comments:

> If the true reality of life is not threatened by death, it is menaced by the perversion which consists in an unphilosophical outlook, in the abandonment of ἀρετή and in the surrender to eternal life and its goods. And since this consists in a threat to real life, it can be described as death or dying and the body and external goods as dead. Indeed, men who are not awakened to the philosophical life are called dead (νεκρός), as are their relationships to life.[133]

Stoics consider those who do not actively seek virtue to be dead. Only those who pursue virtue via the philosophical life are alive. Epictetus, for example, says that if a Stoic philosopher does not benefit those who come to listen to him, both he and his message are 'dead'.[134] This idea

129. Pseudo-Diogenes, *Ep.* 39 (166, 1-22). This epistle may be as late as the fourth century CE.

130. Plato, *Phaed.* 66c, 82c, 83b, 107c, d, 114c.

131. See A.J. Malherbe, ' "Gentle as a Nurse": The Cynic Background to 1 Thess. 2', in *idem, Paul and the Popular Philosophers* (Minneapolis: Fortress Press, 1989), pp. 35-48 (38) n. 16; 'Beasts at Ephesus', p. 82 nn. 19 and 20; and *Paul and the Thessalonians*, p. 48.

132. The use by different philosophical groups of death and life as a metaphor for immoral or moral living is affected by each group's view of the meaning of natural life and the physical body in the face of physical death.

133. Bultmann, 'θάνατος, κτλ', p. 12.

134. 'it is lifeless and so is the speaker himself (νεκρός ἐστί καὶ αὐτὸς ὁ λέγων)' (*Diss.* 3.23.28). In *Diss.* 1.9.19 he describes a teacher and his pupils as both being dead: νεκρὸς μὲν ὁ παιδευτής, νεκροὶ δ' ὑμεῖς. See also Seneca, *Ep.* 1.2. Compare Jesus' saying, placed by Luke at the start of the travel narrative: ἄφες τοὺς νεκροὺς θάψαι τοὺς ἑαυτῶν νεκρούς (Lk. 9.60; Mt. 8.22).

is also found in Juvenal's eighth *Satire:* the man who lives dishonourably (that is, by greedy acts of plunder) is already dead inside.[135]

The same ethical interpretation of life and death is found in Judaism as a result of Hellenistic influence. Philo reflects both Stoic and Neoplatonic ideas of life and death. A good example of this, which also relates closely to Lk. 15.24b-d, is found in *On Flight and Finding*:

> Some people are dead while living, and some alive while dead (ζῶντες ἔνιοι τεθνήκασι καὶ τεθνηκότες ζῶσι). Bad people prolonging their days to extreme old age, are dead men, deprived of life in association with virtue, while good people, even if cut off from their partnership with the body, live for ever, and are granted immortality.[136]

Elsewhere, Philo allegorizes Joseph's 'death' at the hands of wild beasts and Jacob's mourning in terms of those who are 'killed' by the wild beasts of covetousness and knavery (πλεονεξία καὶ πανουργία). They are 'the subject of mourning, as though they were dead, even while they still live (ἔτι ζῶσιν αὐτοῖς ὡς νεκροῖς), since the life they obtain is meet to be lamented and wailed'.[137] Philo's stylized use here of death and life as a pair of metaphors to denote immoral and moral behavior shows the likelihood that Luke is employing the death and life contrast in the same way.

This is supported by similar usage in early Christian literature. 1 Timothy 5.6 says that the well-off, self-indulgent Christian widow is dead while she lives, ζῶσα τέθνηκεν.[138] James 2.17 calls faith νεκρός if it

---

135. Juvenal, *Sat.* 8.83-94. See also Seneca, *Ep.* 1.2

136. Philo, *Fug.* 55. Compare *Fug.* 58, 'goodness and virtue is life (ζωή), evil and wickedness is death'; and *Leg. All.* 1.108

137. Philo, *Somn.* 2.66. Compare *Rer. Div. Her.* 292: 'Learn then thy lesson and hear how the lawgiver tells us that happy old age and longest span of life is only for the good, but briefest is the life of the wicked, since he is ever studying to die or rather has died already to the life of virtue (ἀρετῆς ζωή).'

138. A.T. Hanson, *The Pastoral Epistles* (NCB; Grand Rapids: Eerdmans; London: Marshall, Morgan & Scott, 1982), p. 97, thinks that the widow's self-indulgence implies the possession of some wealth, and, in this instance, perhaps also sexual indulgence. On the vice of self-indulgence (σπατάλημα) see also Jas 5.5; Ezek. 16.49; Sir. 21.15; 27.13; *1 En.* 94.7-9; 103.5-7; Hermas, *Man.* 6.1.6; 6.2.6; *Barn.* 10.3. P.H. Davids, *The Epistle of James: A Commentary on the Greek Text* (NIGTC; Exeter: Paternoster Press, 1982), p. 178, explains it as the vice of the rich man in Lk. 16.18-31, and describes it as 'self-indulgence in the face of the poverty of others'. J.B. Mayor, *The Epistle of St James: The Greek Text with*

does not lead to compassionate, practical sharing of material resources. Hermas (*Vis.* 1.1.8-9) says that those who desire wealth bring upon themselves death and captivity. 'Their hearts will repent; yet they have no hope, but they have abandoned themselves and their life [ἑαυτοὺς ἀπεγνώκασιν καὶ τὴν ζωὴν αὐτῶν]'. These examples all use death and life as metaphors for the wrong or right use of possessions.

b. *Ruin and Recovery*

The verb ἀπόλλυμι is an important one in Luke 15. Outside this parable, in vv. 4 (twice), 6, 8 and 9, it regularly means to be lost. As I noted in Chapter 3, it is likely that one of the reasons Luke adds the 'lost-found' metaphor in the father's refrain is to provide a link between the first two parables (Lk. 15.4-6 and 8-9) and the third. The fact that the first is not an L parable (similar parables to the first are found in Mt. 18.12-13, *Gos. Thom.* 107 and the *Gos. Truth* 31.35–32.9) means that some sort of redactional relationship between the three has to be posited.[139]

As argued in Chapter 3, I prefer to read Lk. 15.11-32 together with the other L parables, and to see it therefore as having a closer relationship with the parables of Luke 16 than Lk. 15.1-10. One of the reasons for grouping the L parables together is that they all deal with matters dealt with under the topos On Covetousness.

In the context of discussions of prodigality, meanness and liberality, ἀπόλλυμι can be used to describe the loss of a possession, but is used much more frequently to describe the ruin or death of those who fail to act with liberality.

Examples of this come readily to hand.[140] Cynic writers warn that prodigality and meanness lead to ruin. An epistle of Pseudo-Anacharsis warns in typical Cynic fashion of the dangers of attachment to gold and

Introduction, Notes and Comments (London: MacMillan, 1892), p. 148, adds the nuance 'self-indulgence without distinct reference to squandering'.

139. Fitzmyer, *Luke*, pp. 1071-74, discusses the pre-Lukan origins of the first two parables.

140. The same is not true of εὑρίσκω in the passive with the meaning 'to recover' or 'to prosper'. This meaning is not distinguished in BAGD or LSJ, the nearest example being the present subjunctive in Lev. 25.47. This supports the view that εὑρίσκω has been added here to harmonize this parable with the two preceding lost-and-found parables in Lk. 15.4-6 and 8-9. 'Since B. Weiss, commentators have at times queried whether Luke has added this to the inherited parable ... This is highly probable' (Fitzmyer, *Luke*, p. 1090).

pleasure, and ends with Anacharsis urging Croesus to take his advice to Cyrus and to all tyrants. 'For it [sc. my advice] will flourish better among those in power than among those who are ruined [ἀπόλλυμι]'.[141] Cercidas speaks of the spendthrift as 'the ruin of money' and the usurer as 'ready to perish for gold'.[142] These warnings are extended to all people by the moderate Cynic Dio Chrysostom. He notes that greed destroys (διαφθείρω) the prosperity of families and states, and leads to a neglect of the human law requiring the honouring of equality (τὸ ἴσον).[143] This leads to wars through which both parties are deprived even of what is sufficient (ἱκανός). For money, men will destroy (ἀπόλλυμι) life (ζωή) and cause even their own fatherlands to be laid waste (πατρίδας τὰς αὐτῶν ἀναστάτους ἐποίησαν).[144] Luke demonstrates the damaging effects of greed on the individual and the community in the life of the younger son, who embarks upon a spendthrift life of luxury and wantonness, and ends up facing death.

Prodigals are not the only ones to bring ruin. The eclectic follower of the Academy, Plutarch, likens the avarice of the mean and illiberal (μικρολογία καὶ ἀνελευθερία) to the avarice of a beast of prey which kills and destroys (κτείνει καὶ ἀπόλλυσιν), without using what it destroys.[145]

This trend is found also in Hellenistic-Jewish and early Christian authors. In a passage dealing with the evil 'offspring' of the love of money, which occurs both in the *Sibylline Oracles* and *Pseudo-Phocylides*, gold is apostrophized as the originator of evil and the destroyer of life (βιοφθόρος).[146] A similar thought is found in Sir. 8.2: 'gold has ruined [ἀπόλλυμι] many, and has perverted the minds of kings [καρδίας βασιλέων ἐξέκλινε]'. Philo says that the generation which craved meat in the desert was destroyed by its greed.[147]

141. Pseudo-Anacharsis, *Ep.* 9 (50, 11); also Pseudo-Anacharsis, *Ep.* 7 (44, 2-3): 'No good ruler ruins (ἀπόλλυμι) his subjects, nor does a good shepherd harm his sheep.' Only despots ruin their subjects and soldiers, by plundering funds needed for communal use.
142. Cercidas, *Meliamb.* 2.6-17.
143. Dio Chrysostom, *Or.* 17.10.
144. He concludes the point by saying that it is the absence of greed among the θεῖοι that makes them indestructible (ἄφθαρτος) (Dio Chrysostom, *Or.* 17.10-11).
145. Plutarch, *Mor.* 525f.
146. Ps.-Phoc. 44; Sib. Or. 2.115.
147. 'With both hands they pulled in the creatures and filled their laps with them, then put them away in their tents, and, since excessive avidity knows no bounds (αἱ

Luke uses ἀπώλεια to refer to the destruction caused by avarice in Acts 8.20. Barrett comments that 'the work of the magus is financially motivated, and the end of such motivation is ἀπώλεια'.[148] As far as other Christian writers are concerned, I noted above the warning found in 1 Tim. 6.9 that the avaricious are subject to 'many senseless and hurtful desires (ἐπιθυμίας πολλὰς ἀνοήτους καὶ βλαβεράς)'. The warning continues with the mention of 'ruin and destruction (ὄλεθρον καὶ ἀπώλειαν)'. Such ruin is the final consequence of the evils that come from φιλαργυρία (6.10). In contrast, εὐσέβεια μετὰ αὐταρκείας leads to πορισμὸς μέγας (6.6). In *Herm. Sim* 6.2.1-2, the shepherd/ angel of luxury and deceit (τρυφῆς καὶ ἀπάτης) mentioned wears out and deceives souls with evil desires until they are destroyed (ἀπόλ-λυμι), 'some to death and some to corruption'. Death is the penalty for blasphemy and results in eternal destruction, while those who have been corrupted by luxury and deceit may still hope for renewal.[149]

Thus, both the younger and elder sons demonstrate the common philosophical view that covetous desires (whether motivated by prodigality or meanness) lead to destruction. The only way to reverse this, and be restored to a state of health and prosperity, is to adopt the values of temperate sufficiency and liberality. In the parable, these are exemplified by the father.

c. *Application*

The use of the two word-pairs (νεκρός-ζάω and ἀπόλλυμι-εὑρίσκω) in Greco-Roman and Hellenistic Jewish moral literature as metaphors for moral regress or progress, suggests that Luke's readers would have understood the refrain of v. 24a-24d and v. 32b-32d in this way. This is particularly true for the first pair. Luke gives force to his gentle appeal for liberality by reminding his readers that Christians do not consider morality in the area of money and possessions as an optional extra. The

---

γὰρ ἄγαν πλεονεξίαι μέτρον οὐκ ἔχουσι), went out to catch others, and after dressing them in any way they could devoured them greedily (ἀπλήστως), doomed in their senselessness to be destroyed (ἀπόλλυμι) by the surfeit' (Philo, *Spec. Leg.* 4.129-31). The place where they died was called 'Monuments of Lust (ἐπιθυμία)'.

148. C.K. Barrett, 'Light on the Holy Spirit from Simon Magus', in J. Kremer (ed.), *Les actes des apôtres: Traditions, rédaction, théologie* (BETL, 48; Leuven: Leuven University Press, 1979), pp. 281-95 (294).

149. Hermas, *Sim.* 6.2.4.

use or abuse of material resources brings life or death, both to the individual and his or her community. As we shall see in the following chapters, this appeal is undergirded with other significant metaphors, such as that of physical health.

From this perspective, the father's words express a recognition that the son has gone through a life-changing experience. What is celebrated is not the son's restoration to his former state (which was one of moral death leading to physical death, v. 17c), but a celebration of his new state, which is one of moral life. There is also the implication that part of this recovery of life is also a recovery of relationship.

The father's declaration that his son was 'alive and found' affirms powerfully that the younger son has completely turned away from his life of prodigal excess, and has already begun to strive after the ideals of moderation and liberality. The father's words give no support to those exegetes who question the genuineness of the younger son's repentance and see his return as an act of selfish expediency.

Chapter 6

THE LIBERAL FATHER

In this chapter, I begin with an overview of the philosophical ideal of liberality, before proceeding to show that Luke's description of the father reveals that he thought of him as an exemplar of this ideal. The words and actions of the father fit together to form a composite picture of a person who has the right attitude to possessions. As with the description of the prodigality of the younger son, many details of the father's behavior gain fresh meaning when understood as expressions of his liberality.

Luke adds a Christian dimension to the father's liberality by also focusing on his compassion. While he shows liberality to all, his dealings with his two sons are distinguished by the further quality of compassion.

1. *The Ideal of Liberality*

Luke's picture of the father's liberality is firmly grounded in an established and widespread view of liberality which can be traced back to Aristotle. For this reason, Aristotle's treatment of liberality forms the basis of my discussion here. However, related terms, used by other philosophical movements to describe their view of the right use of possessions, are also considered.

As I noted in Chapter 4, liberality (ἐλευθεριότης) is Aristotle's term for the temperate approach to giving and receiving wealth. Right giving involves giving the right amount, at the right time, to the right recipients. It also requires the giver to keep within his means.[1]

Right receiving likewise involves deriving income from the right sources. The liberal man is not overly concerned with gaining wealth,

---

1. This paragraph summarizes Aristotle, *Eth. Nic.* 4.1.1-28.

but manages his own property correctly to ensure that he has the means to give. The fact that he does not value money highly makes him vulnerable to being cheated. When he gives, he is prone to give to excess, leaving himself with the smaller share.[2] He is seldom a rich person, for he is more interested in giving wealth away than in getting or keeping it.

Though the representatives of different philosophical schools hold differing views on what constitutes the right amount, the right time and the right recipients, this Peripatetic ideal of liberality is widely influential. Whenever Greco-Roman,[3] Hellenistic-Jewish or Christian[4] authors touch on the topos On Covetousness, the ideal of liberality is advocated in one way or another, with different groups providing their own emphases reflecting their central beliefs.

2. *Indicators of the Father's Liberality*

In the parable the father is not explicitly called liberal. In accordance with his literary technique, Luke prefers his readers to infer this from his presentation of the father's behavior.

2.   Compare Menander, *Kol.* 41-45: 'No one gets rich quickly if he is honest. For the honest man collects and saves up for himself, while the one of the other sort gets all by plotting against the one who has long been careful.' Menander's interaction with the topos On Covetousness is evident from Miller's summary of the damaged first 13 lines of the play: 'After an initial (and conventional) piece of moralizing ("You never can tell in this life"), there are references to fathers and sons, to administrators (perhaps trustees) and provision for a son, to unhappiness, to action required, and the provision of a dinner for fellow-members of a club' (N. Miller (trans.), *Menander: Plays and Fragments* (Harmondsworth: Penguin Books, 1987), p. 195.

3.   For example, Theophrastus, *Char.* 10, 22 and 30; Pseudo-Anacharsis, *Ep.* 9 (48, 1-2); Dio Chrysostom, *Or.* 21.9; Pseudo-Crates, *Ep.* 10. (62, 8-11); Pseudo-Diogenes, *Ep.* 28 (122, 20-30); Pseudo-Aristippus, *Ep.* 27; Dio Chrysostom, *Or.* 17.18; Horace, *Sat.* 2.3.77-239; Seneca, *Ep.* 17.6-12; Musonius, *Frag.* 34; Epictetus, *Diss.* 4.11.23; Plutarch, *Mor.* 527b; Cicero, *Off.* 2 passim; Juvenal, *Sat.* 14.321; Pseudo-Pythagoras, *Carm. Aur.* 37-38.

4.   For example, *Ep. Arist.* 205, 209; Sir. 11.23-25, 27; *4 Macc.* 1.3-4; Hermas, *Man.* 8.1, 3, 5, 10; *Sim.* 10.1.3; Philo, *Omn. Prob. Lib.* 78, 84; Heb. 13.5; *Sent. Sextus* 13, 50, 88; 1 Tim. 6.6-10; Polycarp, *Phil.* 2.2.

a. *Willingness to Divide Up his Possessions*
The first indication is given in the introduction to the parable (vv. 11b-12c), when the father shows his willingness to divide up his possessions between his two sons, without any protest about the cost of such an action to himself. Such behavior was certainly not normal, and would have been out of the question for ordinary citizens of limited means. The more expected response is illustrated in a diatribe by Pseudo-Socrates:

> 'But you', perhaps some citizen who is angry at his sons for setting their hearts on their inheritance might say, 'Is it your intention not to leave me alone when I die? Will you, the living, even ask the dead for food?'[5]

Some popular philosophers, especially the austere Cynics, advocate the division of wealth among one's family, but such radical renunciation is intended to secure philosophical benefits for the giver. Epistle 38 of Pseudo-Diogenes, for example, concludes with a story about a rich young man deciding to follow Diogenes thus: 'From the next day, after he distributed his property to his relatives (διανείμας τὴν οὐσίαν τοῖς αὐτοῦ), he took up the wallet, doubled his coarse cloak, and followed me'.[6]

Other Cynics, Stoics[7] and Platonists[8] take a less extreme position, teaching that people should be willing to give up their possessions when asked. This is because the wise person is free from desire, [9] is satisfied with only a few necessities, [10] and knows that happiness does not come from either spending or hoarding money. Hellenistic Jews[11]

---

5.   Pseudo-Socrates, *Ep.* 6 (236, 6-11).

6.   Pseudo-Diogenes, *Ep.* 38 (162, 12-29).

7.   Epictetus (*Diss.* 4.7.35), for example, urges people to be willing to let all their possessions go, even their families and own bodies. The loss of property is not a misfortune (*Diss.* 1.9.27). When a man weeps when a child goes on a journey or at the loss of property (ἢ ἀποδημοῦντος τέκνου ἢ ἀπολωλεκότα τὰ ἑαυτου), it is not the event, but his judgment about it that distresses him (Epictetus, *Ench.* 16).

8.   The Neoplatonic *Sentences* of Sextus also advise the wise to give up their possessions freely: 'If when asked you are quite willing to give something up, do not deem it of more worth than the person who would receive it' (329).

9.   Seneca, *Ep.* 115.18. Epictetus (*Diss.* 4.11.23) cites the examples of Diogenes and Socrates. Like them, the philosopher can say: 'I have nothing, need nothing.'

10.   Pseudo-Crates (*Ep.* 11 [62, 14-16]) advises his students to practise being in need of only a few things, 'for this is the closest thing to God'.

11.   Sir. 31.5-8; 2 Macc. 10.20; *Sib. Or.* 2.111; 3.234-36; 8.17-18; *Ps.-Phoc.* 42;

and Christians[12] would notice and value the father's freedom from φιλαργυρία or πλεονεξία.

The popular philosophers also supply a religious reason for having a
liberal attitude to possessions. Stoics and Cynics say that God is the
supreme illustration of the truth that we are happiest without possessions or needs.[13] But the father shows none of these self-oriented motivations.

b. *Readiness to Use his Possessions*
The father's willingness to divide up his property between his sons can
be viewed more generally as the liberal virtue of using what one has.
This is a point often stressed by philosophers writing on aspects of the
topos On Covetousness. It is the opposite position from that of the
mean person who does not even use his possessions for himself, a vice
to which the elder son is prone. Horace ridicules those who justify such
behavior by saying that they are keeping their wealth for their heirs. He
says that they are foolish because heirs usually squander the wealth
they inherit as soon as they get it.[14]

Teles the Cynic illustrates the importance of the right use of possessions with an example from Xenophon which is similar to the parable
under discussion.

> For not ineptly does Xenophon say, 'If I show you two brothers who
> have divided an equal sum (δύο ἀδελφῶν τὴν ἴσην οὐσίαν διελομένων),
> one of whom is in utter distress while the other is quite content (τὸν μὲν

Philo, *Poster. C.* 116; *Gig.* 37; *Conf. Ling.* 47-49, esp. 48; *Spec. Leg.* 1.23-24, 4.65;
Omn. Prob. Lib. 78, 84.

12. 1 Tim. 3.3; 2 Tim. 3.2; Heb. 13.15; 2 Pet. 2.2, 3, 14; *2 Clem.* 4.3; 6.1-4; *Did.*
3.5; 15.1; Polycarp, *Phil.* 2.2; 5.2; 6.1; Hermas, *Sim.* 9.19.3; *Mart. Isa.* 3.23-26;
Sent. Sextus 76; *T. Lev.* 17.2, 8-11 (negatively); *T. Jud.* title, 17.1; 18.2; 19.1.

13. See Pseudo-Socrates, *Ep.* 6 (234, 5-9); Pseudo-Crates, *Ep.* 11 (62, 14-16) and
Ep. 15 (64, 18-19). For a Stoic expression of this theme, see Musonius, *Frag.* 17
(108, 11-18): 'Therefore, as God, through the possession of these virtues, is uncon-
quered by pleasure (ἡδονή) or greed (πλεονεξία), is superior to desire, envy, and
jealousy (ἐπιθυμία, φθόνος, ζηλοτυπία), is high-minded, beneficient, and kindly
(μεγαλόφρων δὲ καὶ εὐεργετικὸς καὶ φιλάνθρωπος) (for such is our conception of
God), so also man in the image of Him, when living in accord with nature, should
be thought of as being like Him, and being like Him, being enviable, and being
enviable, he would forthwith be happy, for we envy none but the happy.'

14. Horace, *Sat.* 2.3.111-23.

ἐν τῇ πάσῃ ἀπορίᾳ, τὸν δὲ ἐν εὐκολίᾳ), isn't it obvious that the money (τὰ χρήματα) is not to be blamed but something else?'[15]

Here, Teles illustrates the view that the right use of wealth is determined by the character of the user, rather than the quantity of wealth. Conversely, the way people use their possessions reveals their characters. Luke illustrates this in the contrasts between the use made of wealth by the three central characters in Lk. 15.11-32.

c. *Good Management of his Resources*
The father's liberality is also evident in his good management of his farm, the source of his wealth. He pays his workers well, and the farm prospers even after the younger son has impoverished it by leaving with some of the family wealth. The fact that his hired workers have 'bread enough and to spare (περισσεύονται ἄρτων)' (v. 17b) is a mark of his generosity. It is the recollection of this fact that encourages the humiliated younger son to dare to return home.

d. *Liberality as an Expression of Wisdom*
More generally, the father's liberality can be seen as an expression of his wisdom. Peripatetics, Stoics and Cynics would think of the father as a virtuous man. Peripatetics would be struck by the apparently effortless, godlike quality of his virtue.[16] Stoics would see him as someone who had completely subjected his impulses to the control of reason.[17] The father exhibits many of the attractive virtues of Lucian's mild Cynic Demonax.[18]

Texts dealing with the topos On Covetousness frequently make the point that wisdom is preferable to wealth. In Aristotle, the temperate man gives his money wisely, not indiscriminately.[19] Cynics and Stoics

---

15. Teles 2 (περὶ αὐταρκείας), (12, 94-98), with reference to Xenophon, *Sym.* 4.35, with slightly different wording.

16. Aristotle, *Eth. Nic.* 7.1.

17. See Dibelius and Greeven, *James*, 116-20, with examples from Diogenes Laertius, 7.121; Epictetus, *Diss.* 4.1 passim; Seneca, *Vit. Beat.* 15.7; Philo, *Omn. Prob. Lib.* 45; and *4 Macc.* 14.12. See also Horace, *Sat.* 2.7; and Persius, *Sat.* 5.

18. Lucian, *Demon.* 3-10.

19. Aristotle, *Eth. Nic.* 4.1.17.

urge the wise person to pursue wisdom and not wealth.[20] Plutarch insists that the philosophic virtues, epitomized by σωφροσύνη, cannot be bought, and calls φιλαργυρία and πλεονεξία a mental disorder (ψυχικὴ νόσος). Hellenistic Judaism also teaches that wisdom is better than riches.

e. *Readiness to Risk and to Trust*
The father's division of his living involves both benefits and risks for him and his sons. Sirach warns that those who give their property prematurely to their relatives, place themselves in their power.[21] Thus, his action displays unusual trust in his sons and gives them the freedom to make choices. Their choices in turn reveal their inner dispositions. Pseudo-Heraclitus says that wealth given to the wicked serves to expose and convict them.[22] Pseudo-Socrates warns that if children are left money without having learnt to be good, they will die in misery and hunger.[23]

From the point of view of freedom, the rest of the parable is an exploration of how the two sons use their freedom: the younger by license (v. 13b ζῶν ἀσώτως), and the elder by a legalistic failure to appropriate his liberty (v. 29b οὐδέποτε ἐντολήν σου παρῆλθον).[24] The father does not treat his sons as possessions or extensions of himself, but free agents. He does not manipulate their behavior, but he does rejoice in the younger son's return to himself (v. 17a), to moral health (v. 27d) and hence to life itself (vv. 24a-d, 32b-d), and he exhorts his elder son to recognize the meaning of compassionate liberality at the end of the parable (vv. 28c-32d).

20. For example, Seneca, *Ep.* 17.3, 5, 6, 10; and Epictetus, *Diss.* 3.17.1-6; 3.26 passim; 4.9.1-2. Horace, *Sat.* 2.3, describes avarice, ambition, self-indulgence and superstition all as forms of madness.

21. Sir. 33.20-22.

22. 'God punishes, not by taking away wealth (πλοῦτος), but rather by giving (δίδωμι) it to the wicked so that, since they have the means to err (ἁμαρτάνω), they might be convicted, and by abounding in wealth, they might expose their own wickedness' (Pseudo-Heraclitus, *Ep.* 8 [208, 5-8]).

23. Pseudo-Socrates, *Ep.* 6 (236, 1-6.). See the criticism of the father who paid for his prodigal son's vices in Martial, *Epigr.* 3.10.

24. This is why it is appropriate to describe the behavior of the elder son as ἀνελευθεριότης/ἀνελευθερία.

3. *Liberality Shown by Example and Word*

In the following sections I consider other ways in which the father's liberality is expressed towards his two sons by example and word.

The father functions as a moral example to both his sons. It is the recollection of his behavior as an employer which encourages the younger son to return home. The elder son's resistance to his father's example is seen in his criticism in vv. 29b-30b, and his father's exhortation begins with the reminder to him that they have been together all along.[25]

While Greco-Roman parenesis usually includes the offer of an example for imitation, different philosophical schools make different uses of the motif. Cynics, particularly the austere Cynics, sometimes hold themselves up as examples to others, [26] while Stoics are more hesitant to do so.[27]

a. *Liberality by Example*

Apart from the indicators already mentioned in section 2 above, the father's liberality is revealed in the way he treats his younger son with compassion, and celebrates his return to himself with joy.

(i) *Liberality Motivated by Compassion*. In the literary analysis of the parable in Chapter 2, I noted the emphasis placed upon the compassion

---

25. One of the thematic reasons for upholding the unity of the parable is that the liberality of the father is expressed in each of the four sections I distinguished in Chapter 2.

26. C.R. Holladay, '1 Corinthians 13: Paul as Apostolic Paradigm', in D.L. Balch, E. Ferguson and W.A. Meeks (eds.), *Greeks, Romans and Christians: Essays in Honor of Abraham J. Malherbe* (Minneapolis: Fortress Press, 1990), pp. 80-98 (86), refers to the way the Cynic preacher holds himself up as an example in περὶ κυνισμοῦ in Epictetus, *Diss.* 3.22.47-49. The more cautious Stoic view is seen in Epictetus, *Diss.* 4.8.28-29.

27. See A.J. Malherbe, 'Exhortation in 1 Thessalonians', in *idem, Paul and the Popular Philosophers* (Minneapolis: Fortress Press, 1989), pp. 49-66 (57-58); *Moral Exhortation*, pp. 124-29; *Paul and the Thessalonians*, p. 58; and 'Pseudo-Heraclitus', p. 54. Plutarch, a Middle Platonist, argues that we should avoid speaking about ourselves, unless it is beneficial either to ourselves or to our hearers. See Plutarch, *Mor.* 539a-547f; and the commentary in H.D. Betz, '*De Laude Ipsius (Moralia 539A-547F)*', in H.D. Betz (ed.), *Plutarch's Ethical Writings and Early Christian Literature* (SCHNT, 4; Leiden: E.J. Brill, 1978), pp. 367-93.

of the father. Menken identifies the verb σπλαγχνίζεσθαι in v. 20c as the central aorist indicative.[28] This is the most distinctive expression of his liberality, just as the most prominent expression of the younger son's prodigality is his return to himself in repentance, and the most distinctive expression of the elder son's meanness is his anger.[29]

Koester provides a useful overview of the development in meaning of the verb σπλαγχνίζομαι.[30] In secular Greek usage, the verb σπλαγχνεύω means to eat the inner parts at a sacrificial meal, [31] or to use the entrails for divination. Pre-Christian Greek has occasional examples of the compound form ἄσπλαγχνος, with the meaning cowardly, and εὐσπλαγχνία, with the meaning of boldness or magnanimity.[32] A fragment from the Stoic Chrysippus[33] explains ἄσπλαγχνος as τὸ μηδὲν ἔχειν ἔνδον συναλγοῦν, suggesting that in postclassical times there was a change in meaning from courage to mercy/sympathy.[34]

The only instance in the LXX of the middle σπλαγχνίζομαι with the sense 'to be merciful' is found in Prov. 17.5.[35] This sense comes to the

---

28. Menken, 'Σπλαγχνίζεσθαι', p. 108. This verb also has a central position in the other two L narratives in which it occurs: Lk. 7.13; 10.33.

29. Bovon states that the three characters in the parable are each characterized by a well-chosen verb: 'the prodigal "came to himself", (vs. 17), the father "had compassion" (vs. 20), and the elder brother "was angry" (vs. 28). The three parts of the story correspond to these three verbs' ('First Reading', p. 60).

30. H. Koester, 'σπλάγχνον, σπλαγχνίζομαι, κτλ', *TDNT*, VII, pp. 548-59. I only make use of his discussion of verbal forms here, with additional observations that relate to the perspective of this study.

31. The only secular inscription reported by Koester is a fourth-century BCE inscription from Cos using σπλαγχνίζω in this sense.

32. Euripides, *Rhes.* 191f.

33. H. von Arnim, *SVF* 2.249, 11-19 (*Frag.* 902).

34. A.J. Malherbe, '"Pastoral Care" in the Thessalonian Church', *NTS* 36 (1990), pp. 375-91 (380), notes, with reference to Cicero, *Tusc.* 4.46, 56, that moral philosophers gave help to people 'out of compassion, especially desiring to relieve the misfortunes of people who did not deserve them'.

35. The only other examples of the verb in the LXX are 2 Macc. 6.8; the Symmachus translation of 1 Kgs 23.21; and Ezek. 24.21. The noun σπλάγχνα occurs a number of times in 4 Macc. Where it does not refer to entrails, it frequently bears the transferred sense of natural parental affection: 4 Macc. 14.13; 15.23; 15.29. Wis. 10.5; and Sir. 30.7 also use the word to refer to the compassion which a father has for his son. Koester, 'σπλάγχνον, κτλ', p. 551, observes that 4 Macc. 14.20; 15.28; and Wis. 10.5 all cite Abraham as an example of how to control such powerful emotions.

fore in the *Testaments of the Twelve Patriarchs*, particularly *The Testament of Zebulon*, entitled ΠΕΡΙ ΕΥΣΠΛΑΓΧΝΙΑΣ ΚΑΙ ΕΛΕΟΥΣ,
which deals extensively with this theme and provides an important illustration of Luke's use of the term. σπλαγχνίζομαι is found in *T. Zeb.*
4.2; 6.4; 7.1, 2; 8.1, 3, 4.[36] The first reference is simply to 'compassion',
but, in the other passages, the verb expresses 'the guiding inner disposition which leads to mercy'.[37] In both Prov. 17.5 and *T. Zeb.* compassion and mercy are related to issues traditionally dealt with in the topos
On Covetousness. Proverbs 17.5 is part of a unit (vv. 1-5) dealing with
themes relating to covetousness and possession.[38] In *Testament of
Zebulon*, Zebulon argues for his innocence and goodness in terms that
relate to the topos.[39]

Philo uses σπλάγχνα mostly to refer to the inner organs. Because
these organs are hidden they may refer, figuratively, to the inward
being, heart or soul.[40] One passage in Philo, which does *not* use σπλαγχνίζομαι, is nevertheless valuable for showing that good parents
were expected to show compassion to their prodigal children.

> Now parents do not lose thought for their wastrel children [ἀσώτων υι-
> 'έων], but in pity [οἶκτος] for their unhappy state, bestow on them care
> and attention, deeming that it is only mortal enemies who take advantage
> of others to trample on them, while friends and kinsmen should lighten
> their downfall. Often too they lavish their kindness on the wastrels more
> than on the well-behaved, knowing well that these have in their sober
> disposition [σωφροσύνη] a plentiful source of prosperity while the wast-
> rels' one hope is in their parents, and if this fail them, they will lack the
> very necessaries [ἀναγκαῖα] of life. In the same way God too, the Father
> of all reasonable intelligence has indeed all who are endowed with rea-
> son under his care, but takes thought also for those who live a misspent

---

36. Other forms found in *T. Zeb.* are εὐσπλαγχνία (*T. Zeb.* title 5.1; 8.1; 9.8),
εὔσπλαγχνος (*T. Zeb.* 9.7), and references to τὰ σπλάγχνα as the seat of compassion in the inner being of a person (*T. Zeb.* 2.2, 4; 5.3, 4; 7.3, 4; 8.2, 6).

37. Koester, 'σπλάγχνον, κτλ', p. 551.

38. Words and phrases such as ψωμὸς μεθ' ἡδονῆς; πολλῶν ἀγαθῶν καὶ
ἀδίκων θυμάτων; οἰκέτης νοήμων; δεσποτῶν ἀφρόνων; διελεῖται μέρη; ἄργυρος
καὶ χρυσός; δίκαιος; πτωχοῦ; ἐπιχαίρων ἀπολλυμένῳ; ἐπισπλαγχνιζόμενος
ἐλεηθήσεται.

39. See *T. Zeb.* 1.3; 3.1; 4.1-3; 5.2; 6.1-2, 5-6; 7.2-4.

40. Koester, 'σπλάγχνον, κτλ', p. 553, identifies two definite examples, Philo,
Leg. Gai. 368, and *Jos.* 25.

life, thereby giving them time for reformation but also keeping within the bounds of his own merciful nature which has for its attendant virtue [ἀρετή] and loving kindness [φιλανθρωπία] well fitted to keep watch as sentry around God's world.[41]

Here, Philo says that compassionate behavior is in accordance with 'the Father of all reasonable intelligence' who orders the universe. Dibelius and Greeven mention other places in his writings where Philo seeks to bridge Judaism and Stoicism by relating obedience to the Jewish Law to living in harmony with nature or cosmic reason. Thus, in Philo at least, there is a point of contact between God's Law, his compassionate action, and Stoic notions of cosmic harmony.[42]

This association of the ideas of cosmic reason and compassion may help to explain the Christian understanding of σπλαγχνίζομαι as a divine emotion. In the New Testament σπλαγχνίζομαι is only found in the synoptic gospels. In the parables[43] it denotes a special human attitude[44] and elsewhere it is used only of Jesus.[45] Hermas quite frequently uses the verb to explain that all repentance derives from the mercy or compassion of the Lord.[46] In one instance, Hermas, *Vis.* 3. 12. 3, the Lord's merciful action (ἐσπλαγχνίσθη) is likened to the way the despair, weakness and poverty of old age may be removed by the news

41. Philo, *Prov.* 2.4-6. This reference, and Philo, *Praem. Poen.* 116, are suggested by Downing, *Strangely Familiar*, p. 124, as worth comparing with Lk. 15.18-20.

42. Dibelius and Greeven (*James*, p. 117) refer to Philo, *Op. Mund.* 3; *Vit. Mos.* 2.48 and 2.52. Compare the reference to the σπλάγχνα of God in *T. Zeb.* 8.2 and the explanation of God's mercy in Acts 17.30. See the discussion of harmony in Chapter 7. The Roman view of *misericordia* as a weakness (Cicero, *Tusc.* 4.80) is softened in Virgil's *Aeneid*, according to Cox. See A.S. Cox, 'To Do as Rome Does?' *GR* NS 12 (1965), pp. 85-96 (91).

43. Mt. 18.27 (with μακροθυμέω and ἐλεέω); Lk. 10.33; and 15.20.

44. Koester, 'σπλάγχνον, κτλ', p. 554, calls σπλαγχνίζομαι 'the basic and decisive attitude in human and hence Christian acts'.

45. Mt. 9.36; 14.14; 15.32; 20.34; Mk 1.41; 6.34; 8.2; 9.22; Lk. 7.13. Luke omits the verb from his account of the feeding of the five thousand (Lk. 9.10-17), thereby departing from Mt. 14.14 and Mk 6.34.

46. σπλαγχνίζομαι is seen in Hermas to be an attribute of God alone: *Man.* 4, 3, 5; 9, 3; *Sim.* 7.4; 8, 6, 3; 8, 11, 1; and 9, 14, 3. In contrast, the angel of punishment in *Sim.* 6.3.2 shows no compassion.

of a sudden inheritance. The only other occurrence of this verb in the Apostolic Fathers is found in 2 Clem. 1.7, where it refers to the mercy of God in saving Christians from their inherent 'error and destruction (πλάνη καὶ ἀπώλεια)'. However, in the light of our interest in the relation of the word to the topos On Covetousness, we ought to note that in Polycarp, *Phil.* 5.2 and 6.1 Christian leaders are required to be εὔσπλαγχνοι and free from other vices, such as injustice and the love of money, which are associated with covetousness.[47]

This information indicates that this verb was used primarily by Hellenistic Jews and Christians to describe a divine activity. When it was used to describe human actions, such behavior would be viewed as a reflection of divine compassion. This verb is thus one of Luke's most important Christian qualifications of the Greco-Roman virtue of liberality.

(ii) *Liberality Expressed in Celebration.* May we describe the manner in which the father celebrates his younger son's return as 'liberal'? Aristotle does not specify how a liberal man should celebrate, but we can easily deduce a few guidelines: he should keep his spending within his means[48] and he should spend gladly and lavishly, particularly if his spending is on a large enough scale to be called magnificent.[49] Unlike the mean person, he will spend freely, and, unlike the prodigal, he will not spend on debauchery (ἀκολασία) and pleasure (ἡδονή).[50]

It is possible to use these criteria to argue that the father's spending was prodigal. This is the view that his elder son takes. He maintains that it is inappropriate to throw a lavish party for someone who has already wasted much of the family's hard-earned wealth. It is inappropriate to do so on the large scale reflected in the killing of the prize calf[51] and the invitation to the whole community to rejoice.[52] It is also

---

47. Polycarp, *Phil.* 5.2: 'ἀφιλάργυροι, ἐγκρατεῖς περὶ πάντα, εὔσπλαγχνοι, ἐπιμελεῖς'; Polycarp, *Phil.* 6.1: 'ἀπεχόμενοι πάσης ὀργῆς, προσωποληψίας, κρίσεως ἀδίκου, μακρὰν ὄντες πάσης φιλαργυρίας.'

48. Aristotle, *Eth. Nic.* 4.1.23.

49. Aristotle, *Eth. Nic.* 4.2.8.

50. Aristotle, *Eth. Nic.* 4.1.35, 37-39.

51. The phrase ὁ μόσχος ὁ σιτευτός means the fattened, and hence prize, calf. See LNSM, s.v. μόσχος. Fitzmyer (*Luke*, p. 1090) apparently follows BAGD in considering that ὁ μόσχος ὁ σιτευτός derives from the LXX of Judg. 6.28 (A) and Jer. 26.21.

52. The shift from the second-person plural imperative θύσατε to the first-per-

unfair to act in this way because he, the faithful elder son, has never been given any kind of party, let alone one on this scale.

The recurrent use of the verb εὐφραίνω in the father's speech would have suggested to some readers, especially those with ascetic inclinations, that the father's celebration was an intemperate act. Two of the other parables in the L collection, Lk. 12.16-20 and 16.19-31, use it in the context of accusations of excessive or luxurious eating and drinking, [53] reflecting an issue often discussed by moral philosophers in the process of teaching on the nature of true happiness.

Against this interpretation, it needs to be recognized that all the major schools of Greco-Roman philosophy affirm that εὐδαιμονία is the proper goal of a well-lived life. Both Platonists and Stoics insist that real happiness has to be distinguished from apparent happiness and transient pleasures.[54] The Stoic ideal of ἀπάθεια does not imply absence of feelings. Long points out that 'it means suppression of judgments based on false assessments of pleasure and pain (or good and bad)'. Thus, despite the differences in their understanding of the origins of moral virtue, Stoics and Peripatetics agree that a good man will not only perform acts of virtue, but will feel pleasure while doing so.[55]

All the moral philosophers advocate moderation in the areas of eating and drinking simply because such excesses do not lead to true pleasure. This is true also of Epicureanism. Epicurus of course does not advocate excesses, as his *Letter to Menoecus* makes clear: 'Plain fare gives as

son plural of φαγόντες εὐφρανθῶμεν has the effect of shifting the attention of the reader from the duties of the slaves to the celebration of the whole community.

53. Lk. 12.19: φάγε, πίε, εὐφραίνου; Lk. 16.19: εὐφραινόμενος καθ' ἡμέραν λαμπρῶς.

54. W.A. Meeks, *The Moral World of the First Christians* (London: SPCK, 1986), pp. 46-47.

55. A.A. Long, 'Aristotle's Legacy to Stoic Ethics', *BULICS* 15 (1968), pp. 72-85 (79 and 82). Striker cites Aristotle, *Eth. Nic.* 2.3 ('An index of our dispositions is afforded by the pleasure or pain that accompanies our actions') to illustrate the view that 'morality provides the framework within which human beings try to achieve happiness' (G. Striker, 'The Role of *Oikeiosis* in Stoic Ethics', in J. Annas [ed.], *Oxford Studies in Ancient Philosophy* [Oxford: Clarendon Press, 1983], pp. 145-67 [166]).

much pleasure as costly diet'.[56] His teaching needs to be contrasted with that of popular misunderstandings of the Epicurean position.[57]

The austere Cynics are the strongest advocates of frugality. Pseudo-Diogenes, for example, contrasts a sumptuous meal with happiness. He prefers a simple 'banquet' of water and cresses. 'Therefore, you too, set dinners like this before me, imitating the fairest thing in life, Happiness [εὐδαιμονία]. As for the objects of wealth [πλούτου], send them to those who miss the road to happiness'.[58]

Other epistles by Pseudo-Diogenes use the verb εὐφραίνω in the context of accusations that intemperance and greed impede the experience of true joy. In Epistle 28, Pseudo-Diogenes accuses the 'Greeks' of enjoying little and being much distressed (μικρὰ μὲν γὰρ εὐφραίνεσθε, πολλὰ δὲ λυπεῖσθε) because of their ignorance, envy and greed.[59] He asserts that he is 'more capable of gladness (εὐφραίνεσθαι) than sadness, and knowledge than ignorance'.[60] In *Epistle* 32, he criticizes

56. Diogenes Laertius, 10.130. The frugal eating habits of Epicurus are mentioned in Diogenes Laertius, 10.11.

57. This is evident in epitaphs such as

Εὐφροσύνη, πόθος, οἶνος, ὕπν[ος, ταῦτ᾽ ἐστὶ βροτοῖσι
πλοῦτος· ἀνευφράντων Ταντάλ[ου ἐστὶ βίος.

(Mirth, love, wine, sleep, these are men's riches; the mournful lead the life of Tantalus.)

Sometimes they relate well to the issues of those parables, as in the so-called epitaph of Sardanapalus:

ταῦτ᾽ ἔχω, ὅσσ᾽ ἔφαγον καὶ ἐφύβρισα, καὶ μετ᾽ ἐρώτων
τέρπν᾽ ἔπαθον· τὰ δὲ πολλὰ καὶ ὄλβια κεῖνα λέλειπται·

(I keep what I ate, my dissipation, the pleasures I had in love; all those many other splendid things are left behind.)

For a discussion of these and other examples of popular Epicureanism, see R. Lattimore, *Themes in Greek and Latin Epitaphs* (Urbana: University of Illinois Press, 1962), pp. 260-63.

58. Pseudo-Diogenes, *Ep.* 37 (158, 9-12).

59. See Pseudo-Diogenes, *Ep.* 28 (120, 19-21; 122, 10-13, 21-22; 122, 30-124, 3): They are unable even to enjoy a wedding day, because they are spoiled and hard to please. At festivals or games they eat, drink, get drunk, have intercourse and act effeminately. They suffer illness through intemperance. If they have any sense and wish to be saved they must learn self-control (σωφρονεῖν μάθετε).

60. Pseudo-Diogenes, *Ep.* 28 (124, 13). This combination of gladness and sadness is found also in 2 Cor. 2.2-3.

Aristippus for being delighted by eating and drinking at extravagant dinners (ἐσθίων καὶ πίνων τὰ πολυτελῆ δεῖπνα), at which cruel and immoral things take place.[61]

The same ascetic view of celebration is also found in some early Christian writings. Hermas reflects a Stoic ideal in advising his readers to adopt God's 'perfection and moderation' (maturitatem... et modestiam), [62] and the Neoplatonic *Sentences* of Sextus repeatedly advocate moderation, particularly in the areas of eating and drinking.[63] However, Lk. 15.11-32 does not support the ascetic viewpoint that happiness and wealth are mutually exclusive. The elder son's objections are not based on an ascetic ideal. Rather, to his mean view, this particular act of celebration seems excessive and unjust.

Moreover, other Hellenistic Jewish texts which draw on Stoic ethics, such as Sirach, Wisdom and the works of Philo, frequently use εὐφραίνω to refer to legitimate causes of rejoicing. Sirach teaches that it is right and good to rejoice in one's children (Sir. 16.1-2; 25.7; 30.1, 5).[64]

Rejoicing in one's children is one of the rewards given to those who honour their father and mother (Sir. 3.5-7). While it is not right for a stingy (μικρολόγος) or envious person to enjoy riches, the generous man should enjoy his own wealth, [65] for gladness is a consequence of

61. Pseudo-Diogenes, *Ep.* 32 (138, 5-15).

62. Hermas, *Sim.* 10.1.3. K. Lake says that this is a translation of either σωφροσύνη or of εὐταξία, meaning propriety of conduct, a word used especially by the Stoics. See *The Apostolic Fathers* (2 vols.; trans. K. Lake; LCL; Cambridge, MA: Harvard University Press, 1913), II, p. 299.

63. *Sent. Sextus* 265, 268, 269, 345, 412.

64. Compare *T. Jud.* 13.8, in which Judah says that he was punished by the Lord for having no delight in the children of Tamar. While Epictetus does teach that people should train themselves not be affected by what happens to their children, because this is one of the many things which is outside their control (*Diss.* 4.1.67, 110), such ἀπάθεια does not deny paternal affection. See Epictetus, *Diss.* 1.11.6: 'This is the way, said the man, all, or at least most, of us fathers feel.—And I do not contradict you either, answered Epictetus...'; and Seneca, *Ep.* 75.3: 'yet in the father's embrace also, holy and restrained as it is, plenty of affection is disclosed'. Hopkins points out that although Roman philosophical consolation literature advised against unseemly or excessive mourning, this advice was rarely followed in practice. See Hopkins, 'Death in Rome', pp. 218-19.

65. 'Whoever accumulates by depriving himself, accumulates for others (ὁ συνάγων ἀπὸ τῆς ψυχῆς αὐτοῦ, συνάγει ἄλλοις) and others will live in luxury on his goods. If a man is mean to himself (πονηρὸς ἑαυτῷ), to whom will he be generous? He will not enjoy (εὐφραίνω) his own riches' (Sir. 14.3-5).

generosity to others. With wisdom[66] and God's mercy[67] it ought to be rejoiced in.[68] Sirach condemns those who rejoice in great luxury, wickedness or the fall of the pious.[69] Wisdom 14.28 condemns the ecstatic raving of idolatrous worship.[70] Sirach makes one reference that suggests that it is right to rejoice at a feast.[71]

Philo's Middle Platonism is evident when he says that Moses doubted whether anyone could hold a feast in the true sense of finding 'delight and festivity [ἐνευφραινόμενος καὶ ἐντρυφῶν] in the contemplation of the world', because of the 'numberless evils generated by the greedy desires [αἱ ψυχῆς πλεονεξίαι] of the soul', as well as the other causes of the weakness of the body, the vicissitudes of fortune and the wrongs which people do to one another.[72]

1 Maccabees links rejoicing with victories over the wicked[73] or the establishment of friendships.[74]

In the *Testaments of the Twelve Patriarchs*, rejoicing is linked with the removal of evil, repentance and the keeping of the Law. When the corrupt priesthood of *Testament of Levi* 17 is replaced by a new priest, it is said that the heavens shall rejoice and the Lord shall rejoice over his children (*T. Levi* 18.5, 13).[75] In *T. Dan.* 5.7-12 rejoicing follows repentance of acts of greed. In *T. Zeb.* 10.2, the dying Zebulon says that

---

66. Sir. 4.18; 40.20. Compare Wis. 7.12, where the writer looks back on his life and rejoices in all the good things and innumerable riches (ἀναρίθμητος πλοῦτος) that have come to him together with wisdom.

67. Sir. 32 (35).19; 51.29.

68. Commenting on the LXX citation of Deut. 32.43 in Rom. 15.10, Cranfield, *Romans*, p. 746, says that the passive of εὐφραίνειν is specially used in the LXX with reference 'to rejoicing in God's protection and help, to the exultant joy expressed in cultic worship, and to the joy of the eschatological fulfilment'. Compare the LXX citation of Isa. 54.1 in Gal. 4.27.

69. Sir. 18.32; 19.5; 27.29.

70. 'For they either rave in exaltation (εὐφραίνω), or prophesy lies, or live unrighteously, or readily commit perjury.' Reese comments that the list of vices in Wis. 14.25-27 exhibits points of contact with Stoicism and Epicureanism, especially that of Philodemus (J.M. Reese, *Hellenistic Influence on the Book of Wisdom and its Consequences* [AnBib, 41; Rome: Biblical Institute Press, 1970], pp. 20-21).

71. Sir. 35 (32).2

72. Philo, *Spec. Leg.* 2.52.

73. 1 Macc. 3.7; 7.48; 11.44; 14.11. Compare 2 Macc. 15.11, 27; and *4 Macc.* 8.18.

74. 1 Macc. 12.12; 14.21.

75. Compare Rev. 11.10; 12.12; and 18.20.

he will (metaphorically) rise again and be glad in the midst of his tribe with those who keep the Law of the Lord and his commandments.

Thus, it would appear that the motif of rejoicing derives more from Hellenistic Jewish than Greco-Roman treatments of the topos On Covetousness. However, as there is no suggestion of excessive eating or drinking at the feast by anyone, let alone the father, Greco-Roman readers too would have had no reason to question his behavior. They are likely to have interpreted it as an act of generous, heartfelt celebration, reflecting the moderate Aristotelian virtues of ἐλευθεριότης and σωφροσύνη, the respective means of the vices of ἀσωτία and ἀκολασία. Luke's Christian readers would agree, as the celebration described was clearly not an occasion for the kind of idolatrous worship mentioned in Acts 7.41, the only other place in the New Testament in which similar language is used.[76]

Such recognition that the father's celebration was appropriate shows that the elder son's viewpoint is wrong. This is why the father does not justify his generosity in terms of the elder son's meanness, saying for example that he could afford to kill the calf, or that the family could easily have spared a kid for a party for the elder son's friends. He explains his actions in terms of the principles of liberality. Regardless of how much one has, possessions should always be shared, with compassion and joy.

---

76. In Acts 7.41 the making of a golden calf (μοσχοποιέω) is the cause of idolatrous sacrifices and rejoicing (ἀνήγαγον θυσίαν τῷ εἰδώλῳ καὶ εὐφραίνοντο). Most of the papyrus references to μόσχος given by MM, 418, mention it as a sacrificial animal and this trend is also evident in early Christian literature. Apart from the occurrences in our parable, Acts 7.41 and a symbolic reference in Rev. 4.7, the only other occurrences of μόσχος in the New Testament are in Heb. 9.12 and 19. There the reference is to the blood of calves used in the Yom Kippur ritual and in the establishment of the Sinai covenant. (The corresponding LXX references are Lev. 16.6, 11, μόσχος; and Exod. 24.5, μοσχάρια.) *1 Clem.* 52.2, citing Ps. 69.30-32, uses μόσχος and εὐφραίνω in a sacrificial context, contrasting the sacrifice of a calf with the sacrifice of a broken spirit.

F.F. Bruce, *The Acts of the Apostles: The Greek Text with Introduction and Commentary* (London: Tyndale Press, 2nd edn, 1952), p. 173, points out that Justin in *Dial.* 19, 73, 102 and 132 uses the noun μοσχοποιία to describe the Jews' action in making the golden calf.

b. *Liberality by Word: Moral Exhortation*
The elder son's complaint to his father and the father's appeal (v. 28c
uses παρεκάλει) to his elder son in vv. 28c-32d can be compared in
form and content with the parenesis given by moral philosophers to
change the behavior of those they were training.[77] The art of giving
moral guidance through speech, which follows the way fathers seek to
guide their sons, [78] originated in philosophical rhetoric and can be traced
back to Plato's *Phaedrus*.[79]

The most general of the terms used to describe such moral exhortation is παρακαλέω, [80] although a wide range of other terms is also used
for particular kinds of exhortation, each carefully adapted to the needs
of the hearers.[81]

In paraenesis, hearers are not given additional instruction, but are
reminded of what they already know. All paraenesis has the aim of
helping the weak: 'those who have difficulty living up to the demands
of the philosophical life'. One sign of such weakness is a susceptibility
to anger, to taking offence and to retaliation.[82] The philosopher has
compassion on such people and is patient in his appeal to them, often
treating them as a father would his sons.[83] He focuses his appeal on the
characters of the persons being appealed to, each time addressing the

77. This section draws upon A.J. Malherbe's work on the relationship between
New Testament and philosophical paraenesis, particularly, 'Exhortation in 1 Thessalonians', pp. 49-66; and ' "Pastoral Care" ', pp. 375-91.

78. See the comments on 1 Thess. 2.11-12 (ὡς ἕνα ἕκαστον ὑμῶν ὡς πατὴρ
τέκνα ἑαυτοῦ παρακαλοῦντες ὑμᾶς) in Malherbe, 'Exhortation in 1 Thessalonians', pp. 53-55.

79. Malherbe, ' "Pastoral Care" ', pp. 376-77.

80. Malherbe, ' "Pastoral Care" ', p. 378. Commenting on Heb. 12.5 (τῆς
παρακλήσεως, ἥτις ὑμῖν ὡς υἱοῖς διαλέγεται), Moffat says that παράκλησις is the
regular term in Alexandrian Judaism for an appeal to an individual to rise to the
higher life of philosophy (J. Moffatt, *A Critical and Exegetical Commentary on the
Epistle to the Hebrews* [ICC; Edinburgh: T. & T. Clark, 1924], p. 200).

81. See Malherbe, 'Exhortation in 1 Thessalonians', p. 53. Malherbe, ' "Pastoral
Care" ', p. 382 n. 33, refers to lists in Seneca, *Ep.* 64.7-10; *Consol. ad Marc.* 1.8;
2.1; *Ira* 1.6; Dio Chrysostom, *Or.* 9.7-8; Lucian, *Nigr.* 35-37. A good example,
frequently cited by Malherbe, is the ideal Cynic described by Dio Chrysostom in
Or. 77/78.37-8. Compare the description in Musonius, *Frag.* 1 (34, 34-36, 6).

82. Malherbe, ' "Pastoral Care" ', pp. 379-80. See Chapter 8 below.

83. Malherbe, ' "Pastoral Care" ', pp. 379 and 391.

moral issue in question, [84] making his appeal in private, without anger or harshness. [85]

(i) *Patient Reminder*. These typical elements are all present in vv. 28c-32d. The elder son is revealed to be a weak person by the way he takes offence at his father's liberality. He seeks to retaliate by accusing his father of treating him unjustly (see Chapter 8). The father's response to the accusation is patient and compassionate. He does not become angry or retaliate, because he recognizes that his son's meanness is the cause of his behavior. He addresses him compassionately as τέκνον. [86] The conversation takes place outside the house, and so presumably in private.

Because his son's root problem is meanness, the father explains the meaning of liberality, relating what he says to his son's reference to his friends and to other matters that his son already knows: his liberality is not new, for they live together; he should not have waited for him to provide food for a feast, for their goods are held in common; it is right to celebrate the return of a son, particularly when he has repented of his wrongs. He makes clear that his liberal actions are just.

The son's complaint focuses on the injustice of his father's treatment of him, and illustrates this with a reference to the fact that he has never been given a young goat to enjoy with his friends (v. 29f ἵνα μετὰ τῶν φίλων μου εὐφρανθῶ). [87] The father answers this by showing that both

---

84. Malherbe, 'Exhortation in 1 Thessalonians', p. 55 n. 32.

85. Malherbe, ' "Pastoral Care" ', p. 384. Seneca illustrates this in his advice on how to heal anger in *Ira* 3.39.1–40.2. Compare Lucian's description of the absence of anger in Demonax in *Demon*. 7. The Cynic author of Pseudo-Socrates, *Ep*. 6 (236, 16), condones the angry way a father speaks to his sons about their desire for their inheritance, by saying that his paternal prerogative and civic freedom of speech (πατρικὴν ἅμα πολιτικῇ παρρησίᾳ ἄγων) allow this. Compare the criteria for exhortation in Epicurean groups, derived from περὶ παρρησίας by Philodemus, identified in N.W. de Witt, 'Organization and Procedure in Epicurean Groups', *CP* 31 (1936), pp. 205-11 (209).

86. The father's compassion closely reflects the paraenetic instructions on anger and compassion in Eph. 4.31–5.1. The writer uses the terms ὀργή and εὔσπλαγχνος (in each case together with other synonyms). Those who imitate God by their compassion are called God's 'beloved children (τέκνα ἀγαπητά)'.

87. The Western textual tradition (D) enhances the self-pitying note of his complaint by replacing εὐφρανθῶ with ἀριστήσω, perhaps from Lk. 11.37.

justice and friendship depend upon the virtue of liberality.[88]

(ii) *The Issue in Question: Shared Possessions.* Because of the importance of friendship in Greco-Roman culture, [89] friends are an important subject in Luke–Acts.[90] Other references to friends in Luke–Acts show Luke's awareness of Greco-Roman attitudes to friendship, even when he sometimes inverts them to reveal the special concerns of the Gospel.[91] These factors make it likely that the reference to friends in vv. 29-30 is a significant detail, which the father develops when he refers to a theme that is common to friendship and liberality: the ideal of shared possessions.

The Greco-Roman topos On Friendship has attracted much attention in recent years, with a number of full-scale studies of its use by New Testament authors. Malherbe cites P. Marshall's study of Paul's relations with the Corinthians, M. White and K. Berry's studies of the topos in Philippians, his own illustration of the friendly relationship between Paul and the Thessalonians, and H.D. Betz's claims of the influence of the topos in Gal. 4.12-20.[92]

88. The correspondence between the phrases μετὰ τῶν φίλων in vv. 29-30 and μετὰ πορνῶν in v. 30a gives the impression that the elder son saw both these two groups of people in a utilitarian way. If so, this is a further criticism of his judgment. Just as it is wrong to attempt to buy pleasure from prostitutes, so it is wrong to think that friendship can be bought.

89. Stählin points out that the φίλος word-group entered Jewish and Christian literature under Hellenistic influence and that New Testament usage is almost entirely confined to the Lukan and Johannine writings (Stählin, 'φίλος, κτλ', *TDNT*, IX, pp. 146-71).

90. 17 of the 29 occurrences of φίλος in the New Testament are found in Luke–Acts.

91. Greco-Roman readers would recognize the following actions as normal in the behavior expected of friends: share griefs (Lk. 7.6); invite one another to meals (Lk. 7.34; 14.12, norm inverted; 15.29); give material help to one another (Lk. 11.5-8, norm inverted; 16.9; Acts 27.3); share joys (Lk. 15.6, 9); share important occasions (Acts 10.24); are concerned for one another's welfare (Lk. 12.4; Acts 19.31); would die for one another (21.16, norm inverted); are of one mind, for good or ill (Lk. 23.12).

92. See Malherbe, 'Hellenistic Moral Philosophy', pp. 23-25. The works referred to are those of P. Marshall, *Enmity in Corinth: Social Conventions in Paul's Relations with the Corinthians* (WUNT, 2.23; Tübingen: J.C.B. Mohr [Paul

Friendship is another example of a topos that addresses some of the themes in this parable, but which does not provide a comprehensive explanation for the parable as a whole.[93] This means that the following discussion does not constitute a full treatment of the topos On Friendship. All I do here is look at one of the themes that this topos shares with the topos On Covetousness: the justice of holding property in common.

This ideal, which is central to the parable from the moment the father is asked to divide the family's common property, is raised explicitly in vv. 31b-c: 'you are always with me, and all that is mine is yours', σὺ πάντοτε μετ' ἐμοῦ εἶ, καὶ πάντα τὰ ἐμὰ σά ἐστιν. As Johnson has observed, this strikingly 'anticipates the language and thought of Acts 4.32ff, particularly in the note that those who are together in unity share *all* with each other'.[94] The ideal is epitomized in Barnabas (Acts 4.36-37; 11.22-30).

The ideal of commonly held property, which I discussed in the preceding chapter from the perspective of the injustice of covetousness, is also central to the topos On Friendship. This is evident in the well-known proverbs: 'For friends all things are common', κοινὰ τὰ φίλων and 'friendship is equality', φιλίαν ἰσότητα.[95] As I noted in Chapter 5, this ideal is said to have originated with the Pythagoreans and is

Siebeck], 1987); L.M. White, 'Morality between Two Worlds: A Paradigm of Friendship in Philippians', in D.L. Balch, E. Ferguson and W.A. Meeks (eds.), *Greeks, Romans and Christians: Essays in Honor of Abraham J. Malherbe* (Minneapolis: Fortress Press, 1990), pp. 201-15; K.L. Berry, 'The Function of Friendship Language in Paul's Letter to the Philippians' (PhD dissertation, Yale University); A.J. Malherbe, *Social Aspects of Early Christianity* (Philadelphia: Fortress Press, 2nd edn, 1983), pp. 25-28; *idem, Paul and the Thessalonians*, pp. 72-73; and Betz, *Galatians*, pp. 220-37. A study which examines the social function of the topos in Luke–Acts (and which makes reference to many of the important studies) is that of A.C. Mitchell, 'The Social Function of Friendship in Acts 2.44-47 and 4.32-37', *JBL* 111 (1992), pp. 255-72.

93. Other examples of topoi are those on physical health, anger, and love for children.

94. Johnson, *Literary Function*, p. 161.

95. This motif is discussed in Johnson, *Sharing Possessions*, pp. 119-26, 128-29, with reference to Plato, *Resp.* 449c,d; 450c; Aristotle, *Eth. Nic.* 9.8.2; Iamblichus, *VP* 17.72, 73; 18.81; and Diogenes Laertius, 8.10. For Epicurus, see Diogenes Laertius, 10.11.

advocated by Plato[96] and the Peripatetics.[97] The Stoics based their belief in equality and community upon their understanding of friendship as a divine gift: 'All things belong to the gods; the wise are friends of the gods; among friends everything is common property; all things belong to the wise'.[98] This Stoic belief in equality and community underlies attacks on the concepts of 'mine' and 'yours' in Hellenistic Jewish[99] and Christian writers.[100]

Because of this ideal of shared possessions, treatments of the topos On Covetousness make it clear that meanness and friendship are antithetical.[101] Misers are harsh with their friends, [102] or try to profit from them in unworthy ways, such as gambling.[103] Theophrastus illustrates

96. Plato, *Resp.* 462c; compare *Phaed.* 279c. Plutarch (*Mor.* 484b) cites with approval 'Plato's advice to the citizens of his state, to abolish, if possible, the notion of "mine" and "not mine" '.

97. In *De Fraterno Amore* Plutarch (*Mor.* 490e) quotes Theophrastus as developing the maxim κοινὰ τὰ φίλων to mean that friends should have friends in common (εἰ κοινὰ τὰ φίλων ἐστί, μάλιστα δεῖ κοινοὺς τῶν φίλων εἶναι τοὺς φίλους).

98. See R.M. Grant, *Early Christianity and Society: Seven Studies* (London: Collins, 1987), pp. 102-103; and Malherbe, 'Pseudo-Heraclitus', p. 49. The syllogism is Cynic in origin, attributed to Diogenes in Diogenes Laertius, 6.37; and found in Pseudo-Crates, *Epp.* 26 and 27. See also Diogenes Laertius, 6.72; Seneca, *Ben.* 7.4.1; Philo, *Vit. Mos.* 1.156-59; *De Sobr.* 56-57 and *Sent. Sextus* 228: 'It is impious for those who share God in common, and indeed as Father, not to share possessions in common.' The common idea that God is the owner and giver of all good gifts is also found in Christian writings: 1 Cor. 10.26; Jas 1.17; Hermas, *Sim.* 1.6-8; Tertullian, *Apol.* 39.5-7. See Hengel, *Property*, pp. 68-69, 58.

99. Philo stresses the importance of the idea of ἰσότης (equality) of distribution. See Philo, *Mut. Nom.* 103; *Vit. Mos.* 1.324; *Spec. Leg.* 4.54; *Vit. Cont.* 70; *Conf. Ling.* 48 and *Omn. Prob. Lib.* 79.

100. See Erskine, *Hellenistic Stoa*, pp. 103-22, especially pp. 110-14. Epictetus uses the language of 'I' and 'mine' to teach that the only thing that is truly ours is the power to deal with external impressions. See Epictetus, *Diss.* 3.24.68-69, and his discourse on friendship (*Diss.* 2.22, esp. 2.22.19).

101. Paul implies this in *Phil.* 4.10-20: despite his claim to be αὐτάρκης, he values the friendship which the Philippian church has shown him in the partnership of giving and receiving (ἐκοινώνησεν εἰς λόγον δόσεως καὶ λήψεως).

102. Pseudo-Socrates, *Ep.* 6 (236, 22-23) says that those who treat their friends badly are even worse at managing money. Plutarch (*Mor.* 525c) describes the money-lover in terms that suggest the elder brother.

103. Aristotle, *Eth. Nic.* 4.1.43. In Pseudo-Anacharsis, *Ep.* 3 (40, 6-9), the tyrant Hipparchus is advised to: 'renounce dice games and drunkenness (κύβους καὶ

the vice of meanness (αἰσχροκέρδεια) with a man who sells watered-down wine to his friend.[104] All covetousness is actively hostile to the ideals of true friendship.[105] Nearly all the philosophical schools make the point that friendship is not based upon self-interest. Only the Epicureans take a different view, and they are criticized for thinking of friendship as a means of gaining practical benefits and as a source of pleasure.[106]

Thus, from the perspective of the topos On Covetousness, true friendship is an important social expression of liberality. It is ultimately concerned with giving, not getting.[107] The reason why friends hold all

μέθην), and turn to the things through which you will rule, doing good, and you follow the custom of your father's beneficence (εὐεργεσία), to your friends as well as to beggars'.

104. Theophrastus, *Char.* 30.1.

105. The point is made strongly by Philo (*Conf. Ling.* 48): 'He takes no heed of equity, but pursues the inequitable (ἰσότητος ἀλογεῖ, τὸ ἄνισον διώκει). He eschews thoughts of fellowship, and his eager desire is that the wealth of all should be gathered in his single purse. He hates others, whether his hate be returned or not. His benevolence is hypocrisy. He is hand in glove with canting flattery, at open war with genuine friendship, an enemy to truth, a defender of falsehood, slow to help, quick to harm, ever forward to slander, backward to champion the accused, skilful to cozen, false to his oath, faithless to his promise, a slave to anger (δοῦλος ὀργῆς), a thrall to pleasure, protector of the bad, corrupter of the good (φύλαξ κακῶν, φθορεὺς ἀγαθῶν).'

106. Cicero, *Fin.* 2.82-85. Seneca, *Ep.* 9, differentiates the Cynic-Stoic view of friendship from the Epicurean one. See Rist, 'Epicurus on Friendship', pp. 123 and 125: 'For Epicurus, friendships arise in order that very tangible and specific benefits can be obtained.' However, friendships are not merely the exchange of pleasantness for material goods. 'Just as the wise man's needs are simple and limited, so his requests of his friends will be moderate and reasonable.' An outline of the Epicurean understanding of friendship is given in Long and Sedley, *Hellenistic Philosophers*, I, pp. 137-38.

107. Generosity to friends was not an entirely disinterested virtue. For while the friend gained money, the giver gained nobility, a greater good (Aristotle, *Eth. Nic.* 9.8.9.; and *Pol.* 2.2.6). Even Epicurus held that it was more pleasant to confer a benefit than receive one. Rist ('Epicurus on Friendship', p. 127) comments: 'Here at least he is not far from Greek sentiment, for the opportunity for liberality was always regarded as a blessing, and in Epicurean society a giver could always be sure of a grateful response among his friends.' To prevent generosity from being taken to excess, leading to ruin just as surely as prodigality, Dio Chrysostom adds the principle that when money is used rightly and justly it does not harm the user nor his family and friends (*Or.* 13.16.)

things in common is not that they might feast together, but so that they can help one another in times of need.[108] This is similar to the other frequently stated point that wealth ought to be used for the benefit of family, friends and the wider community.[109]

The motif of friendship also helps to illustrate the father's liberality. Friendship is based on the principle of equality (ἰσότης).[110] This is true for social equals, like brothers, but friendship between a father and son is more like that which exists between a god and a man, or between a benefactor and beneficiary.[111] A son has certain specific obligations towards his father in the area of possessions, as Epictetus explains:

> to treat everything that is his own as belonging to his father [πάντα τὰ αὐτοῦ ἡγεῖσθαι τοῦ πατρός], to be obedient to him in all things [πάντα ὑπακούειν], never to speak ill of him to anyone else [μηδέποτε ψέξαι πρός τινα], nor to say or do anything that will harm him... helping him as far as is within his power.[112]

Though indebted to his father, the elder son fails to do any of these things. Greco-Roman readers would consider such behavior reprehen-

---

108. See the references in Betz, *Galatians*, p. 224 n. 46, and p. 227 n. 90. Compare Sostratos's advice to his father Kallipides in Menander's *Dyskolos* about the instability of money: 'So long as you control it, father, you yourself, I say, should use it generously, aid everyone, and by your acts enrich all to whom you can. Such conduct never dies. If you by chance should ever stumble, it will yield you a like repayment. Better far than hidden wealth kept buried is a visible true friend' (*Dys.* 805-12).

109. Musonius, *Frag.* 19. (122, 12-32); *Frag.* 20. (126, 11-31); Philo, *Omn. Prob. Lib.* 8; Sir. 29.10-11; and Cicero, *Off.* 2.16 (55-56): 'The generous, on the other hand, are those who employ their own means to ransom captives from brigands, or who assume their friends' debts or help in providing dowries for their daughters, or assist them in acquiring property or increasing what they have.'

110. Dio Chrysostom, *Or.* 17.9. Moxnes (*Economy*, p. 70) says that relationships of inequality are balanced by the motif of friendship in Lk. 11.5-8; 15.9; 15.29; 16.9.

111. Aristotle, *Eth. Eud.* 7.10.8-9. Moxnes (*Economy*, p. 94) points out that the function of the verb δίδωμι in Lk. 11.7-8; 15.11-32; and 16.20-25 is similar in each. 'Persons who have the means and opportunity to "give" are in a position to be patrons to others. Here patronage must be understood in its widest sense, including also relations between relatives (father–son) and neighbours.'

112. Epictetus, *Diss.* 2.10.7.

sible, because of the importance that they accorded to gratitude to parents.[113] This serves to emphasize the gentleness of the father's exhortation. Far from angrily insisting on the respect that is his due, he simply explains that his treatment of his younger son is governed by the same principles of liberality which he has always practised at home. He has always treated his sons equally: how then can this be called unjust? This reveals that the real basis of the elder son's complaint is his dislike of his father's liberality, not his father's perceived unfairness in applying it.

113. See J.W. Hewitt, 'Gratitude to Parents in Greek and Roman Literature', *AJP* 52 (1931), pp. 30-48 (33).

Chapter 7

THE YOUNGER SON LEARNS LIBERALITY

At its simplest, the moral teaching of the parable is that the prodigal younger son learns to appreciate and adopt the virtue of liberality, which is exemplified by his father, while his mean elder brother does not. At a moral level, the perennial fascination of the story lies in the question of the *causes* of moral virtue, and of moral change and resistance to change, as they are exemplified in the dispositions and actions of the father and the younger and elder sons respectively.

In this chapter, I look at the milestones within the parable which mark the various stages of the younger son's adoption of a life of virtue: desperation, turning, acknowledgment of culpability, moral choice, restoration, harmony and good health. These are all represented by motifs in the parable that are found in texts representative of the topos On Covetousness. We see again here how Luke uses themes, motifs and terminology that relate the conversion of the younger son to well-known philosophical notions of conversion.

1. *Desperation*

I noted in Chapter 5 that the first event that disturbs the younger son's prodigal lifestyle is the arrival of a famine. While this event lies outside his control, his response to it—that of seeking employment—begins his movement away from prodigality towards liberality. While his motives are still entirely selfish, and his moment of inner moral conversion still lies ahead, this experience of adverse circumstances (the first mentioned in the parable) prepares him for inner change. At the start of Chapter 6 we saw that one of the marks of the liberal person is his willingness to be liberal with *his own* resources.[1] Although the young man is forced

---

1. Aristotle, *Eth. Nic.* 4.1.15-17.

by hunger to seek work, he is at last trying to become self-supporting.[2] By this step, taken under duress, he makes his first adult acquaintance with manual labor. This experience is bad, because of the injustice of his foreign employer. However, Luke stresses that his repentance involves his willingness to work as a manual labourer for his father.[3] This decision would have been viewed positively by those familiar with the teachings of the moral philosophers.

In the part of the parable dealing with the younger son, Luke's text interacts with a variety of philosophical perspectives on manual labor. In vv. 15a-16c he first draws his readers' attention to the unpleasant side of manual labor when he describes the younger son as working with pigs. We saw in Chapter 5 that this particular task would have been abhorrent to Hellenistic Jews, and distasteful to well-to-do Greeks or Romans. By giving this task to a formerly well-off young prodigal, Luke underscores the negative consequences of prodigality. This also enables him to engage with the opinion, held by the rich of every age, that manual labor is unattractive. The statement of the Epicurean Philodemus is a good example of this: 'Miserable also is the lot of the farmer who works with his own hands. "But", says he, "to live off the land while others farm it—that is truly in keeping with wisdom".'[4] Malherbe reminds us that even those philosophers who commended manual labor seldom performed manual labor in practice.[5]

However, other more positive views of manual labor were widely current. The rich sometimes romantically idealized the life of the farmer. The idealistic view of manual labor cherished by aristocratic landowners bore little resemblance to the harsh toil and poverty that marked

---

2. *Ps.-Phoc.* 5-6: 'Do not become unjustly rich (πλουτεῖν ἀδίκως), but live by honourable means. Be content (ἀρκεῖσθαι) with what you have and abstain from what is another's.' Compare Heb. 13.5. Simpson notes the occurrence of the phrase ἀρκοῦνται τοῖς παροῦσιν in Vettius Valens 5.9 and suggests that it is proverbial (E.K. Simpson, 'Vettius Valens and the New Testament', *EvQ* 2 [1930], pp. 389-400 [392]).

3. The point is emphasized by being repeated (vv. 19b and 21d ποίησόν με ὡς ἕνα τῶν μισθίων σου). The importance of this decision to work is one internal reason for retaining ποίησόν με ὡς ἕνα τῶν μισθίων σου in v. 21d. See the comments on the text in Chapter 2.

4. Philodemus, *Oiko.* 23 (trans. A.J. Festugière; and cited in Malherbe, *Paul and the Thessalonians*, p. 103).

5. Malherbe, *Paul and the Thessalonians*, pp. 19-20; and *idem*, *Social Aspects of Early Christianity*, p. 25.

the lives of real tenant farmers and farm labourers.[6] Lutz cites Horace's mention of the land-owner Ofellus, who gained new satisfaction as a tenant farmer, and Columella's view that farming is the only suitable occupation for a free man.[7] Moreover, the moral philosophers, particularly Cynics and Stoics, taught that farming was a good manual occupation for the philosopher.[8] Hierocles argues that even in an age of luxury and idleness most people are persuaded of the value of agricultural work.[9] Plutarch tells that Numa countered the 'rapacity and injustice [ἀδικία καὶ πλεονεξία]' of his warriors by 'administering agriculture to his citizens as a sort of peace potion, and well-pleased with the art as fostering character rather than wealth [ἠθοποιὸν ἢ πλουτοποιὸν], divided the city's territory into districts ...'[10] A similarly positive view of farming is found in Hellenistic Jewish texts with Stoic leanings,[11] and Paul's practice of working with his hands reflects the positive philosophical view of manual work (both in his own writings: 1 Cor. 4.12; 1 Thess. 2.9; 4.10b-12; 2 Thess. 3.8, and Luke's description of him in Acts 18.3; 20.34).[12]

6. J. Shelton, *As the Romans Did: A Source Book in Roman Social History* (New York: Oxford University Press, 1988), pp. 163-64.

7. Horace, *Sat.* 2.2; and Columella, *Rust. praef.* 10-11, in Lutz, 'Musonius', p. 81. Shelton, *As the Romans Did*, pp. 165-66 cites the examples of Cicero, *Sen.* 16.55-56; Horace, *Epod.* 2.1-16, 23-26; and Tibullus, *Elegies* 1.1.1, 5-8, 25-32, 43-46.

8. Musonius, *Frag.* 11. (80, 10-84, 27).

9. Hierocles, *On Duties.* (Stobaeus, *Anth.* 4.28.21 = 5.696, 21-699, 15 Hense), cited in Malherbe, *Moral Exhortation*, p. 98. Jaeger notes that Catullus adds 'a moral as a last stanza [to his translation of Sappho's famous poem] and admonishes his better self not to indulge too much in otium (leisure, ease) which "has already ruined powerful kings and prosperous cities"' (Jaeger, *Early Christianity*, p. 114).

10. Plutarch, *Num.* 16.3, 4.

11. Sir. 7.15 speaks of husbandry as being divinely ordained. *T. Iss.* 3.1-3 and 5.3-6 associates farming with blessing, and *T. Iss.* 6.1-2 associates giving up agriculture with embracing insatiable desire (κολληθήσονται τῇ ἀπληστίᾳ) and the pursuit of evil schemes (ἀφέντες τὸ γεώργιον ἐξακολουθήσουσι τοῖς πονηροῖς διαβουλίοις αὐτῶν). Philo speaks of Issachar as the figure of him who is engaged in noble deeds: 'for he submitted his shoulder to labor and became a tiller of the soil' (*Leg. All.* 1.80, cited by Hollander and de Jonge, *Commentary*, p. 240).

12. Malherbe observes that while Paul mentions manual labor in 1 Thess. 2.9 (cf. 4.11), and elsewhere indicates that the Macedonian church was very poor (2 Cor. 8.2), Luke does not mention Paul's manual labor at Thessalonica in Acts 17.1-15. He thinks that Luke may have omitted this because of the negative attitude to

The positive view of manual labor is represented by the son's re-peated resolve (vv. 19b and 21d) to return to his father's farm as a hired worker.[13] Thus, having confirmed his readers' view that the son's task as a swineherd was the disastrous consequence of his prodigal living, Luke reminds his readers that manual labor could also be used to aid moral living.

Luke also shows that a worker's experience of manual labor is deeply affected by the justice and liberality of his employer. This is demon-strated in the younger son's experience as a farm worker in the foreign country. We saw in Chapter 5 that the younger son's departure with his share of his father's wealth violated the ideal of shared possessions. Now, when his situation changes and he has to seek employment, he tries to attach himself (v. 15a, κολλάω)[14] to a rich landowner like his father. He may have been hoping to have been adopted as a client. Skemp believes that

> ... settlers who had lost or abandoned other citizenships and lacked legal status were the original clientes, and they attached themselves to leading Roman citizens... This close and personal concern weakened as time went on and as whole communities became clientes during Rome's polit-ical and strategic advances. Yet even in classical times its reflection in the salutationes of the great and in the sportulae, the baskets containing food (and sometimes money), which he distributed we can see a debased but surviving sense of personal concern of the leading citizen as such for the underprivileged who attached themselves to him personally. Empty bellies were often filled by this means.[15]

manual labor held by people of high social standing who were his intended readers (*Paul and the Thessalonians*, pp. 16-17). The influence of the perceptions of his readers may also underlie Luke's omission of Paul's Great Collection, except for a reference in Acts 24.17, which differs considerably from the epistles. Barrett ('Light on the Holy Spirit from Simon Magus', p. 290) asks, 'Was it because it made Paul look too much like a money-collecting quack? Had some people brought this charge against him?'

13. Betz *et al.* ('*De Sera Numinis Vindicta*', p. 220) compare the behavior of the prodigal in Lk. 15.14-16 with that of the prodigal described by Plutarch in *De Sera Numinis Vindicta* (*Moralia* 563c). Unlike Plutarch, Luke does not say that his prodigal son becomes 'evil' (πονηρός) as a result of his prodigal living.

14. 'Luke uses κολλᾶσθαι of attaching oneself to somebody without a regular introduction, which may sometimes be successful (Acts 7.29) but not always (Acts 9.26)' (F.C. Burkitt, *JTS* 20 [1919], p. 326, cited by Bruce, *Acts*, p. 137, comment-ing on Acts 5.13).

15. J.B. Skemp, 'Service to the Needy in the Graeco-Roman World', in J.I.

Epictetus refers to a similar practice when he mentions how the wise man seeks to protect himself from the difficulties of life by attaching himself (προσκατατάσσω ἑαυτόν) to a rich or powerful person. He argues that it is useless even to become a friend of Caesar. The only way to pass through the world in safety is to attach oneself to God.[16]

However, the younger son's attempt to support himself fails miserably. The man who employs him cares as little for the ideal of shared possessions as he himself had formerly done. Instead of experiencing the kind of justice and generosity which his father shows to his hired workers, the younger son now experiences what it is like to be treated unjustly by a rich employer.[17] The employer's injustice and meanness would not be a surprise to Luke's readers, as it is conventional in Greco-Roman and Hellenistic Jewish literature to see city-dwellers (v. 15a, πολίτης) as immoral and unjust.[18] Luke's readers would appreciate this ironic twist to the plot. The younger son, who has acted unjustly and covetously towards his own family, and has moved to a place where his prodigality could be indulged to the full, now experiences what it is like to be treated unjustly himself. This experience of a mean employer does not deter him from performing manual labor, but it does encourage him to seek a liberal employer in the person of his father.

McCord and T.H.L. Parker (eds.), *Service in Christ: Essays Presented to Karl Barth on his 80th Birthday* (London: Epworth Press, 1966), pp. 17-26 (23).

16. Epictetus, *Diss.* 4.1.91-98.

17. With their pastoral heritage, reflected, for example, in the treatises on farming by Varro and Columella, Roman readers would view his employer's land-ownership as a conventional indicator of wealth. R.H. Barrow, *The Romans* (Harmondsworth: Penguin Books, 1949), p. 31, points out that *pecunia* means 'head of cattle'.

18. Plato (*Leg.* 677b) states the common view that primitive people were morally better than the civilized city-dwellers of his day, while a Sibylline Oracle describing the eschatological woes predicts that 'love of gain will be shepherd of evils for cities' (Sib. *Or.* 3.642). Teles also reports the popular view that 'in the cities the rich are more honoured than the poor' (φασὶ δὲ καὶ ἐν ταῖς πόλεσιν ἐντιμοτέρους εἶναι μᾶλλον τοὺς πλουσίους τῶν πενήτων, Teles 4B [50, 46-52, 67]). Philo (*Omn. Prob. Lib.* 78) describes those who avoid covetousness as living in villages rather than among city-dwellers. This is why Plutarch's flatterers disparage frugality as 'rusticity' when they speak to prodigals: 'Among the profligate they condemn frugality as "rusticity" (σωφροσύνην τε γὰρ ὡς ἀγροικίαν ψέγουσιν ἐν ἀσώτοις)' (*Mor.* 57c). Moles, 'Cynicism', p. 40, notes that Epicureans preferred the simple life of the country.

Hellenistic Jewish readers would be particularly aware of the loss of status implicit in the son's request after his conversion to be taken on as a μίσθιος.[19] The references to μίσθιος in Sirach imply that such people were defined in terms of their employment contract only: they did what they were hired to do and were paid for their labor.[20] Sirach 7.20 and 37.11 further suggest that levels of loyalty or understanding of the interests of the employer were not usual.[21] Employers found such employees more profitable than slaves, as they were under no obligation to continue to pay them and care for them if they became ill.[22] The son is thus willing to accept a considerable loss of status in return for the relative security of working for a liberal employer.[23]

The conventional link between love of status and love of money would further suggest to Greco-Roman readers that he had turned away from avarice. While freedom from avarice only follows his conversion, the younger son's experience of manual labor, forced upon him by necessity, creates the conditions for this moral change. This illustrates Aristotle's observation that poverty is one of the circumstances which leads to the cure of prodigals.[24]

---

19. See Lev. 19.13; 25.50; Tob. 5.11; and Job 7.1 (where μίσθιος translates words from the root שכר [hire]). The three occurrences of μίσθιος in Sirach (Sir. 7.20; 34.22; and 37.11) all point to the hired status of such workers.

20. Sir. 34.22b: to deprive an employee of his wages (ἀποστερῶν μισθὸν μισθίου) is to shed blood. Danker translates μισθωτός as a 'part-time labourer' in Menander, *Dys.* 331, where it is to be differentiated from the permanent help of household slaves and the friendly assistance of neighbours (F.W. Danker, 'Menander and the New Testament', *NTS* 10 [1963–64], pp. 365-68 [367]).

21. Reiling and Swellengrebel, *Translator's Handbook*, p. 549, point out that the paid worker would expect less affection from his master than a slave.

22. See Varro, *Rust.* 1.17.2, 3, in Shelton, *As the Romans Did*, p. 159. She comments in n. 176 that while owners of slaves had to feed them during illnesses and had a vested interest in their recovery because they owned them, landowners had no obligation to feed sick hired workers, and they represented no loss to the owner if they died.

23. For additional literature on the low status and poor conditions of service pertaining to hired workers see G.H.R. Horsley (ed.), *New Documents Illustrating Early Christianity. IV. A Review of the Greek Inscriptions and Papyri Published in 1979* (The Ancient History Documentary Research Centre, North Ryde, Australia: Macquarie University, 1987), pp. 97-98.

24. Aristotle, *Eth. Nic.* 4.1.31, 36.

2. *Turning and Returning*

One of the important indicators that this parable is addressed to a
Greco-Roman audience is the fact that Luke relates his conversion story
to the common philosophical understanding of the self as both the agent
and the place of moral guidance.[25] The philosophical doctrine of the
care of the self was taught by Platonists, Epicureans and Stoics and
enjoyed something of a 'golden age' in the first two centuries of the
imperial epoch.[26] Luke's reference to the self as the place of moral
guidance here and elsewhere[27] does not mean that he shared the Stoic
assumptions of the self's disposition to virtue, nor endorsed the pes-
simistic view of the austere Cynics that in *practice* the self was diseased
and corrupt.[28] In Luke's Gospel, the self has no inherent moral orientation, but is rather the place of spiritual struggle. Its importance for
moral behavior lies in its being the locus of individual personality and
action.[29]

25. Hellenistic Judaism and Christianity prefer to think of the heart as the source
of moral guidance. For example, *T. Gad* 5.3: 'For he who is righteous and humble
is ashamed to do what is wrong, being reproved not by another but by his own heart
(ὑπὸ τῆς ἰδίας καρδίας), for the Lord looks upon his (inner) disposition (τὸ
διαβούλιον αὐτοῦ).' It is striking that the only occurrences of καρδία in the Travel
Narrative are in Lk. 10.27 (an Old Testament citation of Deut. 6.5); 12.34 and 45
(both Q) and Lk. 16.15 (L).

26. M. Foucault, *The History of Sexuality*. III. *The Care of the Self* (trans.
R. Hurley; Harmondsworth: Penguin Books, 1990), p. 45. Part II provides a useful
overview of the range of citation, associated activities, purpose, procedures and
goals of the doctrine of 'self cultivation'.

27. For example, in the other soliloquies of the L parables (Lk. 12.17, 19; 18.4,
11), in phrases such as ἐν ἑαυτῷ διηπόρει (Acts 10.17) and ἐν ἑαυτῷ γενόμενος
(Acts 12.11), and in exhortations to 'take heed to yourselves' (Lk. 17.3; 21.34; Acts
5.35; 20.28). Johnson's statement that 'Luke sees possessions as a primary symbol
of human existence, the immediate exteriorization of and manifestation of the self'
suggests his intuitive recognition that the care of the self is part of the topos On
Covetousness. See Johnson, *Sharing Possessions*, p. 221; and Verhey, *Great Reversal*, p. 94.

28. Cynics believed people to be fundamentally innocent, but profoundly corrupted by the evils of civilization (such as greed, the love of glory and addiction to
pleasures). For a discussion of the Cynic understanding of vice see J. Moles,
'"Honestius Quam Ambitiosius?" An Exploration of the Cynic's Attitude to Moral
Corruption in His Fellow Men', *JHS* 103 (1983), pp. 103-23 (116-20).

29. This is evident even if we limit examples to those found only in the L

The phrase in v. 17a, εἰς ἑαυτὸν δὲ ἐλθών, marks the most important milestone in the son's change from prodigality to liberality. It defines the process of the change in his attitude towards possessions and, as a consequence, social relationships. It also defines the means by which these changes took place. In view of this, it is surprising that there has not been any prior study of the Greco-Roman philosophical associations of this phrase. Where such associations are mentioned, commentators have been content to repeat the parallels in the philosophical works cited by Wettstein,[30] without examining the meaning and function of such phrases in these texts. They have not indicated what associations this phrase might have had for Luke's intended audience, and hence what it might have signified to them. Here I explore its relationship to philosophical conversions and philosophical teaching on the care of the self.

Through philosophical conversion, people turned away from lives of luxury, self-indulgence and superstition to lives of discipline and, sometimes, contemplation.[31] Philosophy offered explanations for why things were the way they were, and, more importantly, gave people ways of living in accordance with these explanations. The philosophical systems were not always internally consistent and differed from one another. There were also differences between the ways of life advocated, for example, in the degree of asceticism required, or the degree of involvement with society permitted. However, they all began with a process of conversion.

From the time of Socrates onwards, becoming a true philosopher involved a change of life.[32] Nock notes that while philosophical conver-

parables, together with their immediate frames: Lk. 7.39; 10.29; 12.17, 19, 21; 14.27, 33; 15.17; 16.3, 9, 15; 18.4, 11, 14. See also Lk. 17.3.

30. Wettstein, *Novum Testamentum Graecum*, I, p. 760, refers to similar phrases in Epictetus, *Diss.* 3.1.15; Horace, *Ep.* 2.2.136; Lucretius, 4.1016 and 994; Terence, *Andr.* 3.5.16; Seneca, *Ben.* 7.20; Hesychius and Diodorus Siculus 13.95. Price, *Commentarii*, p. 594, offers a more extensive range of parallels mentioning, in addition to most of these, Philo, *Somn.* I, p. 179; Cicero, *Tusc.* 4.36.78; Seneca, *Consol. ad. Marc.* 2.; Philostratus, *Vit. Soph.*; Claudianus Mamercus and John Chrysostom.

31. A.D. Nock, *Conversion: The Old and New in Religion from Alexander the Great to Augustine of Hippo* (Oxford: Clarendon Press, 1993), p. 179.

32. 'Even the word "conversion" stems from Plato, for adopting a philosophy meant a change of life in the first place' (Jaeger, *Early Christianity*, p. 10; and

Prodigality, Liberality and Meanness

sions sometimes occurred during or soon after adolescence, they took place throughout life.[33] He places such conversions into three broad categories: an early call to a serious life with a greater or smaller philosophical content; an enthusiasm for a particular cult; or a return, in mature life, to normal piety.[34] The younger son's return to himself described in v. 17a should be classified as a conversion that took place during, or soon after, adolescence.

I have already observed that Luke intended his readers to recognize that the younger son's conversion involved his rejection of the evils of prodigality, and a recognition of his need to work to support himself. The phrase εἰς ἑαυτὸν δὲ ἐλθών gives us some indication of how they would have understood this process of moral change to take place. First, they would have understood the phrase εἰς ἑαυτὸν δὲ ἐλθών either to suggest a moment of sudden conversion, or to mark an important point within a longer process. Second, they would have understood his conversion to be the result of some form of self-analysis,[35] or the pressure of adverse circumstances.[36]

In Roman Stoicism, the self is both the site and the agent of moral change, and 'coming to oneself' is a phrase which represents the process of moral reform. This can be seen most clearly in Epictetus, and hence I focus upon his work to address this issue.[37] Another reason for focusing upon a Stoic author is that Stoic οἰκείωσις (appropriation) theory provides a useful explanation for much of the younger son's

W. Jaeger, *Paideia: The Ideals of Greek Culture* [3 vols.; trans. G. Highet; Oxford: Basil Blackwell, 1947], II, pp. 285 and 295ff).

33. A wide range of examples of youthful conversions is given in A.D. Nock, 'Conversion and Adolescence', in Z. Stewart (ed.), *Arthur Darby Nock: Essays on Religion and the Ancient World* (2 vols.; Oxford: Clarendon Press, 1972), I, pp. 469-80 (470-73).

34. Nock, 'Conversion and Adolescence', pp. 474-78.

35. There is no explicit reference to the foolishness or wisdom of the central characters in the parable as there is in Lk. 12.20 (ἄφρων); and Lk. 16.8 (φρονίμως).

36. Dio Chrysostom, *Or.* 27.7-9, mentions death, loss of wealth and social status as adverse circumstances which drove people to the comfort of philosophy (Malherbe '"Pastoral Care"', p. 383).

37. Sevenster considers the gap between the view of the self in Epictetus and Christianity to be too wide for Epictetus to be used to understand Christian conversion. However, Sevenster's understanding of Christian conversion is based on an interpretation of sin that is not found in Luke, as I show below. See Sevenster 'Education or Conversion', pp. 256-61.

behavior: his movement from self-interest to moral virtue; his impulse towards self-preservation; and his growing awareness of the importance of social relationships and duties.[38] Kerford describes οἰκείωσις as, 'the process by which an organism "comes to terms with itself"', and the process of self-recognition which leads to a sense of personal identity.[39]

Book 3 of Epictetus's *Discourses* contains three accounts of young men coming to themselves. In the first, Epictetus articulates, in diatribal style, the complaint of a young man who thinks that Epictetus has neglected him:

> 'What did Epictetus observe in me,' you will say to yourself, 'that, although he saw me in such a condition and coming to him in so disgraceful a state [οὕτως αἰσχρῶς], he should let me be so and say never a word to me? Was I not young [νέος]? Was I not ready to listen to reason [λόγου ἀκουστικός]? And how many other young fellows make any number of mistakes of the same kind in their youth [πόσοι δ᾽ ἄλλοι νέοι ἐφ᾽ ἡλικίας πολλὰ τοιαῦτα διαμαρτάνουσιν]?[40] I am told that once there was a certain Polemo who from being a dissolute young man [ἀκολαστοτάτου νεανίσκου] underwent such an astonishing transformation [μεταβολὴν μεταβαλεῖν]. Well, suppose he did not think that I should be another Polemo; he could at least have set my hair right... But although he saw me looking like—what shall I say?—he held his peace'.[41]

Epictetus's reply is that it is no good for him to tell the young man what he looks like: he must realize this for himself. This will only happen when he comes to himself.

> As for me, I do not say what it is you look like, but you will say it, when you come to yourself, [εἰς σαυτὸν ἔλθεις] and will realize [γνώσει] what it is and the kind of people those are who act this way.[42]

Here, εἰς ἑαυτὸν ἔρχεσθαι means to arrive at a true understanding of one's moral condition. It is a process of self-recognition that arises out of the correct interpretation of circumstances, and cannot be induced by

---

38. See D.B. George, 'Lucan's Caesar and Stoic οἰκείωσις Theory: The Stoic Fool', *TAPA* 118 (1988), pp. 331-41 (331-34).

39. G.B. Kerford, 'The Search for Personal Identity in Stoic Thought', *BJRL* 55 (1972), pp. 177-96 (186).

40. He compares his state with that of others (πόσοι δ᾽ ἄλλοι νέοι) in a way that is similar to the son's rhetorical question in Lk. 15.17b (πόσοι μίσθιοι).

41. Epictetus, *Diss.* 3.1.14.

42. Epictetus, *Diss.* 3.1.15.

persuasion alone. This is evident from the stock example of Polemo. Epictetus says that it was not so much the words of Xenocrates that converted him, but the fact that he already had the 'glimmerings of a zeal for the beautiful'.[43] Lucian's description of his conversion in *The Double Indictment* also qualifies the picture of Polemo's sudden change from drunkenness to sober study by the assertion that he was not naturally bad or inclined to drunkenness. He had been led astray by pleasure and his conversion was more like waking up from a profound sleep.[44]

Similarly, in the second instance, the phrase describing a process of returning to oneself does not mark a sudden moment of conversion, but is part of a wider process of honest self-evaluation:

> Has he settled down? Has he come to himself [ἐπέστραπται ἐφ' αὐτόν]? Has he realized the evil plight in which he is? Has he cast aside his self-conceit? Is he looking for the man... who will teach him how to live? No, fool, but only how he ought to deliver a speech; for that is why he admires even you.[45]

The behavior here associated with the return to oneself is easily identified within the parable. The 'evil plight' is represented by the son's degradation, his working as a swineherd and his desire for pig food—all the result of his greed. His abandonment of wrong views about himself is shown in his willingness to accept the humble status of a hired worker. His father is now seen as a man who can teach him how to live. Before he came to himself all he said to his father was, 'Father, give me', πάτερ, δός μοι; after coming to himself he says, 'Father, ...I am no longer worthy to be called your son; treat me like one of your hired hands', πάτερ,... οὐκέτι εἰμὶ ἄξιος κληθῆναι υἱός σου· ποίησόν με ὡς ἕνα τῶν μισθίων σου.

Later in this same discourse (*Diss.* 3.23) Epictetus again speaks of turning to oneself, this time suggesting that it can also mark an important moment of self-recognition:

> Or tell me, who that ever heard you reading a lecture or conducting a discourse felt greatly disturbed about himself, or came to a realization of the state he was in [περὶ αὑτοῦ ἠγωνίασεν ἢ ἐπεστράφη εἰς αὑτὸν], or

43. Epictetus, *Diss.* 4.11.30. In Lk. 15.17a-20a, the younger son's decision to return home can be seen as a return to goodness, wisdom or beauty which he had known before but only now truly understands or appreciates.
44. Lucian, *Bis. Acc.* 16 and 17.
45. Epictetus, *Diss.* 3.23.16.

on going out said, 'The philosopher brought home to me in fine style; I must not act like this any longer'?[46]

However, the notion of process is still present in that the moment of self-insight is followed by a change of behavior.

A further example from Epictetus reminds us that the Stoic understanding of coming to oneself involves not just self-recognition, but also self-rescue. The self is not just the place, but also the agent of moral change. Epictetus describes someone who had once decided to live a moral life but had become shameless. He is described as having dislodged (ἐκσέσεισαι) himself, and is being encouraged to recover himself:

> And now, therefore, are you not willing to come to your own rescue [σαυτῷ βοηθῆσαι]? ... [you have only] to talk to yourself [αὐτὸν αὐτῷ λαλῆσαι] ... And first of all condemn what you are doing; then, when you have passed your condemnation, do not despair of yourself [μὴ ἀπογνῷς σεαυτοῦ], nor act like the spiritless people who, when once they have given in, surrender themselves [ἐπέδωκαν ἑαυτοὺς] completely, and are swept off by the current, as it were, but learn how the gymnastic trainer of boys acts. The boy he is training is thrown; 'get up, ' [ἀνίστημι], he says, 'and wrestle again till you get strong'. React in some such way yourself, for I would have you know that there is nothing more easily prevailed upon than a human soul. You have but to will a thing and it has happened ... on the other hand, you have but to drop into a doze and all is lost. For it is within you that both destruction and deliverance [ἀπώλεια καὶ βοήθεια] lie.[47]

The practical steps for self-rescue that Epictetus mentions here can again be paralleled in vv. 17a-20a of the parable: talk to yourself, condemning what you are doing, but without despair or self-surrender; then get up and wrestle again. As in the parable, the escape from destruction (ἀπώλεια, compare the use of ἀπόλλυμι in the parable) is effected by a decision to get up (ἀνίστημι is used in both texts).

Many other descriptions of conversion or ongoing moral progress presented in terms of returning to oneself and heeding the guidance of oneself are found in other Stoic writings.[48] It is part of their doctrine of

---

46. Epictetus, *Diss.* 3.23.37.

47. Epictetus, *Diss.* 4.9.13-16.

48. As well as Seneca, *Consol. ad. Marc.* 2.3 and *Ben.* 7.20.3-4 (cf. *Ep.* 81) there are frequent references to this theme in his epistles (e.g. *Epp.* 2.1; 6; 10.1-2; 25.6, 7; 41.1, 9; 53.7-8). He recognizes that the self needs the guidance of friends

self-sufficiency, derived from the Cynics.[49] However, as Roman Stoicism would have been one of the philosophical systems most familiar to Luke's Greco-Roman readers, these examples from Epictetus are sufficient to indicate that Luke's readers would have thought of the younger son's return to himself as a process which was the result of self-examination.[50]

While the phrase he came to himself, εἰς ἑαυτὸν δὲ ἐλθὼν might have been understood to indicate the moment of turning, this would have presupposed a period of prior internal preparation. Most philosophical groups thought of conversion as a gradual process.[51] Even

and moral guides. There are also a number of references to retiring into oneself (τὰ εἰς ἑαυτόν) in Marcus Aurelius's *Med.*, 4.3.1, 4; 7.28, 33, 59; 8.48. See too Horace, *Ep.* 2.2.136-40; Persius, *Sat.* 4.23 and Philo, *Somn.* 1.180. As the examples from Wettstein and Price given in n. 30 above show, the motif is not limited to Stoic authors. See also Philostratus, *Vit. Ap.* 4.20e; Plutarch, *Mor.* 563d (παρ' αὐτῷ γεν-όμενος); and Dio Chrysostom, *Or.* 20.4.

49. D. Sedley, 'The Protagonists', in M. Schofield, M. Burnyeat and J. Barnes (eds.), *Doubt and Dogmatism: Studies in Hellenistic Epistemology* (Oxford: Clarendon Press, 1980), pp. 1-119 (5), comments on the 'pervasive influence of the Cynic doctrine of self-sufficiency, particularly among the Stoics'.

50. Malherbe's statement that Luke describes Christian conversion as an instantaneous response to preaching is correct, as long as it is understood to allow for a process of growing moral or spiritual need prior to the moment of conversion. See A.J. Malherbe, ' "Not in a Corner": Early Christian Apologetic in Acts 26.26', in *idem, Paul and the Popular Philosophers* (Minneapolis: Fortress Press, 1989), pp. 147-63 (162). Zacchaeus's strong desire to see Jesus (Lk. 19.3-4) suggests moral or spiritual hunger, while Lydia, found on the Sabbath at a place of prayer and described as σεβομένη τὸν θεόν (cf. Acts 10.2), is hardly unprepared. The same phrase is true of those converted in Acts 13.43 and 17.4. Even these conversions are seldom instantaneous, with periods of one or more weeks between preaching and conversion often being explicitly mentioned (Acts 13.42; 17.2). It has often been argued (e.g. in E.P. Sanders's popular work, *Paul* [Oxford: Oxford University Press, 1991], pp. 8-12) that Paul's conversion is better described as a call, leading to a change of direction, rather than a change of religion. This makes it problematic to use Paul's accounts of his call in Acts 9, 22 and 26 as examples of sudden conversions. This leaves the story of the Philippian jailer in Acts 16.29-33 as the only example of sudden conversion—a conversion precipitated by a crisis, itself the result of an earthquake.

51. See Malherbe, *Paul and the Thessalonians*, p. 25 and ' "Not in a Corner" ', p. 161, and the primary and secondary references given there.

Stoics, who allowed for the idea of instantaneous philosophical conversion, [52] understood this to take place only in those who had been making consistent moral progress beforehand. While some Platonists also thought that sudden change could happen, we find Plutarch scorning the idea that someone could change from being worthless or wicked, φαῦλος, to wise, σοφός in the course of a day, or overnight.[53] Lucian's testimony that he had been suddenly transformed by his meeting with the Platonist Nigrinus is questioned by his hearer.[54]

The younger son's return to himself differs from the usual philosophical conversions in not being the result of eloquent persuasion. Luke here presents a view of conversion that does not conform to the philosophers' belief that people could be converted through verbal appeal.[55] Having said that, we should remember that even philosophical conversions were not the result of intellectual conviction alone, but took place through the appeal of personal example, virtue and belief as well.[56] This is the basis of the father's appeal to the elder brother. The process of philosophical conversion required honest self-examination and a willingness to replace false self-love with right self-care.[57]

Thus, while the younger son's conversion is not caused by external difficulties, poverty and hunger do start the process by which he comes to recognize the seriousness of his condition.[58] Those who question the

52. Moles, 'Cynicism', p. 39.

53. See Plutarch, *Mor.* 75e. Malherbe also cites *Mor.* 1057e-1058c and *Mor.* 1062b, noting that these latter dialogues attack an earlier form of Stoicism. Malherbe, ' "Not in a Corner" ', p. 161. Plutarch does record one notable example of a sudden moral change in a prodigal brought about through a return from death to life in *De Sera Numinis Vindicta* 563c-e. See Nock's discussion of this incident in 'Conversion and Adolescence', p. 476; and Betz *et al.* '*De Sera Numinis Vindicta*', pp. 219-21.

54. Lucian, *Nigr.* 1, 3-5. On the possibility that Lucian is speaking of his own conversion, Malherbe, *Paul and the Thessalonians*, p. 27, cites W. Schmid and O. Stählin, *Geschichte der griechischen Literatur* 2.2 (Munich: Beck, 6th edn, 1920), pp. 712-13.

55. This is evident in some of the accounts mentioned in Nock, 'Conversion and Adolescence', pp. 470-72. A valuable summary of how philosophers called people to conversion is given in Malherbe, *Paul and the Thessalonians*, pp. 21-28.

56. Nock, *Conversion*, pp. 175-81.

57. The case of Polemo, who was converted to philosophy without a period of prior self-examination, is the exception rather than the rule.

58. The Cynic author of Pseudo-Socrates, *Ep.* 6, recognizes that the person who

prodigal's motives for repentance fail to recognize that the external circumstances leading to it, the famine, his hunger and his unjust employer, all make the negative consequences of his prodigal behavior plain to him, and enable him to come to the point of self-recognition.[59] This is in accordance with the way writings On Covetousness stress the negative consequences of wrong behavior. Philosophical texts on the topos equally recognize that conversion is the result of an inner change of perspective, and is not merely the result of external circumstances.[60]

Thus, Greco-Roman readers of Luke's Gospel would have recognized in the phrase εἰς ἑαυτὸν δὲ ἐλθών an echo of philosophic psychagogia on proper care for the self. They would also have appreciated the way Luke was showing that a return to the self led to a change in attitudes to possessions, pleasure and people.

3. *Acknowledgment of Culpability and Confession*

a. *Culpability*
The philosophical view of prodigality is that it is both foolish and culpable, but, as we saw in Chapter 5, opinion is divided on who is to blame. Plato blames the prodigal, who, he says, makes the mistake of thinking that all pleasures are equal, and fails to distinguish between honourable and good (καλός καὶ ἀγαθός) desires and those that are base (πονηρός).[61] However, Plato also places the blame upon the democratic rulers. They are to blame because, owing their own positions to wealth, they are unwilling to make laws to prevent prodigals from spending and wasting their resources.[62]

is oppressed by poverty eventually comes to his senses, while one who has false ideas about happiness never does.

59. Scott, *Hear Then the Parable*, pp. 115-16, recognizes that 'By coming to himself he begins to overcome his self-destructive pattern of behavior' even though 'his stomach induced his return'.

60. Sellew is an example of the recurrent tendency to question the authenticity of the younger son's change. However, he fails to recognize the moral conventions with which Luke is engaging (Sellew, 'Interior Monologue', p. 246).

61. Plato, *Resp.* 561c, with reference to *Gorg.* 494e.

62. Plato, *Resp.* 555c.

Aristotle echoes Plato when he says that prodigals ruin themselves: 'to waste one's substance seems to be in a way to ruin oneself, inasmuch as wealth is the means of life'.[63] Plato and Aristotle both see a link between the use of possessions and the development of character, in that both maintain that in learning to curb their extravagance prodigals are able to avoid self-destruction.

As a Cynic, Teles believes that people are responsible for their behavior and able to make moral progress. He argues that the Cynic way is superior in teaching people to live in such a way that they are freed from want and scarcity (ἔνδεια καὶ σπάνις). Crates, he declares, 'could change men from insatiable and extravagant to liberal and unpretentious (ἐξ ἀπλήστων καὶ πολυτελῶν ἐλευθερίους καὶ ἀφελεῖς)'.[64]

Other philosophers place the blame for the prodigality of children on faulty attitudes to wealth instilled in them by their parents or their society. As mentioned in Chapter 5, the Middle Platonist Plutarch[65] emphasizes the role of parents in the promotion of the twin vices of prodigality and illiberality. Peripatetic influence on his Platonism may be detected in his use of Aristotle's terminology and views (for example prodigality, ἀσωτία and illiberality, ἀνελευθερία, and his harsher criticism of misers than prodigals in 525b11-e3). The satirists Horace[66], Juvenal[67] and Martial, [68] who all broadly employ the ethics of Roman Stoicism, emphasize the responsibility of the father. The eclectic Lucian, however, reminds us that prodigality was a crime that entitled a father to disinherit his son.[69]

In the parable, because Luke emphasizes the father's virtue, he apparently shares the Academic/Peripatetic and Cynic view that the son is responsible for his own actions. Hence, the son's recognition of his guilt in his soliloquy (vv. 17b-19b), and the repetition of this acknowledgment in his confession to his father. He does not blame his father, his family, or the unjust treatment he received in the foreign country. Luke's position is based on the Christian belief in human responsibility for sin. Unlike the philosophers (and the author of the Gospel of John),

63. Aristotle, *Eth. Nic.* 4.1.5 . Compare Plato, *Resp.* 555c.
64. Teles 4A (40, 100-119). See too Teles 2 (14, 128-145).
65. Plutarch, *Mor.* 523c-528b.
66. Horace, *Sat.* 1.4.103-11.
67. Juvenal, *Sat.* 14.107-108.
68. Martial, *Epi.* 3.10.
69. Lucian, *Abd.* 21.

he does not explore the causes of vice or sin. His focus in this parable is not on the reasons for the covetousness of the two sons, but on the possibility of moral change through conversion.

b. *Confession*

The younger son's confession acknowledges sin in two directions: 'I have sinned against heaven and before you', ἥμαρτον εἰς τὸν οὐρανὸν καὶ ἐνώπιόν σου. While this suggests the classic conception of sin as offence against both God and humanity, reference to God in the parable is limited to the metonym 'heaven'. Greco-Roman readers would have understood οὐρανός to refer to τὸ θεῖον in some sense, with each person or group filling out the concept according to their own cosmology and theology.[70] They would accord it greater or lesser importance depending on their view of the relationship between heaven and earth.[71] Within the framework of Luke's Gospel, 'heaven' clearly refers to God, as for example in the confession of the tax collector in Lk. 18.13. However, the absence of explicit reference to God within the parable strengthens the view that the parable has a strong focus on the ethics of human relationships.

Luke's use of the verb ἁμαρτάνω supports this perspective. Apart from vv. 18c and 21b he uses it only twice, in Lk. 17.3-4 and Acts 25.8. In these two places, sinful actions are viewed primarily as offences against other human beings or institutions. In Lk. 17.3-4 the focus is on interpersonal sin (ἡμαρτήσῃ εἰς σὲ), while Acts 25.1-12 focuses on the issue of injustice and justice: 'If then I am a wrongdoer [ἀδικῶ], and have committed anything for which I deserve to die [ἄξιον θανάτου πέπραχά τι], I do not seek to escape death...' (Acts 25.11a). In this parable, the son confesses the sin of coveting his inheritance from his father. Although vv. 18c and 21b place εἰς τὸν οὐρανόν before ἐνώπιόν σου, Luke's employment of metonymy, and his view of sin as an

---

70. Horsley cites an epigram for Apollonius of Tyana in which οὐρανός is used 'as a periphrasis or euphemism for god/the gods' (G.H.R. Horsley [ed.], *New Documents Illustrating Early Christianity. III. A Review of the Greek Inscriptions and Papyri Published in 1978* [The Ancient History Documentary Research Centre, North Ryde: Macquarie University, 1983], p. 50).

71. Plato uses οὐρανός as a figure for the perfect, Aristotle uses it to refer to the cosmos and the divine, the Stoics see it both as the physical limit of the aether and as the commanding faculty of the cosmos, and so on. See H. Traub, 'οὐρανός, κτλ', *TDNT*, V, pp. 497-502 (498-99).

offence against human relationships, both stress the human dimension. Thus, we may say that Luke uses the verb ἁμαρτάνω to refer to the breaking of divine or human law in such a way as to commit an offence against other human beings.[72] Schottroff and Stegemann summarize Luke's position in this way:

> For Luke the transgressions from which human beings must desist are of course sins in God's eyes. But they are also concretely verifiable in the inter-human sphere: arrogance, self-righteousness, extortion, robbery, wastefulness. Therefore the concept 'sinner' takes a socially concrete form in Luke. It serves as the basis on which he develops his soteriological program. In Lk. 15.1f the word 'sinner' has as it were both of the extensions (the social and theological we have distinguished).[73]

Luke's Greco-Roman readers would therefore have interpreted the son's prodigality as a breach of filial love: an offence against his father that also has a religious dimension, not an offence against God that also has a social dimension.

Only when the father-son relationship is allegorized to represent the divine-human relationship is this order of priority reversed. Then the son's sin against his father is *reinterpreted* to refer to human sin against God, and the father's response becomes an illustration of God's mercy to sinners. Yet even when this is done, the ethical dimension reappears via the principle that human behavior should imitate divine behavior.[74]

72. This reflects the main use of the verb elsewhere in the New Testament. Of all the occurrences of ἁμαρτάνω listed in the *Concordance* of Moulton and Geden, only half the references suggest that the sin is primarily an offence against God (Jn 5.14; 8.11; 9.2, 3; Rom. 2.12; 3.23; 5.12, 14, 16; 6.15; 1 Cor. 7.36; Heb. 3.17; 10.26; 2 Pet. 2.4; 1 Jn 1.10; 2.1; 3.6, 8, 9; 5.16, 16, 18). Of these, 2 Pet. 2.4 speaks of angelic sin, while the Johannine writings stress the effect that sin against God has upon human relationships. This reduces the examples to some from Paul and two from Hebrews. All the others speak of sin as an offence against other people.

73. L. Schottroff and W. Stegemann, *Jesus and the Hope of the Poor* (trans. M.J. O'Connell; Maryknoll, NY: Orbis Books, 1986), p. 106.

74. See, for example, P. van Staden, 'Compassion—The Essence of Life: A Social-Scientific Study of the Religious Symbolic Universe Reflected in the Ideology/Theology of Luke' (DD dissertation, University of Pretoria, 1990), p. 242: 'Luke understood God's actions towards man as characterized by the element of compassion, and ... he advocated this value and recommended that it become part of the expectations attendant upon especially the roles that were linked to a high

Recent studies of synoptic parables have emphasized that the way parables change human behavior is by describing it in such a way that the divine perspective is revealed.[75] But this study aims to point out the priority of the parable's moral thrust.

c. *Repentance of Prodigality*

In his confession, the younger son repents of the way his relationship with his father has been damaged by his prodigality, saying: 'Father... I am no longer worthy to be called your son', πάτερ ... οὐκέτι εἰμὶ ἄξιος κληθῆναι υἱός σου.

Prodigality is, as we have seen, an expression of πλεονεξία. While some Christian texts associate πλεονεξία with idolatry, [76] J. Weiss argues for the view that it is more properly the sin of excessive egoism.[77] The younger son's return to himself is therefore quite the opposite of the vice of self-love (φιλαυτία). After his return to himself he has a new concern for healthy relationships with other people.

Sound social relationships are built on justice and equality, as the Cynic Dio Chrysostom argues.[78] This is seen in the Stoicism underlying Hellenistic Jewish authors too. Using the metaphor of moving to a new home, Philo describes repentance as a process of leaving covetousness and injustice and returning to soberness and justice:

> [Repentance] has been suddenly possessed with an ardent yearning for betterment, eager to leave its inbred covetousness and injustice [πλεον-εξίαν καὶ ἀδικίαν] and come over to soberness and justice [σωφρο-σύνην καὶ δικαιοσύνην] and the other virtues.[79]

status (i.e. the rich, the powerful, the authoritative).' Human forgiveness and compassion are endorsed in this way by the frame of the L parables in Lk. 7.43; 10.36-37; 11.9; 13.5 (referring ahead to 13.6-9); 16.8b-9; and 18.14.

75. See, for example, Thiselton's comments on the views of Fuchs and Via in A. C. Thiselton, 'Reader-Response Criticism, Action Models and the Parables of Jesus', in *idem, The Responsibility of Hermeneutics* (Grand Rapids: Eerdmans, 1985), pp. 79-113 (108-109).

76. For example, *T. Jud* 19; Col. 3.5; Lk. 16.13; and 2 *Clem.* 6.1-4. φιλαργυρία leads to εἰδωλολατρία and to a state of mental ἔκστασις in *T. Jud.* 19.1-3. In a way that resembles the message of Lk. 15.11-24, Judah receives pardon through his own penitence and humility, the prayers of his father, and the compassion of God.

77. Comment on 1 Cor. 6.1-11 (*Der Erste Korintherbrief* [KEK, 5; Göttingen: Vandenhoek & Ruprecht, 1970], pp. 141-42).

78. Dio Chrysostom, *Or.* 17 passim.

79. Philo, *Praem. Poen.* 15.

There, the movement is *away* from the distractions of home, country, family and friends, while the parable under discussion describes repentance in terms of *return* to his father and home. The same motif of abandoning one's natural family is found in Dio Chrysostom (*Or.* 12.10) and Lk. 14.26.[80] The difference between these examples and the parable can be explained by remembering that the father is a living example of the philosophical ideals of σωφροσύνη and δικαιοσύνη, which are the ideals which the son finds attractive.

In another figurative reference to πλεονεξία, Philo says that the mind that has received the gift of quietude should not be distracted or 'dominated by the πάθη through greed [ἐπιτιθέμεναι κατὰ πλεονεξίαν παθῶν δυναστείας]'.[81] This point is stated more positively by the author of *4 Maccabees*. He thinks of repentance of covetousness in terms of the Stoic idea of the conquest of avarice through the power of reason.[82] Such a conquest of avarice involves the prior recognition that its pleasures are deceptive. Sometimes such a realization can be overwhelming, as Plutarch recognizes.

> For as Simonides used to jest that he found his coffer of money always full, but his coffer of thanks empty, so, when evil men see through the wickedness within them, they find it bare of pleasure, which allures for a moment with delusive hope, but always full of terrors, sorrows, dismal memories, misgiving for the future, and mistrust of the present.[83]

The son's repentance therefore involves a recognition of the full effects of his prodigality on himself and his family, and a decision to renounce his greed by turning to a life based on the ideals of equality, justice and simplicity.[84]

4. *Moral Choice*

A further motif that can be compared with Luke's description of the younger son's moral change is the doctrine of the two ways (δύο τρίβοι), which was commonly illustrated by the fable of Heracles at the cross-roads.[85] In the myth, which originated with the Sophist Prodicus

---

80. See van Unnik, 'Words Come to Life', p. 207.
81. Philo, *Praem. Poen.* 121.
82. *4 Macc.* 2.8.
83. Plutarch, *Mor.* 555f-556a.
84. Philo, *Praem. Poen.* 15; Josephus, *Apion* 2.291.
85. A.D. Nock describes the fable as a vivid metaphor for the fundamental

but is best known from Xenophon's *Memorabilia*, [86] Heracles arrives at the crossroads and has to choose between Virtue and Vice. The story was popular in philosophical literature. In Philostratus's *Life of Apollonius of Tyana*, for example, Apollonius describes Heracles' decision as being a choice between the different philosophical schools.[87] Heracles is a Cynic (and Stoic) exemplar and the idea that labors (πόνοι) lead to virtue is a Cynic idea.[88]

Both the fable of Heracles and the parable of the prodigal son can be seen as narrative expressions of the two ways doctrine, which goes back at least as far as Hesiod, [89] and was widespread.[90] Neopythagorean examples include a popular philosophical treatise, the *Pinax of Cebes*, which describes a picture of the two ways found among the votive gifts in a temple of Kronos, [91] and a first-century CE sepulchral inscription

choice urged by moral philosophers. See Nock, *Conversion*, p. 167.

86. Xenophon, *Mem.* 2.1.19-33. Also Philo, *Sacr.* 20-34.

87. Philostratus, *Vit. Ap.* 6.11.

88. Diogenes Laertius, 6.2; Dio Chrysostom, *Or.* 31.16; and other references in Malherbe, 'Pseudo-Heraclitus', p. 59 n. 131; and D.E. Aune, 'Heracles and Christ: Heracles Imagery in the Christology of Early Christianity', in D.L. Balch, E. Ferguson and W.A. Meeks (eds.), *Greeks, Romans and Christians: Essays in Honor of Abraham J. Malherbe* (Minneapolis: Fortress Press, 1990), pp. 3-19 (8-11). Aune notes that one of the objectives of Cynic propaganda concerning Heracles was to counter the popular idea of Heracles as 'a muscle-bound moron, athlete, glutton, and boor (as he was depicted in comedy, satyr plays, and Euripides' *Alcestis*)'. Compare H. J. Rose, 'Heracles and the Gospels', *HTR* 31 (1938), pp. 113-42 (121). The proverbial contrast between Heracles (labor) and Sardanapalus (sensual pleasure) is, however, not limited to Cynic authors (e.g. Juvenal, *Sat.* 10.360-62; Plutarch, *Mor.* 1065c; Maximus of Tyre, *Disc.* 1.9; 32.9). See Malherbe, 'Beasts at Ephesus', p. 85.

89. Hesiod, *Op.* 287-92.

90. For literature on this motif see W. Michaelis, 'ὁδός, κτλ', *TDNT*, V, pp. 42-114 (42-96). Thom, 'Golden Verses', p. 153, also refers to the literature in Betz, 'Lukian von Samosata', pp. 205-206; and J. Bergman, 'Zum Zwei-Wege-Motif: Religionsgeschichtliche und exegetische Bemerkungen', *SEÅ* 41-42 (1976–77), pp. 27-56. See also Betz, *Sermon on the Mount*, pp. 521-53.

91. Jaeger, *Early Christianity*, pp. 8-9. Thom, 'Golden Verses', p. 154, classifies the Tabula Cebetis as 'Pythagorean'. Nock (*Conversion*, p. 180) summarizes its message thus, 'It describes the good and bad life: the only deliverance from the bad life is given by Metanoia. The man who chooses the good life is safe (ch. 26). "He will never be disturbed by pain or grief or incontinence or avarice or poverty or any other evil thing. For he is the master of all things and is superior to all that formerly distressed him ..."'

from the Lydian Philadelphia, contrasting the two ways of ἀρετή and ἀσωτία:

> The inscription contains an epigram in which the author, named Pythagoras, claims to have become like his famous namesake in wisdom, and states that he also considered labor [πόνος] as something to be preferred in life. Next to the epigram is a depiction of the Pythagorean symbol Υ (denoting the two ways), with a woman (identified by an inscription above her head) on each side. On the left we find Ἀσωτία ('Prodigality') next to a depiction of the prodigal life (a man making love to a woman on a couch). On the right is Ἀρετή with a depiction of the virtuous life (a man plowing a field in one scene and sleeping peacefully in his bed in another).[92]

The first indication of the doctrine of the two ways in Jewish Hellenistic literature is found in texts with a Stoic ethical orientation, such as Sir. 2.12 and *T. Ash.* 1.3, 5.[93] While the doctrine has 'little or nothing that could be called specifically Christian',[94] Christianized forms of the doctrine are found in the Sermon on the Mount, e.g. Mt. 7.13-14, and in the *Didache, Barnabas* and Hermas.[95] Luke's use of the doctrine is evident in his contrast of the behavior of the two sons, and the results of their behavior. The Christian dimension of his use of the doctrine can be seen by comparing it with a similar example in Philo.[96]

Philo's treatise *On the Sacrifices of Abel and Cain* contains two long discourses, from Pleasure and Effort (πόνος), and two long lists of virtues and vices.[97] It is remarkable for containing a long list of the vices that are attributed to the pleasure-lover.[98] At the end of the discourse on

---

92. Thom, 'Golden Verses', p. 154. The inscription is reported with text on p. 616 and a photograph on p. 622 of A. Brinkmann, 'Ein Denkmal des Neupythagoreismus', *RhM* NS 66 (1911), pp. 616-25. The Υ symbol is referred to by the Stoic Persius as a symbol of the two ways in Persius, *Sat.* 3.56-57.

93. M. Hengel, *The 'Hellenization' of Judaea*, p. 48, and p. 92 n. 256.

94. Jaeger, *Early Christianity*, pp. 110-11.

95. *Did.* 1-6; *Barn.* 18; Hermas, *Sim.* 4.5.

96. See Betz, *Sermon on the Mount*, pp. 81-82 and 520-27 and J. Laporte, 'Philo in the Tradition of Biblical Wisdom Literature', in R.L. Wilken (ed.), *Aspects of Wisdom in Judaism and Early Christianity* (Notre Dame: University of Notre Dame Press, 1975), pp. 111-12.

97. Philo, *Sacr.* 19-44.

98. Philo, *Sacr.* 32. Strangely, ἀσωτία is omitted from Philo's list of 146 associated vices, but, as many of the other vices linked in the topos with ἀσωτία are

effort, we find the way of toil commended in the context of a discussion of the birthrights of the elder and younger sons. Philo argues that, by choosing the path of virtue through toil, the younger son may receive privileges usually reserved for the elder. This is very similar to the situation reflected in the parable from v. 22 onwards.

> Never then despise toil, that from the one you may reap a multitude, even the harvest of every good thing. And so though you be the younger (νεώτ-ερος) in birth you shall be accounted the elder (πρεσβύτερος) and judged worthy (ἀξιωθήσῃ) of the elder's place. And if your life to the end be a progress to the better, the Father will give you not only the birthright of the elder, but the whole inheritance, even as he did to Jacob, who overthrew the seat and foundation of passion—Jacob who confessed his life's story in the words 'God has had mercy on me and all things are mine' (Gen 33.11), words of sound doctrine and instruction for life, for on God's mercy [ἐλέῳ], as a sure anchor, all things rest.[99]

The differences between Luke and Philo at this point reflect their different perspectives.[100] While both celebrate the mercy of the father, in Philo this is expressed in the transfer of the blessings of the elder to the younger son. In Luke's Christian treatment of the doctrine, the elder son is not deprived of anything, and is reminded by his father that he retains a full share in all of his father's possessions.

5. Restoration

The younger son's adoption of the virtue of liberality is symbolized by the special clothes that his father gives to him. Just as the father's welcome shows his own liberality, so the special clothes the son is given signify his adoption of the way exemplified by his father.

mentioned, it illustrates just how seriously the vice of φιληδονία was viewed by Middle Platonists.

99. Philo, *Sacr.* 42. The whole passage from para. 19 should be noted.

100. Another contrasting use of the two-ways motif is noted by van Unnik in 'Corpus Hellenisticum', p. 27. He observes with puzzlement that Mt. 7.13-14 says that the way leading to life is narrow and the way leading to death is broad, while the opposite situation is found in Dio Chrysostom, *Or.* 1.67-84. The difference between Dio Chrysostom and Matthew may be explained by Dio's Cynic belief that virtue and wisdom were readily attainable.

While it is recognized that the gift of a fine robe, a ring and sandals represents his new status, commentators usually explain this with examples drawn from the Old Testament or Palestinian Judaism.[101] Here I consider what significance his 're-investiture' would have had for Hellenistic Jewish and Greco-Roman readers, focusing particularly on the first and most prominent of the items mentioned, the best robe, [τὴν] στολὴν τὴν πρώτην.[102]

BAGD suggests that πρῶτος here simply means 'best', perhaps with the added implication of 'most important'.[103] The same combination of the ideas of 'best' and 'most important' is found in πρωτοκλισία in Lk. 14.7, 8; 20.46. The study by Wilckens traces the meaning of the word στολή from the meaning 'equipping' of an army or fleet, or the equipping of a person with clothing, through to specific items of clothing such as the 'upper garment' of priests or the special robes of hierophants.[104]

Wilckens comments on the *olympiaca stola* which Lucius puts on at the culmination of his initiation into the mysteries of Isis, but makes no mention of the use of the term στολή by Cynics. In the Cynic epistles στολή is sometimes used to refer to the cloak of the true Cynic.[105] στολή may be used in these places instead of the more usual τρίβων for apologetic reasons. True Cynics are not simply those who put on the

---

101. For example, Jeremias, *Parables*, p. 130; and Marshall, *Luke*, pp. 610-11. See especially K.H. Rengstorf, *Die Re-investitur des Verlorenen Sohnes in der Gleichniserzählung Jesu: Luk. 15, 11-32* (Arbeitsgemeinschaft für Forschung des Landes Nordrhein-Westfalen, Geisteswissenschaften, 137; Cologne/Opladen: Westdeutscher-Verlag, 1967).

102. In the light of our interest in the Greco-Roman reception of this parable, it is interesting to note that external evidence favors the retention of the shorter reading, which omits the article before the noun, rather than the more Semitic τὴν στολὴν τὴν πρώτην, found in P[75], D[2], R and f[1] and f[13].

103. See BAGD, s.v. 'πρῶτος', p. 726. C. Burchardt links Lk. 15.22 with *Jos. Asen.* 15.10 (and 18.5): 'your wedding robe, the ancient and first robe which is laid up in your chamber since eternity', in Charlesworth, *OTP*, II, p. 227. See also C. Burchardt, 'The Importance of Joseph and Asenath for the Study of the New Testament', *NTS* 33 (1987), pp. 102-34 (106). Wettstein refers to Athenaeus, *Deipn.* 5.197b: 'couches spread with purple rugs made of wool of the first quality (τῆς πρώτης ἐρέας)'.

104. U. Wilckens, 'στολή', *TDNT*, VII, pp. 687-91.

105. Pseudo-Crates, *Ep.* 13 (64, 2.7); and Pseudo-Diogenes, *Ep.* 7 (98, 13.23); *Ep.* 10 (102, 15); and *Ep.* 34 (144, 2).

cloak, but those who truly live out their profession.[106] The diminutive, στολίον, also means philosophical dress. It is used in this sense, though ironically, by Epictetus.[107]

In Hellenistic Judaism, στολή refers primarily to clothing in general, though frequently it is also an indicator of status.[108] Fitzmyer comments:

> In the LXX στολή is often used to translate the generic word for clothing, Hebrew *beged*. E.g. Gen 27.15; Exod 29.5, 21; 31.10. But it came to be also used for priestly robes (Philo, *Leg. ad Gaium* 37 § 296; Josephus, *Ant.* 3.7, 1 § 151; 11.4, 2 § 80).[109] According to Str-B (2.31-33) στολή refers here to the *tallit*, a Hebrew word not found in the OT or in Qumran literature, but used in later Jewish literature, for the outer cloak (= Latin *pallium*) that most people wore, but which lawyers and officers used in more ornamented or voluminous fashion, as a mark of distinction. K.H. Rengstorf[110] would rather understand it of festive garments which Jews would don for the celebration of the Sabbath.[111]

Examples of LXX usage indicating various kinds of status are, first, *royal* status: 2 Chron. 18.9; Est. 6.8; 8.15; Jon. 3.6; 1 Macc. 10.21. In two instances, Gen. 41.42 and 1 Macc. 6.15, στολή and δακτύλιος are mentioned together. Second, Exod. 28.2-4; 29.5, 21; Sir. 45.7, 10; 50.11 and 2 Macc. 3.15 use the word in connection with *priestly* status. Third, Gen. 27.15 uses it to denote the status of the *elder son*. Fourth, in Sir. 6.29, 31 it points to the glory of *those who possess wisdom*.

In the *Testaments of the Twelve Patriarchs*, while the word refers simply to clothing (e.g. *T. Jud.* 3.6; *T. Jos.* 5.2), sometimes this clothing has special significance, such as the vestments of priests in *T. Lev.* 8.2,

---

106. In Pseudo-Crates, *Ep.* 19 (68, 13-14, 19-26), it is argued that Diogenes, not Odysseus, is the true father of Cynicism. Odysseus 'put pleasure above all else', and only once donned the garb of the Cynic, while Diogenes put on the cloak throughout his life. Pseudo-Crates, *Ep.* 13 (64, 2-7) says that the στολή (cloak) of Diogenes brings greater security than the Carthaginian 'στολή' (robe).

107. See Epictetus, *Diss.* 3.23.35. LSJ, s.v. 'στολίζω' cite a further example of στολίον referring to philosopher's dress in *Anth. Pal.* 11.157.

108. See Wilckens, 'στολή', *TDNT*, VII, pp. 689-90.

109. Also: Josephus, *Ant.* 20, 7; *Life* 334.

110. K.H. Rengstorf, 'Die *stolai* der Schriftgelehrten: Eine Erläuterung zu Mark. 12, 38', in O. Betz (ed.), *Abraham unser Vater: Juden und Christen im Gespräch über die Bibel* (Festschrift Otto Michel; Leiden: E.J. Brill, 1963), pp. 383-404 (402).

111. Fitzmyer, *Luke*, p. 1317-18, commenting on στολή in Lk. 20.46.

5, and symbolic of virginity in *T. Jos.* 19.8. At the close of the *Letter of Aristeas*, the translators of the LXX are honored with fine robes and are also given robes, among other gifts, to take back to Eleazar.[112]

In the New Testament, the word occurs most often in Revelation, where it refers to the clothing of those who have been slain (Rev. 6.11), or who have come through the great tribulation, and washed their robes in the blood of the Lamb (Rev. 7.9, 13, 14 and 22.14). This heavenly dress is also worn by the young man in the empty tomb in Mk 16.5.[113]

In all these examples, the στολή is only put on by those who are morally or spiritually worthy to wear it. This helps to bring out the significance of the only other occurrence of the term in Luke: Lk. 20.47. There it refers to the distinctive robes of the scribes. However, both Luke and Mark (Mk 12.38-40) attack the scribes for being unworthy of the honor they are given. They are charged with being those who devour widows' houses, ὃι κατεσθίουσιν τὰς οἰκίας τῶν χηρῶν, a similar charge to that made by the elder brother. This reflects the grouping of ambition and avarice within the topos On Covetousness: wearing the στολή is only appropriate for those who are not guilty of unjust and covetous behavior.[114]

By placing the best robe upon him, the father not only shows his own magnanimity and generosity, but also that he considers his son worthy to wear it. In the same way, the other gifts of a ring and sandals also speak of a deserved status.[115] It is not necessary to seek separate expla-

---

112. *Ep. Arist.* 319-20.

113. Compare the clothing of the heavenly horsemen in 2 Macc. 5.2.

114. That ambition, avarice and sensual pleasure were traditionally associated is evident from the way Cynics strove against these three vices. See Malherbe, 'Gentle as a Nurse', p. 39; and the references in Gerhard, *Phoinix*, pp. 58-62 and 87-88. Mendell, 'Satire as Popular Philosophy', p. 150, cites Horace, *Sat.* 1.4.25-27, and other examples of attacks on φιλοπλουτία, φιλοτιμία and φιληδονία in Horace's *Satires* and *Epistles*.

115. In Epictetus, *Diss.* 4.1.38, a gold δακτύλιος is mentioned as denoting membership of the Equestrian order. Compare Epictetus, *Diss.* 1.22.18. δακτύλιος is hapax legomenon in the New Testament, but refers to a signet ring conferring authority in LXX Gen. 41.42; Est. 3.10; 8.8, 10; *1 Clem.* 43.2. Compare *T. Jud.* 12.4 and Diogenes Laertius, 4.59.

For the ὑποδήματα see *T. Zeb.* 3.2, 4, 5, referring back to Deut. 25.5-10. Pseudo-Socrates, *Ep.* 6 (232, 19), says that it is part of the Cynic lifestyle to do without sandals. This is related to not wearing fine clothes or seeking political fame. All the

nations for the ring and the shoes under the pressure of exegetical tradition.[116]

It is significant that Luke does not simply narrate the giving of special clothes to the son, but dramatizes the action with the father giving instructions to his servants. This serves to emphasize his liberality. His gifts symbolize his joyful conviction that the son has discovered true virtue.

6. *Harmony*

The father's joy at his son's adoption of a life of liberality is expressed in the celebration that follows. This is symbolized by a word-pair which commentators usually under-interpret: music and dancing, συμφωνία καὶ χοροί (v. 25c). συμφωνία, a hapax in early Christian literature, is usually understood to refer to the musical harmony, either of a single instrument, such as a kind of bagpipe, or of a band or orchestra made up of a number of instruments and voices.[117] While it might be argued that this is the only possible interpretation, since the harmony is *heard* by the elder son, this is not literally true of the χοροί, usually interpreted as (choral) dancing.[118] Moreover, even literally interpreted, συμφωνία καὶ χοροί imply something more. They symbolize the joy, interdependence and mutual enrichment of healthy human community.[119]

Since Plato, συμφωνία has been used to mean concord, both between reason and the emotions in the individual, and between rulers and subjects in the state. It is an expression of the rational life: 'For without harmony [ξυμφωνία], my friends, how could even the smallest fraction of wisdom exist?... He who is devoid thereof will always prove to be a home-wrecker [οἰκοφθόρος] and anything rather than a saviour of the

---

references to ὑποδήματα in Epictetus think of them as everyday articles: Epictetus, *Diss.* 1.16.1; 2.14.4; 2.22.31; 2.23.26; 3.24.44; and 4.1.80.

116. For an account of the extensive patristic allegorization of the robe, ring and shoes see Tissot, 'Patristic Allegories', pp. 377-79.

117. So BAGD, p. 781, and Spicq, *Notes de lexicographie*, p. 847.

118. BAGD, p. 883. Choral dancing is Greek rather than Roman. The picture of the head of a household singing and dancing with joy would suggest to a Roman reader extreme, though undignified joy, as in Terence, *Adelph.* 754.

119. On hearing that Theophrastus was admired for having many pupils, Zeno is reported to have said, 'It is true his chorus (χορός) is larger, but mine is more harmonious (συμφωνότερος)' (Plutarch, *Mor.* 78e).

city [περὶ πόλιν οὐδαμῇ σωτήρ]'.[120] This is why he says in the *Republic* that children have to be guided from childhood 'to likeness, to friendship, to harmony with beautiful reason [ξυμφωνίαν τῷ καλῷ λόγῳ ἄγουσα]'.[121] Cicero roots the political ideal of concord specifically in the maintenance of economic justice and equity: 'Harmony (*concordia*) ... cannot exist when money is taken away from one party and bestowed upon another'.[122]

The importance of the idea of harmony in personal relationships as well as politics is clear from Plutarch, who calls the bad relationships between brothers expressions of πλεονεξία, and good relationships examples of συμφωνία in his treatise *On Brotherly Love*.[123] Cicero's essay *Laelius: On Friendship* extols friendship as more completely in harmony with nature than anything else in the whole world, and utterly right, both in prosperity and adversity.[124]

The concept was also important to the Stoics to express their ideal of living in harmony with nature.[125] Epictetus illustrates the Delphic precept 'know thyself', by saying that a singer in a chorus seeks to know himself 'by paying attention both to his fellows in the chorus and to singing in harmony with them [καὶ τῶν συγχορευτῶν καὶ τῆς πρὸς αὐτοὺς συμφωνίας]?'[126]

---

120. Plato, *Leg.* 3.689d. For a discussion of this, and many of the other references to συμφωνέω, συμφώνησις, συμφωνία and σύμφωνος cited below, see Spicq, *Notes de lexicographie*, pp. 847-50.

121. Plato, *Resp.* 3.401d. Compare Plato, *Tim.* 47d and Aristotle, *Pol.* 7.15.7. In *Apion* 2.170 Josephus lists the four primary virtues, but replaces the usual φρόνησις (wisdom) with συμφωνία. See also Josephus, *Apion* 2.179, and the use of συμφωνῶν in 2.181.

122. Cicero, *Off.* 2.78. Compare the way harmony is restored through restitution of injustices relating to property by Aratus in Cicero, *Off.* 2.81-82.

123. Plutarch, *Mor.* 478f-479a. See Betz, '*De Fraterno Amore*', p. 239.

124. Cicero, *Amic.* 4.16–5.18.

125. This was the ideal of Chrysippus. See, for example, Diogenes Laertius, 7.88; Epictetus, *Diss.* 1.4.14-15, 18, 29, and 1.12.16. Spicq, *Notes de lexicographie*, p. 847, cites Stobaeus, *Anth.* 2.74, 4: συμφωνίαν δὲ ὁμοδογματίαν περὶ τῶν κατὰ τὸν βίον. See N.P. White, 'The Basis of Stoic Ethics', *HSCP* 83 (1979), pp. 143-78 (177).

The Stoics adopted the medical idea of the body having a shared spirit (σύμπνοια) from the Hippocratic text περὶ τροφῆς 23 ('One confluence, one conspiration, all in sympathy with one another'), and related it to the life of the universe via their theory of φύσις. See Jaeger, *Early Christianity*, pp. 22-23 and 115-16.

126. Epictetus, *Frag.* 1 (LCL).

The role of reason in bringing about harmony is seen in *4 Macc.* 14.2-8, where the kingly and free (ἐλεύθερος) reasoning (λογισμός) of the seven brothers leads them to face death. Their agreement (συμφωνία) to go in harmony to death (συνεφώνησαν θάνατον) is likened to movement of the hands and feet in sympathy (συμφωνία) with the directions of the soul. They defeat fear by dancing (χορεύω) around the number seven in harmony (σύμφωνος), just as the seven days of creation form a harmonious pattern for religion.[127] Here we see the familiar Stoic notion that right actions are an expression of acting in harmony with reason and the cosmos. The idea of the sage as being in harmony with the law and with the divine is also found in *4 Macc.* 7.7.

Harmony and the right use of possessions are also linked by moderate Cynics. Dio Chrysostom argues for the importance of having only moderate possessions: 'what exceeds the right proportion is very troublesome [τὸ γὰρ πλέον, οἶμαι, τοῦ συμμέτρου παγχάλεπον]'. He illustrates this by referring to the harmony of the organs in our bodies. We would die if each part of our bodies wished to have the advantage. 'And in the harmonies [ἁρμονίαι] of these instruments of our bodies, if any one of the strings should get more [πλεονεκτέω] than its share of tension, . . . must not the harmony of the whole be destroyed?'[128]

Other examples in which the words συμφωνία, συμφώνησις and σύμφωνος are used with the general meaning to agree, agreement, or in agreement, could be given from Luke's own writings and texts broadly contemporary with them.[129]

---

127. *4 Macc.* 14.7-8 is not easy to picture. H. Anderson, in Charlesworth (ed.), *Pseudepigrapha*, II, p. 559, commends the transposition of ἑβδομάδα in v. 7 and εὐσέβειαν in v. 8 suggested by Hadas, yielding the translation: 'Just as the seven days of creation move around the hebdomad, so did the youths in chorus circle around piety.' Compare Ignatius, *Eph.* 19.2, where at the birth of Christ 'all the other stars, with the sun and the moon, gathered in chorus (χορός) round this star'. Lake, *Apostolic Fathers*, I, p. 193, comments: 'The metaphor is probably from the chorus or choir which gathered round the altar in heathen ceremonial, and sang a sacrificial hymn.'

128. Dio Chrysostom, *Or.* 17.18-19. The following paragraph, 20, describes behavior similar to that of the rich fool in Lk. 12.16-20.

129. Acts 15.15; Lk. 5.36; Mt. 20.2, 13; Eph. 4.1, 2; Josephus, *Apion* 2.169, 180-1; *Ant.* 1.107; 10.106; 15.174, 408; *4 Macc.* 16.4; Philo, *Somn.* 1.28; *Sacr.* 74; *Deus Imm.* 25; and *Mut. Nom.* 200. Spicq, *Notes de lexicographie*, pp. 847-50, cites many examples from the papyri. *1 Clement* makes extensive use of the related term ὁμόνοια which is sometimes found together with συμφωνία. See BAGD, s.v. 'ὁμόνοια'.

Thus, Luke's use of this word-pair indicates that the virtue of liberality leads to social order and happiness. The father's liberality results in an harmonious household: his workers are well-paid (v. 17b) and his servants are obedient (v. 22a), joyful (vv. 24e, 25b, c) and helpful (v. 26a). The younger son's return enhances this domestic harmony, showing the important social consequences of his conversion from prodigality to liberality.[130] The only dissonant note is struck by the elder brother, who rejects the celebrations and refuses to participate in the social concord.

7. *Good Health*

When the elder son asks his παῖς to explain the sounds of harmony and choral dances, he is told that his father has received his brother back in good health (ὅτι ὑγιαίνοντα αὐτὸν ἀπέλαβεν). English translations invariably translate the participle ὑγιαίνοντα as 'safe and sound', [131] revealing that in conventional use, such as in letters, ὑγιαίνω means not much more than to be well or to fare well.[132]

Such an interpretation of ὑγιαίνω in v. 27d neglects the relationship between safety and physical health in Greco-Roman thought.[133] With the exception of an occurrence in 3 John 2, the New Testament usage of the verb ὑγιαίνω is limited to Luke's Gospel and the pastoral epistles. In all three places where Luke uses ὑγιαίνω, the participle is used with the literal meaning of being healthy. In one of these, Lk. 7.10, ὑγιαίνοντα describes the healthy condition of a slave who was formerly on the point of death, and in another, Lk. 5.31-32, ὑγιαίνοντα is a metaphor for being in a sound moral or spiritual condition. These indicate that in Lk. 15.27 we should recognize that Luke says that the

---

130. Compare *T. Jos.* 17.3: 'God is delighted by harmony among brothers (ὁμονοίᾳ ἀδελφῶν) and by the intention of a kind heart that takes pleasure in goodness (προαιρέσει καρδίας εὐδοκιμούσης εἰς ἀγάπην).'

131. In the AV, RSV, NRSV, NASB, TEV and the NIV. Fitzmyer, *Luke*, p. 1091, says that ὑγιαίνοντα is used in a figurative sense. This is correct, but overlooks the importance of the relationship between the literal and figurative meaning.

132. MM, p. 647. A New Testament example of such literal, conventional use is 3 Jn 2. Yet even here it is enclosed within wishes for general and spiritual well-being.

133. This is shown by the more common verb σῴζω, which also refers initially to physical health and well-being. See BAGD, s.v. σῴζω.

younger son has returned in good health, and ask what significance this might have had for his Greco-Roman audience.[134]

The earliest traces of rational medical teaching are found in the fragments of the pre-Socratic philosophers.[135] From the second half of the fifth century BCE onwards, Greek medicine and philosophy cross-fertilized one another.[136] Jaeger sums up the fourth-century Greek view of health as: a symbol of the harmonious integration of the life of body and soul in the individual. He argues that because equality and harmony are seen as the essence of health, health becomes

> a universal standard of value applying to the whole world and to the whole of life. For its foundations, equality and harmony, are the forces which (according to the ideas underlying this doctrine) create that which is good and right, while pleonexia, aggrandizement, disturbs it.[137]

While Plato and Aristotle had different concepts of how medicine was to be understood, they both held it in high esteem.[138] They, and their followers, believed that a close relationship existed between the correct care and treatment of the body and that of the soul.[139] Epicurus also took this view.[140] The metaphor continued to be widely used in the

---

134. 'To the pagans salvation was safety, health, prosperity; but even in pagan usage "the word never wholly excludes a meaning that comes nearer to reality and permanence"; it is never wholly material and ephemeral; "there is latent in it some undefined and hardly conscious thought of the spiritual and moral, which made it suit Paul's purpose admirably" ' (W.M. Ramsay, *The Bearing of Recent Discovery on the Trustworthiness of the New Testament* [London: Hodder & Stoughton, 2nd edn, 1915], p. 173, author of citation not identified).

135. Particularly Alcmaeon of Croton, Empedocles, Diogenes of Apollonia and Anaxagoras. See *OCD*, s.v. 'Medicine', p. 946.

136. The story is told by Jaeger in *Paideia*, III, pp. 3-45.

137. Jaeger, *Paideia*, III, p. 45.

138. For Plato medicine was the knowledge of health, as philosophy was the knowledge of the good. Aristotle saw medicine as part of the practical discipline of ethics. See Jaeger, 'Aristotle's Use of Medicine as Model of Method in his Ethics', in *idem*, *Scripta Minora* (2 vols.; Rome: Edizioni di Storia e Letteratura, 1960), II, pp. 491-509 (492).

139. Plato, *Resp.* 9.591c-e, ultimately values the health of the soul above that of the body. Nevertheless, physical training of the body provides a good analogy for the development of virtue. Plato, *Gorg.* 527e; *Resp.* 407a. Compare Pseudo-Pythagoras, *Carm. Aur.* 13, and Musonius, *Frag.* 6.

140. See Diogenes Laertius, 10.122, 128.

Hellenistic era, particularly by Cynics and Stoics,[141] who held stronger views than the Academic and Peripatetic schools on the danger of passions.[142] Malherbe details the way Cynics and Stoics described vices and passions as diseases which could only be cured through the reasoned instruction and exhortation of the philosopher.[143]

We saw in Chapter 4 that πλεονεξία was widely regarded by Greco-Roman moralists as one of the chief causes of vice. A further example of this is found in Longinus, who attributes moral decline to the love of money and pleasure:

> For the love of money [φιλοχρηματία] (a disease from which we all now suffer sorely [πρὸς ἣν ἅπαντες ἀπλήστως ἤδη νοσοῦμεν]) and the love of pleasure make us their thralls, or rather, as one might say, drown us body and soul in the depths, the love of riches being a malady which makes men petty [φιλαργυρία μὲν νόσημα μικροποιόν], and the love of pleasure one which makes them most ignoble.[144]

This use of literal ill-health as a metaphor for vice is found also in Cynic and Stoic descriptions of gold, luxury, intemperance and superfluity.[145]

---

141. See, for example, Cicero's extended discussion of this Stoic approach in *Tusc.* 4.10-13 and 23-33 (also Diogenes Laertius 7.115), and Seneca's frequent use of medical metaphors in *De Ira*. Hellenistic Jewish authors who engage with Stoicism also reflect a concern with physical health, as the treatment of the topos περὶ ὑγιείας in Sir. 30.14-25 attests. (This heading is given in the Sixtine edition of the LXX at Sir. 30.14.) Also Philo, *Abr.* 223.

142. The Academic-Peripatetic approach to health is related to their view that passions should be moderated (μετριοπάθεια), while the Stoic position reflects their position of ἀπάθεια. According to Thom, 'Golden Verses', pp. 140-41, Pythagoreans tended to take the former position. This different approach to passions is seen in their different attitudes to anger, which is discussed in the following chapter.

143. See A.J. Malherbe, 'Medical Imagery in the Pastoral Epistles', in *idem, Paul and the Popular Philosophers* (Minneapolis: Fortress Press, 1989), pp. 127-30. Pseudo-Diogenes attacks the folly of those who eat and drink to excess and then entrust themselves to doctors. He calls doctors 'public executioners' (κοινοὶ δήμιοι) and scoffs at the way such people thank the gods if they recover, but blame the doctors if they do not. Pseudo-Diogenes, *Ep.* 28 (124, 4-12).

144. Longinus, *Subl.* 44.6-10. Text and translation from W.R. Roberts, *Longinus On the Sublime: The Greek Text Edited after the Paris Manuscript with Introduction, Translation, Facsimilies and Appendices* (Cambridge: Cambridge University Press, 1899), pp. 156-61.

145. For example, Dio Chrysostom, *Or.* 17.11: 'When therefore greed (πλεονεξία) would bring destruction even to the divine beings, what disastrous effect must we believe this malady (νόσος) causes to human kind?' In *Or.* 13.32-33. he

In this way they take the popular idea that sickness and death are evils and transfer this association to vice.[146]

Cynics enhance this argument by adding that vice leads to actual disease. This is particularly evident among the rich who can afford to indulge in luxury and excess.[147] Such people foolishly look to physicians to restore their physical health, instead of heeding the advice of philosophers to live temperately. Austere Cynics see themselves as physicians, whose teaching is the only way to enjoy both physical health and moral freedom. They therefore call on people to see their folly as the cause of their sickness and to seek the health and wisdom of their practical moral philosophy.[148] They offer the cure of living in accordance with nature,[149] and the experience of being thrice-blessed: having temperate souls, healthy bodies and sufficient possessions.[150]

describes the teacher of temperance, manliness and justice (σωφροσύνην δὲ καὶ ἀνδρείαν καὶ δικαιοσύνην) as a physician who is able to heal such diseases of the soul (ψυχῆς νόσους) as licentiousness and covetousness (ἀκολασία καὶ πλεονεξία). It is also frequent in the Cynic epistles, for example: Pseudo-Anacharsis, *Ep.* 9 (46, 26-48, 12); Pseudo-Crates, *Ep.* 10 (62, 8-11); *Ep.* 13 (64, 6-11); Pseudo-Diogenes, *Ep.* 28 (122, 20-22); *Ep.* 34 (144, 4-11); Pseudo-Antisthenes, *Ep.* 8 (244, 16-18). Evidence of the widespread use of the metaphor in antiquity is given by F. Kudlien, 'Der Arzt des Körpers und der Arzt der Seele', *Clio Medica* 3 (1968), pp. 1-20; and 'Gesundheit', *RAC* 10 (1978), pp. 902-45. These references are cited by Thom, 'Golden Verses', p. 140 n. 289.

146. See Pseudo-Diogenes, *Ep.* 36 (148, 28-30); and Epictetus, *Diss.* 3.20.4; 4.8.28-29.

147. For example, Pseudo-Anacharsis, *Ep.* 9 (46, 27-48, 12); and Pseudo-Diogenes, *Ep.* 28 (122, 20-22). Pseudo-Crates, *Ep.* 13 (64, 2-11) contrasts the Cynic life with the life of the proverbially rich such as the Carthaginians and Sardanapalus. See also Dio Chrysostom's description of the condition of the dissolute and intemperate (ἄσωτοι καὶ ἀκρατεῖς) after feasting. They 'are pulled and dragged away by their slave attendants with discomforts and spells of sickness, shouting and groaning the while, and having no knowledge whatever where they have been or how they have feasted ...' (Dio Chrysostom, *Or.* 30.43).

148. Pseudo-Antisthenes advises Aristippus to go to Anticyra and drink the hellebore, which is much stronger than the wine of Dionysus. 'The one produces great madness (μανία) and the other cures (ἀποπαύει) it. Therefore, to the degree that health and wisdom differ from sickness and folly (ὑγίειά τε καὶ φρόνησις νόσου τε καὶ ἀφροσύνης διαφέρει), to that degree you would surpass your present condition' (Pseudo-Antisthenes, *Ep.* 8 [244, 11-19]).

149. Pseudo-Heraclitus, *Ep.* 5 (194, 1-13), especially lines 9-11: ἐγὼ εἰ οἶδα κόσμου φύσιν, οἶδα καὶ ἀνθρώπου, οἶδα νόσους, οἶδα ὑγίειαν.

150. Pseudo-Crates, *Ep.* 10 (62, 6-11).

For our purposes, it is important to note how the Cynics relate the right attitude to and use of possessions to their ideals of physical health and moral freedom.

A similar picture emerges in the writings of the Roman Stoics. Musonius argues that the negative effects of luxurious and intemperate living are cumulative. It weakens the health.[151] It corrupts body and soul. It begets the damaging social vices of covetousness and injustice.[152]

Epictetus's description of the lecture room of the philosopher is well-known. He likens their various moral illnesses to those of a dislocated shoulder, abscess, ulcer or headache.[153] However, he tries to discourage those who turn to philosophy seeking a quick moral cure, like those who seek to cure a sick stomach with a fad diet. Philosophy requires hard training. The true philosopher will have his own good health as proof of the genuineness of his profession.[154]

Seneca's *Epistle* 75 uses the metaphor of disease to discuss different degrees of moral progress. Diseases of the mind are 'hardened and chronic vices such as greed (*avaritia*) and ambition', while passions of the mind are objectionable impulses of the spirit that occur often enough to cause a disease. Those who have made least moral progress have not yet escaped all the vices/diseases, while those who are most advanced

151. Musonius, *Frag.* 18a (114, 8-12). Compare Philo, *Gig.* 34: 'For there are some things which we must admit, as, for instance, the actual necessities of life, the use of which will enable us to live in health and free from sickness (ἀνόσως καὶ ὑγιεινῶς). But we must reject with scorn the superfluities which kindle the lusts (ἐπιθυμίαι) that with a single flameburst consume every good thing.'

152. Musonius, *Frag.* 20 (126, 15-18); Seneca, *Ep.* 17.11-12; Philo, *Rer. Div. Her.* 285; and *Vit. Cont.* 2: '[the Therapeutae and Therapeutrides] profess an art of healing better than that current in the cities which cures only the bodies, while theirs treats also souls oppressed with grievous and well-nigh incurable diseases, inflicted by pleasures and desires and griefs and fears, by acts of covetousness, folly and injustice (ἡδοναὶ καὶ ἐπιθυμίαι καὶ λῦπαι καὶ φόβοι πλεονεξίαι τε καὶ ἀφροσύναι καὶ ἀδικίαι) and the countless host of the other passions and vices (παθῶν καὶ κακιῶν) ...'

153. Epictetus, *Diss.* 3.23.30. When the Platonist Plutarch describes the way a false and unreflecting judgment (κρίσις φαύλη) leads to insatiability and avarice, he likens it to a tapeworm in the mind. The desire for money is like a mental illness (ψυχικὴ νόσος) (Plutarch, *Mor.* 524d). Malherbe, 'Medical Imagery', p. 128 n. 18, comments on the extensive use of the medical metaphor in Plutarch's *Quomodo adulator ab amico internoscatur*.

154. Epictetus, *Diss.* 4.8.34-35, 28-29.

have laid aside passions and vices.[155] The Stoic satirist Persius also likes the early detection of disease to learning to live wisely, making special mention of the use of money.[156]

This widespread philosophical use of health as a metaphor for moral progress is clearly reflected in the vocabulary Luke uses for the slave's speech to the elder son. The clause ὑγιαίνοντα αὐτὸν ἀπέλαβεν in v. 27d would have suggested to Luke's Greco-Roman readers that the younger son had undergone a moral transformation of lasting significance. They would have seen that the hunger of the younger son had done him more good than the luxuries that he had eaten during his period of dissolute living, ζῶν ἀσώτως, and that his health was a sign of his recovery not only from the physical ailments associated with πλεονεξία, but also the spiritual ones.

The last part of the parable shows the elder brother's failure to understand this. His anger contrasts sharply with the good health of his younger brother, and shows that he too needs to be cured.[157]

---

155. Seneca, *Ep.* 75.11-12, 14 and 9.

156. Persius, *Sat.* 3.63-72. See Nock, *Conversion*, p. 183.

157. Note the medical metaphors in Plutarch's *De cohib. ira* 453d-464d. These are discussed in the next chapter. The rather corrupt end of the fragment 'On Rage' suggests that the man who practises being good-tempered at home is the physician of his own soul (Plutarch, *Frag.* 148 [LCL]).

Chapter 8

THE MEAN ELDER SON

The literary analysis of Lk. 15.11-32 in Chapter 2 revealed vv. 29a-32b to be the climax of the parable. It functions as a climax because of the importance of the conversation between the elder son and his father and the father's appeal. I also noted that the part dealing with the elder son is composed of two balanced parts. This means that vv. 25a-28b ought not to be neglected in the evaluation of the last part of the parable.

So, having looked at the moral behavior of the younger son and the father in the preceding chapters, I now turn my attention to that of the elder son. I examine his meanness in the context of discussions of meanness relating to the topos On Covetousness, and its emotional correlatives: his anger and his lack of brotherly love.

The whole section dealing with the elder son is necessary to give the parable a balanced moral structure. It enables Luke to dramatize the negative consequences of both forms of covetousness, prodigality and meanness, and to motivate his readers to embrace the ideal of liberality. The part dealing with the elder son does not merely reinforce what has already been said about covetousness in the preceding discussions of prodigality and liberality, but adds additional perspectives. Given the fact that exegetes have generally neglected the moral dimension of the parable, it is not surprising that the meanness of the elder son has also been neglected. Commentators make few references to it, and never devote to it any systematic moral analysis.[1]

---

1. J.M. Derrett ('The Parable of the Prodigal Son', in idem, *Law in The New Testament* [London: Darton, Longman & Todd, 1970], p. 117) is one of the few to mention it, when he describes the elder brother as 'niggardly'. Yet he makes no further mention of this and bases his observation on a questionable inference from Philo's comment on Gen. 4.4-5 in *Quaest. in Gen.* that Cain is a 'lover of self'.

1. *The Meanness of the Elder Son*

The discussion of the topos On Covetousness in Chapter 4 made repeated reference to meanness as a vice, and the discussions of prodigality and liberality in Chapters 5 and 6 mention various aspects of the meanness of the elder son. Here I gather together and review these observations in the context of moral philosophical treatments of the vice.

The elder son's meanness is best accounted for by the Aristotelian notion of deficiency. Not only does he lack his father's liberal virtues of compassion and generosity, he also lacks his prodigal brother's attractive qualities of initiative, decisiveness, readiness to act, generosity, self-assessment, repentance and desire for good relationships with his family and friends.

Luke describes the elder son almost entirely in terms of inactivity or opposition to the actions of others. His only positive activity in the parable is the years of obedient service that he has given to his father. Yet he speaks of them as years of slave labor, not partnership with his father, or the development of his own wealth. This is all the more striking in that the parable makes clear at the start that he too has received his share of the inheritance (v. 12c). The parable ascribes to him only one active emotion, anger.

This would add up to a one-dimensional picture of the elder son as an irredeemable miser. But at the end of the parable Luke adds another important dimension: he is also a beloved son. This is evident in the tenderness of the father's appeal to him in vv. 31a-32d. He addresses him as 'child', 'τέκνον', and reminds him that he retains all the privileges of a son: 'you are always with me, and all that is mine is yours', 'σὺ πάντοτε μετ' ἐμοῦ εἶ, καὶ πάντα τὰ ἐμὰ σά ἐστιν'. By describing the father's appeal in this way, Luke enhances the significance of the elder son in the eyes of his readers.[2]

Four aspects of the elder son's meanness have already been noted in the previous chapters either as the opposite of the vice of prodigality, or as a deficiency of liberality:

---

2.   This observation is of importance even for those who think that the elder son represents the Pharisees and scribes of Lk. 15.2: the part dealing with the elder son does not constitute an attack upon them, but a compassionate appeal to them.

1. The elder son fails to understand the ideal of shared posses-
    sions when he does not protest at his father's division of his
    living at the start of the parable.
2. He shows himself to be covetous when he accepts his share of
    the inheritance at the start of the parable.[3] He later reveals
    himself to be more covetous than his younger brother when he
    fails to use what he has been given, not even offering hospital-
    ity to his friends.
3. His meanness is evident in his objections to the liberal wel-
    come which his father gives to his younger brother. By his
    refusal to join in the celebrations, he disturbs the harmony of
    the whole community.
4. The seriousness of his meanness is emphasised by the negative
    consequences of his behavior: he is angry with his father,
    neglects his friends and does not love his brother. In drawing
    attention to these things, Luke further illustrates the damaging
    social effects of covetousness.

The most significant difference between him and his younger brother
is that he undergoes no moral or spiritual transformation. There is
nothing in his story which corresponds to the conversion of the younger
son. At the end of the parable he is still in a state of profound depriva-
tion, symbolized in the parable by the twin ideas of ruin, ἀπώλεια and
lifelessness, νέκρωσις. This dramatizes the plight of the mean person:
although he has everything, he possesses nothing.[4] While the younger
son departs and returns, the elder son remains at home. Here the literal
absence of change is also a metaphor for failing to undergo a process of
moral change. In the Hellenistic romance of *Daphnis and Chloe* the

---

3. Plutarch notes that those who spend their father's money freely before it
becomes their own, become miserly once they inherit it: 'Instead there is the
interrogation of servants (οἰκετῶν ἀνάκρισις), inspection of ledgers (γραμματείων
ἐπίσκεψις), the casting up of accounts with stewards and debtors (καὶ πρὸς
οἰκονόμους ἢ χρεώστας διαλογισμός), and occupation and worry that deny him
his luncheon and drive him to the bath at night' (Plutarch, *Mor.* 526f). The resemblance between this description and the actions of the rich man in Lk. 16.1-8a,
suggests that Luke may have been characterizing the elder son as a miser.
4. Paul describes an exact reversal of the situation in 2 Cor. 6.10.

development of the central characters only begins once they are free from parental influence. This principle may be operating here too.[5]

I now turn to a more detailed evaluation of his meanness, before considering the effect that his meanness has upon his relationships with his father and brother, and examining the relationship between covetousness and anger.

2. Philosophical Views of Meanness

Moral philosophers engaging with the topos On Covetousness take a serious view of meanness.[6] Many of their comments correspond well with Luke's portrayal of the elder son and enable us to understand the particular form of the vice that he represents.

a. Academics

Plato's representative of timarchy in *The Republic* reminds us that those who are disdainful of wealth in their youth grow to love it more as they get older. The causes of this are: a covetous nature (μετέχειν τῆς τοῦ φιλοχρημάτου φύσεως), combined with the absence of educated reason to protect his virtue.[7] The view that meanness gets worse with age is recurrent in texts on the topos.

In a collection of Platonic extracts illustrating covetousness and injustice, Stobaeus cites an extract from the *Crito*, in which Socrates shows that 'we ought neither to requite wrong with wrong nor to do evil to anyone, no matter what he may have done to us [οὔτε ἄρα ἀντα-δικεῖν δεῖ, οὔτε κακῶς ποιεῖν οὐδέν' ἀνθρώπων, οὐδ' ἂν ὁτιοῦν πάσχῃ ὑπ' αὐτῶν]'. Socrates says that this is never a popular view, and that there is no common ground between those who hold it and those who reject it.[8] This fundamental moral division, which is widely attested in classical literature[9] and is also found in Luke's sermon on the plain

---

5. See P. Turner, '*Daphnis and Chloe*: An Interpretation', GR NS 7 (1960), pp. 117-23 (122).

6. As early as the third century BCE we find Pseudo-Pythagoras warning against stinginess. *Carm. Aur.* 38 states: μηδ' ἀνελεύθερος ἴσθι.

7. Plato, *Resp.* 549b. Translators struggle to give an adequate English expression for Plato's Λόγου... μουσικῇ κεκραμένου. Suggestions range from Shorey's 'reason blended with culture' (LCL) to Lee's 'a properly trained mind'. See Lee, *Plato: The Republic*, p. 320.

8. Plato, *Crit.* 49c.

9. See also Plato, *Gorg.* 509c; *Resp.* 366e, 367d; Plutarch, *Mor.* 190a; 239a;

in the context of teaching about giving,[10] underlies the disagreement between the father and the elder son in the parable.[11] The father advocates forgiveness as well as generosity and his elder son opposes him on the grounds that such behavior is unjust.

b. *Peripatetics*

Aristotle's description of meanness in the *Nicomachean Ethics* is once again important.[12] Mean people are those who care more than they should (μᾶλλον ἢ δεῖ) about wealth.[13]

Aristotle's distinction of various forms of meanness is important to our understanding of the parable. While there are many and varied forms of meanness, mean actions can basically be divided into those that are deficient in giving, and those that are excessive in taking.[14] People subject to the former condition profess not to covet the possessions of others, either because they do not want to be thought guilty of disgraceful conduct, or because they are afraid of having their own possessions taken away by others.[15] The elder son's meanness is of this type. Those who are obsessed with taking, usually get their money from sordid activities such as keeping a brothel or petty money-lending. This is true αἰσχροκέρδεια.[16] Only small-scale improper gains can be considered meanness: when rulers act this way on a large scale they are called wicked, impious or unjust.

While prodigals can change as they get older, meanness is incurable (ἀνίατος). Aristotle's observations of human behavior confirm the infer-

Musonius, *Frag.* 3 (40, 30-31); Seneca, *Ep.* 95.52; *Ira* 2.34; Juvenal, *Sat.* 13.190-91; and Epictetus, *Diss.* 4.5.10.

10. Lk. 6.27-35. Compare Mt. 5.38-39; Rom. 12.17; 1 Thess. 5.15; and 1 Pet. 3.9. For a discussion of the retaliation and non-retaliation in Hellenistic and Roman periods see Betz, *Sermon on the Mount*, pp. 286-93 and 591-619.

11. 1 Pet. 3.8-9a says that this principle is part of being ὁμόφρων, συμπαθής, φιλάδελφος, εὔσπλαγχνος and ταπεινόφρων.

12. Aristotle, *Eth. Nic.* 4.1.

13. Aristotle, *Eth. Nic.* 4.1.3.

14. Aristotle, *Eth. Nic.* 4.1.8, 29, 38.

15. Aristotle, *Eth. Nic.* 4.1.39.

16. Aristotle, *Eth. Nic.* 4.1.40-41. Other examples given are gaining money from friends through gambling, stealing clothes from bathers, or robbery (*Eth. Nic.* 4.1.43).

ence already made from Plato that the innate human tendency to be mean gets worse with old age and disability.[17]

Three of Theophrastus's *Characters* are illustrations of how the Peripatetics viewed aspects of the vice of meanness.[18] As with all the other vices which he lampoons, Theophrastus attacks meanness via a string of concrete examples. The pettiness of the mean person is illustrated with biting humour. Theophrastus distinguishes μικρολογία (stinginess or excessive economy of expenditure),[19] ἀνελευθερία (meanness or illiberality), and αἰσχροκέρδεια (avarice or sordid love of gain). The latter two are useful for illustrating the vice of the elder son. Ἀνελευθερία, introduced as 'the neglect of honour when it comes to expense',[20] is illustrated by a father who does not share the sacrificial meat with his guests and servants at his daughter's wedding.[21] The elder son exhibits this attitude when he criticizes his father for killing and sharing the prize calf.

He is not guilty of αἰσχροκέρδεια, however, for he fails to understand the ideal of shared possessions, even when it works to his advantage. This is quite unlike the examples given by Theophrastus.[22]

17. Aristotle, *Eth. Nic.* 4.1.37. Compare the comment in Terence, *Adelph.* 833-34 and 953-54. Terence's Peripatetic views reached him via Menander who was a pupil of the Peripatetic school. See J. Barsby, *Terence: The Eunuch, Phormio, The Brothers. A Companion to the Penguin Translation* (Bristol: Bristol Classical Press, 1991), p. 8.

18. Theophrastus, *Char.* 10, 22 and 30.

19. Theophrastus, *Char.* 10. The example given in *Char.* 10.6 bears a striking resemblance to Lk. 15.8: 'Should his wife drop a half-farthing, he is the one that will shift pots, pans, cupboards, and beds, and rummage the curtains.'

20. Theophrastus, *Char.* 22.1.

21. Theophrastus, *Char.* 22.4.

22. Theophrastus, *Char.* 30.7: 'When he goes into foreign parts (ἀποδημέω) on the public service, he leaves at home the travel money given him by the State, and borrows, as occasion demands, of his fellow-ambassadors.' *Char.* 30.9: 'He is apt also, when his servants find ha'pence in the streets, to cry, "Shares in thy luck!" and claim his part (ἀπαιτῆσαι τὸ μέρος, κοινὸν εἶναι φήσας τὸν Ἑρμῆν).' *Char.* 30.15: 'Receiving hire-money from a servant, he demands the discount on the copper; and coming to a reckoning with his steward, requires the premium on the silver.' *Char.* 30.16-17: 'If he travels abroad with men he knows, he will make use of their servants and let out his own without placing the hire-money to the common account (καὶ μὴ ἀναφέρειν εἰς τὸ κοινὸν τὸν μισθόν).'

c. *Cynics*

Teles follows the Peripatetics and the Middle Platonists in believing that rich people who are illiberal and mean suffer want. This is because they do not use what they have. The elder son reveals this in his complaint that he has not been able to feast with his friends, while he has all along shared the resources of the farm with his father.

Even if they lose their riches, they are not automatically freed from their ἀπληστία and ἀνελευθερία.[23] This only happens when they become Cynic philosophers.[24] This comment is one I have already considered in the discussion of liberality. Liberality is not a matter of how much one possesses, but of the generous use of whatever one has. The father's appeal to his son is an attempt to explain this to him.

The conventional association of meanness with age and prodigality with youth is found in an illustration by Dio Chrysostom. He illustrates the impossibility of meeting the incompatible demands of public opinion by describing someone trying to serve a mean (ἀνελεύθερος) old man who has two 'youthful sons, bent on drinking and extravagance [παῖδες νεανίσκοι πίνειν καὶ σπαθᾶν θέλοντες]'.[25]

d. *Stoics*

As I noted in Chapter 4, Stoics warn against the idea that the acquisition of wealth brings happiness. Seneca teaches that the opposite is true: the rich find it hard to gain wealth and painful to lose it. Yet they always want more.[26] Epictetus explains that this is because actions have the effect of strengthening character: avarice is strengthened each time people receive more than they give.[27] The elder son, as we have seen, does not desire more wealth, yet he is pained by his father's generous spending of what they share.

Musonius addresses the problem of the way avarice gets worse with age by stressing that the possession of wealth does not provide for a happy and contented old age. Wealth cannot buy cheerfulness of spirit, nor freedom from sorrow (οὔτε δὲ εὐθυμίαν οὔτε ἀλυπίαν). Many rich men think themselves to be wretched (ἀθλίους νομίζοντες εἶναι

23. Teles 4A (34, 1-46).
24. Teles 4A (38, 76-40, 102).
25. Dio Chrysostom, *Or.* 66.13.
26. Seneca, *Ep.* 115.16-17.
27. 'Deeds that correspond to his true nature strengthen and preserve each particular man' (Epictetus, *Diss.* 2.9.10, 12).

234 Prodigality, Liberality and Meanness

αὐτούς). The best preparation for old age is the Stoic solution of living in accordance with nature, doing and thinking what one ought (τὸ ζῆν κατὰ φύσιν ἃ χρὴ πράττοντα καὶ διανοούμενον).[28] Luke's readers would not have a problem in seeing the father as a Christian expression of this Stoic ideal.

Other Stoic views of meanness can be illustrated from Hellenistic Jewish writings influenced by Stoic ethics: (1) reason alone has the power to change the behavior of the mean lover of money (*4 Macc.* 2.8). This is why the father appeals to his elder son; (2) Sirach describes the mean person as being mean even to himself (Sir. 14.3-10). The elder son similarly fails to understand that generosity is part of appropriate self-care; (3) avarice causes conflict instead of social harmony.[29] This is evident in the disharmony which the elder son's anger brings.

e. *Middle Platonists*
In Chapter 6 I noted that Plutarch's description of the way of life of the miser resembles that of the elder son: 'unsocial, selfish, heedless of friends, indifferent to country [ἀνελευθέρως καὶ ἀπανθρώπως καὶ ἀμεταδότως καὶ πρὸς φίλους ἀπηνῶς καὶ πρὸς πόλιν ἀφιλοτίμως]'[30] Plutarch makes a number of other comments about meanness as a form of avarice, making use of the Peripatetic categories of prodigality, meanness and liberality. For example, in Pelopidas he writes:

> For most wealthy men, as Aristotle says, either make no use of their wealth through avarice [μικρολογίαν], or abuse it through prodigality [ἀσωτίαν], and so they are forever slaves, these to their pleasures [ἡδο-ναῖς], those to their business [ἀσχολίαις]. The rest, accordingly, thankfully profited by the kindness and liberality [ἐλευθεριότητι καὶ φιλαν-θρωπίᾳ] of Pelopidas towards them ...[31]

---

28. Musonius, *Frag.* 17 (110, 16-27).

29. *Ps.-Phoc.* 44-47, paralleled in Sib. *Or.* 2, 114-18. The section ends: 'For your sake [sc. gold] there are battles and plunderings and murders, and children become the enemies of their parents and brothers [the enemies] of their kinsmen (συναίμοις).'

30. Plutarch, *Mor.* 525c.

31. Plutarch, *Pelop.* 3.2. For other examples of his use of this Peripatetic moral framework see Plutarch, *Galb.* 16.3-4: ἀνελεύθερον... μικρολόγον ... χρώμενος ἀσώτως; *Mor.* 60d: ἀνελευθερώτατον καὶ φιλαργυρώτατον ... ἀσώτους; *Mor.* 88f: μηδ' ἄσωτον, αὐτὸς ὢν ἀνελεύθερος; and *Mor.* 445a: τὴν δ' ἐλευθεριότητα μικρολογίας καὶ ἀσωτίας.

Here Plutarch shows his dependence on the moral classification of Aristotle.

His discourse *On the Love of Wealth* also follows Aristotle in viewing both meanness and prodigality as abuses of wealth, and in being more critical of the former than the latter. While his attacks on excessive acquisition do not apply to the elder son, some of Plutarch's objections to loving wealth are applicable: the miserly fail to use what they take, and they are never satisfied with what they have.[32]

f. *Summary*

This review of philosophical attitudes to meanness yields the following insights into Luke's treatment of the elder son:

1. The Peripatetic distinction between deficiency in giving and excessive taking enables us to see that Luke places the emphasis on the problem of his reluctance to give. The elder son is not guilty of αἰσχροκέρδεια, for he does not take advantage of the ideal of shared possessions. The reluctance to give or to share wealth may have been problems in the Christian communities Luke was addressing. This would support the view that Luke's teaching on poverty and wealth is primarily addressed to those who have wealth.[33]

2. The absence of any hint at the end of the parable that the father's appeal is going to change his elder son's attitude is in accordance with the Peripatetic view that meanness is hard to cure, gets worse with age, and is therefore more serious than prodigality.

3. The sharp contrast at the end of the parable between the elder son's unhappiness and his father's joy is a concrete illustration of the teaching of both Cynics and Stoics, that only those who

---

32. Those 'whose rapacity springs from meanness and illiberality (μικρολογία καὶ ἀνελευθερία) disgust us more than those in whom it springs from prodigality (δεῖ μᾶλλον δυσχεραίνειν τῶν δι' ἀσωτίαν τοὺς διὰ μικρολογίαν καὶ ἀνελευθερίαν πονηρούς), since the miserly take from others what they have no power or capacity to use themselves'. Prodigals suspend their greed once their needs or pleasures have been fulfilled, but mean people have no similar respite from their greed, 'as they are forever empty and still want the world' (Plutarch, *Mor.* 525f-526a).

33. See Karris, 'Poor and Rich', p. 124.

make use of their possessions and live in accordance with the right philosophical principles, are happy.

4. The father's response to the elder son's complaint that he is being unjust, reflects Christian support for the common moral ideal that it is never fair to requite wrong with wrong.

From this, it is clear that Luke's Greco-Roman readers would have disapproved of the elder son's meanness.

3. The Consequences of Meanness

As with prodigality, meanness has social consequences. Luke illustrates this by showing the elder son's inability to develop healthy relationships with his father, his younger brother and his friends.

I observed in Chapter 6 that his meanness prevents him from enjoying friendship. This is also true of his family relationships. His first words placed in direct speech in the parable are: 'Listen! For all these years I have been working like a slave for you, and I have never disobeyed your command', ἰδοὺ τοσαῦτα ἔτη δουλεύω σοι καὶ οὐδέποτε ἐντολήν σου παρῆλθον, (v. 29b-d). These reveal that the elder son sees himself as a slave, not a son. Danker has suggested that the elder son saw himself as a 'good slave'.[34] His language, especially the use of δουλεύω and ἐντολή, refers to the unquestioning obedience of slavery, not the responsible obedience of sonship. Ironically, Greco-Roman literature more often presupposes the venality of slaves than their trustworthiness.[35]

He lacks the inner freedom that is the driving force of true morality. Freedom is a part of the topos On Covetousness that is particularly stressed by Stoics and Cynics.[36] The elder son's lack of freedom is further evident in his failure to realize that all his father's possessions were available to him, and that he did not have to wait for his father to give him a young goat to share with his friends. Luke thus dramatizes the

---

34. Danker, *Luke*, p. 277.

35. See M.A. Beavis, 'Ancient Slavery as an Interpretive Context for the New Testament Servant Parables with Special Reference to the Unjust Steward (Luke 16.1-8)', *JBL* 111 (1992), pp. 37-54 (41).

36. For example, by Teles 4A; Pseudo-Crates, *Epp.* 7, 8 and 13; Seneca, *Ep.* 17; Musonius, *Frag.* 17; and Epictetus, *Diss.* 4.1. Epicurus teaches freedom from pain. See also Malherbe, *Moral Exhortation*, pp. 158-59.

message that meanness obstructs the process of interchange and sharing which is the life-blood of all healthy relationships.

a. *The Absence of Brotherly Love*

His view of himself as a slave rather than a son is consistent with his subsequent refusal to accept his younger brother. In v. 30a he avoids describing the younger son as his brother, and says, 'this son of yours', ὁ υἱός σου οὗτος, rather than, 'this brother of mine', ὁ ἀδελφός μου οὗτος. Luke emphasizes this point by describing the father as correcting his son in v. 32b with the words, 'this brother of yours', ὁ ἀδελφός σου οὗτος. By making this prominent change to the father's repeated refrain, Luke indicates that the elder son's failure to understand the true meaning of brotherhood is a significant deficiency.[37]

The elder son's denial of the ethical requirements of brotherhood, particularly those related to sharing of possessions, would have been noted by Greco-Roman readers, for whom brotherly love was an important topos. Although Stobaeus gives a collection of extracts on the topos, Plutarch's discourse *On Brotherly Love* gives the best systematic treatment of the ethical issues involved.[38]

Betz provides a useful study of Plutarch's discourse, in which he illustrates many of the points made by Plutarch with examples from Lk. 15.11-32.[39] The issue raised by Plutarch's discourse that is most pertinent to this parable is the view that, when brothers fight over the distribution of their father's goods, as they often do, they are motivated by

37. T. Corlett, 'This *brother* of yours', *ExpTim* 100 (1989), p. 216.

38. Betz, '*De Fraterno Amore*', p. 232. The largest extracts in Stobaeus, *Anth.* 4.27 (4.656, 1-4.675, 16; Wachsmuth-Hense) are from Hierocles' *De frat. amor.*; Musonius, *Frag.* 15 (98, 28-100, 16); Xenophon, *Mem.* 2.3; *Cyr.* 8.7.13-16; and Plutarch, *Frat. Amor.* (479a, 480d-f, 483c, 482b, 489d and 479b). The extracts from Hierocles are translated in Malherbe, *Moral Exhortation*, pp. 93-100. A further example of this topos is found in *4 Macc.* 13.1–14.10, especially 13.19–14.1. See H.-J. Klauck, 'Brotherly Love in Plutarch and in 4 Maccabees', in D.L. Balch, E. Ferguson and W.A. Meeks (eds.), *Greeks, Romans and Christians: Essays in Honor of Abraham J. Malherbe* (Minneapolis: Fortress Press, 1990), pp. 144-56 (150-55).

39. This is another of the topoi with which the parable also engages, but which is not comprehensive enough to account for all the contents of the parable and those of its co-texts.

πλεονεξία.[40] Plutarch provides a list of ethical principles that should govern the distribution of paternal property, all of which are violated by the events in the parable.[41] The central one is that of Plato: brothers should see themselves as dividing up the 'care and administration' of the estate, with the 'use and ownership' being left 'unassigned and undistributed for them all in common'.[42] Plutarch recognizes the problems in implementing this ideal, given practical differences such as those of physical separation, age and abilities.[43]

He also points out that a sound relationship between children and parents and between brothers is essential if people are to be able to develop proper friendships.[44] The elder son's hostility towards his younger brother therefore not only robs his father of joy,[45] but also further prevents him from experiencing true friendship and social harmony.[46] Brothers ought to share everything, even friends, but brothers who are hostile to one another do not share anything.[47]

Musonius weaves the motifs of brothers and possessions very closely together, by arguing that brothers are a more precious inheritance than money: brothers discourage intrigue; they give greater support than possessions or friends; and they are most disposed to share common goods

---

40. Plutarch, *Mor.* 482d-483a. Epictetus touches on this common issue in a diatribe that recalls the situations of Lk. 12.13 and Lk. 15.11-32: ' "My father is taking away my money". But he is doing you no harm. "My brother is going to get the larger part of the farm". Let him have all he wants. That does not help him at all to get a part of your modesty, does it, or of your fidelity, or of your brotherly love? Why, from a possession of this kind who can eject you?' (*Diss.* 3.3.9-10). See also Epictetus, *Diss.* 2.10.9, with its play on the word πλεονεξία. Oldfather comments: 'πλέον ἔχης (πλεονεξία), "getting the best of it", usually had a bad sense, but there is a πλεονεξία which should attract the good man' (Oldfather, *Epictetus*, I, p. 276).

41. Plutarch, *Mor.* 483d-484a.

42. Plutarch, *Mor.* 483d, with reference to Plato, *Crit.* 109b. See also Plutarch, *Mor.* 484b, which repeats Plato's advice 'to abolish, if possible, the notion of "mine" and "not mine" ' found in Plato, *Resp.* 462c.

43. Plutarch, *Mor.* 487f, 484c, 486b and 486f.

44. Plutarch, *Mor.* 479c-d. Friendship is an image of the natural relationship children have with their parents and siblings. 'This means that a relationship like friendship cannot possibly be authentic if the foundational relationship of brother toward brother is in disorder' (Betz, '*De Fraterno Amore*', p. 241).

45. Plutarch, *Mor.* 480a-b.

46. See Chapters 6 and 7 above.

47. Plutarch, *Mor.* 490e, 481e.

(κοινωνὸν ἀγαθῶν).[48] This shows the folly of the elder son's rejection of his younger sibling because of lost patrimony. His covetousness leads him to fail to recognize that he has recovered a greater good than money. Longus appears to cite as proverbial the statement, 'To wise men no fortune is worth a brother [κρεῖττον γὰρ τοῖς εὐφρονοῦσιν ἀδελφοῦ κτῆμα οὐδέν]'.[49]

Thus, the elder son's meanness has far-reaching effects upon his social relationships, robbing him of a good relationship with his father, his brother and his friends.

b. *Anger*

Apart from his meanness, the most distinctive characteristic of the elder son is his anger (v. 28a, ὀργίζομαι). G. Stählin describes his anger well as 'indignant selfishness'.[50] He is angry with his father for treating him unjustly: he complains that he has served his father for many years without any reward, while his brother is being lavishly rewarded after years of prodigal living. This is a distorted perception of the situation. It is true that the younger son had squandered his inheritance, but, as the readers of the parable would know, he had also experienced injustice and heartlessness from his former employer and other foreigners, while the elder son had remained at home and daily experienced his father's compassion and generosity. His inability to reflect clearly upon the situation reflects not only the distorted perspective of the mean person, but also the irrationality of anger. This is a particular concern of Cynics and Stoics.[51]

(i) *Anger and Meanness in the Elder Son.* The son's outburst would have been noted by Greco-Roman readers, as anger was also a topos much discussed by moral philosophers. Cicero speaks of 'the repeated

48. Musonius, *Frg.* 15 (100, 1-15).

49. Longus, *Daphn. Chloe.* 4.24. This statement is made in the context of Dionysophanes's 'consideration of the delicate matter of what this returning son means to the other brother'. See Hock, 'The Greek Novel', p. 140.

50. G. Stählin, in H. Kleinknecht *et al.*, *Wrath* (trans. D. M. Barton; London: A. & C. Black, 1964), p. 76. Bromiley's translation in Kleinknecht *et al.*, 'ὀργή, κτλ', p. 420, is the less elegant 'aroused self-seeking'.

51. Compare Cicero, *Tusc.* 4.77, where anger (*ira*) is understood as unsoundness of mind: 'And so we say appropriately that angry men have passed beyond control, that is, beyond consideration, beyond reason, beyond intelligence (*de consilio, de ratione, de mente*); for these should exercise authority over the entire soul.'

utterances of the greatest philosophers on the subject of irascibility (iracundia)',[52] and it is discussed at some length by Seneca in *De ira* and Plutarch in *De cohibenda ira* and a lost work 'On Rage' (περὶ ὀργῆς), of which Stobaeus preserves only a fragment.[53] All agree that anger is an important emotion, which has to be rightly handled if one is to make moral progress. However, they are divided on whether it can make a positive contribution to the moral life. Followers of the traditions of Plato and Aristotle believe that anger is a necessary part of the moral life, provided it is controlled. Others, influenced by Cynic and Stoic traditions, see it as a dangerous passion which the good person has to overcome. However, even authors leaning towards an Academic-Peripatetic position see anger as a 'sickness or passion'.[54]

Aristotle teaches that the ideal emotional state is to be good-tempered, but that there is a legitimate place for moderate anger.[55] For him, the mean is gentleness (πραότης), the excess, irascibility (ὀργιλότης), and the deficiency, spiritlessness (ἀοργησία) or an inability to get angry in the right manner, at the right time and with the right people.[56] Of the various forms of excessive anger mentioned by Aristotle, the elder son is similar to the harsh-tempered person (χαλεπός)[57] who loses his temper at the wrong things, and more and longer than he ought, and who refuses to be reconciled without obtaining redress.[58]

The condition of freedom from anger (ἀοργησία) which Aristotle sees as a deficiency, is regarded by Cynics and Stoics as the ideal. This is because of their concern for the control of all passions. Plutarch views anger as the most hated and despised of the passions. Following Zeno, he thinks of it as a mixture of pain, pleasure, insolence, envy, and, the most unattractive desire of all, 'the wish to cause pain to

---

52. See Cicero, *Quint. Frat.* 1.1.37.

53. Fragment 148 in Plutarch, *Fragments* (LCL), pp. 274-76.

54. See Aulus Gellius, *NA* 1.26.3.

55. Kleinknecht ('ὀργή, κτλ', pp. 384-85) cites the criticisms of this by Cicero in *Tusc.* 4.43-44; and Seneca in *Ira* 3.3. Cicero continues his attack in *Tusc.* 4.79: 'Where are the wiseacres who say that irascibility is useful (can unsoundness of mind be useful?) or natural? or is anything in accordance with nature which is done in opposition to reason?'

56. Aristotle, *Eth. Nic.* 2.7.11; and 4.5.1-15.

57. Aristotle, *Eth. Nic.* 4.5.7-11.

58. Aristotle, *Eth. Nic.* 4.5.11.

others'.[59] From this point of view, both the elder son's anger and his covetousness are passions that must be eradicated.

As examples of the Cynic position I consider the austere Cynic author of Pseudo-Heraclitus *Epistle* 4, and the mild Cynic, Dio Chrysostom. The former claims to have overcome pleasures (ἡδονή), money (χρήματα), ambition (φιλοτιμία), cowardice (δειλία) and flattery (κολακεία), to have authority over fear (φόβος) and drunkenness (μέθη) and to be respected by grief (λύπη) and anger (ὀργή).[60] Dio Chrysostom gives similar lists of πάθη over which the philosopher must gain control.[61]

The Stoic fondness for classification of moral disorders is well-known. Cicero shows this when he lists the Stoic definitions of different kinds of anger:

> The divisions again under the head of lust are defined in such a way that *anger* (*ira*) is the lust of punishing the man who is thought to have inflicted an undeserved injury; *rage* (*excandescentia*) on the other hand is anger springing up and suddenly showing itself, termed in Greek θύμωσις: *hate* (*odium*) is inveterate anger; *enmity* (*inimicitia*) is anger watching an opportunity for revenge; *wrath* (*discordia*) is anger of greater bitterness conceived in the innermost heart and soul...[62]

For our purposes, it is significant to note that Cicero's list continues immediately with the mention of greed (*indigentia*) as 'insatiable lust' (*libido*), thus showing his perception of a close relationship between these passions.

Seneca provides a full account of the Stoic understanding of anger in *De ira*. It is valuable for being in dialogue with the views of other schools, noting points of agreement and disagreement. His Stoic position is the same as that advocated by Plutarch in *De cohibenda ira*.

59. Plutarch, *Mor.* 455e, 463a. This is similar to the popular view of prodigality, which sees it as a vice that combines the worst passions; see Chapter 5.

60. Pseudo-Heraclitus, *Ep.* 4 (192, 1-5). The epistle is Cynic, despite the Platonic and Stoic parallels. See Malherbe, 'Pseudo-Heraclitus' passim. Gore comments on the relationship between the ideas contained in this Cynic epistle and Stoic and Platonic texts, and compares it with Acts 16.15-18 and 17.22-29. See C. Gore, *St Paul's Epistle to the Ephesians: A Practical Exposition* (London: John Murray, 1898), p. 254.

61. Dio Chrysostom, *Or.* 1.13; 2.75; 49.9; and 62.2.

62. Cicero, *Tusc.* 4.9.21.

Here I note only three aspects that have a bearing upon the covetous behavior of the elder son.

First, Seneca defines ὀργή as the desire to repay suffering.[63] It is caused by the impression of having received an injury, particularly when the injury is perceived to be unjust.[64] Seneca also here mentions money as a frequent cause of anger.[65] Thus, a Stoic view would be that the elder son was angry because he felt that his father was being unfair to him in the way he was using his resources.

Second, Seneca's *Epistle* 75 mentions anger and avarice (*ira* and *avaritia*) as equally serious vices.[66] Those who have begun to make moral progress are still subject to one or the other.[67] The fact that the elder son is prone to *both* vices shows that he is not yet on the path of moral reform. Indeed, his angry response to perceived injustice in the use of possessions suggests that he himself may be guilty of this shortcoming, for Seneca argues that people are most angry with others for failings of which they themselves are guilty: '... hence it happens that a father who is even worse than his son rebukes his son's untimely revels, that a man does not pardon another's excesses who sets no bound to his own...'[68]

A further indication of the elder son's poor moral state is that he does not learn the control of anger through the example of his father.[69]

(ii) *The Control of Anger by the Father*. Plutarch's essay on the control of anger[70] is essentially Stoic in orientation. It illustrates the pervasiveness of the Stoic view of anger, even among people with other philosophical affiliations. He considers weak people to be most prone to anger. One example of this is the miser (φιλάργυρος).[71] Children, too,

---

63. The definition, drawn from Posidonius, was in part of the text which has been lost, but is preserved by Lactantius, *Ira Dei* 17: *ira est cupiditas ulciscendae iniuriae*. Seneca, *Ira* 1.3.3. The definition is similar to that by Aristotle in *Rhet.* 2.2.

64. Seneca, *Ira* 2.1.3; 2.31.1.

65. Seneca, *Ira* 3.33.

66. Seneca, *Ep.* 75.14. In *Ira* 1.21.1-4 he equates anger with luxury, avarice, lust and ambition.

67. See Malherbe, *Moral Exhortation*, p. 157.

68. Seneca, *Ira* 2.28.8.

69. Seneca, *Ira* 3.8.3.

70. Plutarch, *De Cohibenda Ira* (*Mor.* 452e-464d).

71. Plutarch, *Mor.* 457b.

are weak. Hence, angry behavior is like the behavior of children.[72] He also mentions that anger is caused by a selfish attachment to luxuries and superfluities, a familiar motif in the topos On Covetousness.[73] In a description of the fine nature of Brutus, Plutarch links his freedom from anger with his freedom from pleasurable indulgence and greed (καὶ πρὸς πᾶσαν ὀργὴν καὶ ἡδονὴν καὶ πλεονεξίαν ἀπαθής).[74] Again we see the close link between anger and greed.

As I noted in Chapter 6, the father shows marked control of his passions. He shows himself to be free of anger, despite the fact that he has good reason to be angry with both of his sons.[75] Stoics teach that reason can be used to control both anger and avarice.[76] Seneca gives examples of reasonable responses to anger and other vices, including those that are expressions of covetousness, which illustrate the father's behavior.

Seneca says that the man of sense does not hate those who make mistakes, for all people err. 'How much more human to manifest toward wrong-doers a kind and fatherly spirit, not hunting them down but calling them back'.[77] It is wrong for the wise man to be angry at base deeds, because he will meet many people who are happy to be criminals, misers, spendthrifts or profligates.[78] The father illustrates Seneca's

72. Plutarch, *Mor.* 458d; 447a.
73. Plutarch, *Mor.* 461a.
74. Plutarch, *Brut.* 29.2.
75. See Kleinknecht *et al.* 'ὀργή, κτλ', p. 442 n. 409.
76. Epictetus repeatedly mentions anger as an emotion the philosopher must overcome. See Epictetus, *Diss.* 1.13.1-5; 1.26.7; 2.10.18; 3.10.17; 3.13.11; 3.15.10; 3.22.13; and *Frag.* 20 (LCL). Thom observes that it is a Greek commonplace to think of passions such as anger being healed through the use of reason. Thom, 'Golden Verses', p. 125.
77. Seneca, *Ira* 1.14.2-3; 2.10; 2.28; 3.24. Plutarch takes the same view: 'And if we keep repeating to ourselves Plato's question, "Can it be that I am like that?" and turn our reason inward instead of to external things, and substitute caution for censoriousness, we shall no longer make much use of "righteous indignation" towards others when we observe that we ourselves stand in need of much indulgence' (*Mor.* 463e).
78. Seneca, *Ira* 2.7.2. Epictetus (*Diss.* 2.18.5, 12-13) says that, as with any other habit, the way to control anger is never to 'feed' it. Compare the advice given in *T. Gad* 7, especially 7.3-6: 'Search out the Lord's judgments, and thus you shall gain an inheritance and your mind will be at rest. Even if someone becomes rich by evil schemes, as did Esau, your father's brother, do not be jealous; wait for the Lord to set the limits... The man who is poor but free from envy, who is grateful to the

advice that the intention, motives and age of the offender should be
taken into account.[79] The younger son did not intend to harm his family,
and was young when he spent his money wastefully. Thus, the father
illustrates the Stoic view, upheld by Plutarch against the Peripatetics,
that reason is at all times more fit to govern us than anger.[80]

This view is also found in Hellenistic Jewish texts which show Stoic
influence. As part of its teaching on the way reason masters the passions,[81] *4 Macc.* 2.15 mentions that the love of money,[82] like wrath, is
one of the violent passions which reason is able to master. In *Pseudo-
Phocylides* anger is rejected together with excess (πλεονάζον), great
luxuriousness (ἡ πολλὴ δὲ τρυφή) and great wealth (πολὺς πλοῦτος).[83]
The same orientation is found in the *Testaments of the Twelve Patriarchs*,[84] Sirach,[85] Philo and Josephus.[86]

While most early Christian writers tend to agree with the Peripatetic
view that there is a place for righteous indignation,[87] Trench overstates

---

Lord for everything, is richer than all, because he does not love the foolish things
that are a temptation common to mankind.'

79. Seneca, *Ira* 3.12.2.

80. Plutarch, *Mor.* 459d. Compare the third sentence of the fragment 'On Rage'
(περὶ ὀργῆς): 'A man ought then to make reason his guide and so set his hand to
life's tasks, either pushing aside his feelings of wrath whenever they assail him, or
finding a way past ...' (*Frag.* 148 [LCL]).

81. *4 Macc.* 1.3-4.

82. Sinaiticus reads φιλαργυρίας in place of the φιλαρχίας found in Alexan-
drinus.

83. See *Ps.-Phoc.* 60-62, which relates the ideas of excess and wealth, and
vv. 63-64, which mentions various types of anger: 'Anger (θυμός) that steals over
one causes destructive madness. Rage (ὀργή) is a desire, but wrath (μῆνις) sur-
passes it.' See too v. 57b: 'bridle your wild anger (ὀργή)'.

84. *T. Dan* 2-4. Power and wealth are mentioned as the allies of anger in *T. Dan*
3.4.

85. Sir. 28.10b: 'in proportion to his wealth he will heighten his wrath (ὀργή)'.
Compare Sir 27.30: 'Malice and wrath (μῆνις καὶ ὀργή) are both abominations: and
the sinful man shall have them both.'

86. For examples from these two authors see Kleinknecht *et al.*, 'ὀργή, κτλ',
pp. 417-18. In Philo, *Conf. Ling.* 48, ὀργή is one of the vices of the covetous
person. In contrast with Philo, Josephus is more influenced by the Old Testament
and rabbinic usage. This can be seen in his report of Arion's anger (ὀργίζω) at the
prodigal way of life (ἀσώτως ζῆν) of Hyrcanus in Josephus, *Ant.* 12.203.

87. Betz and Dillon '*De Cohibenda Ira*', pp. 171, 179-81. The principal reason
for this is the Christian acceptance of the wrath of God. Luke only uses the noun

matters when he says, 'The Scripture has nothing in common with the Stoics' absolute condemnation of anger. It inculcates no ἀπάθεια, but only μετριοπάθεια, a moderation, not an absolute suppression, of the passions, which were given to man as winds to fill the sails of his soul, as Plutarch excellently puts it (*De virt. mor.* 12)'.[88] Early Christian writers either condemn anger[89] or urge that it be carefully controlled.[90] The approach to anger in the *Shepherd of Hermas* is even closer to that of the Stoics.[91]

In common with moderate Cynics and Roman Stoics, Luke takes a negative view of the ὀργή of the elder son.[92] The son's words and actions are not manifestations of the milder emotion of θυμός, but express an angry desire (ὀργή) to punish his father for acting unjustly towards him.[93]

ὀργή twice (Lk. 3.7; 21.23), both times with reference to the eschatological wrath of God.

88. Trench, *Synonyms*, p. 133.

89. Eph. 4.25 is a citation of Ps. 4.5. Compare Eph. 4.31, which equally condemns πικρία, θυμός and ὀργή; and Eph. 6.4. See also *1 Clem.* 29.7; *Did.* 3.2; Polycarp, *Phil.* 6.1.

90. Mt. 5.21-26; Eph. 4.26; Jas 1.19-21.

91. Hermas, *Man.* 5.2.4, describes the progress from ill temper (ὀξυχολία) to silliness (ἀφροσύνη), bitterness (πικρία), wrath (θυμός), rage (ὀργή) and, finally, fury (μῆνις), which is the source of great and inexpiable sin. Compare the marks of the presence of the angel of wickedness in *Man.* 6.2.5: 'When ill temper or bitterness (ὀξυχολία... ἢ πικρία) come upon you, know that he is in you. Next the desire of many deeds and the luxury (πολυτέλειαι) of much eating and drinking and many feasts, and various and unnecessary foods (πολλῶν καὶ ποικίλων τροφῶν), and the desire (ἐπιθυμίαι) of women, and covetousness and haughtiness, and pride...'

92. The only other Lukan use of ὀργίζομαι is found in Lk. 14.21, where the master exhibits righteous anger. The frame of the parable suggests that he may allegorically represent God: compare the reference to the kingdom of God in Lk. 14.15. However, exegetes have never understood the elder son to represent God, and his anger has seldom been considered righteous. Moreover, the punitive expression of anger found in Mt. 22.7 is notably absent from Lk. 14.21-24.

93. Kleinknecht notes that in post-Homeric usage, ὀργή denoted the impulsive state of the human disposition, in contrast with the more inward and quiet ἦθος. It developed the meaning of anger orientated towards revenge through its use in Attic tragedy (Kleinknecht *et al.*, 'ὀργή, κτλ', pp. 383-84).

In the fragment 'On Rage' (περὶ ὀργῆς) (*Frag.* 148 [LCL]) Plutarch distinguishes θυμός from ὀργή. Anger (θυμός) can be virtue's ally, but people should try to rid themselves of excesses such as rage (ὀργή), asperity (πικρία) or quick temper (ὀξυθυμία).

Thus, the anger of the elder son is a further consequence of his meanness. As in the case of his younger brother, he can only be healed by turning to liberality. However, because of the more serious nature of meanness, Luke leaves the question of his moral change open. This means that the joyful note on which the parable ends also carries a silent warning to those of Luke's readers who have not learnt liberality. Not surprisingly, Luke 16 continues with a parable about a rich man.

Trench, *Synonyms*, p. 132; and van der Horst, *Pseudo.-Phocylides*, p. 156, both refer to the definitions in Diogenes Laertius 7.113, 114: 'Anger (ὀγρή) is a craving or desire to punish one who is thought to have done you an undeserved injury... Wrath (μῆνις) is anger which has long rankled and has become malicious, waiting for its opportunity... Resentment (θυμός) is anger at an early stage.'

Chapter 9

CONCLUSION

The heart of the above study has been the recognition and examination of the relationship between Lk. 15.11-32 and the Greco-Roman topos On Covetousness. In this chapter I sum up the nature of this relationship and its effect on the interpretation of the parable.

1. *Similarities and Differences between the Parable and the Topos*

The parable has many points of contact, both thematic and formal, with the writings of moral philosophers on the same topos. The differences between the parable and other texts On Covetousness are fewer, yet also significant.

a. *Similarities*

The most obvious area of agreement between the parable and other texts on the topos is that they are all about different aspects of the use of possessions. The recognition, via a literary analysis, that the parable gives teaching on the right use of possessions, was the first indicator that the topos has strongly influenced the composition of the parable in its present form.

The broad moral area covered by the topos is demarcated by Stobaeus in terms of the three vices of ἀδικία, φιλαργυρία and πλεονεξία. This area contains a cluster of interrelated vices, which are condemned in different ways by particular texts. A number of these vices, such as ἐπιθυμία, ἀσωτία and πορνεία are explicitly mentioned in a negative way in Lk. 15.11-32. Others are opposed implicitly by the positive example of the father. For example, readers knowing the conventions of the topos would not understand his joyful celebration to include eating and drinking to excess

In addition to condemning the same vices as other texts on the topos, the parable advocates a similar group of associated virtues. Examples of these are the virtues of φιλία, ὑγίεια, σωφροσύνη, πόνος, ἰσότης and συμφωνία.

Thus, an important area of agreement between the parable and other texts on the topos is that of shared moral concerns, expressed in a common message and a common moral vocabulary. As well as references to vices and virtues, language which makes explicit reference to the use of possessions, such as δίδωμι, συνάγω and δαπανάω, is prominent.

The parable also makes contact with the topos in its method of moral organization and argumentation. This is evident in the way it: (1) presents a preferred virtue as the mean of two opposing vices; (2) describes virtues in terms of their opposite vices; and (3) presents the negative consequences of particular vices and the positive results of following a particular virtue. Like other texts on the topos, Lk. 15.11-32 discusses vice and virtue by means of character studies. The whole parable can be seen as an example of the way texts on the topos illustrate moral points about inheritances, the correct upbringing of children, and relationships between siblings and their use of wealth, by means of short narratives or examples. Both the parable and these other illustrations have a hortatory function.

b. *Differences*

There are three ways in which the parable differs from other texts on the topos.

(1) At a number of points in the parable Luke adopts a particular position on issues over which there was division between the different philosophical groups. An example of this is the question of how possessions should be owned and used. Within the topos, different texts take up different positions between the extremes of ascetic renunciation of all possessions and the private ownership of great wealth. The parable reveals Luke's support for the ideals of the common ownership and shared use of possessions. It also shows that he advocates the practical virtues of moderation and liberality in the use of possessions. Unlike many other Jewish and Christian texts on the topos, the parable does not constitute an attack upon the rich. Instead, Luke's message is that those who have wealth ought to share it. This accords with Luke's teaching elsewhere in Luke–Acts.[1]

---

1. See Fitzmyer, *Luke*, p. 249.

(2) A distinctive element in the parable that is not prominent in Greco-Roman and Hellenistic Jewish texts on the topos is the theme of compassion. The father is identified as the central figure of the parable, and his liberality is marked by the exercise of compassion towards both of his covetous sons. He celebrates the younger son's return home as a turning to liberality and he exhorts the elder son to understand the meaning of his liberal actions.

The Christian roots of the ideal of compassion are evident in its being an attribute of God in Hellenistic Jewish texts and of Jesus in the synoptic gospels. However, even at this, the point of the widest difference between Luke and other Greco-Roman texts, Philo reveals a point of contact between God's compassion and the cosmic harmony of Stoicism.

(3) One prominent motif that is not found in other texts on the topos is the use of εὑρίσκω with the sense 'to recover'. The absence of a point of contact here is striking in view of the many points of contact which exist between the use of the terms νεκρός, ζάω and ἀπόλλυμι in the parable and in other texts on the topos. This suggests that Luke's use of εὑρίσκω does not derive from the topos, but arises out of his desire to link this parable with the preceding two lost and found similitudes. The provision of such links is typical of Luke's compositional method. However, exegetical history has overemphasized the importance of this link, neglecting in the process the thematic and terminological links between the parable and Luke 16.

All these resemblances and differences reveal Luke's creative Christian engagement with the topos.

2. *Luke's Philosophical Affiliation*

While the parable interacts closely with the teachings of the Greco-Roman moral philosophers on the use of possessions, the findings of this study do not suggest that Luke consistently follows the views of any single philosophical tradition. Instead, he tells a simple narrative which, through its form, themes and language, uses a topos that influenced all the philosophical traditions.

He is least close to the ascetic views of the austere Cynics and Epicureans, and has most in common with the attitudes of mild Cynic and Stoic authors. Like many other authors, his treatment of the virtue of liberality is shaped by peripatetic distinctions and categories. However, he does not follow Aristotle slavishly. The view of anger found in the parable, for example, is closer to that of the Cynics and Stoics than the Peripatetics. Thus, his philosophical position is essentially eclectic.

The clearest indicator of his Christian perspective is his emphasis upon compassion.

3. *Gains from Recognizing the Relationship between the Parable and the Topos*

The recognition of Luke's engagement with the topos On Covetousness yields many exegetical insights. It provides a sound reason for paying fresh attention to two neglected features of the parable: its language of possessions and its hortatory function. Their importance is confirmed by their prominence in the other L parables and by the gnomic aspect of the Lukan travel narrative.

a. *Meaning*

Two exegetical cruxes are decisively addressed by this moral reading, the unity of the parable and the nature of the younger son's repentance. In addition to these, the moral resonances of many other terms become evident and we are enabled to identify accurately the particular types of vice and virtue being addressed.

As I have already noted, the parable is unified by being an expression of the topos. Many of the words have related moral functions when used by texts on the topos, and each of the major units of the parable is seen to be dealing with prodigality, liberality and meanness, respectively. Apart from this simple configuration, the two opposing vices each interact individually with the virtue of liberality. As a whole, the parable emerges as a valuable illustration of the Lukan ideal of shared possessions, which sheds light on the summaries of this in Acts 2.44-46 and 4.32-35. Thus, by reading the parable as an exhortation to liberality, the close relationship between the structure and language of the parable becomes apparent, and it is seen to be a unified whole with a coherent moral message.

The authenticity of the younger son's repentance is shown in various ways. His repeated request to be taken on as a hired worker takes on new significance when the moral value of manual labor is recognized. The use of the phrase εἰς ἑαυτὸν ἔρχεσθαι in discussions of moral conversion, the importance of death-alive antithesis in moral discussions, and the importance of health as a metaphor for the life of virtue, all support the view that his moral change is genuine.

Many other words and phrases gain new significance by being viewed from a moral perspective: συνάγειν is recognized to be an activity of the rich; εἰς ἑαυτὸν ἔρχεσθαι is seen to be an indicator of moral conversion; συμφωνία and φιλία are recognized to be important social ideals, and so on. All these support the overall message of the parable and further enrich its meaning.

Comparison with other texts using the topos allows for the moral issues being addressed to be identified with greater precision. Examples of this are: (1) The two sons are seen to represent opposing forms of the vice of covetousness, while the father represents the virtuous mean; (2) prodigality is seen to be a vice which is curable while meanness is not; (3) meanness is seen to be the more serious of the two vices; (4) the particular form of meanness represented by the elder son is deficiency in giving. Overall, Luke reveals a more positive moral view of the self than that of other New Testament writers.

b. *Function*
This perspective indicates a clear moral function for the parable. It reveals Luke's engagement with an issue of great concern to his intended audience: the destructive effects of greed upon society. Through the parable he illustrates the negative consequences of greed, whether it is expressed in excessive consumption or the accumulation of wealth. He shows that liberality provides the only path to social justice and harmony, in the home and in society. Through the joyful welcome that the father gives to his younger son, and the tender appeal that he makes to the elder, Luke appeals to his readers to be generous in their compassion and compassionate in their generosity. He tells the parable to illustrate that liberality is a source of joy and harmony for the individual and the community.

4. *Further Research*

These results indicate that a study of the relationship between Greco-Roman moral topoi and the other L parables would be rewarding. Some, like those in Lk. 12.16-20 and 16.1-8a, appear to be closely related to the topos On Covetousness.[2] This may be true of the others too. If not,

2. Since this study was completed Malherbe has demonstrated the important

their form and contents may be better accounted for by investigating Luke's employment of related topoi. The results of such inquiries should yield further insights into Luke's creative interaction with the Greco-Roman morality of the late first century, and his commitment to relating some of the deepest ideals of Greco-Roman culture to 'all that Jesus began to do and teach until the day that he was taken up' (Acts 1.2).

function of this topos in Lk. 12.13-34. See Malherbe, 'Christianization of a *Topos*', p. 135.

BIBLIOGRAPHY

Aalen, S., 'St Luke's Gospel and the Last Chapters of 1 Enoch', *NTS* 13 (1966–67), pp. 1-13.

Aland, K., and B. Aland, *The Text of the New Testament: An Introduction to the Critical Editions and to the Theory and Practice of Modern Textual Criticism* (trans. E.F. Rhodes; Grand Rapids: Eerdmans, 1987).

A'Lapide, C., *Commentarii in Scriptorum Sacram.* VIII. *Complectens Expositionem Litteralem et Moralem in Quattuor Evangelia Matthaei, Marci, Lucae, et Joannis* (London: J.B. Pelagaud, 1864).

Alexander, L., 'Luke's Preface in the Context of Greek Preface Writing', *NovT* 28 (1986), pp. 48-73.

—'The Living Voice: Scepticism towards the Written Word in Early Christian and in Graeco-Roman Texts', in D.J.A. Clines, S.E. Fowl and S.E. Porter (eds.), *The Bible in Three Dimensions: Essays in Celebration of Forty Years of Biblical Studies in the University of Sheffield* (JSOTSup, 87; Sheffield: Sheffield Academic Press, 1990), pp. 221-47.

Alford, H.A., *The Greek Testament: With a Critically Revised Text: A Digest of Various Readings: Marginal References to Verbal and Idiomatic Use: Prolegomena: And a Critical and Exegetical Commentary.* I. *The Four Gospels* (London: Rivingtons; Cambridge: Deighton, Bell, 1856).

Allinson, F.G. (trans.), *Menander: The Principal Fragments* (LCL; New York: G.P. Putnam, 1921).

Almqvist, H., *Plutarch und das Neue Testament: Ein Beitrag zum Corpus Hellenisticum Novi Testamenti* (ASNU, 15, Appelbergs boktr.: Uppsala, 1946).

American and British Committees of the International Greek New Testament Project (ed.), *The New Testament in Greek.* III. *The Gospel According to St Luke.* Part 2. *Chapters 13–24* (Oxford: Oxford University Press, 1987).

Angus, S., *The Religious Quests of the Greco-Roman World: A Study in the Historical Background of Early Christianity* (New York: Charles Scribner & Sons, 1929).

Antoine, G., 'The Three Parables of Mercy: Exposition of Luke 15.11-32', in F. Bovon and G. Rouiller (eds.), *Exegesis: Problems of Method and Exercises in Reading (Genesis 22 and Luke 15)* (trans. D.G. Miller; Pittsburgh: Pickwick Press, 1978), pp. 183-96.

Armstrong, A.A., (ed.), *Classical Mediterranean Spirituality: Egyptian, Greek, Roman* (New York: Crossroad, 1989).

Armstrong, A.H., *An Introduction to Ancient Philosphy* (University Paperbacks Series; London: Methuen, 3rd edn, 1965).

Arnim, H. von , *Stoicorum Veterum Fragmenta* (4 vols.; Leipzig: B.G. Teubner, 1903–24).

Arnold, E.V., *Roman Stoicism* (Cambridge: Cambridge University Press, 1911).

Arnott, W.G., 'Time, Plot and Character in Menander', in F. Cairns (ed.), *Papers of the Liverpool Latin Seminar: Second Volume 1979* (ARCA Classical and Medieval Texts, Papers and Monographs, 3; Liverpool: Francis Cairns, 1979), pp. 343-60.

Attridge, H.W., 'The Philosophical Critique of Religion under the Early Empire', *ANRW*, II.16.1, pp. 45-78.

Aune, D.E., 'The Literary Background of the Gospels', review of *Documents for the Study of the Gospels* (Cleveland: Collins) by David Cartlidge and David Dungan, *Int* 35 (1981), pp. 293-97.

—'Greco-Roman Biography', in *idem* (ed.), *Greco-Roman Literature and the New Testament: Selected Forms and Genres* (SBLSBS, 21; Atlanta: Scholars Press, 1988), pp. 107-26.

—'Heracles and Christ: Heracles Imagery in the Christology of Early Christianity', in Balch, Ferguson and Meeks (eds.), *Greeks, Romans and Christians*, pp. 3-19.

Aus, R.D., 'Luke 15.11-32 and R. Eliezer ben Hyrcanus's Rise to Fame', *JBL* 104 (1985), pp. 443-69.

Austin, M.R., 'The Hypocritical Son', *EvQ* 57 (1985), pp. 307-15.

Baasland, E., 'Zum Beispiel der Beispielerzählungen: Zur Formenlehre der Gleichnisse und zur Methodik der Gleichnisauslegung', *NovT* 28 (1986), pp. 193-219.

—'Die περί-Formel und die Argumentation(ssituation) des Paulus', *ST* 42 (1988), pp. 69-87.

Balch, D.L., 'Household Ethical Codes in Peripatetic, Neopythagorean and Early Christian Moralists', in P.J. Achtemeier (ed.), *Society for Biblical Literature Seminar Papers 1977* (Missoula: Scholars Press, 1977), pp. 397-404.

—*Let Wives Be Submissive: The Domestic Code in 1 Peter* (SBLMS, 26; Chico: Scholars Press, 1981).

—'Household Codes', in D.E. Aune (ed.), *Greco-Roman Literature and the New Testament: Selected Forms and Genres* (SBLSBS, 21; Atlanta: Scholars Press, 1988), pp. 25-50.

—'The Areopagus Speech: An Appeal to the Stoic Historian Posidonius against Later Stoics and the Epicureans', in Balch, Ferguson and Meeks (eds.), *Greeks, Romans and Christians*, pp. 52-79.

—'The Greek Political Topos περὶ νόμων and Matthew 5.17, 19 and 16.19', in *idem* (ed.), *Social History of the Matthean Community: Cross-Disciplinary Approaches* (Minneapolis: Fortress Press, 1991), pp. 68-84.

—'The Neopythagorean Moralists and the New Testament', *ANRW*, II.26.1, (1992), pp. 380-411.

Balch, D.L., E. Ferguson and W.A. Meeks (eds.), *Greeks, Romans and Christians: Essays in Honor of Abraham J. Malherbe* (Minneapolis: Fortress Press, 1990).

Barclay, W., 'Hellenistic Thought in New Testament Times: The Cyrenaics. The Way of Pleasure', *ExpTim* 72 (1960–61), pp. 28-31.

—'Hellenistic Thought in New Testament Times: The Way of Tranquillity. The Epicureans I', *ExpTim* 72 (1960–61), pp. 79-81.

—'Hellenistic Thought in New Testament Times: The Way of Tranquillity. The Epicureans II', *ExpTim* 72 (1960–61), pp. 101-104.

—'Hellenistic Thought in New Testament Times: The Way of Tranquillity. The Epicureans III', *ExpTim* 72 (1960–61), pp. 146-49.

—'Hellenistic Thought in New Testament Times: The Way of The Will of God. The Stoics I', *ExpTim* 72 (1960–61), pp. 164-66.

—'Hellenistic Thought in New Testament Times: The Way of The Will of God. The Stoics II', *ExpTim* 72 (1960–61), pp. 200-203.

—'Hellenistic Thought in New Testament Times: The Way of The Will of God. The Stoics III', *ExpTim* 72 (1960–61), pp. 227-30.

—'Hellenistic Thought in New Testament Times: The Way of The Will of God. The Stoics IV', *ExpTim* 72 (1960–61), pp. 258-61.

—'Hellenistic Thought in New Testament Times: The Way of The Will of God. The Stoics V', *ExpTim* 72 (1960–61), pp. 291-94.

—*Turning to God: A Study of Conversion in the Book of Acts and Today* (A.S. Peake Memorial Lecture, 8; London: Epworth Press, 1963; Edinburgh: The Saint Andrew Press, repr. 1978).

Barr, D.L., 'Speaking of Parables: A Survey of Recent Research', *TSFBul* 6 (1983), pp. 8-10.

Barr, D.L., and J.L. Wentling, 'The Conventions of Classical Biography and the Genre of Luke–Acts: A Preliminary Study', in C.H. Talbert (ed.), *Luke–Acts: New Perspectives from the Society of Biblical Literature Seminar* (Crossroad: New York, 1984), pp. 63-88.

Barrett, C.K., *Luke the Historian in Recent Study* (London: Epworth Press, 1961).

—'Light on the Holy Spirit from Simon Magus', in J. Kremer (ed.), *Les actes des apôtres: Traditions, rédaction, théologie* (BETL, 48; Leuven: Leuven University Press, 1979), pp. 281-95.

—*The Epistle to the Romans* (BNTC; London: A. & C. Black, 1957, 1991).

Barrow, R.H., *The Romans* (Harmondsworth: Penguin Books, 1949).

Barsby, J., *Terence: The Eunuch, Phormio, The Brothers. A Companion to the Penguin Translation* (Bristol: Bristol Classical Press, 1991).

Bauckham, R., 'The Rich Man and Lazarus: The Parable and the Parallels', *NTS* 37 (1991), pp. 225-46.

Bayreuther, E., 'ἡδονή', *NIDNTT*, I, pp. 459-60.

Beare, W., *The Roman Stage: A Short History of Latin Drama in the Time of the Republic* (London: Methuen, 3rd rev. edn, 1964).

Beavis, M.A., 'Parable and Fable', *CBQ* 52 (1990), pp. 473-98.

—'Ancient Slavery as an Interpretive Context for the New Testament Servant Parables with Special Reference to the Unjust Steward (Luke 16.1-8)', *JBL* 111 (1992), pp. 37-54.

Beck, B.E., 'Luke's Structure', in *idem*, *Christian Character in the Gospel of Luke* (London: Epworth Press, 1989), pp. 145-69.

Benko, S., *Pagan Rome and the Early Christians* (London: B.T. Batsford, 1985).

Berger, K., 'Gleichnisse als Texte: Zum lukanischen Gleichnis vom "verlorenen Sohn" ', in K.-H. Bender, K. Berger and M. Wandruszka (eds.), *Imago Linguae* (Festschrift F. Paepcke; Munich: Wilhelm Fink Verlag, 1977), pp. 61-74.

—'Hellenistische Gattungen im Neuen Testament', *ANRW*, II.25.2 (1984), pp. 1031-432, 1831-1885.

Berger, K., and C. Colpe, *Religionsgeschichtliches Textbuch zum Neuen Testament* (TNT, 1; Göttingen: Vandenhoeck & Ruprecht, 1987).

Bergman, J., 'Zum Zwei-Wege-Motif: Religionsgeschichtliche und exegetische Bemerkungen', *SEÅ* 41-42 (1976–77), pp. 27-56.

Berry, K.L., 'The Function of Friendship Language in Paul's Letter to the Philippians' (PhD dissertation, Yale University,).

Betz, H.D., 'Lukian von Samosata und das Christentum', *NovT* 3 (1959), pp. 226-37.

—*Lukian von Samosata und das Neue Testament: Religionsgeschichtliche und paränetische Parallelen. Ein Beitrag zum Corpus Hellenisticum Novi Testamenti* (TU, 76; Berlin: Akademie Verlag, 1961).

—(ed.) *Plutarch's Theological Writings and Early Christian Literature* (SCHNT, 3; Leiden: E.J. Brill, 1975).

—'Introduction', in *idem* (ed.), *Plutarch's Ethical Writings*, pp. 1-10

—'*De Fraterno Amore (Moralia* 478A-492D)', in *idem* (ed.), *Plutarch's Ethical Writings*, pp. 231-63.

—'*De Laude Ipsius (Moralia* 539A-547F)', in *idem* (ed.), *Plutarch's Ethical Writings*, pp. 367-93.

—'*De Tranquillitate Animi (Moralia* 464E-477F)', in *idem* (ed.), *Plutarch's Ethical Writings*, pp. 198-230.

—*Galatians: A Commentary on Paul's Letter to the Churches in Galatia* (Hermeneia; Philadelphia: Fortress Press, 1979).

—'The Delphic Maxim "Know Yourself" in the Greek Magical Papyri', *HR* 21 (1981), pp. 156-71.

—'Cosmogeny and Ethics in the Sermon on the Mount', in *idem*, *Essays on the Sermon on the Mount* (trans. L.L. Welborn; Philadelphia: Fortress Press, 1985), pp. 89-123.

H.D. Betz (ed.), *Plutarch's Ethical Writings and Early Christian Literature* (SCHNT, 4; Leiden:, E.J. Brill, 1978).

Betz, H.D., *2 Corinthians 8 and 9: A Commentary on Two Administrative Letters of the Apostle Paul* (Hermeneia; Philadelphia: Fortress Press, 1985).

Betz, H.D., *The Sermon on the Mount: A Commentary on the Sermon on the Mount, including the Sermon on the Plain (Matthew 5:3–7:27 and Luke 6:20-49)* (Hermeneia; Minneapolis: Fortress Press, 1995).

Betz, H.D., and J.M. Dillon, '*De Cohibenda Ira (Moralia* 452E-464D)', in Betz (ed.), *Plutarch's Ethical Writings*, pp. 170-97.

Betz, H.D., P.A. Dirkse and E.W. Smith, Jr, '*De Sera Numinis Vindicta (Moralia* 548A-568A)', in H.D. Betz (ed.), *Plutarch's Theological Writings and Early Christian Literature* (SCHNT, 3; Leiden: E.J. Brill, 1978), pp. 181-235.

Betz, H.D., and E.W. Smith, Jr, '*De E apud Delphos (Moralia* 384C-394C)', in H.D. Betz (ed.), *Plutarch's Theological Writings and Early Christian Literature* (SCHNT, 3; Leiden: E.J. Brill, 1975), pp. 85-102.

Bevan, E., 'Hellenistic Popular Philosophy', in *The Hellenistic Age* (Cambridge: Cambridge University Press, 1925), pp. 79-107.

Billerbeck, M., 'Aspects of Stoicism in Flavian Epic', in F. Cairns (ed.), *Papers of the Liverpool Latin Seminar: Fifth Volume 1985* (ARCA Classical and Medieval Texts, Papers and Monographs, 19; Liverpool: Francis Cairns, 1986), pp. 341-56.

Black, M., *An Aramaic Approach to the Gospels and Acts* (Oxford: Clarendon Press, 3rd edn, 1967).

Blomberg, C.L., 'Midrash, Chiasmus and the Outline of Luke's Central Section', in R.T. France and D. Wenham (eds.), *Gospel Perspectives: Studies in Midrash and Historiography* (6 vols.; Sheffield: JSOT Press, 1983), III, pp. 217-61.

—*Interpreting the Parables* (Downer's Grove, IL: InterVarsity Press, 1990).

—'Interpreting the Parables of Jesus: Where Are We and Where Do We Go from Here?' *CBQ* 53 (1991), pp. 50-78.

Bonhöffer, A., *Epiktet und das Neue Testament* (RVV, 10; Giessen: Alfred Töpelmann, 1911; repr., 1964).

Bonus, A., 'Luke XV. 30', *ExpTim* 31 (1919–20), p. 476.

Boring, M.E., K. Berger and C. Colpe, *Hellenistic Commentary to the New Testament* (Nashville: Abingdon Press, 1995).

Botha, J., *Semeion: Inleiding tot die interpretasie van die griekse Nuwe Testament* (Potchefstroom: Dept. Sentrale Publikasie, PU vir CHO, 1989).

Bovon, F., 'The Parable of the Prodigal Son (Luke 15.11-32): First Reading', in F. Bovon and G. Rouiller (eds.), *Exegesis: Problems of Method and Exercises in Reading (Genesis 22 and Luke 15)* (trans. D.G. Miller; Pittsburgh: Pickwick Press, 1978), pp. 43-73.

—'The Parable of the Prodigal Son (Luke 15.11-32): Second Reading', in F. Bovon and G. Rouiller (eds.), *Exegesis: Problems of Method and Exercises in Reading (Genesis 22 and Luke 15)* (trans. D.G. Miller; Pittsburgh: Pickwick Press, 1978), pp. 441-66.

—*Luke the Theologian: Thirty-Three Years of Research (1950–1983)* (trans. K. McKinney; Princeton Theological Monograph Series, 12; Allison Park: Pickwick Publications, 1987).

Boyle, M. O'R., 'The Stoic Paradox of James 2:10', *NTS* 31 (1985), pp. 611-17.

Bradley, D.G., 'The *Topos* as a Form in the Pauline Paraenesis', *JBL* 72 (1953), pp. 238-46.

Braumann, G., 'Tot-lebendig, verloren-gefunden', in W. Haubeck and M. Bachmann (eds.), *Wort in der Zeit: Neutestamentliche Studien. Festgabe für Karl Heinrich Rengstorf* (Leiden: E.J. Brill, 1980), pp. 156-64.

Braun, M., *History and Romance in Graeco-Oriental Literature* (Oxford: Basil Blackwell, 1938).

Breech, J., *Jesus and Postmodernism* (Minneapolis: Fortress Press, 1989).

Brinkmann, A., 'Ein Denkmal des Neupythagoreismus', *RhM* NS 66 (1911), pp. 616-25.

Brodie, T.L., 'The Conventions of Classical Biography and the Genre of Luke–Acts', in C.H. Talbert (ed.), *Luke–Acts: New Perspectives from the Society of Biblical Literature Seminar* (Crossroad: New York, 1984), pp. 17-46.

Broer, I., 'Das Gleichnis vom Verlorenen Sohn und die Theologie des Lukas', *NTS* 20 (1974), pp. 453-62.

Brown, S., 'Precis of Eckhard Plümacher, *Lukas als hellenistischer Schriftsteller*', in G. MacRae (ed.), *Society of Biblical Literature Seminar Papers 1974* (Cambridge, MA: Society of Biblical Literature, 1974), pp. 103-13.

Bruce, F.F., *The Acts of the Apostles: The Greek Text with Introduction and Commentary* (London: Tyndale Press, 2nd edn, 1952).

—'The New Testament and Classical Studies', *NTS* 22 (1976), pp. 229-242.

Brunt, J.C., 'More on the *Topos* as a New Testament Form', *JBL* 104 (1985), pp. 495-500.

Brunt, P.A., 'Philosophy and Religion in the Late Roman Republic', in M. Griffin and J. Barnes (eds.), *Philosophia Togata: Essays on Philosophy and Roman Society* (Oxford: Clarendon Press, 1989), pp. 174-98.

Büchsel, F., 'ἐπιθυμία', *TDNT*, III, pp. 168-72.

Bultmann, R., 'εὐφραίνω, εὐφροσύνη', *TDNT*, I, pp. 772-75.

—'θάνατος, κτλ', *TDNT*, II, pp. 4-25.

—'νεκρός, κτλ', *TDNT*, IV, pp. 892-95.

—*Primitive Christianity in its Contemporary Setting* (trans. R.H. Fuller; London: Thames & Hudson, 1956).

—*The History of the Synoptic Tradition* (trans. J. Marsh; Oxford: Basil Blackwell, 1972).

Bultmann, R. *et al.* 'ζάω, ζωή, κτλ', *TDNT*, II, pp. 832-75.

Burchardt, C., 'The Importance of Joseph and Asenath for the Study of the New Testament', *NTS* 33 (1987), pp. 102-34.

Burkitt, F.C., *JTS* 20 (1919).

Burton, E. de W., *Syntax of the Moods and Tenses in New Testament Greek* (Edinburgh: T. & T. Clark, 3rd edn, 1898).

Byington, S.T., '1 Timothy 6.10', *ExpTim* 56 (1944), p. 54.

Cadbury, H.J., 'Luke—Translator or Author?' *AJT* 24 (1920), pp. 436-55.

—*The Style and Literary Method of Luke* (HTS, 6; Cambridge, MA: Harvard University Press, 1920).

—*The Making of Luke–Acts* (New York: Macmillan, 1927).

—*The Book of Acts in History* (New York: Harper & Brothers, 1955).

Cahill, L.S., 'The New Testament and Ethics: Communities of Social Change', *Int* 44 (1990), pp. 383-95.

Caird, G.B., *Saint Luke* (Pelican New Testament Commentaries; Harmondsworth: Penguin Books, 1963).

Callan, T., 'The Preface of Luke–Acts and Historiography', *NTS* 31 (1985), pp. 576-81.

Campbell, J., *The Hero with a Thousand Faces* (Bollingen Series, 17; New York: Pantheon Books, 1949).

Carlston, C.E., 'Reminiscence and Redaction in Luke 15.11-32', *JBL* 94 (1975), pp. 368-90.

Cartlidge, D.R., and David L. Dungan, *Documents for the Study of the Gospels* (Cleveland: Collins, 1980).

Chadwick, H., *Early Christian Thought and the Classical Tradition: Studies in Justin, Clement and Origen* (Oxford: Oxford University Press, 1966).

Charlesworth, J.H., 'Reflections on the SNTS Pseudepigrapha Seminar at Duke on the Testaments of the Twelve Patriarchs', *NTS* 23 (1977), pp. 296-304.

Clarke, M.L., *Rhetoric at Rome: A Historical Survey* (London: Cohen & West, 1953).

—*Higher Education in the Ancient World* (London: Routledge & Kegan Paul, 1971).

Clemen, C., *Religionsgeschichtliche Erklärung des Neuen Testaments: Die Abhängigkeit des ältesten Christentums von nichtjüdischen Religionen und philosophischen Systemen* (Giessen: Alfred Töpelmann, 1924; Berlin: W. de Gruyter, repr. 1973).

Coenen, L., 'νεκρός', *NIDNTT*, I, pp. 443-46.

Colish, M.L., *The Stoic Tradition from Antiquity to the Early Middle Ages. I. Stoicism in Classical Latin Literature, with addenda and corrigenda* (Leiden: E.J. Brill, 2nd edn, 1990).

Colwell, E.C., 'Method in Evaluating Scribal Habits: A Study of P45, P66, P75', in *Studies in Methodology in Textual Criticism of the New Testament* (NTTS, 9; Leiden: E.J. Brill, 1969).

Colwell, E.C., and E.W. Tune, 'Method in Classifying and Evaluating Variant Readings', in *Studies in Methodology in Textual Criticism of the New Testament* (NTTS, 9; Leiden: E.J. Brill, 1969).

Copleston, F., *A History of Philosophy. I. Greece and Rome* (London: Burns & Oates, 1966).

Copley, F.O., *Latin Literature: From the Beginnings to the Close of the Second Century A.D.* (Ann Arbor: University of Michigan Press, 1969).

Corlett, T., 'This *brother* of yours', *ExpTim* 100 (1989), p. 216.

Corrington, G.P., (trans.), 'Philo On the Contemplative Life: Or, On the Suppliants (The Fourth Book on the Virtues)', in V.L. Wimbush (ed.), *Ascetic Behavior in Greco-Roman Antiquity* (Minneapolis: Augsburg, Fortress, 1990), pp. 134-55.

Cosgrove, C.H., 'The Divine Δεῖ in Luke–Acts: Investigations into the Lukan Understanding of God's Providence', *NovT* 26 (1984), pp. 168-90.

Cox, A.S., 'To Do as Rome Does?', *GR* NS 12 (1965), pp. 85-96.

Cranfield, C.E.B., *A Critical and Exegetical Commentary on the Epistle to the Romans* (ICC; 2 vols.; Edinburgh: T. & T. Clark, 1975, 1979).

Creed, J.M., *The Gospel According to St Luke: The Greek Text with Introduction, Notes and Indices* (London: Macmillan, 1930).

—'Some Outstanding New Testament Problems. II. 'L' and the Structure of the Lucan Gospel: A Study of the Proto-Luke Hypothesis', *ExpTim* 46 (1934–35), pp. 101-107.

Crescenzo, L. de, *The History of Greek Philosophy. II. Socrates and Beyond* (2 vols.; trans. A. Bardoni; London: Pan, 1990).

Crossan, J.D., (ed.), *Polyvalent Narration* (Semeia, 9; Missoula: Scholars Press, 1977).

Dakin, A., 'The Parable of the Prodigal Son as Literature', *ExpTim* 35 (1924), pp. 330-31.

Danker, F.W., 'Menander and the New Testament', *NTS* 10 (1963–64), pp. 365-68.

—*Benefactor: Epigraphic Study of a Graeco-Roman and New Testament Semantic Field* (St. Louis: Clayton Publishing House, 1982).

—*Luke* (Philadelphia: Fortress Press, rev. edn, 1987).

—*Jesus and the New Age: A Commentary on St Luke's Gospel* (Philadelphia: Fortress Press, rev. edn, 1988).

Davids, P.H., *The Epistle of James: A Commentary on the Greek Text* (NIGTC; Exeter: Paternoster Press, 1982).

Deissman, A., *Light from the Ancient East: The New Testament Illustrated by Recently Discovered Texts of the Graeco-Roman World* (trans. L.R.M. Strachen; London: Hodder & Stoughton, 4th edn, 1927).

Deist, F., *A Concise Dictionary of Theological Terms* (Pretoria: J.L. van Schaik, 1984).

Delling, G., 'πλεονέκτης, πλεονεκτέω, πλεονεξία', *TDNT*, VI, pp. 266-74.

Derrett, J.D.M., 'The Parable of the Prodigal Son', in *idem*, *Law in the New Testament* (London: Darton, Longman & Todd, 1970), pp. 100-125.

—'The Parable of the Prodigal Son: Patristic Allegories and Jewish Midrashim', *SP* 10 (1970), pp. 219-24.

Dibelius, M., *The Message of Jesus Christ: The Traditions of the Early Christian Communities* (trans. F.C. Grant; New York: Charles Scribners Sons, 1939).

—'Paul and the Areopagus', in *idem*, *Studies in the Acts of the Apostles* (ed. H. Greeven; London: SCM Press, 1956), pp. 26-77

—*Studies in the Acts of the Apostles* (ed. H. Greeven; London: SCM Press, 1956).

Dibelius, M., H. Conzelmann, *The Pastoral Epistles: A Commentary on the Pastoral Epistles* (trans. P. Buttolph and A. Yarbro; ed. H. Koester; Hermeneia; Philadelphia: Fortress Press, 1972).

Dibelius, M., and H. Greeven, *James: A Commentary on the Epistle of James* (trans. M.A. Williams; ed. H. Koester; Hermeneia; Philadelphia: Fortress Press, 1976).

Dickie, E.P., 'The Third Gospel: A Hidden Source', *ExpTim* 46 (1934–35), pp. 326-30.

Dillon, J.M., and A.A. Long. *The Question of 'Eclecticism': Studies in Later Greek Philosophy* (Hellenistic Culture and Society, 3; Berkeley: University of California Press, 1988).

Dix, G., *Jew and Greek: A Study in the Primitive Church* (Westminster: Dacre Press; London: A. & C. Black, 1953).

Dormeyer, D., *The New Testament among the Writings of Antiquity* (trans. R. Kossov; Biblical Seminar, 55; Sheffield: Sheffield Academic Press, 1998).

Dörrie, H., 'Die griechischen Romane und das Christentum', *Philologus* 93 (1973), pp. 273-76.

Dover, K.J., *Greek Popular Morality in the Time of Plato and Aristotle* (Oxford: Basil Blackwell, 1974).

Dover, K.J., (ed.), *Ancient Greek Literature* (Oxford: Oxford University Press, 1980).

Downing, F.G., 'Ethical Pagan Theism and the Speeches in Acts', *NTS* 27 (1981), pp. 544-63.

—'Common Ground with Paganism in Luke and Josephus', *NTS* 28 (1982), pp. 546-59.

—'Contemporary Analogies to the Gospels and Acts: "Genres" or "Motifs"?', in C.M. Tuckett (ed.), *Synoptic Studies: The Ampleforth Conferences of 1982 and 1983* (JSNTSup, 7; Sheffield: JSOT Press, 1984), pp. 51-65.

—'Cynics and Christians', *NTS* 30 (1984), pp. 584-93.

—'Reflecting the First Century: 1 Corinthians 13:12', *ExpTim* 95 (1984), pp. 176-77.

—*Strangely Familiar: An Introductory Reader to the First Century* (Manchester: F. Gerald Downing, 1985).

—'Interpretation and the "Culture Gap" ', *SJT* 40 (1987), pp. 161-71.

—'The Social Contexts of Jesus the Teacher: Construction or Reconstruction', *NTS* 33 (1987), pp. 439-51.

—'A bas les aristos: The Relevance of Higher Literature for the Understanding of the Earliest Christian Writings', *NovT* 30 (1988), pp. 212-30.

—*Christ and the Cynics: Jesus and Other Radical Preachers in First-Century Tradition* (JSOT Manuals, 4; Sheffield: JSOT Press, 1988).

—'Compositional Conventions and the Synoptic Problem', *JBL* 107 (1988), pp. 69-85.

—'Quite like Q: A Genre for "Q": The "Lives" of the Cynic Philosophers', *Bib* 69 (1988), pp. 196-225.

—'The Ambiguity of "The Pharisee and the Toll-Collector" (Luke 18.9-14) in the Greco-Roman World of Late Antiquity', *CBQ* 54 (1992), pp. 80-99.

Drake, L.K., 'The Reversal Theme in Luke's Gospel' (PhD dissertation, Saint Louis University, 1985).

Drury, J., *The Parables in the Gospels: History and Allegory* (Crossroad: New York, 1985).

Duncan, A.A., 'The Prodigal Son', *ExpTim* 28 (1917), p. 327.

Easterling, P.E., 'The Fable', in P.E. Easterling and B.M.W. Knox (eds.), *The Cambridge History of Classical Literature. I. Greek Literature* (Cambridge: Cambridge University Press, 1985), pp. 699-703.

Edwards, R.A., and R.A. Wild (eds.), *The Sentences of Sextus* (SBLTT, 22; Chico: Scholars Press, 1981).

Ehrhardt, A.A.T., 'Greek Proverbs in the Gospel', in A. Ehrhardt (ed.), *The Framework of the New Testament Stories* (Manchester: Manchester University Press, 1964).

Ellis, E.E., *The Gospel of Luke* (NCB; Grand Rapids: Eerdmans; London: Marshall, Morgan & Scott, rev. edn 1974).

Entrevernes Group, The, *Signs and Parables: Semiotics and Gospel Texts* (trans. G. Phillips; Pittsburgh: Pickwick Press, 1978).

Erskine, A., *The Hellenistic Stoa: Political Thought and Action* (Ithaca, NY: Cornell University Press, 1990).

Esler, P.F., *Community and Gospel in Luke–Acts: The Social and Political Motivations of Lucan Theology* (SNTSMS, 57; Cambridge: Cambridge University Press, 1987).

Evans, C.F., 'The Central Section of St. Luke's Gospel', in D.E. Nineham (ed.), *Studies in the Gospels: Essays in Memory of R.H. Lightfoot* (Oxford: Basil Blackwell, 1957), pp. 37-53.

—*Saint Luke* (London: SCM Press; Philadelphia: Trinity Press International, 1990).

Evans, G.R., 'The Sentences of Sextus in the Middle Ages', *JTS* NS 34 (1983), pp. 554-55.

Farmer, W.R., 'Notes on a Literary and Form-Critical Analysis of Some of the Synoptic Material Peculiar to Luke', *NTS* 8 (1961–62), pp. 301-16.

Farrar, F.W., *The Gospel According to St Luke* (CGTC; Cambridge: Cambridge University Press, 1893).

Ferguson, E., *Backgrounds of Early Christianity* (Grand Rapids: Eerdmans, 1987).

Fiore, B., 'Passion in Paul and Plutarch: 1 Corinthians 5–6 and the Polemic against Epicureans', in Balch, Ferguson and Meeks (eds.), *Greeks, Romans and Christians*, pp. 135-43.

Fitzmyer, J.A., *The Gospel According to Luke* (AB, 28, 28A; New York: Doubleday, 1983).

Flacelière, R., *A Literary History of Greece* (trans. D. Garman; London: Elek Books, 1964).

Foerster, W., 'ἄξιος, ἀνάξιος, ἀξιόω, καταξιόω', *TDNT*, I, pp. 379-80.

—'ἄσωτος, ἀσωτία', *TDNT*, I, pp. 506-507.

Fortenbaugh, W.W. (ed.), *On Stoic and Peripatetic Ethics: The Work of Arius Didymus* (Rutgers University Studies in Classical Humanities, 1; New Brunswick; London: Transaction Books, 1983).

Foucault, M., *The History of Sexuality. III. The Care of the Self* (trans. R. Hurley; Harmondsworth: Penguin Books, 1990).

Fournier, W.J., 'The Third Gospel: A Hidden Source', *ExpTim* 46 (1934–35), p. 428.

Freeman, A.F., 'Proto-Luke Reconsidered: A Study of Literary Method and Theology in the Gospel of Luke' (PhD dissertation, Duke University, 1968).

Frenzel, E., 'Sohn, Der verlorene', in *idem, Stoffe der Weltliteratur: Ein Lexikon dichtungsgeschichtlicher Längsschnitte* (Stuttgart: Alfred Kröner Verlag, 7th edn, 1988), pp. 702-706.

Funk, R.W., 'Structure in the Narrative Parables of Jesus', *Semeia* 2 (1974), pp. 51-73.

Garnsey P., *Famine and Food Supply in the Graeco-Roman World: Responses to Risk and Crisis* (Cambridge: Cambridge University Press, 1988).

George, D.B., 'Lucan's Caesar and Stoic οἰκείωσις Theory: The Stoic Fool', *TAPA* 118 (1988), pp. 331-41.

Gerhard, G.A., *Phoinix von Kolophon: Texte und Untersuchungen* (Leipzig: B.G. Teubner, 1909).

Gerhardsson, B., *The Origins of the Gospel Traditions* (London: SCM Press, 1979).

Giblin, C.H., 'Structural and Theological Considerations on Luke 15', *CBQ* 24 (1962), pp. 15-31.

Gigon, O., 'Antike Erzählungen über die Berufung zur Philosophie', *MH* 3 (1946), pp. 1-21.

Gill, D., 'Observations on the Lukan Travel Narrative and Some Related Passages', *HTR* 63 (1970), pp. 199-221.

Gilmour, S.M., 'A Critical Examination of Proto-Luke', *JBL* 67 (1948), pp. 143-52.

Glucker, J., 'Cicero's Philosophical Affiliations', in J.M. Dillon and A.A. Long (eds.), *The Question of 'Eclecticism': Studies in Later Greek Philosophy* (Hellenistic Culture and Society, 3; Berkeley: University of California Press, 1988), pp. 34-69.

Gore, C., *St Paul's Epistle to the Ephesians: A Practical Exposition* (London: John Murray, 1898).

Goulder, M.D., *Luke: A New Paradigm* (JSNTSup, 20; Sheffield: JSOT Press, 1989).

Gowler, D.B., 'Characterization in Luke: A Socio-Narratological Approach', *BTB* 19 (1989), pp. 54-62.

Grant, M., *Cicero: On the Good Life* (Harmondsworth: Penguin Books, 1971).

Grant, R.M., 'Early Christianity and Greek Comic Poetry', *CP* 60 (1965), pp. 157-63.

—*Early Christianity and Society: Seven Studies* (London: Collins, 1978).

Green, P., *Alexander to Actium: The Historical Evolution of the Hellenistic Age* (Hellenistic Culture and Society, 1; Berkeley: University of California Press, 1990).

Greenlee, J.H., *Introduction to New Testament Textual Criticism* (Grand Rapids: Eerdmans, 1964).

Grelot, P., 'Le père et ses deux fils: Luc, XV, 11-32: Essai d'analyse structurale', *RB* 84 (1977), pp. 321-48.

—'Le père et ses deux fils: Luc, XV, 11-32: De l'analyse structurale a l'herméneutique', *RB* 84 (1977), pp. 538-65.

Grese, W.C., '*De Profectibus in Virtute* (*Moralia* 75A-86A)', in Betz (ed.), *Plutarch's Ethical Writings*, pp. 11-31.

Grundmann, W., 'δεῖ, δέον ἐστί', *TDNT*, II, pp. 21-25.

Grundy, R.H., 'The Language Milieu of First-Century Palestine', *JBL* 83 (1964), pp. 404-408.

Hadas, M. (trans.), *Three Greek Romances* (New York: Doubleday, 1953).

Hadas, M., and M. Smith, *Heroes and Gods: Spiritual Biographies in Antiquity* (RP, 13; New York: Harper & Row, 1965).

Hadot, I., 'The Spiritual Guide', in A.H. Armstrong (ed.), *Classical Mediterranean Spirituality: Egyptian, Greek, Roman* (trans. M. Kirby; World Spirituality, 15; New York: Crossroad, 1986), pp. 436-59.

Hadot, P., *Exercices spirituels et philosophie antique* (Paris: Etudes Augustiniennes, 2nd rev. edn, 1987).

Haenchen, E., *The Acts of the Apostles* (trans. B. Noble and G. Shinn; Oxford: Basil Blackwell, 1971).

Hägg, T., *Narrative Technique in Ancient Greek Romances* (Göteborg: Paul Astrom, 1971).

—*The Novel in Antiquity* (Oxford: Basil Blackwell, 1983).

Halliday, W.R., *The Pagan Background of Early Christianity* (Liverpool: University Press of Liverpool; London: Hodder & Stoughton, 1925).

Handley, E.W., 'Plautus and his Public: Some Thoughts on the New Comedy in Latin', *Dioniso* 46 (1975), pp. 117-32.

Hands, A.R., *Charities and Social Aid in Greece and Rome* (London: Thames & Hudson, 1968).

Hanson, A.T., *The Pastoral Epistles* (NCB; Grand Rapids; London: Eerdmans: Marshall, Morgan & Scott, 1982).

Harrison, B., 'Parable and Transcendence', in M. Wadsworth (ed.), *Ways of Reading the Bible* (Brighton, UK: Harvester Press; Totowa, NJ: Noble Books, 1981), pp. 190-212.

Hatch, E., *Essays in Biblical Greek* (Amsterdam: Philo Press, 1970).

Hauck, F., *Das Evangelium nach Lukas* (THKNT, 3; Leipzig: Deichert, 1934).

—'ἐπιβάλλω', in *TDNT*, II, pp. 528-29.

—'παραβολή', in *TDNT*, V, pp. 744-61.

Hauck, F., and S. Schulz. 'πόρνη, κτλ', *TDNT*, VI, pp. 579-95.

Hendrickx, H., *The Parables of Jesus* (London: Geoffrey Chapman; San Francisco: Harper & Row, 1986).

Hengel, M., *Judaism and Hellenism* (trans. J. Bowden; 2 vols.; London: SCM Press, 1974).

—*Property and Riches in the Early Church* (trans. J. Bowden; London: SCM Press, 1974).

—*Acts and the History of Earliest Christianity* (London: SCM Press, 1979).

—'Between Jesus and Paul: The "Hellenists", the "Seven" and Stephen (Acts 6.11-15;7.54–8.3)', in *idem*, *Between Jesus and Paul* (London: SCM Press, 1983), pp. 1-29.

—*The 'Hellenization' of Judaea in the First Century after Christ* (London: SCM Press; Philadelphia: Trinity Press International, 1989).

Hershbell, J.P., '*De Virtute Morali (Moralia* 440D-452D)', in Betz (ed.), *Plutarch's Ethical Writings*, pp. 135-69.

—'The Stoicism of Epictetus: Twentieth Century Perspectives', *ANRW*, II.36.3 (1989), pp. 2148-63.

Hewitt, J.W., 'Gratitude to Parents in Greek and Roman Literature', *AJP* 52 (1931), pp. 30-48.

Hickling, C.J.A., 'A Tract on Jesus and the Pharisees? A Conjecture on the Redaction of Luke 15 and 16', *HeyJ* 16 (1975), pp. 253-65.

Hock, R.F., 'Lazarus and Micyllus: Greco-Roman Backgrounds to Luke 16:19-31', *JBL* 106 (1987), pp. 447-63.

—'The Greek Novel', in D.E. Aune (ed.), *Greco-Roman Literature and the New Testament: Selected Forms and Genres* (SBLSBS, 21; Atlanta: Scholars Press, 1988), pp. 127-46.

—'A Dog in the Manger: The Cynic Cynulcus Among Athenaeus' Deipnosophists', in Balch, Ferguson and Meeks (eds.), *Greeks, Romans and Christians*, pp. 20-37.

Hodgson, R., 'Valerius Maximus and Gospel Criticism', *CBQ* 51 (1989), pp. 502-10.

—'Valerius Maximus and the Social World of the New Testament', *CBQ* 51 (1989), pp. 683-93.

Hofius, O., 'Alttestamentliche Motive im Gleichnis vom verlorenen Sohn', *NTS* 24 (1978), pp. 240-48.

Holladay, C.R., '1 Corinthians 13: Paul as Apostolic Paradigm', in Balch, Ferguson and Meeks (eds.), *Greeks, Romans and Christians*, pp. 80-98.

Hollander, H.W., 'The Ethical Character of the Patriarch Joseph: A Study in the Ethics of *The Testaments of the XII Patriarchs*', in G.W.E. Nickelsburg, Jr (ed.), *Studies on the Testament of Joseph* (SBLSCS, 5; Missoula: Scholars Press, 1975), pp. 47-104.

Hollander, H.W., and M. de Jonge, *The Testaments of the Twelve Patriarchs: A Commentary* (SVTP, 8; Leiden: E.J. Brill, 1985).

Hopkins, K., 'Death in Rome', in *idem*, *Death and Renewal* (Sociological Studies in Roman History, 2; Cambridge: Cambridge University Press, 1983), pp. 201-56.

Horn, F.W., *Glaube und Handeln in der Theologie des Lukas* (GTA, 26; Göttingen: Vandenhoeck & Ruprecht, 2nd edn, 1986).

Hornblower, A., and A. Spawforth (eds.), *The Oxford Classical Dictionary* (Oxford: Oxford University Press, 3rd edn, 1966).

Horsley, G.H.R. (ed.), *New Documents Illustrating Early Christianity. III. A Review of the Greek Inscriptions and Papyri Published in 1978* (The Ancient History Documentary Research Centre: Macquarie University, 1983).

—(ed.), *New Documents Illustrating Early Christianity*. IV. *A Review of the Greek Inscriptions and Papyri Published in 1979* (The Ancient History Documentary Research Centre: Macquarie University, 1987).

Horst, P.W. van der, 'Drohung und Mord Schnabend (Acta 9.1)', *NovT* 12 (1970), pp. 257-69.

—'Macrobius and the New Testament', *NovT* 15 (1973), pp. 220-32.

—'Musonius Rufus and the New Testament', *NovT* 16 (1974), pp. 306-15.

—'Hieracles the Stoic and the New Testament', *NovT* 17 (1975), pp. 156-60.

—*The Sentences of Pseudo-Phocylides* (SVTP, 4; Leiden: E.J. Brill, 1978).

—'Cornutus and the New Testament', *NovT* 23 (1981), pp. 165-72.

—'Chariton and the New Testament', *NovT* 25 (1983), pp. 348-55.

—'Hellenistic Parallels to the Acts of the Apostles (1.1-26)', *ZNW* 74 (1983), pp. 17-26.

—'Hellenistic Parallels to the Acts of the Apostles (2.1-47)', in C.A. Evans and S.E. Porter (eds.), *New Testament Backgrounds: A Sheffield Reader* (The Biblical Seminar, 43; Sheffield: Sheffield Academic Press, 1997), pp. 207-219.

—'Hellenistic Parallels to Acts (Chapters 3 and 4)', in Evans and Porter (eds.), *New Testament Backgrounds*, pp. 220-29.

Houlden, J.L., *Ethics and the New Testament* (Harmondsworth: Penguin Books, 1973; London: Mowbrays, repr. 1975).

Howell, E.B., 'St Paul and the Greek World', *GR* NS 11 (1964), pp. 7-29.

Hultgren, A.J., 'Interpreting the Gospel of Luke', *Int* 30 (1976), pp. 353-65.

Inwood, B., and L.P. Gerson, *Hellenistic Philosophy: Introductory Readings* (trans. with introd. and notes; Indianapolis: Hackett, 1988).

Irwin, T.H., *A History of Western Philosophy*. I. *Classical Thought* (Oxford: Oxford University Press, 1989).

—'Aristotle's Defense of Private Property', in D. Keyt and F.D. Miller, Jr (eds.), *A Companion to Aristotle's Politics* (Oxford: Basil Blackwell, 1991), pp. 200-225.

Jaeger, H., 'L'examen de conscience dans les religions non-chrétiennes et avant le christianisme', *Numen* 6 (1959), pp. 175-233.

Jaeger, W., *Paideia: The Ideals of Greek Culture* (trans. G. Highet; 3 vols.; Oxford: Basil Blackwell, 1939, 1943, 1944).

—'Aristotle's Use of Medicine as Model of Method in his Ethics', in *idem*, *Scripta Minora* (Rome: Edizioni di Storia e Letteratura, 1960); also *JHS* 77 (1957), pp. 54-61.

—*Early Christianity and Greek Paideia* (Cambridge, MA: Harvard University Press; London: Oxford University Press, 1962).

Jagu, A., 'La morale d'Epictète et le christianisme', *ANRW*, II.36.3 (1989), pp. 2164-99.

Jellicoe, S., 'St Luke and the Letter of Aristeas', *JBL* 80 (1961), pp. 149-55.

Jeremias, J., 'Zum Gleichnis vom verlorenen Sohn, Luk. 15, 11-32', *TZ* 5 (1949), pp. 228-31.

—'Tradition und Redaktion in Lukas 15', *ZNW* 62 (1971), pp. 172-89.

—*The Parables of Jesus* (London: SCM Press, 3rd edn, 1972).

—*Die Sprache des Lukasevangeliums: Redaktion und Tradition im Nicht-Markusstoff des dritten Evangeliums* (Göttingen: Vandenhoeck & Ruprecht, 1980).

Johnson, L.T., *The Literary Function of Possessions in Luke–Acts* (SBLDS, 39; Missoula: Scholars Press, 1977).

—'On Finding the Lukan Community: A Cautious Cautionary Essay', in P. Achtemeier (ed.), *Society for Biblical Literature Seminar Papers 1979* (Atlanta: Scholars Press, 1979), pp. 87-100.

—*Sharing Possessions: Mandate and Symbol of Faith* (OBT; Philadelphia: Fortress Press, 1981).
—'The Lukan Kingship Parable', *NovT* 24 (1982), pp. 139-59.
—'James 3.13–4.10 and the *Topos* περὶ φθόνου', *NovT* 25 (1983), pp. 327-47.
—*The Writings of the New Testament* (Philadelphia: Fortress Press, 1986).
—'Taciturnity and True Religion', in Balch, Ferguson and Meeks (eds.), *Greeks, Romans and Christians*, pp. 329-39.
—*The Gospel of Luke* (Sacra Pagina, 3; Collegeville, MN: Michael Glazier, 1991).
Jonge, M., de 'Rachel's Virtuous Behaviour in the *Testament of Issachar*', in Balch, Ferguson and Meeks (eds.), *Greeks, Romans and Christians*, pp. 340-52.
—'The Main Issues in the Study of the Testaments of the Twelve Patriarchs', in H.J. de Jonge (ed.), *Jewish Eschatology, Early Christian Eschatology and the Testaments of the Twelve Patriarchs: Collected Essays of Marinus de Jonge* (repr. from *NTS* 26 [1980], pp. 508-24; Leiden: E.J. Brill, 1991), pp. 147-63.
Jonge, M., de *et al.* (eds.) (*The Testaments of the Twelve Patriarchs: A Critical Edition of the Greek Text* (Leiden: E.J. Brill, 1978).
Jones, G.V., *The Art and Truth of the Parables: A Study in their Literary Form and Modern Interpretation* (London: SPCK, 1964).
Judge, E.A., *The Social Pattern of Christian Groups in the First Century* (London: Tyndale Press, 1960).
Jülicher, A., *Die Gleichnisreden Jesu* (Darmstadt: Wissenschaftliche Buchgesellschaft, 1976 [1910]).
Kany, R., 'Der Lukanische Bericht von Tod und Auferstehung Jesu aus der Sicht eines hellenistischen Romanlesers', *NovT* 28 (1986), pp. 76-90.
Karris, R.J., 'The Background and Significance of the Polemic in the Pastoral Epistles', *JBL* 92 (1973), pp. 549-64.
—'Poor and Rich: The Lukan *Sitz im Leben*', in C.H. Talbert (ed.), *Perspectives on Luke–Acts* (Danville, VA: Association of Baptist Professors of Religion, 1978), pp. 112-25.
—'Missionary Communities: A New Paradigm for the Study of Luke–Acts', *CBQ* 41 (1979), pp. 80-97.
Kat, J.F.M., *De Verloren Zoon: Als letterkundig motief* (Bussem: Paul Brand N.V., 1952).
Kee, H.C., 'The Ethical Dimensions of the Testaments of the XII as a Clue to Provenance', *NTS* 24 (1978), pp. 259-70.
Kelley, R.L., 'The Significance of the Parable of the Prodigal Son for Three Major Issues in Current Synoptic Study' (PhD dissertation, Princeton University, 1972).
Kerford, G.B., 'The Search for Personal Identity in Stoic Thought', *BJRL* 55 (1972), pp. 177-96.
Kingsbury, J.D., *Conflict in Luke: Jesus, Authorities, Disciples* (Minneapolis: Fortress Press, 1991).
Kissinger, W.S., *The Parables of Jesus: A History of Interpretation and Bibliography* (ATLA Bibliography Series, 4; Metuchen, NJ: Scarecrow Press, American Theological Library Association, 1979).
Klauck, H.-J., 'Brotherly Love in Plutarch and in 4 Maccabees', in Balch, Ferguson and Meeks (eds.), *Greeks, Romans and Christians*, pp. 144-56.
Klausner, J., 'Pagan Philosophical Thought in the Generation of Paul', in *idem, From Jesus to Paul* (trans. W.F. Stinespring; London: George Allen & Unwin, 1946).
Kleinknecht, H., *et al.*, 'ὀργή, κτλ', *TDNT*, V, pp. 382-447.

Knox, W.L., *Some Hellenistic Elements in Primitive Christianity* (Schweich Lectures of the British Academy, 1942; London: Published for the British Academy by Oxford University Press, 1944).

Koester, H., 'σπλάγχνον, σπλαγχνίζομαι, κτλ', *TDNT*, VII, pp. 548-59.

—*Introduction to the New Testament* (2 vols; Philadelphia: Fortress Press, 1982).

—*Ancient Christian Gospels: Their History and Development* (London: SCM Press; Philadelphia: Trinity Press International, 1990).

Kolenkow, A.B. (trans.), 'Chaeremon the Stoic on Egyptian Temple Askesis', in W.L. Wimbush (ed.), *Ascetic Behavior in Greco-Roman Antiquity* (Minneapolis: Augsburg–Fortress, 1990), pp. 387-92.

Kudlien F., 'Der Arzt des Körpers und der Arzt der Seele', *Clio Medica* 3 (1968), pp. 1-20.

—'Gesundheit', *RAC* 10 (1978), pp. 902-45.

Lacy, P.H. de, 'II.—Lucretius and the History of Epicureanism', *APAT* 79 (1948), pp. 12-23.

Lacey, W.K., 'Patria Potestas', in B. Rawson (ed.), *The Family in Ancient Rome: New Perspectives* (London: Croom Helm, 1986), pp. 121-44.

Lake, K., (trans.), *The Apostolic Fathers* (LCL; 2 vols; Cambridge, MA: Harvard University Press, 1912, 1913).

Lake, K., and S. Lake, *An Introduction to the New Testament* (London: Christophers, 1938).

Lambrecht, J., *Once More Astonished: The Parables of Jesus* (New York: Crossroad, 1981).

Laporte, J., 'Philo in the Tradition of Biblical Wisdom Literature', in R.L. Wilken (ed.), *Aspects of Wisdom in Judaism and Early Christianity* (University of Notre Dame Center for the Study of Judaism and Christianity in Antiquity; Notre Dame: University of Notre Dame Press, 1975).

Lattimore, R., *Themes in Greek and Latin Epitaphs* (Urbana: University of Illinois Press, 1962).

Lee, H.D.P., *Plato: The Republic* (Harmondsworth: Penguin Books, 1955).

Lehnert, G., *Declamationes xix maiores* (Bibliotheca scriptorum Graecorum et Romanorum Teubneriana; Leipzig: Teubner, 1905).

Lewis, J.J., 'The Table Talk Section in the *Letter of Aristeas*', *NTS* 13 (1966–67), pp. 53-56.

Liebeschuetz, J.H.W.G., *Continuity and Change in Roman Religion* (Oxford: Clarendon Press, 1979).

Lightfoot, J.B., *Saint Paul's Epistle to the Philippians* (London: Macmillan, 8th edn, 1888).

—*Saint Paul's Epistles to the Colossians and Philemon* (London: Macmillan, 1892).

Link, H.-G., 'βίος, ζωή', *NIDNTT*, II, pp. 474-83.

Linnemann, E., *Parables of Jesus: Introduction and Exposition* (London: SPCK, 1966).

Little, J.C., 'Parable Research in the Twentieth Century. I. The Predecessors of J. Jeremias', *ExpTim* 87 (1976), pp. 356-60.

—'Parable Research in the Twentieth Century. II. The Contribution of J. Jeremias', *ExpTim* 88 (1976), pp. 40-44.

—'Parable Research in the Twentieth Century. III. Developments Since J. Jeremias', *ExpTim* 88 (1976), pp. 71-75.

Lock, W., *A Critical and Exegetical Commentary on the Pastoral Epistles* (ICC; Edinburgh: T. & T. Clark, 1924).

Long, A.A., 'Aristotle's Legacy to Stoic Ethics', *BULICS* 15 (1968), pp. 72-85.

—*Hellenistic Philosophy: Stoics, Epicureans, Sceptics* (London: Gerald Duckworth, 1974).

—'The Early Stoic Concept of Moral Choice', in F. Bossier (ed.), *Images of Man in Ancient and Medieval Thought: Studia Gerardo Verbeke ab amicis et collegis dicata* (Symbolae Facultatis Litterarum et Philosophiae Louvaniensis: Series A, vol. I; Leuven: Leuven University Press, 1976), pp. 77-92.

—'Post-Aristotelian Philosophy', in P.E. Easterling and B.M.W. Knox (eds), *The Cambridge History of Classical Literature. I. Greek Literature* (Cambridge: Cambridge University Press, 1985), pp. 622-41.

Long, A.A., and D.N. Sedley, *The Hellenistic Philosophers* (2 vols.; Cambridge: Cambridge University Press, 1987).

Louw, J.P., *Semantics of New Testament Greek* (Philadelphia: Fortress Press, 1983).

Louw, J.P., *et al.* (eds.), *Greek-English Lexicon of the New Testament Based on Semantic Domains. I. Introduction and Domains* (New York: United Bible Societies, 1988).

Luck, U., 'σώφρων, κτλ', *TDNT*, VII, pp. 1097-104.

—'ὑγιής, κτλ', *TDNT*, VIII, pp. 308-13.

Lutz, C.E., 'Musonius Rufus: "The Roman Socrates"', *YCS* 10 (1947), pp. 3-147.

MacMullen, R., *Roman Social Relations: 50 B.C. to A.D. 284* (New Haven: Yale University Press, 1974).

—*Paganism in the Roman Empire* (New Haven: Yale University Press, 1981).

Malherbe, A.J., 'Athenagoras on Christian Ethics', *JEH* 20 (1969), pp. 1-5.

—'Athenagoras on the Pagan Poets and Philosophers', in P. Granfield and J.A. Jungman (eds.), *Kyriakon* (Festschrift J. Quasten; Münster: Aschendorff, 1970), pp. 214-25.

—'Pseudo-Heraclitus, Epistle 4: The Divinization of the Wise Man', *JAC* 21 (1978), pp. 42-64.

—Review of *Teles (The Cynic Teacher)*, ed. and trans. by E.N. O'Neil (Missoula: Scholars Press), in *JBL* 97 (1978), pp. 599-600.

—Review of *Plutarch's Ethical Writings and Early Christian Literature*, ed. H.D. Betz (Leiden: E.J. Brill), in *JBL* 100 (1981), pp. 140-42.

—*Social Aspects of Early Christianity* (Philadelphia: Fortress Press, 2nd edn, 1983).

—*Paul and the Thessalonians: The Philosophic Tradition of Pastoral Care* (Philadelphia: Fortress Press, 1987).

—'Greco-Roman Religion and Philosophy and the New Testament', in E.J. Epp and G.W. MacRae (eds.), *The New Testament and its Modern Interpreters* (Scholars Press: Atlanta, 1989), pp. 3-26.

—*Paul and the Popular Philosophers* (Minneapolis: Fortress Press, 1989).

—'Medical Imagery in the Pastoral Epistles', in *idem, Paul and the Popular Philosophers*, pp. 121-36.

—' "In Season and out of Season": 2 Timothy 4.2', in *idem, Paul and the Popular Philosophers*, pp. 137-45.

—'The Beasts at Ephesus', in *idem, Paul and the Popular Philosophers*, pp. 79-89.

—'Exhortation in 1 Thessalonians,' in *idem, Paul and the Popular Philosophers*, pp. 49-66.

—' "Not in a Corner": Early Christain Apologetic in Acts 26.26', in *idem, Paul and the Popular Philosophers*, pp. 147-63.

—'Hellenistic Moral Philosophy and the New Testament: A Retrospective Analysis' (keynote paper presented at the 1990 meeting of the SBL).

—' "Pastoral Care" in the Thessalonian Church', *NTS* 36 (1990), pp. 375-91.

—'Hellenistic Moralists and the New Testament', ANRW, II.26.1 (1992), pp. 267-333.

—'The Christianization of a *Topos* (Luke 12:13-34)', *NovT* 38 (1996), pp. 123-35.

Malherbe, A.J. (ed.), *The Cynic Epistles: A Study Edition* (trans. A.M. McGuire *et al.*; SBLSBS, 12; Missoula: Scholars Press, 1977).

Malherbe, A.J. (ed. and trans.), *Moral Exhortation: A Greco-Roman Sourcebook* (Library of Early Christianity, 4; Philadelphia: Westminster Press, 1986).

Marrou, H.I., *A History of Education in Antiquity* (trans. G. Lamb; London: Sheed & Ward, 1956).

Marshall, I.H., *Luke: Historian and Theologian* (Exeter: Paternoster Press, 1970).

—'Palestinian and Hellenistic Christianity: Some Critical Comments', *NTS* 19 (1972–73), pp. 271-87.

—*The Gospel of Luke: A Commentary on the Greek Text* (NIGTC; Exeter: Paternoster Press, 1978).

—'The Present State of Lukan Studies', *Themelios* 14 (1989), pp. 52-56.

—Review of *Saint Luke* by C.F. Evans (London: SCM Press; Philadelphia: Trinity Press International) in *JTS* NS 42 (1991), pp. 215-18.

Marshall, P., *Enmity in Corinth: Social Conventions in Paul's Relations with the Corinthians* (WUNT, 2.23; Tübingen: J.C.B. Mohr [Paul Siebeck], 1987).

Martin, Francis, *Narrative Parallels to the New Testament* (SBLRBS, 22; Atlanta: Scholars Press, 1988).

Mayor, J.B., *The Epistle of St James: The Greek Text with Introduction, Notes and Comments* (London: Macmillan, 1892).

McCartney, E.S., 'A Bibliography of Collections of Greek and Roman Folklore', *CW* 40 (1947), pp. 99-101.

McCrum, M., and A.G. Woodhead (eds.), *Select Documents of the Principates of the Flavian Emperors: Including the Year of Revolution. AD 68–96* (Cambridge: Cambridge University Press, 1961).

McEleney, M.J., 'The Vice Lists in the Pastoral Epistles', *CBQ* 36 (1974), pp. 203-19.

McIntyre, J., 'The Parabolic Imagination', in *idem, Faith, Theology and Imagination* (Edinburgh: Handsel, 1987).

Mealand, D.L., 'Community of Goods and Utopian Allusions in Acts II–IV', *JTS* NS 28 (1977), pp. 96-97.

—*Poverty and Expectation in the Gospels* (London: SPCK, 1980).

—'The Close of Acts and Its Hellenistic Greek Vocabulary', *NTS* 36 (1990), pp. 583-97.

—' "After not Many Days" in Acts 1.5 and Its Hellenistic Context', *JSNT* 42 (1991), pp. 69-77.

Meeks, W.A., *The First Urban Christians: The Social World of the Apostle Paul* (New Haven: Yale University Press, 1983).

—'Understanding Early Christian Ethics', *JBL* 105 (1986), pp. 3-11.

—*The Moral World of the First Christians* (London: SPCK, 1986).

Mendell, C.W., 'Satire as Popular Philosophy', *CP* 15 (1920), pp. 138-57.

Menken, M.J.J., 'The Position of Σπλαγχνίζεσθαι and Σπλάγχνα in the Gospel of Luke', *NovT* 30 (1988), pp. 107-14.

Metzger, B.M., *The Text of the New Testament: Its Transmission, Corruption and Restoration* (Oxford: Clarendon Press, 1964).

—*A Textual Commentary on the Greek New Testament* (London: United Bible Societies, 2nd edn, 1994).

Michaelis, W., 'ὁδός, κτλ', *TDNT*, V, pp. 42-114.

Miller, N., (trans.), *Menander: Plays and Fragments* (Harmondsworth: Penguin Books, 1987).

Milligan, G., *Selections from the Greek Papyri* (Cambridge: Cambridge University Press, 1927).

Misch, G., *A History of Autobiography in Antiquity* (trans. E.W. Dickes; International Library of Sociology and Social Reconstruction; 2 vols.; London: Routledge & Kegan Paul, 3rd edn, 1950).

Mitchell, A.C., 'The Social Function of Friendship in Acts 2.44-47 and 4.32-37', *JBL* 111 (1992), pp. 255-72.

Mitchell, M.M., 'Concerning περὶ δέ in 1 Corinthians', *NovT* 31 (1989), pp. 229-56.

Moessner, D.P., *The Lord of the Banquet: The Literary and Theological Significance of the Lukan Travel Narrative* (Minneapolis: Fortress Press, 1989).

Moffatt, J., *An Introduction to the Literature of the New Testament* (Edinburgh: T. & T. Clark, 3rd edn, 1918).

—*A Critical and Exegetical Commentary on the Epistle to the Hebrews* (ICC; Edinburgh: T. & T. Clark, 1924).

Moles, J., 'The Career and Conversion of Dio Chrysostom', *JHS* 98 (1978), pp. 79-100.

—' "Honestius Quam Ambitiosius?" An Exploration of the Cynic's Attitude to Moral Corruption in His Fellow Men', *JHS* 103 (1983), pp. 103-23.

—'Cynicism in Horace *Epistles* I', in F. Cairns (ed.), *Papers of the Liverpool Latin Seminar: Fifth Volume 1985* (ARCA Classical and Medieval Texts, Papers and Monographs, 19; Liverpool: Francis Cairns, 1986), pp. 33-60.

Montefiore, H., 'Does "L" Hold Water?' *JTS* 12 (1961), pp. 59-60.

Most, G.W., and G.B. Conte, 'Topos', in S. Hornblower and A. Spawforth (eds.), *Oxford Classical Dictionary* (Oxford: Oxford University Press, 1996), p. 1534.

Mott, S.C., 'The Power of Giving and Receiving: Reciprocity in Hellenistic Benevolence', in Gerald F. Hawthorne (ed.), *Current Issues in Biblical and Patristic Interpretation* (Festschrift Merril C. Tenney; Grand Rapids: Eerdmans, 1975), pp. 60-72.

—'Greek Ethics and Christian Conversion: The Philonic Background of Titus 2:10-12 and 3:3-7', *NovT* 20 (1978), pp. 22-48.

Moulder, J., 'Hellenistic Philosophy', *SAJP* 7 (1988), pp. 183-84.

Moule, C.F.D., *An Idiom Book of New Testament Greek* (Cambridge: Cambridge University Press, 1953).

—'The Use of Parables and Sayings as Illustrative Material in Early Christian Catechesis', in *idem*, *Essays in New Testament Interpretation* (Cambridge: Cambridge University Press, 1982), pp. 50-53.

Moulton, J.H., and G. Milligan, *The Vocabulary of the Greek Testament* (Grand Rapids: Eerdmans, 1982 [1930]).

Moxnes, H., *The Economy of the Kingdom: Social Conflict and Economic Relations in Luke's Gospel* (OBT; Philadelphia: Fortress Press, 1988).

Mullins, T.Y., 'Topos as a New Testament Form', *JBL* 99 (1980), pp. 541-47.

Murray, G., *Five Stages of Greek Religion* (London: C. & A. Watts, 1935).

—*Stoic, Christian and Humanist* (London: C. & A. Watts, 1940).

Mussies, G., *Dio Chrystostom and the New Testament* (SCHNT, 2; Leiden: E.J. Brill, 1972).

Neyrey, J.H., 'Acts 17, Epicureans and Theodicy', in Balch, Ferguson and Meeks (eds.), *Greeks, Romans and Christians*, pp. 118-34.

270   *Prodigality, Liberality and Meanness*

Nickelsburg, G.W.E., 'Riches, the Rich and God's Judgment in 1 Enoch 92-105 and the Gospel According to Luke', *NTS* 25 (1978), pp. 324-44.

—*Jewish Literature between the Bible and the Mishnah: A Historical and Literary Introduction* (London: SCM Press, 1981).

Nida, E.A., *et al.* (eds.), *Style and Discourse: With Special Reference to the Text of the New Testament* (Cape Town: Bible Society, 1983).

Nock A.D., *Conversion: The Old and New in Religion from Alexander the Great to Augustine of Hippo* (Oxford: Clarendon Press, 1933).

—'Christianity and Classical Culture', in Z. Stewart (ed.), *Arthur Darby Nock: Essays on Religion and the Ancient World* (2 vols.; Oxford: Clarendon Press, 1972), II, pp. 676-81.

—'Conversion and Adolescence', in Z. Stewart (ed.), *Arthur Darby Nock: Essays on Religion and the Ancient World* (2 vols.; Oxford: Clarendon Press, 1972), I, pp. 469-80.

—'Early Gentile Christianity and its Hellenistic Background', in Z. Stewart (ed.), *Arthur Darby Nock: Essays on Religion and the Ancient World* (2 vols.; Oxford: Clarendon Press, 1972), I, pp. 49-133.

—'Philo and Hellenistic Philosophy', in Z. Stewart (ed.), *Arthur Darby Nock: Essays on Religion and the Ancient World* (2 vols.; Oxford: Clarendon Press, 1972), II, pp. 559-65.

Noorda, S.J., 'Scene and Summary: A Proposal for Reading Acts 4, 32–5, 16', in J. Kremer (ed.), *Les actes des apôtres: Traditions, rédaction, théologie* (BETL, 48; Leuven: Leuven University Press, 1979), pp. 475-83.

North, H., *Sophrosyne: Self-Knowledge and Self-Restraint in Greek Literature* (CSCP, 35; Ithaca, NY: Cornell University Press, 1966).

O'Neil, E.N., *Teles (The Cynic Teacher)* (SBLTT Graeco-Roman Religion Series, 3; Missoula: Scholars Press, 1977).

O'Neil, E.N., '*De Cupiditate Divitiarum (Moralia* 523C-528B)', in Betz (ed.), *Plutarch's Ethical Writings*, pp. 289-362.

O'Rourke, J.J., 'Some Notes on Luke XV.11-32', *NTS* 18 (1971–72), pp. 431-33.

O'Toole, R.F., 'Why Did Luke Write Acts (Lk–Acts)?' *BTB* 7 (1977), pp. 66-76.

—'Luke's Position on Politics and Society in Luke–Acts', in R.J. Cassidy and P.J. Scharper (eds.), *Political Issues in Luke–Acts* (Maryknoll, NY: Orbis Books, 1983), pp. 1-17.

Oepke, A., 'ἀπόλλυμι', *TDNT*, I, pp. 394-96.

Oldfather, W.A., *Epictetus: The Discourses as Reported by Arrian, the Manual, and Fragments* (LCL; 2 vols.; Cambridge, MA: Harvard University Press, 1928 [1925]).

Oltramere, A. *Les origines de la diatribe romaine* (Lausanne: Librarie Payot, 1926).

Packman, Z.M., 'Ethics and Allegory in the Proem of the Fifth Book of Lucretius' *De Rerum Natura*', *ClJ* 71 (1975), pp. 206-12.

Page, A.F., 'Proto-Luke Reconsidered: A Study of Literary Method and Theology in the Gospel of Luke' (PhD dissertation, Duke University, 1968).

Parrott, D.M., 'The Dishonest Steward (Luke 16:1-8a) and Luke's Special Parable Collection', *NTS* 37 (1991), pp. 499-515.

Pearson, L., *Popular Ethics in Ancient Greece* (Stanford: Stanford University Press, 1962).

Pelling, C., 'Plutarch: Roman Heroes and Greek Culture', in M. Griffin and J. Barnes (eds.), *Philosophia Togata: Essays on Philosophy and Roman Society* (Oxford: Clarendon Press, 1989), pp. 199-232.

Pelser, G.M.M., *et al.*, 'Discourse Analysis of Galatians', addendum to *Neot* 26 (1992).

Perkins, P., 'New Testament Ethics: Questions and Contexts', *RSR* 10 (1984), pp. 321-27.

Perry, B.E. (ed.), *Aesopica: A Series of Texts Relating to Aesop or Ascribed to Him or Closely Connected with the Literary Tradition That Bears his Name. Collected and Critically Edited, in Part Translated from Original Languages, with a Commentary and Historical Essay.* I. *Greek and Latin Texts* (Urbana: University of Illinois Press, 1952).

—(trans.) *Babrius and Phaedrus* (LCL; Cambridge, MA: Harvard University Press, 1965).

Pervo, R.I., *Profit with Delight: The Literary Genre of the Acts of the Apostles* (Philadelphia: Fortress Press, 1987).

Petersen, N.R., 'The Reader in the Gospel', *Neot* 18 (1984), pp. 38-51.

Petzer, J.H., 'A Survey of the Developments in the Textual Tradition of the Greek New Testament since UBS 3', *Neot* 24 (1990), pp. 71-92.

—'Author's Style and the Textual Criticism of the New Testament', *Neot* 24 (1990), pp. 185-97.

Petzke, G., *Die Traditionen über Apollonius von Tyana und das Neue Testament* (SCHNT, 1; Leiden: E.J. Brill, 1970).

Pfitzner, V.C., *Paul and the Agon Motif* (NovTSup, 16; Leiden: E.J. Brill, 1967).

Pilgrim, W.E., *Good News to the Poor: Wealth and Poverty in Luke–Acts* (Minneapolis: Augsburg, 1981).

Piper, J., *'Love Your Enemies': Jesus' Love Command in the Synoptic Gospels and in the Early Christian Paraenesis. A History of the Tradition and Interpretation of its Uses* (SNTSMS, 38; Cambridge: Cambridge University Press, 1979).

Places. E. des, 'En marge du *Theologisches Wörterbuch zum Neuen Testament*: Conscience et personne dans l'antiquité Grecque', *Bib* 30 (1949), pp. 501-509.

Plessis, I.J. du, 'Once More: The Purpose of Luke's Prologue (Lk i 1-4)', *NovT* 16 (1974), pp. 259-71.

—'Die gelykenis van die verlore seun. Lukas 15:11-32', in P.G.R. de Villiers (ed.), *Hoe lees 'n mens die Bybel* (Pretoria: Universiteit van Suid Afrika, 1988), pp. 74-97.

—*'n Kykie in die Hart van God* (Pretoria: N.G. Kerkboekhandel, 1990).

—Review of *Reden in Vollmacht: Hintergrund, Form und Anliegen der Gleichnisse Jesu* by E. Rau (Göttingen: Vandenhoeck & Ruprecht), in *Neot* 25 (1991), pp. 430-32.

Plato, *The Republic* II (2 vols.; trans. P. Shorey; LCL; Cambridge, MA; Harvard University Press, 1935).

Plümacher, E., *Lukas als hellenistischer Schriftsteller: Studien zur Apostelgeschichte* (SUNT, 9; Göttingen: Vandenhoeck & Ruprecht, 1972).

Plummer, A., *A Critical and Exegetical Commentary on the Gospel According to St Luke* (ICC; T. & T. Clark: Edinburgh, 1896).

Pogoloff, S.M., 'Isocrates and Contemporary Hermeneutics', in D.F. Watson (ed.), *Persuasive Artistry: Studies in New Testament Rhetoric in Honor of George A. Kennedy* (JSNTSup, 50; Sheffield: JSOT Press, 1991), pp. 338-62.

Pohlenz, M., *Freedom in Greek Life and Thought: The History of an Ideal* (trans. C. Lofmark; Dordrecht, Holland: D. Reidel, 1966).

Pöhlmann, W., *Der verlorene Sohn und das Haus: Studien zu Lukas 15.11-32 im Horizont der antiken Lehre von Haus, Erziehung und Ackerbau* (WUNT, 68; Tübingen: J.C.B. Mohr [Paul Siebeck], 1993).

Porter, S.E., 'The Parable of the Unjust Steward (Luke 16:1-13): Irony *is* the Key', in D.J.A. Clines, S.E. Fowl and S.E. Porter (eds.), *The Bible in Three Dimensions:*

Essays in Celebration of Forty Years of Biblical Studies in the University of Sheffield (JSOTSup, 87; Sheffield: Sheffield Academic Press, 1990), pp. 127-53.

Powell, J.U., and E.A. Barber (eds.), *New Chapters in the History of Greek Literature: Recent Discoveries in Greek Poetry and Prose of the Fourth and Following Centuries B.C.* (Oxford: Clarendon Press, 1921).

Price, J., *Commentarii in Varios Novi Testamenti Libros* (London: Flescher, 1660).

Price, J.L., 'Luke 15.11-32', *Int* 31 (1977), pp. 64-69.

Prior, W.J., *Virtue and Knowledge: An Introduction to Ancient Greek Ethics* (London: Routledge, 1991).

Radice, B. (trans.), *Terence: The Comedies* (Harmondsworth: Penguin Books, 1976).

Ramaroson, L., 'Le coeur du troisième évangile: Lc 15', *Bib* 60 (1979), pp. 348-60.

Ramsay, W.M., *The Bearing of Recent Discovery on the Trustworthiness of the New Testament* (London: Hodder & Stoughton, 2nd edn, 1915).

Rau, E., *Reden in Vollmacht: Hintergrund, Form und Anliegen der Gleichnisse Jesu* (FRLANT, 149; Göttingen: Vandenhoeck & Ruprecht, 1990).

Rawson, E., *Intellectual Life in the Late Roman Republic* (London: Gerald Duckworth, 1985).

—'Roman Rulers and the Philosophic Adviser', in M. Griffin and J. Barnes (eds.), *Philosophia Togata: Essays on Philosophy and Roman Society* (Oxford: Clarendon Press, 1989), pp. 233-57.

Reardon, B.P., Review of *The Ancient Romances: A Literary-Historical Account of their Origins* by B.E. Perry in *AJP* 89 (1968), pp. 476-80.

—'The Greek Novel', *Phoenix (Toronto)* 23 (1969), pp. 55-73.

—'Aspects of the Greek Novel', *GR* NS 23 (1976), pp. 118-31.

—'Theme, Structure and Narrative in Chariton', *YCS* 27 (1982), pp. 1-27.

—(ed.) *Collected Ancient Greek Novels* (Berkeley: University of California Press, 1989).

Reese, J.M., *Hellenistic Influence on the Book of Wisdom and its Consequences* (AnBib, 41; Rome: Biblical Institute Press, 1970).

Rehkopf, F., *Die lukanische Sonderquelle: Ihr Umfang und Sprachgebrauch* (WUNT, 5; Tübingen: J.C.B. Mohr [Paul Siebeck], 1959).

Reiling, J., and J.L. Swellengrebel, *A Translator's Handbook on the Gospel of Luke* (Leiden: E.J. Brill, 1971).

Rengstorf, K.H., 'Die *stolai* der Schriftgelehrten: Eine Erläuterung zu Mark. 12, 38', in O. Betz (ed.), *Abraham unser Vater: Juden und Christen im Gespräch über die Bibel* (Festschrift O. Michel; Leiden: E.J. Brill, 1963), pp. 383-404.

—*Die Re-investitur des Verlorenen Sohnes in der Gleichniserzählung Jesu: Luk. 15, 11-32* (Arbeitsgemeinschaft für Forschung des Landes Nordrhein-Westfalen, Geisteswissenschaften, 137; Cologne/Opladen: Westdeutscher-Verlag, 1967).

—*Das Evangelium nach Lukas* (Göttingen: Vandenhoeck & Ruprecht, 1978).

Richard, E., 'Luke: Writer, Theologian, Historian. Research and Orientation of the 1970s', *BTB* 13 (1983), pp. 3-15.

Rickards, R., 'Some Points to Consider in Translating the Parable of the Prodigal Son (Luke 15.11-32)', *BT* 31 (1980), pp. 243-45.

Rist, J.M., 'Epicurus on Friendship', *CP* 75 (1980), pp. 121-29.

—*Human Value: A Study in Ancient Philosophical Ethics* (PA, 40; Leiden: E.J. Brill, 1982).

Roberts, W.B., *Longinus on the Sublime: The Greek Text Edited after the Paris Manuscript with Introduction, Translation, Facsimiles and Appendices* (Cambridge: Cambridge University Press, 1899).

Robertson, W.P., ' "The Word of the Cross and the Parable of the Prodigal",' *ExpTim* 25 (1913–14), pp. 181-82.

Rose, H.J., 'Heracles and the Gospels', *HTR* 31 (1938), pp. 113-42.

Sandbach, F.H., *The Stoics* (London: Chatto & Windus, 1975).

Sanders, E.P., *Jesus and Judaism* (London: SCM Press, 1985).

—*Paul* (Oxford: Oxford University Press, 1991).

Sanders, J.T., 'Tradition and Redaction in Luke XV.11-32', *NTS* 15 (1968–69), pp. 433-38.

—*Ethics in the New Testament: Change and Development* (London: SCM Press, 1975).

Sandy, G.N., 'Recent Scholarship on the Prose Fiction of Classical Antiquity', *Classical World* 67 (1974), pp. 321-59.

Saunders, J.L. (ed.), *Greek and Roman Philosophy after Aristotle* (Readings in the History of Philosophy; New York: Free Press; London: Collier-Macmillan, 1966).

Schmid W., and O. Stählin, *Geschichte der griechischen Literatur* (Munich: Beck, 6th edn, 1920).

Schmithals, W., *Das Evangelium nach Lukas* (Zürcher Bibelkommentare; Zürich: Theologische Verlag, 1980).

Schneider, J., 'μέρος', *TDNT*, IV, pp. 594-98.

Schnider, F., *Die verlorenen Söhne: Strukturanalytische und historisch-kritische Untersuchungen zu Lk 15* (OBO, 17; Freiburg: Universitästverlag; Göttingen: Vandenhoeck & Ruprecht, 1977).

Schottroff, L., 'Das Gleichnis vom verlorenen Sohn', *ZTK* 68 (1971), pp. 27-52.

Schottroff, L., and W. Stegemann, *Jesus and the Hope of the Poor* (trans. M.J. O'Connell; Maryknoll, NY: Orbis Books), 1986.

Schrage, W., *The Ethics of the New Testament* (trans. D.E. Green; Edinburgh: T. & T. Clark, 1988).

Schweizer, E., 'Zur Frage der Lukasquellen, Analyse von Luk. 15, 11-32', *TZ* 4 (1948), pp. 469-71.

—'Antwort', *TZ* 5 (1949), pp. 231-33.

—*Luke: A Challenge to Present Theology* (London: SPCK, 1982).

—*The Good News According to Luke* (trans. D.E. Green; Altanta: John Knox Press, 1984).

Scott, B.B., 'The Prodigal Son: A Structuralist Interpretation', *Semeia* 9 (1977), pp. 45-73.

—*Hear Then the Parable: A Commentary on the Parables of Jesus* (Minneapolis: Fortress Press, 1989).

Sedgwick, W.B., 'Covetousness and the Sensual Sins in the New Testament', *ExpTim* 36 (1924–25), pp. 478-79.

Sedley, D., 'The Protagonists', in M. Schofield, M. Burnyeat and J. Barnes (eds.), *Doubt and Dogmatism: Studies in Hellenistic Epistemology* (Oxford: Clarendon Press, 1980), pp. 1-19.

—'Philosophical Allegiance in the Greco-Roman World', in M. Griffin and J. Barnes (eds), *Philosophia Togata: Essays on Philosophy and Roman Society* (Oxford: Clarendon Press, 1989), pp. 97-119.

Seeley, D., *Deconstructing the New Testament* (Leiden: E.J. Brill, 1994).

Sellew, P., 'Interior Monologue as a Narrative Device', *JBL* 111 (1992), pp. 239-53.

Sellin, G., 'Luke as Parable Narrator', *TD* 25 (1977), pp. 53-60.

—'Komposition, Quellen und Funktion des Lukanischen Reiseberichtes (Lk. ix 51-xix 28)', *NovT* 20 (1978), pp. 100-135.

Seng, H.W., 'Der reiche Tor', *NovT* 20 (1978), pp. 136-55.

Senior, F., 'Luke XV.30', *ExpTim* 31 (1919–20), p. 282.

Sevenster, J.N., 'Waarom spreekt Paulus nooit van vrienden en vriendschap?' *NTT* 9 (1954/55), pp. 356-63.

—*Paul and Seneca* (NovTSup, 4; Leiden: E.J. Brill, 1961).

—'Education or Conversion: Epictetus and the Gospels', in J.N. Sevenster (ed.), *Placita Pleiadia: Opstellen aangeboden aan G. Sevenster* (Leiden: E.J. Brill, 1966), pp. 247-62.

—*Do You Know Greek? How Much Greek Could the First Jewish Christians Have Known?* (NovTSup, 19; Leiden: E.J. Brill, 1968).

Sharples, R.W., 'Review Discussion: Accessible Hellenistic Philosophy', *JHS* 110 (1990), pp. 199-202.

Sheeley, S.M., 'Narrative Asides and Narrative Authority in Luke–Acts', *BTB* 18 (1988), pp. 102-107.

Shelton, J., *As the Romans Did: A Source Book in Roman Social History* (New York: Oxford University Press, 1988).

Sherk, R.K., (trans. and ed.), *The Roman Empire: Augustus to Hadrian* (Translated Documents of Greece and Rome, 6; Cambridge: Cambridge University Press, 1988).

Sherwin-White, A.N., 'The Galilean Narrative and the Greco-Roman World', in *idem*, *Roman Society and Roman Law in the New Testament* (Oxford: Oxford University Press, 1963).

Sibinga, J.S., 'Toorn en droefheid in Marcus 3.5: Een bijdrage aan het Corpus Hellenisticum', in I.B. Horst *et al.* (eds.), *De Geest in het geding* (Festschrift J.A. Oosterbaan; Alphen aan den Rijn: Tj. Willink, 1978), pp. 255-67.

—'Zur Kompositionstechnik des Lukas in Lk. 15:11-32', in J.W. van Henten (ed.), *Tradition and Re-Interpretation in Jewish and Early Christian Literature* (Festschrift. J.C.H. Lebram; Leiden: E.J. Brill, 1986), pp. 97-113.

Sider, J.W., 'Rediscovering the Parables: The Logic of the Jeremias Tradition', *JBL* 102 (1983), pp. 61-83.

Simpson, E.K., 'Vettius Valens and the New Testament', *EvQ* 2 (1930), pp. 389-400.

Skemp, J.B., 'Service to the Needy in the Graeco-Roman World', in J.I. McCord and T.H.L. Parker (eds.), *Service in Christ: Essays Presented to Karl Barth on his 80th Birthday* (London: Epworth Press, 1966), pp. 17-26.

Smith, H., *Ante-Nicene Exegesis of the Gospels* (trans. of Christian Literature, 6; London: SPCK, 1928).

Smith, M., '*De Tuenda Sanitate Praecepta* (*Moralia* 122B-137E)', in Betz (ed.), *Plutarch's Ethical Writings*, pp. 32-50.

Snodgrass, K., *The Parable of the Wicked Tenants: An Enquiry into Parable Interpretation* (WUNT, 27; J.C.B. Mohr: Tübingen, 1983).

Spicq, C., *Saint Paul: Les épitres pastorales* (EBib; 2 vols.; Paris: J. Gabalda, 4th edn, 1969).

—*Notes de lexicographie néo-testamentaire* (OBO, 22.1-3; 2 vols. with supplement; Fribourg, Switzerland: Editions universitaires, 1978–82).

Stählin, G., 'φίλος, κτλ', *TDNT*, IX, pp. 146-71.

—in H. Kleinknecht Stählin, G. *et al.* (eds.), *Wrath* (trans. D.M. Barton; London: A. & C. Black, 1964).

Staden, P. van, 'Compassion: The Essence of Life. A Social-Scientific Study of the Religious Symbolic Universe Reflected in the Ideology/Theology of Luke' (DD dissertation, University of Pretoria, 1990).

Stählin, G., and W. Grundmann, 'The Linguistic Usage and History of ἁμαρτάνω, ἁμάρτημα and ἁμαρτία before and in the NT', *TDNT*, I, pp. 293-302.

Stählin, G., and O. Schmitz, 'παρακαλέω, παράκλησις', *TDNT*, V, pp. 773-99.

Starr, R.J., 'The Circulation of Literary Texts in the Roman World', *ClQ* 37 (1987), pp. 213-23.

Stickler, H.E., 'The Prodigal's Brother', *ExpTim* 42 (1930), pp. 45-46.

Stowers, S.K., 'The Diatribe', in D.E. Aune (ed.), *Greco-Roman Literature and the New Testament: Selected Forms and Genres* (SBLSBS, 21; Atlanta: Scholars Press, 1988), pp. 71-83.

Strecker, G., and U. Schnelle (eds.), *Neuer Wettstein: Texte zum Neuen Testament aus Griechentum und Hellenismus* (2 vols.; Berlin: W. de Gruyter, 1995, 1997).

Striker, G., 'The Role of *Oikeiosis* in Stoic Ethics', *Oxford Studies in Ancient Philosophy* 1 (1983), pp. 145-67.

Talbert C.H., *Literary Patterns, Theological Themes and the Genre of Luke–Acts* (SBLMS, 20; Missoula: Scholars Press, 1974).

—(ed.), *Luke–Acts: New Perspectives from the Society of Biblical Literature Seminar* (New York: Crossroad, 1984).

—'Luke–Acts', in E.J. Epp and G.W. MacRae (eds.), *The New Testament and its Modern Interpreters* (Atlanta: Scholars Press, 1989), pp. 297-320.

Tannehill, R.C., *The Narrative Unity of Luke–Acts: A Literary Interpretation*. I. *The Gospel According to Luke* (2 vols.; Philadelphia: Fortress Press, 1986).

Tatum, J., *Apuleius and The Golden Ass* (Ithaca, NY: Cornell University Press, 1979).

Taylor, V., *The Formation of the Gospel Tradition* (London: Macmillan, 1935).

—'Rehkopf's List of Words and Phrases Illustrative of Pre-Lukan Speech Usage', *JTS* 15 (1964), pp. 59-62.

Thiselton, A.C., 'Reader-Response Criticism, Action Models and the Parables of Jesus', in *idem, The Responsibility of Hermeneutics* (Grand Rapids: Eerdmans, 1985), pp. 79-113.

Thom, J.C., 'The Golden Verses of Pythagoras: Its Literary Composition and Religio-Historical Significance' (PhD dissertation, University of Chicago, 1990).

Thompson, J.A.K. (trans.), *The Ethics of Aristotle* (Harmondsworth: Penguin Books, 1955).

Thompson, J.W., *The Beginning of Christian Philosophy: The Epistle to the Hebrews* (CBQMS, 13; Washington, DC: Catholic Biblical Association, 1982).

Thompson, W., *Matthew's Advice to a Divided Community: Mt 17, 22-18, 35* (AnBib, 44; Rome: Biblical Institute Press, 1970).

Tissot, Y., 'Patristic Allegories of the Lukan Parable of the Two Sons', in F. Bovon and G. Rouiller (eds.), *Exegesis: Problems of Method and Exercises in Reading* (trans. D.G. Miller; Pittsburgh: Pickwick Press, 1978), pp. 362-409.

Topel, L.J., 'On the Injustice of the Unjust Steward: Lk 16:1-13', *CBQ* 37 (1975), pp. 216-27.

Traub, H., 'οὐρανός, κτλ', *TDNT*, V, pp. 497-502.

Trench, R.C., *Notes on the Parables of our Lord* (London: Macmillan, 1870).

—*Synonyms of the New Testament* (London: Macmillan, 9th edn, 1880; Grand Rapids: Eerdmans, repr. 1948).

Trenkner, S., *The Greek Novella in the Classical Period* (Cambridge: Cambridge University Press, 1958).

Tuckett, C.M., 'A Cynic Q?' *Bib* 70 (1989), pp. 349-76.

Turner, E.G., 'The Rhetoric of Question and Answer in Menander', *Themes in Drama* 2 (1980), pp. 1-23.

Turner, N., *Grammatical Insights into the New Testament* (Edinburgh: T. & T. Clark, 1965).

—'Jewish and Christian Influence on New Testament Vocabulary', *NovT* 16 (1974), pp. 149-60.

—'The Style of Luke–Acts', in *idem, A Grammar of New Testament Greek. IV. Style* (Edinburgh: T. & T. Clark, 1976).

Turner, P., '*Daphnis and Chloe*: An Interpretation', *GR* NS 7 (1960), pp. 117-23.

Unnik, W.C., van, 'Hugo Grotius als uitlegger van het Nieuwe Testament', *NAK* NS 25 (1932), pp. 1-48.

—'Corpus Hellenisticum Novi Testamenti', *JBL* 83 (1964), pp. 17-33.

—'Die Motivierung der Feindesliebe in Lukas 6:32-35', *NovT* 8 (1966), pp. 284-300.

—'First Century A.D. Literary Culture and Early Christian Literature', *NTT* 25 (1971), pp. 28-43.

—'Words Come to Life: The Work for the "Corpus Hellenisticum Novi Testamenti"', *NovT* 13 (1971), pp. 199-216.

Verhey, A., *The Great Reversal: Ethics and the New Testament* (Grand Rapids: Eerdmans, 1984).

Via, D.O., Jr, *The Parables: Their Literary and Existential Dimension* (Philadelphia: Fortress Press, 1967).

Vielhauer, P., 'Jewish-Christian Gospels', in *New Testament Apocrypha* I. *Gospels and Related Writings* (trans. R.M. Wilson; London: SCM Press, 1963), pp. 117-65.

Villiers, de P.G.R., 'Die diens van die gelowige in die Lukas-geskrifte', *Scriptura* 6 (1982), pp. 13-27.

Vogel, C.J., de 'What Philosophy Meant to the Greeks', *IPQ* 1 (1961), pp. 35-57.

Wachsmuth, C., and O. Hense (eds.), *Stobaeus: Anthologium* (5 vols.; Berlin: Weidmann, repr. 1958).

Walsh, M.J., *A History of Philosophy* (London: Geoffrey Chapman, 1985).

Wedberg, A., *A History of Philosophy*. I. *Antiquity and the Middle Ages* (Oxford: Clarendon Press, 1982).

Weder, H., *Die Gleichnisse Jesu als Metaphern* (FRLANT, 120; Göttingen: Vandenhoeck & Ruprecht, 1978).

Wehrli, F., 'Menander und die Philosophie', in E.G. Turner (ed.), *Ménandre* (Entretiens sur l'antiquité classique, 16; Geneva: Vandoevres, 1969).

Weil, S., *Intimations of Christianity among the Greeks* (London: Ark [Routledge & Kegan Paul], 1987).

Weiss, B., *Die Evangelien des Markus und Lukas* (KEK, 1/2; Göttingen: Vandenhoeck & Ruprecht, 7th edn, 1885).

Weiss, H., 'The *Pagani* among the Contemporaries of the First Christians', *JBL* 86 (1976), pp. 42-52.

Weiss, J., *Der erste Korintherbrief* (KEK, 5; Göttingen: Vandenhoeck & Ruprecht, 1970).

Wellhausen, J., *Das Evangelium Lucae* (Berlin: G. Reimer, 1904).

Wenham, J.W., 'Synoptic Independence and the Origin of Luke's Travel Narrative', *NTS* 27 (1981), pp. 507-15.

West, M.L., 'Near Eastern Material in Hellenistic and Roman Literature', *HSCP* 73 (1969), pp. 113-34.

West, S., '*Joseph and Asenath*: A Neglected Greek Romance', *ClQ* NS 24 (1974), pp. 70-81.

Wettstein, J., *Novum Testamentum Graecum* (2 vols.; Amsterdam 1751/1752; Graz: Akademische Druck- und Verlagsanstalt, repr. 1962).

White, K.D., *Roman Farming* (London: Thames & Hudson, 1970).

White, L.M., 'Morality between Two Worlds: A Paradigm of Friendship in Philippians', in D.L. Balch, E. Ferguson and W.A. Meeks (eds.), *Greeks, Romans and Christians: Essays in Honor of Abraham J. Malherbe* (Minneapolis: Fortress Press, 1990), pp. 201-15.

White, N.P., 'The Basis of Stoic Ethics', *HSCP* 83 (1979), pp. 143-78.

Wilckens, U., 'στολή', *TDNT*, VII, pp. 687-91.

Wiles, M.F., 'Early Exegesis of the Parables', *SJT* 11 (1958), pp. 287-301.

Wilhelm, F., 'Die Oeconomica der Neupythagoreer Bryson, Kallikratidas, Periktione, Phintys', *RhM* 70 (1915), pp. 161-223.

Wilken, R.L., 'Wisdom and Philosophy in Early Christianity', in R.L. Wilken (ed.), *Aspects of Wisdom in Judaism and Early Christianity* (University of Notre Dame Center for the Study of Judaism and Christianity in Antiquity, 1; Notre Dame: University of Notre Dame Press, 1975), pp. 143-68.

Wilken, R.W., 'The Christians as the Romans (and Greeks) Saw Them', in E.P. Sanders (ed.), *Jewish and Christian Self-Definition. I. The Shaping of Christianity in the Second and Third Centuries* (London: SCM Press, 1982), pp. 100-125.

Willcock, J., 'Luke XV.16', *ExpTim* 29 (1917–18), p. 43.

Williams, F.E., 'Is Almsgiving the Point of the Unjust Steward?' *JBL* 83 (1964), pp. 293-97.

Williamson, R., *Jews in the Hellenistic World: Philo* (Cambridge Commentaries on Writings of the Jewish and Christian World 200 BC to AD 200; Cambridge: Cambridge University Press, 1989).

Wimbush, V.L., 'Stobaeus: Anthology (Excerpts)', in *idem, Ascetic Behavior in Greco-Roman Antiquity* (Minneapolis: Augsburg–Fortress, 1990), pp. 169-74.

Windelband, W., *A History of Philosophy. I. Greek, Roman and Medieval* (trans. J.H. Tufts; New York: Macmillan, 1901; New York: Harper & Brothers, repr. 1958).

Winston, D., 'Philo's Ethical Theory', *ANRW* II.21.1 (1984), pp. 372-416.

Witt, N.W. de, 'Organization and Procedure in Epicurean Groups', *CP* 31 (1936), pp. 205-11.

Wordsworth, C., *The New Testament of Our Lord and Saviour Jesus Christ, in the Original Greek with Introductions and Notes. I. The Four Gospels and Acts of the Apostles* (London: Rivingtons, new edn, 1872).

Wuellner, W., 'Paul's Rhetoric of Argumentation in Romans: An Alternative to the Donfried–Karris Debate over Romans', *CBQ* 38 (1976), pp. 330-51.

Yerkes, R.K., *Sacrifice in Greek and Roman Religions and Early Judaism* (New York: Charles Scribners Sons, 1952).

Young, F., 'Traditional Religious Cultures and the Christian Response—I', *ExpTim* 95 (1984), pp. 235-39.

—'Traditional Religious Cultures and the Christian Response—II', *ExpTim* 95 (1984), pp. 265-69.

Ziesler, J.A., 'Luke and the Pharisees', *NTS* 25 (1979), pp. 146-57.

INDEXES

INDEX OF REFERENCES

OLD TESTAMENT

Genesis		24.11	141	65.4	157
4.4-5	227			66.3	157
27.15	216	*Esther*			
33.11	214	3.10	217	*Jeremiah*	
41.42	216, 217	6.8	216	3.3	144
47.14	141	8.8	217	5.1-9	144
		8.10	217	26.21	178
Exodus		8.15	216		
24.5	183			*Ezekiel*	
28.2-4	216	*Job*		16.30-42	144
29.5	216	7.1	197	16.31	141
29.21	216	20.15	141	16.49	163
31.10	216	27.16	141	23	144
				24.21	175
Leviticus		*Psalms*			
11.7	157	4.5	245	*Hosea*	
16.6	183	69.30-32	183	1–4	144
16.11	183	79.14	157		
19.13	197			*Jonah*	
25.47	164	*Proverbs*		3.6	216
25.50	197	7.10	134		
		11.24	141	*Micah*	
Deuteronomy		13.11	141	1.7	141
6.5	198	17.1-5	176		
25.5-10	217	17.5	175, 176	*Zechariah*	
32.43	182	22.15	134	9.3	141
		28.8	141		
Judges				Apocrypha	
6.28	178	*Ecclesiastes*		*1 Esdras*	
		2.8	141	4.18-19	141
1 Kings					
23.21	175	*Isaiah*		*2 Esdras*	
		1.21	144	8.14	141
2 Chronicles		23.15-18	144		
18.9	216	54.1	182	*Tobit*	
24.5	141	57.1-6	144	5.11	197

Wisdom of Solomon
7.12   182
10.5   175
14.12-29   144
14.25-27   182
14.28   182

Ecclesiasticus
2.12   213
3.5-7   110, 181
4.1-4   110
4.18   182
5.1-2   110, 151,
            155
6.29   216
6.31   216
7.15   194
7.20   197
8.2   110, 165
10.8   110
10.9   110
10.22   110
10.30-31   110
11.10-14   111
11.17-28   111
11.19   111
11.23-25   151, 169
11.23-24   111
11.27   169
13.3   111
13.19   111
13.24   111
14.3-16   111
14.3-10   233
14.3-5   181
14.3   141
14.4   141
14.14-16   155
16.1-2   181

18.20   111
18.25   111, 151
18.30–19.1 111, 155
18.32   182
19.5   182
21.8   141
21.15   163
22.23   111
23.4-6   111, 155
23.5   42
23.6   42
25.2   111
25.3   141
25.7   181
27.1   111
27.13   163
27.29   182
27.30   244
28.10   111, 244
29.10-11   111, 190
29.21-23   111
30.1   181
30.5   181
30.7   175
30.14-25   223
30.14   223
30.15-16   111
31.3   141
31.5-8   170
31.5-6   111
31.8   111
32.19   182
33.19-21   111
33.20-22   173
34.22   197
35.2   182
37.11   197
37.29   111
40.12-13   111

40.20   182
40.25-26   111
40.28   111
41.1-2   111
41.14   111
44.6   111
44.7   111
45.7   216
45.10   216
47.18   141
47.19   141
50.11   216
51.25   111
51.28   111
51.29   182

Baruch
1.6   141

1 Maccabees
3.7   182
3.31   141
6.15   216
7.48   182
10.21   216
11.44   182
12.12   182
14.11   182
14.21   182

2 Maccabees
3.15   216
5.2   217
6.8   175
10.20   170
15.11   182
15.27   182

NEW TESTAMENT

Matthew
5.21-26   245
5.38-39   231
6.25-34   96
7.13-14   213, 214
8.22   162

9.36   177
14.14   177
15.17   42
15.19   144
15.32   177
18.12-13   164

18.27   43, 177
20.2   220
20.13   220
20.34   177
21.28-32   31
22.7   245

25.14-30	138	10.30-35	80, 82	12.21	39, 81, 199		
25.24	141	10.30	74, 83	12.34	198		
25.26	141	10.33	43, 83, 175, 177	12.45	198		
				13.3-7	160		
Mark		10.34	83	13.5	210		
1.41	177	10.35-37	69	13.6-9	74, 81, 82, 85, 86, 210		
4.19	156	10.35	82, 83				
6.34	177	10.36-37	210	13.6	83		
6.56	51	10.36	82	13.7-8	82		
7.19	42	10.37	82	13.7	83		
7.21-22	144	11.5-8	74, 80, 82, 84, 86, 186, 190	13.8-9	82		
8.2	177			13.8	83		
9.22	177			14–16	78		
12.38-40	217	11.5-7	82	14	78		
16.5	217	11.5	83	14.7-11	80		
		11.7-8	190	14.7	215		
Luke		11.7	83	14.8-10	74		
1.59	63	11.8	83	14.8	215		
3.7	245	11.9	210	14.11	74		
5.31-32	221	11.15-18	86	14.12-33	78		
5.36	220	11.21-22	71	14.12-14	74		
6.7-9	160	11.23	43, 141	14.12	186		
6.27-35	231	11.37	185	14.15	78, 245		
7.6	186	11.51-54	160	14.21-24	245		
7.10-43	70	12.4	186	14.21	245		
7.10	221	12.12.16	83	14.26	211		
7.13	175, 177	12.13-34	252	14.27	199		
7.34	186	12.13-21	69, 70	14.28-33	86		
7.36-50	74	12.13	133, 161, 238	14.28-32	74, 80, 81, 85		
7.39	199						
7.41-43	71	12.15-21	32, 82	14.28	82, 83		
7.41-42	74, 79, 80, 82, 84, 86	12.15	99, 139, 161	14.30	83		
		12.16-21	81	14.31	82, 83		
7.41	83	12.16-20	69, 70, 74, 77, 80-82, 84, 86, 88, 149, 179, 220, 251	14.33–16.1	69		
7.42	82			14.33	39, 85, 199		
7.43	82, 210			15	20, 27, 29, 30, 38, 69, 70, 72, 73, 75-79, 87, 164		
8.9-14	33						
9.10-17	177						
9.51–19.27	16, 73, 79	12.16	83				
9.51–18.14	74, 79	12.17-20	111	15.1–16.31	72		
9.60	162	12.17-19	82	15.1-32	79		
10.25-37	70	12.17	83, 140, 198, 199	15.1-10	164		
10.27	198			15.1-2	75, 76		
10.28	160	12.18	83, 140	15.1	20, 209		
10.29	83, 199	12.19	83, 88, 179, 198, 199	15.2	77, 228		
10.30-37	70, 80, 81			15.3-11	75		
10.30-36	74, 81, 82, 84, 86	12.20	82, 83, 149, 200				

15.4-10	75		66, 71, 140,	15.22-30	49
15.4-6	73, 81, 164		145, 161,	15.22-24	59, 82, 135
15.4	164		173	15.22-23	52, 66, 71
15.6	164, 186	15.13-24	45	15.22	19, 48, 49,
15.8-10	74, 75, 81,	15.13-26	52		51, 88, 214,
	85	15.13-22	48		215, 221
15.8-9	81, 86, 164	15.13-20	46, 53, 61,	15.23-24	59, 104
15.8	83, 164, 232		66	15.23	49, 51, 52,
15.9	82, 83, 164,	15.14-16	57, 63, 71,		60, 88
	186		195	15.24-32	46
15.10	39	15.14	48, 52, 59,	15.24	43, 49, 52,
15.11-32	13, 14, 16-		66		57, 59-61,
	19, 21, 22,	15.15-16	52, 66, 136,		63, 76, 158,
	26, 28-31,		193		160, 161,
	35-41, 44,	15.15	48, 195, 196		163, 166,
	57, 66, 67,	15.16	41, 42, 48,		173, 221
	69-75, 77-		51, 52, 56,	15.25-32	44, 45, 53,
	85, 87, 88,		66, 158		62
	90, 91, 95,	15.17-27	46	15.25-28	46, 53, 60,
	96, 101, 102,	15.17-20	63, 202, 203		61, 66
	104, 106,	15.17-19	47, 57, 59,	15.25-27	63
	107, 110-12,		82, 207	15.25	43, 49, 51,
	123, 128,	15.17	46, 48, 51,		52, 57, 60,
	132, 133,		52, 58, 59,		61, 66, 218,
	142, 147,		66, 71, 133,		221
	149, 164,		135, 136,	15.26-32	58
	172, 181,		167, 172,	15.26-27	58, 82
	190, 227,		173, 175,	15.26	49, 51, 52,
	237, 238,		199-201,		66, 221
	247, 248		221	15.27	49, 51, 60,
15.11-25	57	15.18-32	60		173, 221,
15.11-24	53, 210	15.18-20	31, 177		226
15.11-20	45	15.18-19	58-60, 158	15.28-32	46, 53, 58,
15.11-16	46	15.18	48, 51, 52,		60, 61, 63,
15.11-12	46, 58, 60,		59, 208		66, 82, 173,
	61, 66, 170	15.19	44, 48, 51,		184, 185
15.11	45-47, 51,		193, 195	15.28	49, 58, 60-
	53, 57, 66,	15.20-24	45, 46, 53,		63, 66, 175,
	71		58, 61, 63,		184, 239
15.12-24	51		66	15.29-32	58, 59, 227
15.12-16	34	15.20	31, 43, 48,	15.29-30	57, 174, 186
15.12	45, 47, 51,		52, 57-59,	15.29	29, 49, 51,
	56-59, 62,		61, 66, 175		56, 59, 66,
	82, 133, 135,	15.21-24	57		173, 186,
	161, 228	15.21	43, 44, 48,		190, 236
15.13	43, 47, 48,		51, 59, 60,	15.30-32	50
	52, 53, 57,		82, 158, 193,		
	58, 61, 62,		195, 208		

Luke (cont.)

15.30	49-51, 59, 60, 113, 161, 177, 186, 237
15.31-32	82, 228
15.31	50, 51, 59, 66, 71, 77, 133, 139, 187
15.32	43, 50, 52, 59, 60, 63, 76, 135, 158, 161, 166, 173, 237
16	70, 73, 77, 78, 164, 249
16.1-31	69
16.1-13	70, 71, 78, 79
16.1-9	33, 72, 81, 82
16.1-8	69, 74, 76, 77, 80-82, 85, 86, 142, 149, 229, 251
16.1	45, 76, 78, 83, 142
16.2	82, 83
16.3-8	78
16.3	82, 83, 199
16.4	83
16.5-7	82
16.5	83
16.6	83
16.7	83
16.8-9	210
16.8	142, 200
16.9	39, 186, 190, 199
16.13	210
16.14	70, 72, 76, 77, 99, 139
16.15	198, 199
16.18-31	163
16.19-31	17, 36, 69-72, 74, 76, 78, 80-82, 85, 86, 161, 179
16.19	83, 88, 179
16.20-25	190
16.21	42, 83
16.24-31	82
16.24	83
16.25	83, 161
16.27	83
16.28	83
16.30	82, 83
16.31	78, 83
17.3-4	208
17.3	198, 199
17.7-10	74, 80, 82, 85, 86
17.7-9	82
17.7	82, 83
17.8	82, 83
17.9	83
17.10	39, 82
18.1-8	33, 82
18.2-5	74, 80-82, 85, 86, 149
18.2	83
18.3	82
18.4-5	82
18.4	82, 83, 198, 199
18.6-8	39
18.7	82
18.9-14	36, 82
18.9	83
18.10-14	70, 74, 80-82, 85, 86
18.10	83
18.11	82, 83, 198, 199
18.13	83, 208
18.14	39, 74, 83, 199, 210
19.3-4	204
19.11-27	71
19.12-27	138
20.9-16	149
20.35-38	160
20.46	215, 216
20.47	85, 217
21.23	245
21.34	198
22.15	156
23.12	186
24	54
24.2-5	159
24.5	160

John

4.15	209
5.25	159
8.11	209
9.2	209
9.3	209
11.52	141

Acts

1.2	252
1.5	62
1.18	142
2	139
2.44-46	250
4	139
4.32–5.16	57
4.32-35	250
4.32	71, 187
4.36-37	187
5.12-16	51
5.13	195
5.35	198
5.37-39	160
7.26	63
7.29	195
7.41	183
8.20	166
9	204
9.26	195
10.2	204
10.17	198
10.24	186
10.42	160
11.22-30	187
12.11	198
13.42	204
13.43	204
15.15	220
16.15-18	241

16.29-33	204	*2 Corinthians*		*1 Timothy*		
17.1-15	194	2.2-3	180	3.2-7	144	
17.2	204	6.9-10	153	3.3	171	
17.4	204	6.10	229	5.6	163	
17.22-29	241	8.2	194	6.6-10	169	
17.23-32	159			6.6	152, 166	
17.24	159	*Galatians*		6.9	156, 166	
17.30	177	4.12-20	95, 186	6.10	166	
18.3	194			6.17-19	80	
19.31	186	*Ephesians*				
20.9-12	160	2.1	159	*2 Timothy*		
20.28	198	2.5	159	3.2-5	144	
20.34	194	4.1	220	3.2	171	
21.16	186	4.2	220	3.4	141	
22	204	4.19	144			
24.17	195	4.25	245	*Titus*		
25.1-12	208	4.26	245	3.3	156	
25.8	208	4.31–5.1	185			
26	204	4.31	245	*Hebrews*		
26.5-8	160	5.3-4	144	3.17	209	
26.11	63	5.3	144	9.12	183	
27.3	186	5.5	144	9.19	183	
27.28-34	160	5.14	159	10.26	209	
28.4-6	160	6.4	245	12.5	184	
				13.5	169, 193	
Romans		*Philippians*		13.15	171	
1.29-31	144	3.19	42			
2.12	209	4.10-20	188	*James*		
3.23	209	4.14	153	1.15-16	156	
5.12	209	4.17	153	1.17	188	
5.14	209			1.19-21	245	
5.16	209	*Colossians*		2.17	163	
6.15	209	2.13	159	3.13–4.10	96	
7.7	156	3.5	144, 210	4.1-4	156	
12.17	231	3.8	144	4.2	156	
15.10	182			5.5	163	
16.18	42	*1 Thessalonians*				
		2.9	194	*1 Peter*		
1 Corinthians		2.11-12	184	2.13–3.7	94	
4.12	194	4.3-6	144	3.8-9	231	
5.10-11	144	4.10-12	194	3.9	231	
6.1-11	210	4.11	194			
6.9-10	144	5.15	231	*2 Peter*		
6.13	42			2.2	171	
7.36	209	*2 Thessalonians*		2.3	171	
10.26	188	3.8	194	2.4	209	
				2.14	171	

1 John

1.10	209
2.10	209
3.6	209
3.9	209
5.16	209
5.18	209

3 John

2	221

Revelation

4.7	183
6.11	217
7.9	217
7.13	217

7.14	217
11.10	182
12.12	182
17.13	93
17.17	93
18.20	182
22.14	217

PSEUDEPIGRAPHA

1 Enoch

92-105	149
94.7-9	163
100.10-13	149
103.5-7	163

4 Maccabees

1.3-4	169, 244
1.13-27	115
1.21	116
1.25-27	116
1.30	116
2.1-9	115, 116
2.8	211, 233
2.15	244
5.6	157
7.7	220
8.18	182
13.1–14.10	237
13.19–14.1	237
14.2-8	220
14.7-8	220
14.7	220
14.8	220
14.12	172
14.13	175
14.20	175
15.23	175
15.28	175
15.29	175
16.4	220

Apocalypse of Sedrach

6	29

Letter of Aristeas

205	169
209	169

277	135
278	135
319-20	217

Joseph and Asenath

15.10	215
18.5	215

Martyrdom of Isaiah

3.23-26	171

Sibylline Oracles

2	233
2.55-149	117
2.109-18	117
2.111	170
2.115-18	134
2.115	165
2.131-34	117
2.133	155
3.234-5	149
3.234-36	170
3.642	196
8.17-18	170
114-18	233

Testament of Asher

1.3	213
1.5	213
4.4	146
5.1	113

Testament of Benjamin

5.1	113, 146
6.1-3	113, 141
6.2	151
10.3-4	113
11.1-2	113

Testament of Dan

2–4	244
3.4	244
5.7-12	182
5.7	113

Testament of Gad

2.3-5	113
5.1	113
5.3	113, 198
7	243
7.1	113
7.3-6	243
7.3-4	113
7.6	113

Testament of Issachar

2.3	141
3.1-3	194
4.2-3	113
4.5	113
5.3-6	194
6.1-2	194

Testament of Joseph

5.2	216
19.8	217
17.3	221

Testament of Judah

1–9	113
3.6	216
10–26	113
11.1	134, 135
12.4	217
13.8	181
16.1-4	92
16.1	113, 146

17 — 113
17.1-3 — 113
17.1 — 113, 171
18 — 113
18.1-4a — 113, 144
18.2 — 113, 171
19 — 113, 210
19.1-3 — 113, 210
19.1 — 171
21.7-8 — 113

Testament of Levi
6 — 113
8.2 — 216
8.5 — 217
14 — 113
17 — 182
17.2 — 113, 171
17.8-11 — 113, 144, 171
18.5 — 182
18.13 — 182

Testament of Naphtali
3.1 — 113

Testament of Reuben
1.6 — 134
2.8 — 141
2.9 — 134
3.2 — 113
3.3 — 42
3.6 — 141

Testament of Zebulun
1.3 — 176
2.2 — 176
2.4 — 176   3.2 — 217
3.1 — 176
3.4 — 217
3.5 — 217
4.1-3 — 176

4.2 — 176
5.1 — 176
5.2 — 176
5.3 — 176
5.4 — 176
6.1-2 — 176
6.4 — 176
6.5-6 — 176
7.1 — 176
7.2-5 — 176
7.2 — 176
7.3 — 176
7.4 — 176
8.1 — 176
8.2 — 176, 177
8.3 — 176
8.4 — 176
8.6 — 176
9.7 — 176
9.8 — 176
10.2 — 182

PHILO

Abr.
24 — 141
26 — 127
133-34 — 127
223 — 223

Agr.
83 — 127, 155

Conf. Ling.
47–49 — 127, 171
48 — 171, 188, 189, 244
166 — 127

Decl.
142-53 — 127
151-53 — 155
155 — 127

Det. Pot. Ins.
32 — 127
34 — 127

Deus Imm.
25 — 220

Ebr.
22 — 43
209 — 151

Flacc.
91 — 127

Fug.
55 — 163
58 — 163

Gig.
34 — 225
35 — 127
37 — 127, 171

Hypoth.
11.4 — 137

Jos.
7 — 216
20 — 216
25 — 176
216 — 127

Leg. All.
1.80 — 194
1.108 — 163
3.8 — 144

Leg. Gai.
37.296 — 216
46.368 — 176

Migr. Abr.
69 — 144

Mut. Nom.
103 — 127, 188
200 — 220
205 — 144

Omn. Prob. Lib.
8   127
21   141
45   172
57   28
65–67   127
76–86   127
78   169, 171,
                   196
79   188
84   169, 171
85–86   137
Op. Mund.
3   177
158   141

Plant.
8   190

Poster. C.
34   127
116   127, 171

Praem. Poen.
15   127, 210
116   31, 177
121   127, 211

De Prov.
2.4-6   177

2.4   31
2.15   29

Quaest. in Gen.
4.198   28

Rer. Div. Her.
285   225
292   163

Sacr.
19–44   213
20–34   212
20–21   144
32   127, 213
42   214
74   220

Sobr.
56-57   188

Somn.
1.28   220
1.179   199
1.180   204
2.66   163
2.149   135

Spec. Leg.
1.21-27   127

1.23-24   127, 151,
                   171
1.150   43
1.278   127
1.281   141
2.43   127
2.52   127, 182
3.51   134
4.5   127
4.54   127, 188
4.65   127, 171
4.79-131   155
4.129-32   166
4.129-31   127

Virt.
39–40   134
179   29

Vit. Cont.
2   127, 225
70   127, 188

Vit. Mos.
1.56   127
1.156-59   188
1.324   127, 188
2.48   177
2.52   177
2.186   127

JOSEPHUS

Ant.
1.107   220
10.106   220
10.277-79   150
12.203   147, 244
14.408   220
15.104   137
15.174   220
17.253   155

18.1.5   137
20.57   151

Apion
2.169   220
2.170   219
2.179   219
2.180-81   220
2.180   150

2.181   219
2.291   211

Life
334   216

War
2.8.3   137

EARLY CHRISTIAN

Diogn.
5.12-13   153

Ignatius
Eph.
19.2   220

Rom.
4.3   157

Lactantius
Ira Dei
17   242

Tertullian
Apol.
39.5-7   188

De Poenitentia
8   20

Pud.
8.9   20

1 Clement
29.7   245
43.2   217
52.2   183

2 Clement
1.7   178
4.3   171
6.1-4   171, 210

Barnabas
10.3   163
18–20   144
18   213

Clement of Alexandria
Paed.
2   141
3.7   141
37   141

Did.
1–6   213
2.1-6   144
3.2   245
3.5   171
15.1   171

Gos. Thom.
63   81
107   164

Gos. Truth
31.35–32.9   164

Hermas
Man.
3   177
4   177
5   177
5.2.4   245
6.1.6   163
6.2   144
6.2.5   245
6.2.6   163
8.1   169
8.3-5   144
8.3   169
8.5   169
8.10   169
9   177

Sim.
1.6-8   188
4.5   213
6.2.1-2   166

6.2.4   166
6.3.2   177
6.5.5   144
7.1   177
7.3   177
7.4   177
7.6   177
7.8   177
7.9   177
7.11   177
7.14   177
9.15   144
9.19.3   157, 171
10.1.3   169, 181

Vis.
1.1.8-9   157, 164

Justin
Dial.
19   183
73   183
102   183
132   183

Polycarp
Phil.
2.2   144, 169, 171
4.3   144, 157
5.2   171, 178
6.1   171, 178, 245

GREEK AND LATIN AUTHORS

Achilles Tatius
Leucippe and Clitophon
1.4.1   159
7.16.3   159

Aeschines
Tim.
96   145

Aeschylus
Ag.
1221   43

Anth. Pal.
11.157   216

Aristophanes
Eccl.
590   137

610   137
670   137

Nu.
899-1104   154

Aristotle
Eth. Eud.
2.7   151
2.8   151

7.10.8-9	190	**P.A.**	
1221a15	103	3.4	43
Eth. Nic.		**Pol.**	
2.3	179	1.3.18-19	103
2.7.4	103	1.13	145
2.7.11	240	1.15	145
3.12.9	103	2.1-2	137
4.1	84, 103, 231	2.2.6	103, 189
4.1.1-36	143	2.4.1	103
4.1.1-28	168	2.4.11	155
4.1.1-2	103	2.6.19	103
		2.9	145
4.1.3	231	2.17	145
4.1.4	143	7.10.6	137
4.1.5	143, 207	7.15.7	135, 219
4.1.8	231		
4.1.15-17	192	*Rhet.*	
4.1.17	172	2.2	242
4.1.23	143, 178	1366b	139
4.1.29	231		
4.1.30	143	Athenaeus	
4.1.31	135, 144, 197	*Deipn.*	
		4.165d-169b	34
4.1.33-35	144	4.166b-c	141
4.1.35	178	4.166d-168e	33
4.1.36	197		
4.1.37-39	178	Aulus Gellius	
4.1.37	232	*NA*	
4.1.38	231	1.26.3	240
4.1.39	231	10.17.3-4	34
4.1.40-41	231		
4.1.43	188, 231	Cercidas	
4.1.140	145	*Meliamb.*	
4.2.5	84	2.6-17	165
4.2.8	84, 178	2.14	157
4.5.1-15	240		
4.5.7-11	240	Cicero	
4.5.11	240	*Amic.*	
4.21.1-22	103	4.16-5.18	219
7.1	172		
8.10.6	102	*Div.*	
9.8.2	187	1.93	150
9.8.9	189		
8.10 (1160a33-34)	102	*Fin.*	
		2.7	146
		2.8	146
		2.82-85	189

Nat. Deor.	
2.73	150
3.77	146
Off.	
1.16.51	137
1.25	138
1.51	138
2	138, 169
2.10.37	159
2.16	190
2.20	135
2.52-71	120
2.54	121
2.58	121
2.59	121
2.72-89	121
2.78	219
2.81-82	219
3.53	138
Quint. Frat.	
1.1.137	240
Sen.	
16.55-56	194
Tusc.	
4.9.21	241
4.10-13	223
4.23-33	223
4.36.78	199
4.43-44	240
4.46	175
4.56	175
4.77	239
4.79	240
4.80	177
Columella	
Rust. praef.	
10-11	194
Cassius Dio	
65.20.3	33
67.6.3	33
67.6.4	33

Dio Chrysostom

Or.

1.13	241
1.14	144
1.67-84	214
2.75	241
4.96-98	145
4.103-104	145
7.133-37	145
8.24-26	158
9.7-8	184
12.10	211
13.16	189
13.32-33	223
17	210
17.4	145
17.7	145
17.9	190
17.10-11	165
17.10	165
17.11	223
17.15	107
17.18-19	220
17.18	169
17.21	156
20.4	145, 204
21.9	169
27.7-9	200
30.33-34	145
30.33	158
30.43	145, 224
31.16	212
33.14	145
49.9	241
66.13	37, 232
62.2	241
77	184
78.37-8	184

Diodorus Siculus

5.45	137
13.95	199

Diogenes Laertius

4.16	123
4.59	217
6.2	212
6.37	188

6.72	137, 188
7.33	137
7.88	219
7.113	246
7.114	246
7.115	223
7.121	172
8.10	136, 187
8.23	137
10.11	120, 180, 187
10.122	222
10.127-32	119
10.127-28	154
10.128	222
10.130	180
10.131	146
10.140-54	119
10.142	146

Dionysius of Halicarnasss

Ancient Orators

1	33

Epictetus

Diss.

1.4.14-15	219
1.4.18	219
1.4.29	219
1.9.19	162
1.9.27	170
1.11.6	181
1.12.16	219
1.13.1-5	243
1.16.1	218
1.22.18	217
1.26.7	243
2.5.25	151
2.9.10	232
2.9.12	232
2.10.7	190
2.10.9	238
2.10.18	243
2.14.4	218
2.16	118
2.17	118
2.18.5	243

2.18.8-10	156
2.18.12-13	243
2.19	118
2.22	188
2.22.19	188
2.22.31	218
2.23.26	218
3.1.8	146
3.1.12-15	142
3.1.13	135
3.1.14-15	37, 123
3.1.14	135, 146, 201
3.1.15	199, 201
3.1.33	146
3.3.9-10	238
3.7.20	119
3.10.17	243
3.13.11	243
3.15.10	243
3.17.1-6	173
3.20.4	224
3.22.13	243
3.22.47-49	174
3.23	202
3.23.16	37, 202
3.23.28	162
3.23.30	225
3.23.35	216
3.23.37	37, 203
3.24	118
3.24.8-10	151
3.24.44	218
3.24.68-69	188
3.26	118, 173
3.26.3	118
3.26.5	118
3.26.8	118
3.26.14	118
3.26.21-22	119
3.26.25-26	119
3.26.28-29	119
3.26.30-32	119
3.26.34	119
4.1	118, 172, 236
4.1.2	146
4.1.10	146

4.1.21	145	2.3.77-83	122		Longus		
4.1.38	217	2.3.77-239	169		*Daphn. Chloe*		
4.1.67	181	2.3.77-257	122		2.30.1	159	
4.1.80	218	2.3.84-102	122		3.7	159	
4.1.91-98	196	2.3.111-23	171		4.22	159	
4.1.110	187	2.3.111	122		4.23.1	159	
4.4	118	2.3.114	122		4.36.3	159	
4.4.33	156	2.3.124-26	122		4.24	239	
4.5-10	231	2.3.142-57	122				
4.6	118	2.3.176-86	122		Lucian		
4.7	118	2.3.168-86	34		*Abd.*		
4.7.35	170	2.3.224-46	34		21	207	
4.8.28-29	174, 224,	2.3.238	135				
	225	2.3.253-57	34		*Bis. Acc.*		
4.8.34-35	225	2.7	172		16	202	
4.9.1-2	173				17	202	
4.9.12	145	Hesiod					
		Op.			*Demon.*		
Euripides		287-92	212		3–10	106, 172	
Phoen.					7	185	
531-40	107	*Od.*					
		17.31-35	32		*Nigr.*		
Horace		23.207-208	32		1	205	
Ars P.					3-5	205	
189-92	34	Iamblichus			35-37	184	
		V.P.					
Ep.		17.72	187		Lucretius		
1.2.23-24	157	17.73	187		4.994	199	
2.2.136-40	204	18.81	187		4.1016	199	
2.2.136	199	30.167-68	137				
Epod.		Juvenal			Marcus Aurelius		
2.1-16	194	*Sat.*			*Med.*		
2.23-26	194	8.83-94	163		1.16	152	
		10.360-62	212		4.3.1	204	
Sat.		13.190-91	231		4.3.4	204	
1.1.28-119	34, 122	14.1-3	123		7.28	204	
1.1.108-12	156	14.31-33	123		7.33	204	
1.1.161-62	156	14.107-108	135, 207		7.59	204	
1.2.1-24	34, 122	14.107-331	123		8.48	204	
1.4.25-27	217	14.226-28	135				
1.4.48-54	34	14.250-51	135		Martial		
1.4.48-53	122	14.321	123, 169		*Epi.*		
1.4.103-11	122, 207				3.10	173, 207	
1.4.105-11	34	Longinus			10.11	158	
1.6.65-71	122	*Subl.*					
2.2	194	20.1	57				
2.3	121, 173	44.6-10	223				

Maximus of Tyre
Disc.
1.9   212
32.9   212

Menander
Aspis
82-86   56
114-89   56

Dys.
331   197
805-12   190

Kol.
41-45   169

Musonius Rufus
Frag.
1 (34, 14-16)   116, 134
1 (34, 31-33)   116, 134
1 (34, 34-
   36, 6)   184
3 (40, 17-20)   116, 146
3 (40, 38)   116
3 (42, 22-29)   146
4 (44, 16-22)   146
4 (48, 9)   116
6 (52, 15-28)   116
6 (56, 8-11)   116
8 (62, 12-23)   146
8 (62, 13-20   116
   11 (80, 10–
84, 27)   194
12 (84, 30–
   88, 6)   145
14 (92, 17-25)   116, 139
15 (98, 17-22)   116
15 (98, 27–
   100, 16)   116, 237
15 (100,
   12-15)   239
17   116, 236
17 (108,
   11-18)   116, 171
17 (110,
   16-27)   116, 233

18a (114,
   8-12)   225
18b (118,
   32-34)   116
19   138
19 (122,
   12-32)   116, 138,
     190
20 (126, 4-8)   116, 138
20 (126,
   11-31)   116, 138,
     190
20 (126,
   15-18)   225
34   116, 169
50   116

Ovid
Met.
1.89-90   137

Persius
Sat.
3.63-72   115, 226
4.23   204
5   172
5.104-88   115
5.132-60   115
5.161-74   115
6   115
6.18-22   115
6.21-22   145
16.27   115

Philodemus
Oiko.
23   193

Philostratus
Vit. Ap.
4.20e   204
6.11   212

Plato
Apol.
28b   161
29a-e   161
39a   161

Crit.
49b   101
49c   230
109b   238

Gorg.
492a   154
492c   154
494c   154
494e   206
509c   230
527e   222

Leg.
689d   219
736e   139
739c   136
677b   196
736e   101
840a-841c   145
941b   101
941c   101

Phaed.
64a   161
66c   162
67e   161
80e   161
82c   162
83b   154, 162
107c   162
107d   162
114c   162
279c   188
238a-b   155

Resp.
331e   139
347b   101
350d   101
361a   101
366e   230
367d   230
401d   219
407a   222
416c-17b   136
449c   187
449d   187

450c 187
462c 188, 238
543c-576b 102
544c 102
545b 102
549b 230
553a-d 102
555c 135, 206, 207
559d-561b 135
559d-562a 102, 142
560d 143
560e-561a 143
561c 206
591c-e 222
591c 222
612e-613a 149
612e-613c 149

Tim.
47d 219

Plutarch
Brut.
29.2 243

Cato Minor
6.7 140
772c 140

Frag.
148 226, 240, 244, 245
276-78 125

Galb.
16.3-4 233
19.3 146

Mor.
5d 151
12 245
56c 146
57c 146, 196
57d 146
593f 155
60d 146, 233
60e 146

75e 205
78e 218
88f 233
139b 141
140f 141
190a 230
239a 230
389b-c 150
445a 146, 233
447a 243
450f 134
451c-d 245
452e-464d 242
453d-464d 226
455e 241
457b 242
458d 243
4596f-497a 134
459d 244
461a 243
463a 241
463b-f 37
463e 243
478f-479a 219
479a 237
479b 237
479c-d 238
480a-b 238
480d-f 237
481e 238
482b 237
482d-483a 238
483c 237
483d 238
483d-484a 238
484b 188, 238
484c 238
486b 238
486f 238
487f 238
489d 237
490e 188, 238
523c-528b 125, 207
524a 127
524c 127
524d 139, 225
525a 127
525b-e 146

525c 188, 233
525f 165
526a-527a 127
525f-526a 146, 234
526b-c 145
525b11-e03 207
526f 229
527b-528b 127
527b 169
539a-547f 174
555f-556a 211
563b-e 147
563c-e 205
563b-f 142
563c 141, 195
563c-e 160, 205
563d 204
1057e-1058c 205
1062b 205
1065c 212
1086c-1107c 150
1092e-1099d 154

Num.
16.3 194
16.4 194

Pelo
3.2 146

Pelop.
3.2 233

Polybius
Hist.
14.12.3 33
32.11.10 33
39.7.7 33

Porphyry
V.P.
20 137

Ps.-Phoc.
3–6 144
5-6 118, 193
5-79 117
27-28 118

27	151	**Pseudo-Crates**		36 (148,	
36-37	118	*Ep.*		28-30)	224
42-47	117	7	236	37 (158, 9-12)	180
42	170	8	236	38 (162,	
44–47	134, 233	10	109	12-29)	170
44	165	10 (62, 6-11)	224	39 (166, 1-22)	162
53-54	118	10 (62, 8-11)	109, 169		
57	244	11 (62, 14-16)	170, 171	**Pseudo-Heraclitus**	
59-69	117	13	236	*Ep.*	
60–62	244	13 (64, 2-11)	224	4	241
63–64	244	13 (64, 2, 7)	215, 216	4 (192, 1-5)	241
109-10	118	13 (64, 6-11)	224	4 (194, 1-13)	224
177	144	15	109	5 (194, 9-11)	224
199	118	15 (64, 18-19)	171	7 (202, 15)	135
		17 (66, 15-25)	42	7 (202, 15-24)	144
Pseudo-Anacharsis		17 (66, 22-25)	152	8 (208, 5-8)	150, 173
Ep.		19 (68, 13-14)	216	8 (208, 9)	150
3 (40, 6-9)	188	19 (68, 19-26)	216	9	43
7 (44, 2-3)	165	22	109	9 (214, 9)	43
9	104	22 (72, 1-5)	145		
9 (46, 2-8)	105	26	188	*Epistle*	
9 (46, 9-26)	105	27	188	9	43
9 (46, 12)	224				
9 (46, 12-14)	137, 224	**Pseudo-Diogenes**		**Pseudo-Pythagoras**	
9 (46, 13-22)	104	*Ep.*		*Carm. Aur.*	
9 (46, 17)	104, 105	7 (98, 13, 23)	215	9-20	124
9 (46, 26-48)	224	10 (102, 15)	215	13	222
9 (46, 26-		28	180	16	151
48, 17)	105	28 (122,		27-44	124
9 (46, 26-49)	104	10-13)	180	32-38	124
9 (48, 1-2)	169	28 (124, 4-12)	223	32-34	124
9 (48, 11)	104, 105	28 (124, 13)	180	35-36	124
9 (48, 18-27)	104, 105	28 (120,		37-38	169
9 (48, 28)	105	19-21)	180	38	124, 230
9 (48, 28-50)	104, 105	28 (122,		38a	137
9 (50, 11)	165	20-22)	224		
		28 (122,		**Pseudo-Quintilian**	
Pseudo-Antishenes		20-30)	169	*Declam*	
Ep.		28 (122,		5	28, 29
8 (244, 11-19)	224	21-22)	180		
8 (244, 16-18)	224	28 (122,		**Pseudo-Socrates**	
		30-124)	180	*Ep.*	
Pseudo-Aristippus		32	180	1 (220, 16)	150
Ep.		32 (138, 5-15)	181	6	109, 205
27	169	33 (140,		6 (232, 19)	217
29 (294,		28-30)	155	6 (234, 5-9)	171
10-13)	150	34 (144, 2)	215	6 (236, 1-6)	173
		34 (144, 4-11)	224	6 (236, 6-11)	170

6 (236, 16)	185	95.51	231	137-140	125
6 (236, 22-23)	188	115	114	137	125
8	108	115.11	135	138	125
		115.16-17	232	139b	125
Seneca		115.16	114	140	125
Ben.		115.18	114, 170	146	125, 156
7.4-12	138			192	125
7.4.1	188	*Ira*		193	125
7.20	199	1.3.3	242	210a	125
7.20.3-4	203	1.6	184	227	125
		1.6.5	152	228	125, 137,
Consol. ad Marc.		1.14.2-3	243		188
1.8	184	1.21.1-4	242	247b	156
2	199	2.1.3	242	260	125
2.1	184	2.7.2	243	263	125
2.3	203	2.10	243	264a	125
		2.28	242, 243	264b	125
Ep.		2.31.1	242	265	181
1.2	162, 163	2.34	231	266	125
2.1	203	3.3	240	267	125
2.6	203	3.8.3	242	268	181
9	152, 189	3.12.2	244	269	125, 181
10.1-2	203	3.24	243	274b	125
14.18	114	3.33	242	294	125
16	114	3.39.1–40.2	185	295	125
17	114, 236			300	125
17.3	173	*Vit. Beat.*		310	125
17.4	152	15.7	172	312	125
17.5	173			329	125, 170
17.6-12	169	Sextus		330	125
17.6	173	*Sent.*		334	125
17.10	173	13	125, 169	345	125, 181
17.11-12	225	15	125	365	125
18.13	114	17	125	371	125
22.12	114	18	125	377	125
25.6	203	19	125	378	125
25.7	203	50	125, 169	379	125
41.1	203	52	125	382	125
41.9	203	73	125	392	125
53.7-8	203	76	125, 171	412	125, 181
64.7-10	184	82b	125	811	125
75	242	88	125, 169		
75.3	181	91b	125	Stobaeus	
75.9	226	98	125	*Anth.*	
75.11-12	226	116	125	1.3-10	99
75.14	226, 242	117	125	1.3.53-54	149
81	203	127	125	2.74	219
90	137	128	125	3.10.1-77	99

3.10.27	101
3.10.59	101
3.10.67	101
3.10.71	101
3.10.72	101
3.10.73	101
3.10.74	101
3.10.75	101
3.10.76	101
3.16.27, 28	159
3.16.28	159
4	219
4.27	237
4.28.21	194
4.31.84	134
4.31.84	134
4.31.85	125
4.31.86	125
4.32.16	125
4.32.16	144
4.32.17	125
4.33.31	106

Strabo
7.3.9	137

Teles
2	37
2 (12, 94-98)	37, 172
2 (12, 95-96)	29, 107
2 (14, 128-45)	207
4A (34, 1-46)	232
4A (36, 35-46)	151
4A (38, 76–40, 102)	232
4A (40, 100-119)	207
4A (40, 103-108)	151
4A (42, 135-44)	151
4B (50, 46-52)	196
4B (50, 67)	196

Autark.
95-96	29

Terence
Andr.
623 (3.5.16)	199

Adelph
500-504	34
707-10	35
754	218
757-62	35
831-34	34
833-34	232
953-54	34, 232
985-95	34
986-95	135

Haut.
439-41	35

Theophrastus
Char.
10	104, 169, 232
10.6	232
22	169, 232
22.1	104, 232
22.4	104, 232
30	104, 169, 232
30.1	155, 189
30.7	232
30.9	232
30.15	232
30.16-17	232

Tibullus
Elegies
1.1.1	194
1.3.43-44	137
1.5-8	194
1.25-32	194
1.43-46	194

Varro
Rust.
1.17.2	197
1.17.3	197

Vettius Valens
5.9	193

Virgil
Georg.
1.125-26	137

Xenophon
Cyr.
8.7.13-16	237

Mem.
2.1.19-33	212
2.3	237

Sym.
4.35	172

Symposium
4.35	107

Achtemeier, P.J. 94
Aland, B. 41, 42
Aland, K. 41, 42
Alexander, L. 17
Allinson, F.G. 35
Almqvist, H. 25
Anderson, H. 220
Anna, J. 179
Antoine, G. 53
Armstrong, A.H. 120
Arnim, H. von 175
Arnott, W.G. 55, 56
Aune, D.E. 32, 35, 95
Austin, M.R. 78

Baasland, E. 97
Bachmann, M. 159
Balch, D.L. 18, 94, 95, 97, 99, 103, 115,
    144, 150, 151, 174, 187, 212, 237
Barber, E.A. 9
Barnes, J. 204
Barrett, C.K. 156, 166
Barrow, R.H. 196
Barsby, J. 232
Bauckham, R. 36
Bauer, W. 24
Beare, W. 34
Beavis, M.A. 32, 33, 82, 236
Beck, B.E. 78
Bender, K.-H. 27
Berger, K. 27-31, 36, 107
Bergman, J. 212
Berry, K. 186
Betz, H.D. 25, 27, 36, 47, 95, 96, 126,
    147, 160, 174, 186, 190, 195, 205,
    212, 213, 219, 231, 237, 238, 244
Betz, O. 216

Billerbeck, M. 24
Black, M. 50, 52
Blomberg, C.L. 45, 76, 77, 79
Bonhöffer, A. 24
Boring, M.E. 29, 36
Botha, J. 47
Bovon, F. 21, 26, 28, 42, 44, 53, 54, 154,
    175
Bradley, D.G. 92-94, 96, 97
Braumann, G. 159
Breech, J. 32
Brinkmann, A. 213
Bruce, F.F. 183, 195
Brunt, J.C. 96, 97
Büchsel, F. 153-55
Bultmann, R. 45, 160-62
Burchardt, C. 215
Burkitt, F.C. 195
Burnyeat, M. 204
Burton, E. de W. 52, 63

Cadbury, H.J. 40, 64
Cairns, F. 55, 152
Campbell, J. 31
Carlston, C.E. 45
Cartlidge, D. 35
Chadwick, H. 19
Charlesworth, J.H. 100, 112, 215, 220
Clemen, C. 24
Clines, D.J.A. 17, 78
Collins, J.J. 117
Colpe, C. 29, 36, 107
Conzelmann, H. 152
Copleston, F. 19
Corlett, T. 237
Cox, A.S. 177
Cranfield, C.E.B. 156

Creed, J.M. 75, 140
Crossan, J.D. 26

Danker, F.W. 36, 59, 78, 84, 197
Davids, P.H. 163
Deissmann, A. 24
Deist, F. 56
Derrett, J.D.M. 21, 227
Dibelius, M. 17, 152, 156, 172, 177
Dillon, J.M. 120, 244
Dirkse, P.A. 147
Dormeyer, D. 26
Downing, F.G. 31, 36, 37, 177
Dungan, D. 36

Edwards, R.A. 124, 125
Ellis, E.E. 79
Epp, E.J. 26
Erskine, A. 136, 138, 188
Evans, C.A. 25, 77, 87
Evans, C.F. 39

Farrar, F.W. 78, 79
Ferguson, E. 18, 100, 101, 115, 120,
    144, 150-52, 174, 187, 212, 237
Festugière, A.J. 193
Fiore, B. 151
Fitzmyer, J.A. 16, 39, 42, 44, 45, 62, 69,
    73, 74, 76, 78-80, 82, 133, 140,
    164, 178, 216, 221, 248
Foerster, W. 33, 148
Foucault, M. 198
Fowl, S.E. 17, 78
France, R.T. 79

George, D.B. 201
Gerhard, G.A. 134, 153, 159, 217
Giblin, C.H. 75
Glucker, J. 120
Gore, C. 241
Goulder, M.D. 31, 57, 64, 80
Grant, M. 120
Grant, R.M. 188
Greenlee, J.H. 44
Greeven, H. 156, 172, 177
Grelot, P. 45
Grotius, H. 19

Hägg, T. 56, 57
Hammond, N.G.L. 9
Hanson, A.T. 163
Harrison, B. 39
Haubeck, W. 159
Hauck, F. 145
Hawthorne, G.F. 121
Heinrici, G. 24
Hengel, M. 21, 112, 137, 188, 213
Hense, O. 97, 99, 101, 106, 125, 134,
    194
Henten, J.W. van 34
Hershbell, J.P. 101, 118
Hewitt, J.W. 191
Hickling, C.J.A. 78
Hock, R.F. 17, 32, 36, 158, 239
Holladay, C.R. 174
Hollander, H.W. 43, 134, 141, 194
Hopkins, K. 33, 181
Horn, F.W. 70
Hornblower, S. 9, 25
Horsley, G.H.R. 197, 208
Horst, I.B. 25
Horst, P.W. van der 25, 136, 151, 246
Houlden, J.L. 87
Hultgren, A.J. 80

Irwin, T.H. 138

Jaeger, W. 19, 134, 194, 199, 200, 212,
    213, 219, 222
Jeremias, J. 20, 21, 27, 42-45, 59, 62,
    140, 215
Johnson, L.T. 16, 40, 55, 57, 59, 70-73,
    79, 90, 95, 96, 138, 148, 187, 198
Jones, G.V. 39
Jones, H. 120
Jones, H.S. 9
Jonge, M. de 43, 112, 141, 144, 156, 194
Jülicher, A. 20, 23, 24, 27, 42

Karris, R.J. 69, 78, 79, 92, 235
Kee, H.C. 113
Kerford, G.B. 201
Keyt, D. 138
Kingsbury, J.D. 55, 81
Kissinger, W.S. 19

Klauck, H.-J. 115, 237
Kleinknecht, H, 149, 239, 240, 243-45
Koester, H. 43, 152, 175-77
Kremer, J. 57, 166
Kudlien, F. 224

Lake, K. 181, 220
Lambrecht, J. 75
Laporte, J. 213
Lattimore, R. 180
Lee, H.D.P. 230
Lehnert, G. 27
Lewis, J.J. 118
Liddell, H.G. 9
Liebeschuetz, J.H.W.G. 149
Lightfoot, J.B. 43, 152
Little, J.C. 20
Long, A.A. 103, 120, 179, 189
Louw, J.P. 47, 64
Lührmann, D. 103
Lutz, C.E. 116, 194

MacRae, G.W. 26
Malherbe, A.J. 13, 26, 36, 37, 90, 94, 98,
    99, 104, 120, 134, 136, 150, 158,
    162, 174, 175, 184-88, 193, 194,
    200, 204, 205, 212, 217, 223, 236,
    237, 241, 242, 251, 252
Marshall, I.H. 21, 27, 28, 42, 44, 70, 75,
    76, 133, 140, 186
Mayor, J.B. 163
McCord, J.I. 196
McCrum, M. 140
Mealand, D.L. 62, 70, 136, 137
Meeks, W.A. 18, 115, 144, 150, 151,
    174, 179, 187, 212, 237
Mendell, C.W. 122, 152, 217
Menken, M.J.J. 43, 53, 175
Metzger, B.M. 42, 44
Michaelis, W. 212
Miller, F.D., Jr 138
Miller, N. 169
Mitchell, A.C. 187
Mitchell, M.M. 97
Moessner, D.P. 79
Moffat, J. 184
Moles, J. 152, 196, 198, 205
Mott, S.C. 121

Moule, C.F.D. 52, 80
Moulton, J.H. 159
Moxnes, H. 88, 133
Mullins, T.Y. 94
Mussies, G. 25, 145

Neyrey, J.H. 150
Nickelsburg, G.W.E. 77, 134, 150
Nida, E.A. 76
Nock, A.D. 19, 199, 200, 205, 211, 212,
    226
Noorda, S.J. 57
North, H. 154

Oldfather, W.A. 238
Oltramare, A. 97
O'Neil, E.N. 96, 106, 126, 146, 147
O'Rourke, J.J. 45

Parker, T.H.L. 196
Parrott, D.M. 74, 81, 82, 84
Pelser, G.M.M. 46
Perry, B.E. 32
Petersen, N.R. 30
Petzer, J.H. 13, 41, 42, 44
Pilgrim, W.E. 69, 70
Piper, J. 27
Plessis, I.J. du 19, 45, 56, 75
Pogoloff, S.M. 96
Pöhlmann, W. 36
Porter, S.E. 17, 25, 78
Price, J. 23, 35, 199

Radice, B. 35
Rahlfs, A. 110
Ramaroson, S. 75
Ramsay, W.M. 222
Rau, E. 27-31
Reardon, B.P. 32, 40, 55, 57, 62, 159
Reese, J.M. 182
Reiling, J. 63, 197
Rengstorf, K.H. 215, 216
Rist, J.M. 120, 189
Roberts, W.R. 223
Rose, H.J. 212
Rouiller, G. 21, 26, 42, 53, 54

Sanders, E.P. 76, 204
Sanders, J.T. 45, 71, 72
Schmid, W. 205
Schmithals, W. 31, 75
Schneider, J. 133
Schnelle, U. 23, 28
Schnider, F. 60
Schofield, M. 204
Schottroff, L. 27-30, 209
Schulz, S. 145
Schweizer, E. 39, 45
Scott, B.B. 30, 51, 52, 56, 206
Scott, R. 9
Scullard, H.H. 9
Sedley, D. 189, 204
Seeley, D. 161
Sellew, P. 149, 206
Sellin, G. 80
Sevenster, J.N. 25, 200
Shelton, J. 194, 197
Sherk, R.K. 140
Shorey, P. 102
Sibinga, J.S. 25, 34, 42, 46, 53
Simpson, E.K. 193
Skemp, J.B. 195
Smith, E.W., Jr 147
Smith, H. 20
Spawforth, A. 9
Spicq, P.C. 36, 93, 157, 218, 219
Staden, P. van 209
Stählin, G. 186, 239
Stählin, O. 205
Stegemann, W. 209
Stewart, Z. 19, 200
Strecker, G. 23
Striker, G. 179
Swellengrebel, J.L. 63, 197

Talbert, C.H. 69
Tannehill, R.C. 54, 75
Thiselton, A.C. 210
Thom, J.C. 13, 47, 124, 139, 151, 212, 213, 223, 224
Thompson, J.A.K. 104

Thompson, J.W. 100
Thompson, W. 51
Thraede, K. 103
Tissot, Y. 21, 22, 218
Traub, H. 208
Trench, R.C. 24, 93, 245, 246
Tuckett, C.M. 37
Turner, E.G. 58
Turner, N. 50, 63
Turner, P. 230

Unnik, W.C. van 19, 21, 24, 25, 93, 94, 211

Verhey, A. 72, 73, 80
Veyne, P. 33
Via, D.O., Jr 34, 54, 210
Villiers, P.G.R. de 13

Wachsmuth, C. 97, 99, 101, 134
Wadsworth, M. 39
Wandruszka, M. 27
Watson, D.F. 96
Weder, H. 67
Weiss, B. 153, 164
Weiss, H. 43
Wellhausen, J. 44
Wenham, D. 79
West, M.L. 122
Wettstein, J.J. 23, 24, 31, 35, 199, 215
White, K.D. 157
White, L.M. 187
White, M. 186
White, N.P. 219
Wilckens, U. 215, 216
Wild, R.A. 124, 125
Wiles, M.F. 20-22
Wilhelm, F. 95
Wilken, R.L. 125, 213
Wimbush, V.L. 97
Witt, N.W. de 185
Woodhead, A.G. 140
Wuellner, W. 97

JOURNAL FOR THE STUDY OF THE NEW TESTAMENT
SUPPLEMENT SERIES

55 L. Ann Jervis, *The Purpose of Romans: A Comparative Letter Structure Investigation*

56 Delbert Burkett, *The Son of the Man in the Gospel of John*

57 Bruce W. Longenecker, *Eschatology and the Covenant: A Comparison of 4 Ezra and Romans 1–11*

58 David A. Neale, *None but the Sinners: Religious Categories in the Gospel of Luke*

59 Michael Thompson, *Clothed with Christ: The Example and Teaching of Jesus in Romans 12.1–15.13*

60 Stanley E. Porter (ed.), *The Language of the New Testament: Classic Essays*

61 John Christopher Thomas, *Footwashing in John 13 and the Johannine Community*

62 Robert L. Webb, *John the Baptizer and Prophet: A Socio-Historical Study*

63 James S. McLaren, *Power and Politics in Palestine: The Jews and the Governing of their Land, 100 BC–AD 70*

64 Henry Wansborough (ed.), *Jesus and the Oral Gospel Tradition*

65 Douglas A. Campbell, *The Rhetoric of Righteousness in Romans 3.21-26*

66 Nicholas Taylor, *Paul, Antioch and Jerusalem: A Study in Relationships and Authority in Earliest Christianity*

67 F. Scott Spencer, *The Portrait of Philip in Acts: A Study of Roles and Relations*

68 Michael Knowles, *Jeremiah in Matthew's Gospel: The Rejected Prophet Motif in Matthean Redaction*

69 Margaret Davies, *Rhetoric and Reference in the Fourth Gospel*

70 J. Webb Mealy, *After the Thousand Years: Resurrection and Judgment in Revelation 20*

71 Martin Scott, *Sophia and the Johannine Jesus*

72 Steven M. Sheeley, *Narrative Asides in Luke–Acts*

73 Marie E. Isaacs, *Sacred Space: An Approach to the Theology of the Epistle to the Hebrews*

74 Edwin K. Broadhead, *Teaching with Authority: Miracles and Christology in the Gospel of Mark*

75 John K. Chow, *Patronage and Power: A Study of Social Networks in Corinth*

76 Robert W. Wall and Eugene E. Lemcio (eds.), *The New Testament as Canon: A Reader in Canonical Criticism*

77 Roman Garrison, *Redemptive Almsgiving in Early Christianity*

78 L. Gregory Bloomquist, *The Function of Suffering in Philippians*

79 Blaine Charette, *The Theme of Recompense in Matthew's Gospel*

80 Stanley E. Porter and D.A. Carson (eds.), *Biblical Greek Language and Linguistics: Open Questions in Current Research*

81 In-Gyu Hong, *The Law in Galatians*

82 Barry W. Henaut, *Oral Tradition and the Gospels: The Problem of Mark 4*

83 Craig A. Evans and James A. Sanders (eds.), *Paul and the Scriptures of Israel*

84 Martinus C. de Boer (ed.), *From Jesus to John: Essays on Jesus and New Testament Christology in Honour of Marinus de Jonge*

85 William J. Webb, *Returning Home: New Covenant and Second Exodus as the Context for 2 Corinthians 6.14–7.1*

86 Bradley H. McLean (ed.), *Origins and Method—Towards a New Understanding of Judaism and Christianity: Essays in Honour of John C. Hurd*

87 Michael J. Wilkins and Terence Paige (eds.), *Worship, Theology and Ministry in the Early Church: Essays in Honour of Ralph P. Martin*

88 Mark Coleridge, *The Birth of the Lukan Narrative: Narrative as Christology in Luke 1–2*

89 Craig A. Evans, *Word and Glory: On the Exegetical and Theological Background of John's Prologue*

90 Stanley E. Porter and Thomas H. Olbricht (eds.), *Rhetoric and the New Testament: Essays from the 1992 Heidelberg Conference*

91 Janice Capel Anderson, *Matthew's Narrative Web: Over, and Over, and Over Again*

92 Eric Franklin, *Luke: Interpreter of Paul, Critic of Matthew*

93 Jan Fekkes III, *Isaiah and Prophetic Traditions in the Book of Revelation: Visionary Antecedents and their Development*

94 Charles A. Kimball, *Jesus' Exposition of the Old Testament in Luke's Gospel*

95 Dorothy A. Lee, *The Symbolic Narratives of the Fourth Gospel: The Interplay of Form and Meaning*

96 Richard E. DeMaris, *The Colossian Controversy: Wisdom in Dispute at Colossae*

97 Edwin K. Broadhead, *Prophet, Son, Messiah: Narrative Form and Function in Mark 14–16*

98 Carol J. Schlueter, *Filling up the Measure: Polemical Hyperbole in 1 Thessalonians 2.14-16*

99 Neil Richardson, *Paul's Language about God*

100 Thomas E. Schmidt and Moisés Silva (eds.), *To Tell the Mystery: Essays on New Testament Eschatology in Honor of Robert H. Gundry*

101 Jeffrey A.D. Weima, *Neglected Endings: The Significance of the Pauline Letter Closings*

102 Joel F. Williams, *Other Followers of Jesus: Minor Characters as Major Figures in Mark's Gospel*

103 Warren Carter, *Households and Discipleship: A Study of Matthew 19–20*

104 Craig A. Evans and W. Richard Stegner (eds.), *The Gospels and the Scriptures of Israel*

105 W.P. Stephens (ed.), *The Bible, the Reformation and the Church: Essays in Honour of James Atkinson*

106 Jon A. Weatherly, *Jewish Responsibility for the Death of Jesus in Luke–Acts*

107 Elizabeth Harris, *Prologue and Gospel: The Theology of the Fourth Evangelist*

108 L. Ann Jervis and Peter Richardson (eds.), *Gospel in Paul: Studies on Corinthians, Galatians and Romans for Richard N. Longenecker*

109 Elizabeth Struthers Malbon and Edgar V. McKnight (eds.), *The New Literary Criticism and the New Testament*

110 Mark L. Strauss, *The Davidic Messiah in Luke–Acts: The Promise and its Fulfillment in Lukan Christology*

111 Ian H. Thomson, *Chiasmus in the Pauline Letters*

112 Jeffrey B. Gibson, *The Temptations of Jesus in Early Christianity*

113 Stanley E. Porter and D.A. Carson (eds.), *Discourse Analysis and Other Topics in Biblical Greek*

114 Lauri Thurén, *Argument and Theology in 1 Peter: The Origins of Christian Paraenesis*

115 Steve Moyise, *The Old Testament in the Book of Revelation*

116 C.M. Tuckett (ed.), *Luke's Literary Achievement: Collected Essays*

117 Kenneth G.C. Newport, *The Sources and Sitz im Leben of Matthew 23*

118 Troy W. Martin, *By Philosophy and Empty Deceit: Colossians as Response to a Cynic Critique*

119 David Ravens, *Luke and the Restoration of Israel*

120 Stanley E. Porter and David Tombs (eds.), *Approaches to New Testament Study*

121 Todd C. Penner, *The Epistle of James and Eschatology: Re-reading an Ancient Christian Letter*

122 A.D.A. Moses, *Matthew's Transfiguration Story in Jewish–Christian Controversy*

123 David Lertis Matson, *Household Conversion Narratives in Acts: Pattern and Interpretation*

124 David Mark Ball, *'I Am' in John's Gospel: Literary Function, Background and Theological Implications*

125 Robert Gordon Maccini, *Her Testimony is True: Women as Witnesses According to John*

126 B. Hudson Mclean, *The Cursed Christ: Mediterranean Expulsion Rituals and Pauline Soteriology*

127 R. Barry Matlock, *Unveiling the Apocalyptic Paul: Paul's Interpreters and the Rhetoric of Criticism*

128 Timothy Dwyer, *The Motif of Wonder in the Gospel of Mark*

129 Carl Judson Davis, *The Names and Way of the Lord: Old Testament Themes, New Testament Christology*

130 Craig S. Wansink, *Chained in Christ: The Experience and Rhetoric of Paul's Imprisonments*

131 Stanley E. Porter and Thomas H. Olbricht (eds.), *Rhetoric, Scripture and Theology: Essays from the 1994 Pretoria Conference*

132 J. Nelson Kraybill, *Imperial Cult and Commerce in John's Apocalypse*

133   Mark S. Goodacre, *Goulder and the Gospels: An Examination of a New Paradigm*

134   Larry J. Kreitzer, *Striking New Images: Roman Imperial Coinage and the New Testament World*

135   Charles Landon, *A Text-Critical Study of the Epistle of Jude*

136   Jeffrey T. Reed, *A Discourse Analysis of Philippians: Method and Rhetoric in the Debate over Lierary Integrity*

137   Roman Garrison, *The Graeco-Roman Context of Early Christian Literature*

138   Kent D. Clarke, *Textual Optimism: A Critique of the United Bible Societies' Greek New Testament*

139   Yong-Eui Yang, *Jesus and the Sabbath in Matthew's Gospel*

140   Thomas R. Yoder Neufeld, *Put on the Armour of God: The Divine Warrior from Isaiah to Ephesians*

141   Rebecca I. Denova, *The Things Accomplished among Us: Prophetic Tradition in the Structural Pattern of Luke–Acts*

142   Scott Cunningham, *'Through Many Tribulations': The Theology of Persecution in Luke–Acts*

143   Raymond Pickett, *The Cross in Corinth: The Social Significance of the Death of Jesus*

144   S. John Roth, *The Blind, the Lame and the Poor: Character Types in Luke–Acts*

145   Larry Paul Jones, *The Symbol of Water in the Gospel of John*

146   Stanley E. Porter and Thomas H. Olbricht (eds.), *The Rhetorical Analysis of Scripture: Essays from the 1995 London Conference*

147   Kim Paffenroth, *The Story of Jesus According to L*

148   Craig A. Evans and James A. Sanders (eds.), *Early Christian Interpretation of the Scriptures of Israel: Investigations and Proposals*

149   J. Dorcas Gordon, *Sister or Wife?: 1 Corinthians 7 and Cultural Anthropology*

150   J. Daryl Charles, *Virtue amidst Vice: The Catalog of Virtues in 2 Peter 1.5-7*

151   Derek Tovey, *Narrative Art and Act in the Fourth Gospel*

152   Evert-Jan Vledder, *Conflict in the Miracle Stories: A Socio-Exegetical Study of Matthew 8 and 9*

153   Christopher Rowland and Crispin H.T. Fletcher-Louis (eds.), *Understanding, Studying and Reading: New Testament Essays in Honour of John Ashton*

154   Craig A. Evans and James A. Sanders (eds.), *The Function of Scripture in Early Jewish and Christian Tradition*

155   Kyoung-Jin Kim, *Stewardship and Almsgiving in Luke's Theology*

156   I.A.H. Combes, *The Metaphor of Slavery in the Writings of the Early Church: From the New Testament to the Begining of the Fifth Century*

158   Jey. J. Kanagaraj, *'Mysticism' in the Gospel of John: An Inquiry into its Background*

159   Brenda Deen Schildgen, *Crisis and Continuity: Time in the Gospel of Mark*

160   Johan Ferreira, *Johannine Ecclesiology*

161   Helen C. Orchard, *Courting Betrayal: Jesus as Victim in the Gospel of John*

162   Jeffrey T. Tucker, *Example Stories: Perspectives on Four Parables in the Gospel of Luke*

163   John A. Darr, *Herod the Fox: Audience Criticism and Lukan Characterization*

164   Bas M.F. Van Iersel, *Mark: A Reader-Response Commentary*

165   Alison Jasper, *The Shining Garment of the Text: Gendered Readings of John's Prologue*

166   G.K. Beale, *John's Use of the Old Testament in Revelation*

167   Gary Yamasaki, *John the Baptist in Life and Death: Audience-Oriented Criticism of Matthew's Narrative*

168   Stanley E. Porter and D.A. Carson (eds.), *Linguistics and the New Testament: Critical Junctures*

169   Derek Newton, *Deity and Diet: The Dilemma of Sacrificial Food at Corinth*

170   Stanley E. Porter and Jeffrey T. Reed (eds.), *Discourse Analysis and the New Testament: Approaches and Results*

172   Casey Wayne Davis, *Oral Biblical Criticism: The Influence of the Principles of Orality on the Literary Structure of Paul's Epistle to the Philippians*

173   Stanley E. Porter and Richard S. Hess (eds.), *Translating the Bible: Problems and Prospects*

174   J.D.H. Amador, *Academic Constraints in Rhetorical Criticism of the New Testament: An Introduction to a Rhetoric of Power*

175   Edwin K. Broadhead, *Naming Jesus: Titular Christology in the Gospel of Mark*

176   Alex T. Cheung, *Idol Food in Corinth: Jewish Background and Pauline Legacy*

177   Brian Dodd, *Paul's Paradigmatic 'I': Personal Examples as Literary Strategy*

178   Thomas B. Slater, *Christ and Community: A Socio-Historical Study of the Christology of Revelation*

179   Alison M. Jack, *Texts Reading Texts, Sacred and Secular: Two Postmodern Perspectives*

180   Stanley E. Porter and Dennis L. Stamps (eds.), *The Rhetorical Interpretation of Scripture: Essays from the 1996 Malibu Conference*

181   Sylvia C. Keesmaat, *Paul and his Story: (Re)Interpreting the Exodus Tradition*

182   Johannes Nissen and Sigfred Pedersen (eds.), *New Readings in John: Literary and Theological Perspectives. Essays from the Scandinavian Conference on the Fourth Gospel in Århus 1997*

184   David Rhoads and Kari Syreeni (eds.), *Characterization in the Gospels: Reconceiving Narrative Criticism*

187   David A. Holgate, *Prodigality, Liberality and Meanness: The Prodigal Son in Greco-Roman Perspective*